Grandpappy's Gourmet Cookbook

Robert Wayne Atkins, P.E.
(Grandpappy)

Detailed instructions on
"How to Become a Gourmet Cook."
Also included are
more than 250 gourmet recipes
for almost any occasion.

For more information please visit: https://www.grandpappy.org

Grandpappy's Gourmet Cookbook
Robert Wayne Atkins, P.E. (Grandpappy)

Some of the recipes in this cookbook may include foods or spices that some people should not eat. For example, a person's physician may have told that person not to consume milk, eggs, gluten, nuts, or sodium. Always follow the advice of your licensed medical practitioner before preparing or consuming any of the dishes mentioned in this cookbook.

First Edition published by Grandpappy, Inc.

Detailed instructions on
"How to Become a Gourmet Cook."
Also included are
more than 250 gourmet recipes
for almost any occasion.

ISBN: 978-0-9850358-8-4

Printed in the United States of America.
10 9 8 7 6 5 4 3

Preface to
Grandpappy's Gourmet Cookbook

My parents raised all of us the same way without regard to whether we were male or female. At age six each of us had to start learning how to cook simple meals, how to wash and dry dishes by hand, how to use hand tools correctly, and how to safely shoot a firearm.

In 1965 I was a Junior in High School and I got my first part-time job as a waiter. Because I knew how to cook simple meals, it was not long before I was doing the cook's job when he took a break or ate a meal. Near the end of my Senior year I was promoted to cook. When I graduated I enrolled in a major Engineering University. I worked a part-time job on weekdays in the university dining room kitchen and occasionally I was able to observe the cooks prepare food. In my Senior year I took on a second part-time job working weekends at a Hardee's fast food restaurant as a cook. When I graduated from college in 1972 I began working as an Engineer.

In June of 1975 I moved my wife and our 3 preschool age children onto 12 acres of land we purchased in the backwoods of Maine. We lived in a tent for about 6 months while I was building a rustic log cabin using pine trees that grew on our land. My wife and I shared the job of cooking meals over the campfire. However, it was not long before I realized I could only cook a few different tasty meals over a campfire. And I began to appreciate the significant impact that good food can have on a person's happiness, energy level, and mental attitude.

In late November of 1975 I accepted an Engineering job in Fort Lauderdale, Florida. For one year I worked two weeks each month in Puerto Rico near the 3 best restaurants on the south side of the island. I ate dinner at one of those restaurants every evening and I became infatuated with the quality and taste of a wide variety of international foods that were prepared by internationally acclaimed chefs. Since I had just recently been humbled by my own shortcomings as a campfire cook, I began to truly appreciate every meal I ate. This motivated me to acquire a better understanding of how high quality food is prepared.

For the next 40 plus years I diligently studied the art and science of cooking. My scientific engineering background helped me to clearly understand the chemical and scientific reasons why some things should be done, and why other things should not be done. This cookbook is the result of my lifetime adventure of learning how to cook.

The recipes in this cookbook are also enhanced by my 30 plus years of teaching at a major state university where I learned how to clearly explain concepts without including unnecessary information, but also without omitting any of the critical facts that are absolutely necessary.

Respectfully, Robert Wayne Atkins, P.E. (Grandpappy), March 1, 2018

Table of Contents

Chapter One
Secrets of Gourmet Cooking

Introduction to Gourmet Cooking

A gourmet cook is an individual, either male or female, of almost any age, who is able to prepare food that is enjoyable to eat. The food may be a common item, such as white rice, or a not-so-common item, such as quail. The recipe may only require two or three ingredients, or the recipe may require more than a dozen ingredients. The food may not require cooking, or the food may be cooked over a campfire, or on a grill, or on a stove, or in an oven. The amount cooked may be just enough for one person or for a large group of people.

A gourmet cook normally prepares meals that accomplish all of the following objectives at the same time:
1. The food has an enticing aroma.
2. The food has a very desirable appearance.
3. The food has a delightful pleasant taste.
4. The food satisfies the person's hunger for at least a few hours.
5. The food can be easily and quickly digested.
6. The vitamins and nutrients in the food have been preserved and they can be easily absorbed into the body.
7. The food facilitates the long-term health of the person who eats it.

A gourmet cook also understands all of the following:
1. People are different.
2. Different foods appeal to different people.
3. Different cooking techniques yield foods that appeal to different people, such as steamed food, or stir-fried food, or baked food.
4. Specific foods may be liked or disliked by different people in the same exact family, such as onions or oysters.
5. There is no single universal recipe that will produce a dish that everyone likes.
6. All recipes can be gradually enhanced based on experience.
7. Cooking is a life-long adventure and a gourmet cook is always willing to learn new things.
8. Almost everyone is a food critic, even if that person cannot cook anything.
9. Most professional food critics are aware that some people may not like a food they really enjoy, and some people may love a food that they detest.
10. A gourmet cook is intellectually prepared to receive positive and negative feedback, and they do not let praise or ridicule impact their humble self-image. Instead they use all feedback in an appropriate manner to help them become better gourmet cooks in the future.

Modifying Recipes

All gourmet cooks gradually modify their recipes as they gain more experience and as they learn new things. The best way to become a great gourmet cook is to start with a great recipe. If you start with an average recipe, or with a good recipe, then it will take more of your time, and more of your money invested in ingredients, in order to gradually convert that recipe into something you can take pride in. There is nothing wrong with this approach if you have the patience, and the time, and the money to invest in gradually and slowing enhancing your cooking skills and your favorite recipes. On the other hand, if you start with a superior recipe then you may discover that you like the recipe exactly the way it is. Or you may decide to gradually make small changes to the recipe to see if those changes impact the results in a favorable or unfavorable manner. By starting very close to your personal finish line, you will be able to arrive there quicker while spending less money.

The recipes in this gourmet cookbook are superior recipes. However, no recipe anywhere in this cookbook will please everyone because different people have different taste preferences, and there is nothing unusual about that.

Taste Buds or Palette

Each person has their own unique ability to taste subtle differences in foods. Some people have extremely sensitive taste buds and they can easily detect all the ingredients that are included in a recipe. On the other hand, some people have extremely weak taste buds and they can barely taste the foods they eat. But most of us have normal or average taste buds and we like or dislike specific foods because of the way those foods taste. However, most of us cannot detect a small difference in the quantity of an ingredient in a recipe, or in some cases the presence or the absence of a specific ingredient in a recipe, especially if the recipe contains many different ingredients. A normal person should not be ashamed of having normal taste buds, just like a normal person should not be ashamed if he or she cannot sing well enough to earn a living as a singer. There is nothing wrong with having normal average taste buds, or normal average hearing, or normal average eyesight.

However, it is possible for a person with normal average taste buds to become a gourmet cook and to prepare culinary miracles that will amaze most of their friends and family members, even if some of those people have remarkably sensitive taste buds.

A Suggestion for New Gourmet Cooks:
"Cook Once and Eat Twice."

Consider cooking enough for two meals. Eat one meal and freeze the other meal so you can thaw it out, reheat it, and eat it on another day.

More Suggestions for New Gourmet Cooks

1. Always read each recipe completely before you begin to follow the instructions.

2. Locate all the ingredients you will need and put them on the counter where you will be using them.

3. Locate all the equipment, bowls, and other items you will need and place then on the counter where you can easily find them.

4. Measure all ingredients before you start cooking so you have the correct amount ready to use when it is needed.

5. If eggs are cold, it is easier to separate the yolks and the whites. If whipping the whites then do not let any of the yolk cling to the whites, not even a small speck. If appropriate, allow the egg yolks and/or whites to come to room temperature.

6. Remove cold butter, eggs, milk, buttermilk, and cream cheese from the refrigerator, measure the amount you need, and allow the measured ingredients to sit for one hour until they come to room temperature. Then use them in your cooking recipes. Ingredients at room temperature mix more easily, more evenly, and more completely with the dry ingredients in a recipe, and this will usually yield a lighter more delicious finished cooked food item.

7. Allow cheese to come to room temperature and then grate or shred it.

8. If fresh vegetables need to be soaked then do so before slicing in order to retain as much of their nutritional value as possible.

9. Cut and prepare all vegetables and meats before you begin combining items using the recipe.

10. Do not cut lettuce. Tear lettuce instead.

11. Cut the ends off onions and tomatoes before you begin to slice, chop, or dice them.

12. If you wish to garnish a dish with raw onions, then soak them in cold water first.

13. If onions need to be sautéd, and if you have the time, then sauté onions over low heat for 15 or 20 minutes instead of 3 to 5 minutes. This will significantly enhance the final flavor of the food.

14. Vegetables that grow above ground should be boiled with **no** cover on the cook pot.

15. When practical, add butter at the end of a recipe. The butter will not blend with the other ingredients and it will add more of its desirable taste to the food. Less butter will also be needed to achieve the same results.

16. Cut meat across the grain before cooking to make it easier to eat after cooking.

17. If a recipe specifies that meat be browned then sear it over high heat to caramelize the surface of the meat. Do not just heat the meat or allow the meat to cook or steam in its own juices. Sear the meat.

18. When cooking pork chops, cut the piece of fat on the outside of the chop. This will help the chop to lay flat in the pan without curling up as it cooks.

19. When fried in a skillet, *crumbled* ground meat should be separated into very small pieces, first by your hands when you put it into the skillet, and then again with the edge of your stirring spoon as you cook the meat. Very small pieces of meat: (a) cook more quickly and more evenly so it is all consistently done, (b) better absorb any herbs, spices, or sauces you may add to the meat, (c) are much easier for older people and very young children to chew, (d) are much easier for most people to digest.

20. Do not add oil to the boiling water when you cook pasta. Oil does not help and it makes the pasta slippery so that the sauce cannot stick to the pasta. Instead add just a little salt to the boiling water.

21. Put a wooden spoon across the top of a boiling pot and the water will not boil over the top of the pot.

22. When available, use lard or shortening to grease baking pans. If you use butter, margarine, or oils then they will be absorbed into the dough or food more quickly and the food may stick to the pan.

23. Put an empty baking sheet in the oven on the shelf below the one that contains the food. The empty baking sheet will absorb some of the heat and keep it off the bottom of the food pan so the food in the pan bakes more evenly.

24. Fill one side of your kitchen sink with hot water and add some dish soap. When you are finished with each cook pot or dish, wait for it to cool, wipe it out with a paper towel, rinse it off under hot water in the other side of your kitchen sink, and put it into the sink with the hot soapy water so it can soak. When you finish eating your meal, your cook pots and dishes will be much easier to clean.

25. Do not soak cast iron pots, or wood bowls, or wood spoons, or items with wood handles, in water. These items should be washed with water but they should not be allowed to soak in water because cast iron will rust, and wood will absorb water, expand, crack, and be ruined.

26. Save your bacon grease and use it to season a variety of beans and vegetables.

27. A practical easy way to use leftovers is to use them to make soup.

28. Instant potatoes work well as a thickener for homemade soups and stews.

29. If a glass pan or a dark colored pan is used for baking then reduce the recommended oven temperature by 25 degrees.

Basic Food Safety Precautions

1. Do not buy dented cans of food or canned foods that show any sign of aging, such as rust on the outside of the can, or labels that show visible signs of aging.

2. Before opening a can of food, rinse the top of the can under cool faucet water to remove any contamination or germs that might be on the top of the can. Dry the top of the can before opening it.

3. If a can is swollen (bulging) around its center then it probably contains poisonous toxins. Do not open the can. Dispose of the can safely. If necessary, bury the unopened can at least one foot under the ground.

4. Before using any item that has been in storage a long time, open it and carefully examine it. It should look okay and smell okay. If it doesn't look and smell okay then it is probably not safe to eat. Never, never eat any food that has an offensive or unusual odor, or that has something growing on it.

5. Wash your hands thoroughly before handling any type of food. Consider wearing disposable single-use kitchen gloves when handling food.

6. Rinse raw food thoroughly before processing it or storing it.

7. Use clean food processing equipment.

8. Always wash utensils before using them on a different food item to prevent a problem of cross-contamination.

9. Use clean storage containers.

10. Examine the food carefully and discard any food that has mold or bruises or slime or insects or other problems.

11. Boiling or cooking food until its internal temperature exceeds 200°F (93°C) will kill almost every harmful microorganism that might be in the food. Therefore all canned meats, vegetables, and soups should be cooked at a high temperature before eating them.

Two Quick Tips

1. Dark soy sauce is a good barbecue sauce because it has more flavor and less salt than light or all-purpose soy sauce. A naturally brewed soy sauce is better than one that is chemically brewed. This information should be on the label. For example, Walmart's Great Value brand is naturally brewed.

2. If your hot coffee or tea is a little too bitter, then sprinkle a tiny bit of iodized salt into the hot beverage instead of adding sugar. The iodized salt will help to neutralize the bitterness and it will bring out some of the subtle flavors in the hot beverage.

Aluminum Foil, Wax Paper, and Parchment Paper

Aluminum Foil: It cannot be used in a microwave oven. However, it can be used to surround soft delicate foods, such as mushrooms or fish, so they can be cooked on a grill surface. It can also be wrapped around a food item to contain its natural moisture when baked in an oven, such as a potato. It can be used to cover a pan placed in an oven to keep the food from becoming too dry, and to protect the top layer of food from overcooking. Aluminum foil helps food retain its natural flavor while it is cooked. It can also be used to line the inside of a broiler pan to make cleanup a lot easier. However, aluminum foil should not be used with high acidic foods, such as tomatoes, because the aluminum may react with the acid in those foods. Nonstick aluminum foil is also available.

Wax Paper: A paper covered with a thin coating of wax that provides a nonstick surface. It is semi-transparent, waterproof, and it won't stick to most foods. In the year 2018 wax paper costs about $0.023 per square foot, whereas parchment paper costs about $0.088 per square foot, or almost 4 times more than wax paper. Wax paper generally should not be used for cooking because it will smoke, and it may catch on fire. It can be used to cover dishes in a microwave to prevent splattering as long as the microwave temperature is not too high and the cooking time is not too long.

Parchment Paper: A nonstick waterproof greaseproof paper that is oven safe and microwave safe. It can be used to line the inside of baking pans and to cover baking sheets to eliminate the need to grease the pans and it makes cleanup easier. If used in a baking pan then cut the paper to fit the shape of the round or rectangular baking pan so it will lie flat on the bottom of the pan. If used to cover a baking sheet then smear a tiny bit of butter on the underside corners of the parchment paper so it will stick to the baking sheet without shifting and to keep it from curling up when baking. This is very useful when baking thin cookies or delicate pastries. It can be used to bake fish or chicken to provide a low-fat method of cooking.

Oven Differences

There are six primary variables that make ovens different:
1. the size of the inside of the oven.
2. the quality of the materials used to build the interior oven walls.
3. the heat insulation inside the oven walls.
4. the possible positions of the shelves up and down inside the oven.
5. the accuracy of the oven temperature control gauge.
6. the fluctuation of the internal oven temperature above and below the set oven temperature before the oven's automatic temperature control is activated.

All of these variables influence how much time will be required for something to be cooked in a specific oven until it is done. That is why there are usually time estimates on each recipe for minimum and maximum baking times.

Most foods should be baked in the middle of an oven, unless the recipe has other instructions.

Stovetop Differences

Different stoves have different indicators on their heat settings. Some have numbers, some have words, and some just have markings. In this cookbook the following cooking terms will apply to the minimum and maximum settings on your stove temperature adjustment dials:

Off = 0% setting.
Very Low = 10% approximately.
Low = 20% approximately.
Medium-Low = 35% approximately.
Medium = 50% approximately.
Medium-High = 75% approximately.
High = 100% approximately.

The above should be used as a guide to help you learn how your stove cooks. When you prepare a recipe in this cookbook make a note on how the food cooked using the recommended stove temperature setting in the recipe. As you gradually collect some data you will be able to set your stove to the correct temperature based on the recommended temperature in the recipe. However, if you cook on someone else's stove then you will need to repeat this procedure until you learn how their stove cooks.

The Minimum Equipment Needed by a Gourmet Cook

Now let's examine the **minimum** equipment that is necessary for a person to prepare gourmet food on a regular basis. The following items are ones you will need at various times when you are cooking:

A Few Good Knives: A gourmet cook needs the following 3 knives: chef's knife with 8-inch blade, small paring knife, serrated bread knife.

Knife Maintenance: Sharpen your knives when they begin to get dull. A dull knife makes cutting more difficult and more dangerous. A dull knife is actually more dangerous and it causes more accidents than a sharp knife. The Bible says, "If the iron is blunt, and one does not sharpen the edge, he must use more strength, but wisdom helps one to succeed." (Ecclesiastes 10:10, English Standard Version.)

An Instant Read Meat Thermometer: This is the secret weapon of a gourmet cook. It allows the cook to know when meat is perfectly done by checking the internal temperature of the meat. The pointed tip of the thermometer is briefly inserted into the thickest part of the meat but not all the way to the bone.

Some Cooking Utensils (spoon, spatula, etc.): Cooking utensils with plastic ends, and comfortable synthetic handles, and that are connected by stainless steel are recommended. The plastic ends will not scratch your cookware. The stainless steel center will allow the utensil (when it has food dripping off its end) to be briefly supported against the edge of a hot cook pot without melting the steel, so the food can drip down into the pot. Stainless steel will not rust or chip. If you have 100% plastic utensils then do not rest them on the edge of a hot cook pot. Instead always put them on a spoon rest when they are not being used. The **minimum** cooking utensils are a regular spoon, a slotted spoon, a ladle, a spaghetti ladle, a spatula with a small end, a spatula with a long wide end, and a fork with hard plastic prongs instead of metal prongs. The fork will be used for stirring and not for piercing.

Spoon Rest: A metal spoon rest is recommended. It should be placed on the counter beside your stove. If necessary, it can be placed on the middle of the stove between the stove cooking elements. Cooking spoons, forks, and spatulas can be placed on this spoon rest so they do not become contaminated while cooking, and they are within easy reach when they are needed. Wash the spoon rest after preparing each meal.

Long Wooden Spoon: Very useful for stirring but it can also be laid across the top of an uncovered cook pot to prevent the pot from boiling over.

Tongs: Cooking tongs, instead of a fork, are needed so you can turn meat over while the meat is cooking. If you use a fork then it will punch holes in the meat and the delicious juices inside the meat will be able to leak out. If the meat loses its natural juices then this will result in a dry bland meat taste instead of a juicy delicious gourmet meat taste.

Other Items: A whisk, a measuring cup, a set of measuring spoons, a flour sifter, a rolling pin, a set of round biscuit/cookie cutters, a large mixing bowl, a medium size mixing bowl, and a cutting board.

A Pair of Oven Mittens: These should be thick enough so you could hold a really hot pot between both hands for a short period of time when you need to move the hot pot somewhere else. If the mittens are not thick enough the hot pot will burn your hands and you will automatically drop your hot pot of food on the floor.

Optional - Disposable Food Handling Clear Plastic Gloves: These are the thin disposable gloves worn by employees in a restaurant kitchen. These gloves prevent human germs from getting on the food, and the odors and chemicals from some foods (garlic, onions) from getting on the hands, and they also prevent food from being touched by human hands which is very, very important to some people. The gloves are sold in one-size-fits-all and they can be purchased at kitchen specialty stores and online. One hundred gloves usually come in one box, and they are available in 3 boxes (300 gloves) for about $6.50, or 10 boxes (1,000 gloves) for about $12.

Some Good Cookware: Good cookware is extremely important. A gourmet cook can prepare culinary miracles in almost any kitchen if the kitchen has some good average cookware. The cookware does not have to be expensive. This is similar to a good musician. A good musician can play beautiful music on almost any good musical instrument even if that instrument is not the most expensive one available. The reason is because the talent is in the musician, or gourmet cook, and not in the equipment being used. Now let's look at cookware in more detail.

How to Select a Good Cookware Set

The first step is to carefully examine all the cookware pieces that you currently own. Any that have loose handles, or scratches on the inside of the pot, or flaking or discoloration on the inside of the pot, need to be thrown away. However, any cookware you currently own that is still in good condition should be kept and not replaced. Remember that the food you cook will depend on your skill and not on how much money you invest in cookware.

Most people will only need to purchase a few pieces of new cookware because most of their current cookware will probably still be in good condition. However, if you need everything, or almost everything, then a new complete set of cookware may be less expensive than buying several individual pieces one-at-a-time.

A higher price is frequently associated with higher quality. However, this is not always true. Sometimes a higher price is due to inefficient and wasteful manufacturing practices at the facility where the product is made. On the other hand, a really cheap price usually means inferior quality. These concepts are true when applied to cookware.

Once I purchased a cheap $20 set of cookware and it lasted about 3 months before I threw it away because the handles were coming loose and the cookware had developed some hot spots in the pans that caused my food to burn.

In 1995 I paid $500 for a set of professional quality cookware (it was on sale for $500) and it lasted about 2 years before I threw it away. The handles did not come loose but the "nonstick" coating gradually acquired some permanent food stains that could not be removed and those stains would occasionally impart some of their flavor into the food being cooked in those pots.

For the last 20 years I have usually paid between $60 to $120 for an average set of good cookware and those cookware sets have usually lasted between two to four years before I replaced them for one reason or another. But while I was using them I was very pleased with them.

Therefore if you are considering the purchase of a complete set of cookware then I suggest that you consider paying between $60 to $120 for an average set of good cookware and be emotionally prepared to replace some or all of the pieces in that set a few years after you buy it. The life of the cookware will depend on how well you take care of it, how you use it, and how often you use it each week. Look carefully at what is included in a set of cookware. The lids count as a piece. One lid can frequently be used on two different pieces of cookware in the set. If utensils are included they are sometimes counted as a piece of the set. Sets sometimes include pieces you will never use. If a set includes a wok then make sure that a wok can be used on your stove.

Now let's take a close look at single piece of cookware.

Handles: All cookware has either one or two handles that allow the hot cookware to be moved. If a pot has two handles then they are usually short and on opposite sides of the pot so it can be lifted using both hands. If a pot only has one handle it should be long enough to be comfortably grasped with one hand. The handles may be made of metal, wood, synthetic material, or plastic. Metal handles are usually oven safe. The handle may or may not have a non-slip grip. You should actually grasp the handle, or handles, and verify that they feel comfortable to you. If a pot feels heavy when empty then consider how heavy it will be when it contains food. Also examine how the handle is attached to the pot. Handles welded to a pot are very nice. Handles attached with a fastener are good if the fastener does not extend into the inside of the pot where the food will be cooked. Small round raised bumps on the inside of the pot where the handle is attached can collect food while it is being cooked and they require more effort to clean properly after cooking. Some handles are oven safe and some are not.

Lids: A lid is an important part of most cookware because sometimes you need to cook food with a cover on the pot. The lids should fit nicely on the pot without being too snug (scratches) or too loose (steam escapes during cooking). Some lids have vents that you can manually open and close to keep steam in the pot, or to release steam from the pot but still keep the food covered while it is cooking to prevent cooking oils or grease from "popping" out of the pot onto you, or onto the stove or floor. Metal lids are common but glass lids are better because glass allows you to see what is happening inside the pot as the food cooks. However, glass lids are heavier and they can sometimes break. The top center of the lid will have some type of handle so you can lift the lid off the pot when necessary. However, you will need a kitchen mitten to move a hot lid regardless of what the lid is made of, or what the lid handle is made of. You should grasp the lid handle and verify that you can get a good grip on it and that it cannot easily slip out of your hand.

Bottom Surface of Pot: Read the information that comes with the cookware, or read the information on the manufacturer's website. The bottom of the pot should disperse heat evenly over the entire bottom of the pot to prevent hot spots inside the pot that will burn your food. This is extremely important for a gourmet cook.

Inside Surface of Pot: Metal interiors can interact with the ingredients used in some recipes and the metal can impart an unexpected flavor in those recipes. Therefore some type of nonstick coating is highly recommended. Sometimes you may have more than one pot on the stovetop and you can only focus your attention on one pot at a time. If most of your pots have a nonstick cooking surface then the food is less likely to burn while you momentarily have your attention focused on a different pot. This is extremely important for a gourmet cook because nobody likes burned food or food that is burnt in one or more spots. There has been a lot of negative publicity about nonstick coatings but I still recommend nonstick coatings and I recommend that you replace your cookware before the nonstick coating begins to negatively impact your food. If you do not invest a lot of money in your cookware then this is easier to do when it becomes necessary.

Compatibility With Your Stovetop: The cookware must be designed to work with your stove, such as gas burners, or electric coils, or an induction cook surface. Glass covered cook surfaces are more easily damaged with heavy cookware, such as cast iron. Induction surfaces are designed to work with pots that have magnetic properties.

Oven-Safe: Some cookware can be used on the stovetop and inside the oven. Some cookware can only be used on the stovetop. All your cookware does not need to be oven-safe but you should have a few oven-safe baking sheets, casserole dishes, and baking pans that are specifically designed to be used in an oven.

Color: A final minor issue, but still an important issue, is that the color of the cookware should compliment your kitchen and not clash with your kitchen. Color has no impact on the way the cookware performs, but color will impact the perception of your cooking ability because people will see the color of the cookware and you do not wish to be ashamed of the color of your cookware.

Rating of Cookware: Before you make your final decision, read all the reviews posted by other people who have already bought the cookware you are considering. These reviews are available on Amazon, and sometimes on other websites. The only reviews that should influence your decision are from people who have something positive or negative to say about the functionality of the cookware. Comments about fast delivery, or late delivery, or delivery problems, or other similar issues are not as relevant as comments about the actual performance of the cookware.

Cookware Materials

Stainless Steel Cookware: Very popular with professional chefs who spend their entire day in the kitchen. However, for the average gourmet cook, stainless steel has a significant learning curve in order to be able to use it correctly, it is more difficult to clean, and it can more easily be scratched or become discolored.

Cast Iron Cookware: Extremely versatile and it can be used on the stovetop or inside the oven. A properly well-seasoned cast iron pot is nonstick and it could last a lifetime if properly maintained. However, it is extremely heavy, it takes longer to heat up, it takes longer to cool down, it can be very challenging to clean if food sticks to the pot, it needs to have its oil coating periodically refreshed, and it can rust if stored in a humid environment. It is also very difficult to use a cast iron skillet to flip food over because of its weight. Cast iron pots have cast iron handles and they heat up just like the pot. Therefore you must use a kitchen mitten when you want to move or adjust a hot cast iron pot. However, one or two cast iron cookware pieces can be extremely useful to a gourmet cook. "Lodge" is an American family-owned company that makes high quality factory-seasoned cast iron cookware. If you invest in cast iron cookware then learn how to take care of it.

Enamel Coated: The enamel does not react with acidic foods. They do extremely well for most cooking tasks. They are sometimes available in a variety of colors. However, they can be heavy and enamel can chip.

Nonstick Cookware: Teflon or ceramic coating. Foods do not easily stick to the pans, it is easier to learn how to cook with nonstick pans, they are easier to clean, and you can cook food using less fat or oil which results in healthier meals. However, food does not brown well on a nonstick cooking surface. Nonstick cookware should not be used on high heat because it can damage the nonstick coating. Cream colored ceramic coated cookware is recommended because you can see the food changing color as it cooks against the cream colored surface. A cream colored cooking surface also vividly reveals any spots that may have been missed during the first washing so you can focus on cleaning those spots to remove any food that is still clinging to the pot.

Other Materials: Copper, aluminum, and carbon-steel are also available. But they are usually combined with one another or with another material. Therefore they need to be evaluated individually based on what they are made of and how that benefits the cookware.

Maintaining Your Cookware: Even if your cookware is dishwasher safe, do not put your cookware in a dishwasher. Instead take the time to carefully wash your cookware in the kitchen sink by hand using hot water, dish soap, and a soft sponge or dishcloth. Do not cook at high temperatures if avoidable. If a recipe has to be cooked at a high temperature then use a special high temperature cook pot for the task, such as cast iron, and not your good cookware. If the cooking surface of one piece of cookware gets scratched, stop using it and replace it.

Recommended Cookware Pieces

Nonstick cookware, and cast iron cookware, and enamel coated cookware are all recommended because each type of coating has it own unique advantages when cooking specific types of food.

1. 10-inch or 12-inch cast iron skillet (a tight fitting lid is optional but nice). Cast iron sears beef quickly and it will fry chicken. Cast iron can be used on the stovetop, or in the oven to prepare foods such as cornbread or deep dish pan pizza.

2. 12-inch straight sided sauté pan with a tight fitting lid. Straight sides contain heat and foods heat faster. Straight sides help keep food and moisture in the pan. This helps foods retain their moisture so they will be juicer when served.

3. 9-inch or 10-inch nonstick skillet with curved sides (a tight fitting lid is optional but nice). Curved sides allow for moisture to more quickly evaporate from the pan in order to reduce liquids and thicken sauces. Curved sides allow for food to be easily slid out of the pan onto a plate, such as an omelet or hash browns.

4. 5-quart, or 5 1/2 quart, or 6-quart enameled Dutch oven with a tight fitting lid (size depends on what you can find in a style and color you like). It can be used on the stovetop and inside the oven. It is great for soups, chili, and slow cooking a roast.

5. Two-quart, three-quart, or four-quart saucer (saucepan) with a tight fitting lid. It can be used for boiling or cooking pasta, soups, vegetables, and a variety of other foods. If you can only afford one size then buy the three-quart. If you can afford two sizes, then buy the two-quart and the four-quart. A cream colored ceramic nonstick saucepan will allow you to clearly see how your food is changing color as it cooks.

6. A large glazed-ceramic casserole dish (9-inch by 13-inch). A plastic tight fitting lid is also recommended for keeping leftover casseroles, or one-layer cakes, or other desserts, in the refrigerator. A Pyrex glass casserole dish with a tight fitting plastic lid is also acceptable and the glass allows you to see what is inside the dish when the lid is attached, and the glass provides visual appeal when serving a dessert because people can see the dessert clearly.

7. Cast iron griddle with a flat surface on one side and an uneven ridged surface on the opposite side. The griddle should fit inside your oven. It should also be long enough to fit across two burners on top of your stove. Or it should be small enough to only touch one stove burner at a time. Cast iron cookware is usually available in the kitchen area, and/or the camping area, of a store. In some stores cast iron cookware is available in both areas but with a different selection of cast iron in each area.

8. Two rimmed nonstick baking sheets and two wire cooling racks that are oven-safe. A baking sheet should fit on one shelf in your oven with space on all sides of the baking sheet so heat can freely circulate around the baking sheet. Measure the inside of your oven before your buy baking sheets.

9. Two 9-inch round nonstick baking pans.

10. Two 9-inch square nonstick baking pans.

11. A cupcake or muffin pan with either 6 or 12 compartments, depending on the size of your family, and the size of your oven.

12. Optional Wok: A wok is a very functional piece of cookware if it will work on your stovetop, and if you plan to cook Asian stir-fried meals on a regular basis. A wok has deep sides and a large cooking area so it helps to contain cooking oils and foods while they are being stir-fried without the food or oils spilling over the sides of the wok.

Chapter Two
Definition of Cooking Words

Al Dente: An Italian word that describes pasta that is not cooked until the pasta is tender. Instead the pasta is only partially cooked and it is still a little difficult to bite into.

Bake: Cooking inside an oven using dry heat.

Barbecue (or Barbeque): Cooking food outdoors over charcoal or wood and the food is usually liberally coated with some type of barbecue sauce.

Baste: Adding moisture, such as pan drippings or a seasoned sauce, to food while it is cooking to prevent the food from drying out.

Batter: A mixture that usually contains flour, or cornmeal, and some type of liquid that will hold together but it is still thin enough to pour.

Blanch: Scalding or parboiling a food, such as a fruit or vegetable, in boiling water for a brief period of time in order to soften it, or to partially cook it, or to remove some of its strong flavor, or to make it easier to remove its skin.

Blend: Thoroughly mixing two or more ingredients together.

Boil: Heating a liquid to approximately 212°F or until bubbles continuously appear on the surface. Once it reaches this temperature it will not get any hotter regardless of how much extra heat is applied. An exception is when food is cooked in a pressure cooker.

Braise: Searing food in hot oil or fat in a hot pan and then covering the pan with a tight fitting lid and slowly cooking the food in some liquid. Braising helps to preserve the natural flavor and juices of the food while slowly tenderizing the food as it cooks.

Broil: Cooking beneath a strong source of dry heat.

Broth: The liquid or juice that results from cooking meat or vegetables for a short period of time in water. The liquid is strained to remove small particles and then salt, spices, or flavorings may be added.

Brown: Cooking a food until its exterior surfaces turn a brown color.

Caramelize: Heating granulated sugar until it turns brown to give it a unique flavor.

Char: Cooking fats or sugars to the point of complete caramelization but stopping just before it is burnt in order to add flavor but not a burnt taste.

Chop: Cutting solid food into pieces with a knife or chopping tool. The pieces do not have to be the same size and the chopped pieces are bigger than diced pieces.

Clarify: Removing solid particles from a liquid to make it clear.

Coddle: Cooking a food item in water that is below the boiling point.

Cream: Beating a room temperature fat, such as butter or lard, to make it soft and smooth, and sometimes combining it with another ingredient.

Cure: Preserving meat by drying, salting, and/or smoking.

Dash: Cooking term used in older recipes to refer to a very small amount. Today it has been defined by different "experts" as equal to 2/32 (1/16) or 3/32 or 4/32 (1/8) of a teaspoon when referring to a dry measurement. A dash is approximately 2 pinches or 4 smidgens.

Deglaze: Dissolving a thin layer of juices and small particles that are clinging to the bottom and sides of a pan that has been used for cooking. This is done by heating the pan and adding a liquid to the pan and stirring and scrapping the bottom and sides of the pan in order to create a sauce that contains the flavors of the cooked food.

Degrease: Removing a layer of fat or grease from the top surface of soups, stews, or stocks. The liquid can be refrigerated and when the fat or grease hardens it can be easily removed.

Dice: Cutting food into small pieces of uniform shape and size. A large dice is a cube between 1/2 inch to 3/4 inch, a medium dice is a cube between 1/4 inch to 1/2 inch, a small dice is a cube between 1/8 inch to 1/4 inch, and a fine dice is a cube 1/8 inch or less is size. Most recipes require diced cubes no larger than 1/4 inch in size.

Dissolve: Converting a dry ingredient into a liquid.

Divided: An ingredient is not added at just one step in the recipe. The ingredient will be added at different steps in the recipe and the amount used at each step will be specified. However, the total amount required is shown in the list of all the ingredients at the beginning of the recipe.

Dredge: Sprinkling or coating the exterior surface of food with flour, cornmeal, or breadcrumbs, in order to help prevent the food from sticking, or to help keep the natural moisture in the food, or to provide a crunchy cooked surface, or to add flavor to the food.

Drizzle: Randomly sprinkling a few small drops of a liquid over food.

Dust: Sprinkling a food with a dry substance, or shaking the food inside a plastic or paper bag that contains the dry substance.

Fillet (or filet): *Verb:* Removing the bones from meat or fish. *Noun:* A piece of meat or fish that has had its bones removed.

Flake: Breaking into small pieces.

Flambe: Dousing food with some type of potable alcohol and then setting it ablaze.

Fold: Retaining the air bubbles in a substance, such as egg whites or whipped cream, by using a spoon to gently and repeatedly move the mixture from the bottom of the bowl to the top while slowly rotating the bowl until the mixture is blended but still fluffy.

Fricassee: Cooking a food, such as fowl or rabbit, by braising.

Fry: Cooking in hot fat or oil. Cooking in a little oil is called sautéing or pan frying. Cooking in one to two inches of oil is called shallow frying. Cooking in a deep layer of oil is called deep frying.

Garnish: Decorating a dish to enhance its appearance and flavor.

Glaze: A thin layer that forms on the outside of food while cooking, or a thin layer of sugar or shiny icing that is added to the food.

Grate: Using a grater to cut food into slices, slivers, or pieces.

Gratin: A French word that means baking a food with a thin layer of breadcrumbs, cheese, or cheese sauce, until it turns golden brown.

Grill: Cooking over high heat on a grill surface.

Grind: Reducing solid food into very small particles.

Julienne: Cutting fruit, vegetables, or cheese into long thin strips using a sharp knife so they will cook faster. Standard julienne is 1/8 inch square and between 1 to 2 inches long. Fine julienne is 1/16 inch square and between 1 to 2 inches long. The easiest way to cut food into thin slices is to use the largest opening in a grater but this will produce slightly rounded edges instead of square edges.

Knead: Working dough by pressing and pulling the dough to develop the gluten in the flour.

Lukewarm: Approximately body temperature and not cold or hot.

Marinate: *Dry:* Rubbing a dry mixture of herbs and spices into the outside surfaces of meat, poultry, or seafood. *Wet:* Moisturizing or soaking a food in a liquid solution, for 30 minutes or a few days, in order to add flavor to the food and make it more tender. An acidic liquid, such as vinegar or fruit juices (lemon), helps to soften the food fibers. The food should be marinated in a bowl that will not react with the acids while marinating. Marinades are only used once and they should be discarded after they have been used.

Mince: The French word is émincé. Chopping food into very tiny pieces. This is the finest of all cutting and chopping techniques.

Mix: Blending items together, usually by stirring.

Parboil: Boiling for a short period of time until partially cooked (blanching the food). The food is then usually cooked in some type of sauce until it is done, or it may be plunged into cold water to halt the cooking process and then the food may be canned or frozen.

Pare (or Peel): Removing the outer layer of skin from a fruit or vegetable while leaving as much of the inner flesh as possible.

Peel (or Pare): Removing the outer layer of skin from a fruit or vegetable while leaving as much of the inner flesh as possible.

Pickle: Preserving meat, vegetables, or meat in a brine solution.

Pinch: The trivial amount you can grasp between your forefinger and thumb. Today it has been defined by different "experts" as equal to 2/64 (1/32) or 3/64 or 4/64 (1/16) of a teaspoon when referring to a dry measurement. It is approximately 1/2 of a dash, or approximately twice as much as a smidgen.

Pit: Removing the interior pit from a fruit.

Plump: Soaking dried fruits in a liquid until they absorb some of the liquid and swell up.

Poach: Cooking gently in a liquid at a temperature between 140°F to 180°F. It produces no agitation in the liquid which makes it perfect for cooking delicate foods such as eggs or fish. The cooked foods retain most of their moisture and they will rarely become overcooked unless they are neglected. If poaching eggs or fish then the addition of a little vinegar to the water will help keep the eggs or fish firm.

Purée: Blending or mashing a food until it is perfectly smooth without any lumps.

Reduce: Boiling a liquid to decrease its volume or to thicken the liquid.

Refresh: Quickly stopping the cooking process by running cold water over parboiled food.

Render: Slowly melting a solid fat into a liquid.

Roast: Cooking by dry heat in an oven.

Roux: A cooked mixture of flour and fat, such as butter or oil or lard. It is used to thicken gravies, sauces, soups, and stews. Usually a roux is made of equal parts of flour and fat. The flour is added to the melted fat, stirred until smooth, and then cooked to the desired degree of brownness. Other ingredients are commonly added to the roux after it has been properly prepared.

Sauté: In French it means "jump" which refers to the continuous tossing or flipping of the food in the pan. Or the food can be stirred and turned over with a spatula. Sautéing is cooking in a small quantity of oil or fat over relatively high heat in order to preserve the food's texture, flavor, and natural moisture. Using too much oil or fat will result in pan frying instead of sautéing. The food is normally cut into thin slices, or pieces, so it will cook faster. Heat the pan first, then add the oil or fat and give it time to heat, and then add the food. The hot fat or oil will coat the food so the food will brown more evenly. Do not overcrowd the food in the pan.

Scald: Bringing a liquid to a temperature just below its boiling point.

Scallop: Baking food in a casserole dish with a liquid or a sauce.

Score: Cutting thin grooves into the top surface of a food.

Sear: Browning very quickly using intense heat to enhance flavor and appearance, and to produce a flavorful brown crust.

Shred: Cutting or tearing into long slender pieces.

Sift: Processing one or more dry ingredient through a sieve or sifter.

Simmer: Heating a liquid to between 180°F to 205°F, or almost to a boil but not to the point where bubbles appear, except occasionally on the sides of the pot. Usually the food must be stirred occasionally to prevent the food from burning or sticking to the bottom of the pot. It is appropriate for cooking rice, and for cooking the cartilage in bones to make stock.

Skim: Removing impurities that float to the surface of a liquid when it is being cooked to improve the flavor and appearance of the food.

Slice: Cutting completely through a food, across the grain, into thin pieces that are of a relatively consistent thickness, usually between 1/16 inch to 3/8 inch.

Smidgen: Cooking term used in old recipes to refer to the most trivial amount of a dry ingredient. It is approximately 1/2 of a pinch, or approximately 1/4 of a dash.

Steam: Cooking over a small quantity of boiling water where the food does not make contact with the boiling water.

Steep: Extracting flavor or color from a dry substance, such as a tea bag, by placing it in almost boiling water and then allowing the water to fall in temperature, but not until the water is cool, until the liquid has the flavor and color of the dry substance.

Sterilize: Killing harmful microorganisms by boiling, steaming, or exposing to high dry heat.

Stew: Simmering very slowly in a little liquid for a long time.

Stir: Mixing ingredients using a circular motion until they are well blended.

Stock: The liquid that results when vegetables or bones (sometimes with small pieces of meat attached) are simmered in water for a long time in order to extract the maximum amount of flavor. Stock is usually thicker than broth.

Toss: Mixing ingredients, such as pasta or a salad, by gently lifting, separating, and dropping the ingredients many times.

Truss: Securing the legs and wings of poultry to keep them in a fixed position while cooking.

Whip: Beating rapidly to add air in order to expand egg whites or cream.

Chapter Three
Herbs, Seasonings, and Spices

Terminology: In this chapter herbs, seasonings, and spices will all be referred to simply as herbs.

Storage of Dried Herbs: Store all herbs in airtight containers at normal room temperatures in a dry cool dark area. Do not store above an oven, or dishwasher, or sink, or in front of a window that receives direct sunlight during the day. Do not freeze herbs that are used on a regular basis because freezing will not extend their shelf-life. Each time a regularly used herb is removed and then returned to the freezer, condensation will form inside the container which will reduce the aroma and flavor of the herb.

Fresh or Dried: Usually the taste of most fresh herbs are significantly more flavorful and more complex than the same herb after it has been dried. When a recipe only requires a total of three of four ingredients and a fresh herb is recommended then most people will be able to detect a taste difference if a dried herb is substituted. However, dried herbs can usually be substituted for fresh herbs in recipes that require eight or more different ingredients if the recipe only requires a small quantity of the herb because its contribution to the final flavor and texture of the finished recipe is minor and most people will not be able to detect a noticeable difference in the final recipe results.

Substituting Dried Herbs for Fresh Herbs: If a recipe specifies fresh herbs then use 1/4 the amount of freshly dried herbs or freshly purchased dried herbs up to three months old. Or use 1/3 the amount for older dried herbs between four to six months old.

Shelf Life of Herbs: The shelf life of herbs varies based on the herb itself, how it is stored, and how old it was when you acquired it. The printed expiration date on the herb container can be very useful. However, you may wish to replace any unused herbs after they have been in your possession for six months. The easiest way to do this is to use a permanent marker and write your own expiration date on each container when you first purchase it.

Information on Different Herbs

Basil: Also called sweet basil. It is a member of the mint family and it has a warm mild sweet licorice flavor, and a pleasant odor. Basil is usually added at the last step in a recipe because heat rapidly diminishes its flavor. Good with beef, dressing, eggs, fish, lamb, and vegetables.

Bay Leaves: Also called bay laurel. A whole bay leaf is put in a muslin bag or tea ball so it can be easily removed from the food after cooking. If eaten whole a bay leaf has a sharp bitter taste and it can be abrasive in the digestive system. Ground dried bay laurel does not have to be removed after cooking. Used with seafood, stews, and vegetables.

Caraway Seed: It is not a seed but the dried fruit of a caraway plant. It is a member of the carrot family and is related to parsley and coriander. It has a mild sweet flavor with a subtle licorice and citrus hint. In the USA it is used on rye bread, soda bread, in soups, and in sauerkraut.

Celery Seed: It has a strong celery flavor and it should be used sparingly on beef, dips, dressing, fish, marinades, and salads.

Chives: The smallest member of the onion family with long slender leaves that have a very mild onion flavor. Usually sprinkled on food just before serving, such as fish, potatoes, salads, and soups.

Cilantro: "Cilantro" is the Spanish translation of the English word "coriander." In the USA, cilantro refers to the lacy green leaves of the plant. It has a lemon-like or lime-like flavor. In the USA the seed of the same plant is called "coriander" and it has a total different flavor. Use cilantro with beans, chicken, fish, Mexican dishes, rice, and salads.

Cinnamon: Obtained from the inner tree bark of a specific type of tropical evergreen tree. It is used for its aromatic scent and warm, sweet flavor, and it is frequently used with sugar. Used in baked sweets, cheesecake, chocolate, and hot drinks.

Coriander: It has a mild, sweet, orange taste. Ground coriander seed quickly loses its flavor and therefore it is usually ground when it is needed. Roasted coriander seeds are common in some Indian dishes. Use with baked goods, beef, casseroles, and Greek recipes.

Cream of Tartar: A fine white powder. It is acidic and when used with baking powder it will cause baked goods to rise. It is also a stabilizing agent and it helps egg whites reach their maximum volume and hold high peaks when whipped. It also helps to prevent sugar from crystallizing when cooked. It will last indefinitely if stored in an airtight container in a cool dark area.

Cumin Powder or Seed: It is a member of the parsley family. It has a distinctive flavor that is used to compliment the natural sweet flavor of some foods. It has a sharp slightly bittersweet taste. It is a major ingredient in curry powder.

Curry Powder: A mixture of a variety of dried herbs, including coriander, turmeric, cumin, fenugreek, chili pepper, garlic, and ginger. It is a common spice in Indian and Mexican recipes. It can produce a distinctive skin odor in people who eat it frequently. Use on beef, fish, poultry, and vegetables.

Dill: A member of the celery family. Its leaves and fruit are used. The fresh aromatic leaves are called "dill weed" and the dried fruit are called "dill seed" even though they are not seeds. Dill leaves are best used fresh because home dried dill leaves quickly lose their flavor. However, commercially "freeze-dried" dill leaves retain their flavor for several months. Dill weed is commonly used with chives or parsley. Dill seed has a flavor similar to caraway but with a hint of the flavor of dill weed. It is a primary ingredient in dill pickles. Dill is usually added at the last step in a recipe because heat rapidly diminishes its flavor. Use as a garnish on beans, dressings, fish, potatoes, soup, or vegetables.

Fennel: A member of the carrot family. The bulb, leaves, and seed are used. It is aromatic and it has a slightly sweet taste similar to licorice and anise. The bulb can be eaten raw or cooked like a vegetable. The fresh leaves are commonly added to a salad, or used as a garnish. Dried fennel seed is used as a spice in small quantities in baked goods. Fennel is common in Italian recipes.

Ginger: An underground root that is common in Indian and Asian recipes. Powdered dried ginger root is used as a spice. It can be added to hot coffee or tea. In the USA ginger is normal used as a sweet spice in ginger ale, gingerbread, and ginger snaps. Modern scientific research has shown that ginger is effective in helping to relieve gastrointestinal stress, eliminate intestinal gas, and it has antioxidant and anti-inflammatory benefits. May be used in cakes, cookies, preserves, meat dishes, and soups.

Italian Seasoning: A mixture of herbs in the proportions commonly preferred by most good Italian-American cooks

Lawry's® Seasoned Salt: Created in 1938 for use in the world-famous Lawry's® Prime Rib Restaurant in Beverly Hills, California to season prime rib beef. It is currently used to season prime rib, beef, chicken, potatoes, and casseroles.

Marjoram: It is in the mint family. It has a mild bittersweet oregano flavor but its gentle flavor is a little sweeter than oregano. It is popular in English, French, German, Greek, Italian, and Polish recipes. It retains its flavor when dried. It is usually added at the last step in a recipe because heat rapidly diminishes its delicate flavor. Use with eggs, fish, lamb, poultry, stuffing, stew, and tomato juice.

Mace and Nutmeg: Nutmeg is the hard brown seed of the nutmeg tree. Mace is the dried lacy membrane around the nutmeg seed. Nutmeg has a pungent aroma and a warm slightly sweet taste, and mace has a more delicate flavor. Nutmeg grinders are available and some chefs prefer freshly ground nutmeg. Use with cakes, custards, fish, pies, poultry, milk pudding, soup, and veal.

Nutmeg: See Mace. Freshly ground nutmeg can enhance the flavor of a creamed dish, such as creamed spinach or mashed potatoes.

Old Bay Seasoning: Created in 1939 by a German immigrant named Gustav Brunn in the Chesapeake Bay area for the purpose of seasoning crabs with a salt mixture that would encourage restaurant customers to purchase more beverages. It gradually became a standard seasoning on Navy ships. It was named after the passenger ship called "The Old Bay Line" that sailed the Chesapeake Bay in the early 1900s between Baltimore, Maryland and Norfolk, Virginia. The seasoning is primarily used to season crabs and shrimp, and sometime clams and oysters.

Oregano: It is one of the most widely used herbs in the world. Its leaves are more flavorful when dried than when fresh. It has a warm slightly bitter taste and a strong smell. It is frequently used in Italian-American recipes. Oregano and rosemary can be substituted for one another in equal amounts in a recipe. Use with chili, eggs, fish, pizza, poultry, stew, and vegetables.

Paprika: A red powder made by air-drying and grinding sweet red peppers. It can be sprinkled raw as a garnish, or it can be heated in oil to help release its flavor and to infuse its color into a dish. Paprika deteriorates quickly and should be replaced in 6 months. Use with beef, fish, soups, vegetables, and as a garnish on eggs, potatoes, and salads.

Parsley: One of the most popular herbs in the world. Widely used as a green garnish. The leaves are normally used, but the stalks can be used to add flavor to stocks. Use on beef, eggs, fish, stuffing, and soup.

Pepper, Black: Dried ground black pepper is one of the most common and most popular spices added to foods worldwide. It is normally used as a companion to salt. Black pepper is a good source of manganese and iron. It helps the stomach to digest fats and meat proteins, and it aids the body in the absorption of the nutrients and the vitamins in food. Black pepper is grown in tropical regions and when the pepper fruit is dried it is called a black peppercorn. The black peppercorn can be course ground, normal ground, or fine ground. Fine grind is normally used when cooking because there are more particles per teaspoon and therefore it distributes itself more evenly with the rest of the ingredients in the recipe. Coarse grind is good when a burst of pepper flavor is desired while eating. Black pepper has a distinctive aroma. Ground black pepper can gradually lose its flavor and aroma so many chefs prefer to grind peppercorns when pepper is needed. Black pepper stimulates the taste buds on the tongue and this sends a message to the brain and stomach to start producing digestive compounds. This enhances digestion because food is processed quicker by the stomach and when food spends less time in the stomach it reduces the chance of heartburn or indigestion. It also enhances digestion in the intestines and this results in easier, more gentle bowel movements because the food is more fully digested. Black pepper helps to prevent both constipation and diarrhea. Black pepper is a carminative (prevents gas) and a diaphoretic (promotes sweating) and a diuretic (promotes urination). In addition, black pepper has antioxidant and antibacterial properties. It also stimulates the breakdown of fat cells to help a person stay slimmer while giving the person extra energy and vitality. Therefore a smart cook will add a little black pepper to almost every recipe (when practical) usually in the form of fine grind black pepper, for the following reasons: (1) to enhance the flavor of the food, (2) to make the food easier to digest, (3) to make the food more pleasant for people to eat and enjoy, (4) to decrease the chance of heartburn or indigestion, and (5) to enhance the overall health and happiness of a person. Since black pepper is the most important herb of a gourmet chef, you should consider buying superior quality, organically grown, black peppercorns from a spice specialty store, or online, and expect to pay a premium. Tellicherry (India), Malabar (India), and Lampong (Indonesia) are three good black peppercorns. The good news is that black peppercorns will remain fresh almost indefinitely if stored in an airtight container in a cool dark area. Black pepper loses some of its flavor the longer it is cooked so it should normally be added near the last step in a recipe if the food will be cooked a long time.

Pepper, White: The inside of a black peppercorn after its black outer skin is removed. It does not have a pepper smell and it has a different flavor than black pepper because the black skin of a peppercorn has its own unique flavor and chemical compounds. Since an important part of the peppercorn has been removed, white pepper does not have the documented health benefits of black pepper. White pepper usually costs more than black pepper because of the extra processing steps and not because of its quality. It can go stale faster than black pepper so purchase smaller quantities more often. White pepper is used in Chinese and Thai dishes. The French use it in white sauces. More white pepper is required to approximate the taste of black pepper, if that is important. White pepper can be used if the color of black pepper is not desired in the dish, or if the full taste of black pepper is not desired in the dish. However, the easiest way to reduce the taste impact of black pepper is to use less of it instead of using white pepper. White pepper is recommended in some recipes in this cookbook only because it is a "traditional" ingredient in those recipes.

Rosemary: It has a bitter astringent taste and a pleasant aroma which enhances some foods. Dried rosemary has almost the same qualities as fresh rosemary but use 1/3 less dried than fresh. Oregano and rosemary can be substituted for one another in equal amounts. Use with beef, breads, dressing, eggs, fish, lamb, potatoes, poultry, and stuffing.

Sage: It has a mild sweet peppery flavor. Sage and poultry seasoning can be substituted for one another in equal amounts in a recipe. Use with beef, bread, eggs, fish, poultry, and stuffing.

Salt: It helps extend the shelf life of food and helps prevent the growth of harmful microorganisms. **Kosher salt** has large irregularly shaped salt flakes that can help beef, chicken, and pork remain tender, moist, and juicy while cooking. One teaspoon of regular salt is equal to about three teaspoons of Kosher salt. **Sea salt** is made by evaporating sea water and it contains insignificant amounts of other minerals. **Regular table salt**, from a salt mine, contains about the same amount of iodine as sea salt, or an insignificant 2 mcg of iodine per gram. **Iodized salt** contains potassium iodine plus an anti-caking agent and it dissolves quickly. Iodine deficiency in a pregnant woman is the most common preventable cause of mental retardation in her baby. It can contribute to miscarriages and stillbirths. Iodine deficiency can result in goiter (enlarged thyroid gland), reduced metabolism, weight gain, fatigue, cold intolerance, an impaired immune system, an increase in bodily toxins, and neurological, gastrointestinal, and skin abnormalities. *The salt in processed food and fast foods is non-iodized.* Regular salt and sea salt are widely available as iodized or non-iodized. **Regular iodized table salt, or Morton's® Lite Iodized Salt, is recommended for cooking, baking, and for foods that require no cooking.** A teaspoon of iodized table salt contains about 280 mcg (or µg) of iodine. The recommended amount of **iodine** per day for a young child is 90 mcg to 250 mcg, and for an adult is 150 mcg to 1,100 mcg. The recommended **minimum** amount per day for a pregnant mother is 220 mcg, and 270 mcg for a mother who breast feeds her baby. Too much **sodium** can cause a rise in blood pressure and increase the chance of heart disease. A teaspoon of salt contains 2,300 mg sodium. The recommended adult amount of **sodium** is 1,500 to 2,300 mg per day. Some people who do not understand the importance of **iodine** will criticize cooks who use iodized salt -- so be prepared for criticism.

Tarragon: The leaves have a hot pungent flavor and it can easily overpower other flavors so it should be used sparingly. Fresh leaves are preferred because dried leaves are very weak in flavor. Use with carrots, dressing, eggs, fish, poultry, salads, sauces, and tomatoes.

Thyme: Dried thyme retains most of its flavor and is a good substitute for fresh thyme. Use on fish or poultry before baking or broiling.

Turmeric: It has a pleasant aroma and a slightly bitter mustard-like taste. An important ingredient in many Asian recipes. Most turmeric is used as a powder but it can be used fresh. It is an important ingredient in curry powder. It should be used sparingly in rice recipes.

Chapter Four
Common Recipe Ingredients

Baking Powder, Baking Soda, and Yeast

Baking soda is pure sodium bicarbonate.

Baking powder is baking soda plus cream of tartar plus a starch (such as cornstarch). A homemade baking powder recipe is in chapter six.

If necessary, you may use baking powder in place of baking soda in a recipe but do **not** use baking soda in place of baking powder in a recipe.

Baking powder or **yeast** will cause your bread to rise. But both baking powder and yeast have relatively short shelf lives.

Baking Powder Shelf Life: Baking powder gradually looses its effectiveness as time passes. Old baking powder can completely ruin a great recipe. The day you buy your baking powder write the date on the can with a permanent marker. If you haven't used all the baking powder within three months then throw the unused baking powder in the trash. Baking powder is really cheap when compared to all the other ingredients in your recipes (plus your time) and you shouldn't gamble on old baking powder being potent enough to do its job, regardless of the manufacturer's preprinted expiration date on the container.

Yeast: Yeast multiplies rapidly at a temperature between 100 to 115°F. Yeast converts sugar into alcohol and carbon dioxide. The carbon dioxide bubbles cause the dough to expand and become light and fluffy. The alcohol quickly cooks out of the dough when it is heated. Yeast begins to die at temperatures above 120°F. One-half ounce of yeast will double the size of 4 cups of dough in 1.5 to 2 hours.

Rapid Rise or Fast Acting Yeast: Smaller grains of yeast that can reduce the time it takes for bread to rise by one-half. However, unless it is specified in a recipe, use regular yeast instead.

Yeast Storage: If you do not need your yeast when you buy it, then freeze store bought yeast until it is needed. Before using the yeast allow it to gradually warm up to room temperature.

Yeast Water: Hot faucet water may be used if it is well water and it does not contain chlorine. Water that contains chlorine will transfer its taste into your bread. If your water contains chlorine then consider using bottled water for baking purposes and for activating your yeast.

Proofing the Yeast: Crumble yeast and stir into 1/4 cup very warm water (100°F to 115°F). Test the water on your wrist. It should feel warm but not hot. If the water is too hot it will kill the yeast. If the water is too cold it will slow down the process. Adding a pinch of sugar to the water will speed up the process. Adding salt or fat will slow it down. Good yeast will become foamy and creamy in about 10 to 12 minutes.

Kneading Dough: Kneading helps to evenly distribute the yeast throughout the dough so the dough will rise uniformly, and it also helps develop a firm gluten structure for the carbon dioxide bubbles.

Butter, Margarine, Bacon Grease, Lard, and Shortening

Butter, margarine, bacon grease, lard, and shortening are different types of fats. Each has its own advantages and shortcomings. Therefore the decision on which one to use in a recipe requires good judgment.

Recommendation: If a recipe for a baked good specifies either butter or shortening (or lard), then you may wish to consider using half butter and half lard to get the benefits of lard and the taste of butter.

Greasing Baking Pans: Lard is the best choice for lightly greasing a baking pan because lard will not be absorbed into the food as it bakes.

Butter: Butter is a dairy product made by churning cream to separate the butterfat from the buttermilk. Butter contains cholesterol and saturated fat. Different brands of butter have different amounts of cholesterol and fat (read the label). Butter is a good choice for baking cakes, cookies, pastries, and pies because it yields butter flavored, tender, flaky baked goods. Butter is also good for frying some foods.

Whipped Butter: Butter with air added to it. It is easier to spread but more of it is required to yield the same flavor because it contains air.

Unsalted Butter: Unsalted butter does not contain any salt. It is recommended in most recipes because the appropriate amount of salt can added separately if salt is needed in the recipe.

Salted Butter: Salted butter contains salt and it may be used at the table to put on bread, rolls, pancakes, waffles, corn, and potatoes. If you use salted butter in a recipe then omit the salt in the recipe.

Butter Blends: Butter that is blended with canola oil or olive oil are healthier choices for use as a table butter, but not for baking.

Margarine: It is a non-dairy product made from different vegetable oils that have significantly different flavors. Stick margarine may be hydrogenated and contain trans fat. The USDA recommends that trans fat not be eaten. Margarine must contain 80% fat by law. If it contains less than 80% it must be labeled as a "spread." If a tub margarine contains enough fat then it may be used for baking. It may also be used to make cookies or pastries but it will not add the butter flavor that most people prefer. If it contains very little fat then it will normally contain more water and if used for baking it will produce flatter, tougher, less flavorful baked goods that may have burned bottoms. Most good cooks do not use margarine for anything because it increases LDL (bad cholesterol) and decreases HDL (good cholesterol) and it decreases the body's automatic immune response to invading microorganisms.

Bacon Grease: When bacon is fried it produces grease. The hot grease should be allowed to cool a little and then it should be poured into a special container that is only used to save bacon grease. In some recipes bacon grease can be used to add a bacon flavor to the food. Bacon and bacon grease are not appropriate if you will be serving the food to a Jewish guest.

Lard: Lard is rendered (melted) pork fat. Lard in not appropriate if you will be serving the food to a Jewish guest.

Lard has all the following advantages:

1. Lard has a neutral flavor and it does **not** add a pork flavor to food.
2. Lard is heat stable. Lard contains about 48% monounsaturated fat (heart healthy fat) and 40% saturated fat. Saturated fat helps keep other fats from oxidizing when exposed to heat. If the fats oxidize then they create free radicals which are harmful to the human body.
3. Until 1900 lard was the primary cooking fat used in most restaurants and in homes. Our ancestors used lard and prior to the 1900s heart disease was **not** as common as it is today.
4. Modern scientific research has **not** been able to show any correlation between saturated fat and an increased risk of heart disease or cancer. Instead research has found just the opposite -- saturated fat decreases the risk of heart disease. On the other hand, a **low fat** diet has been shown to increase triglycerides which can increase the chance of heart disease.
5. Lard is the 18th richest food in good HDL cholesterol, which helps to control inflammation and improve hormone production, which helps control many of the body's important functions. Research has shown a correlation between **low** blood cholesterol and an increased risk of depression, dementia, Alzheimer's disease, suicide, and committing violent crimes.
6. Lard has a smoking point of about 370°F and it is excellent for frying and deep frying at temperatures of 370°F or below.
7, Lard is excellent for baking and it produces the best tasting fried chicken, biscuits, rolls, cookies, and piecrusts.
8. Lard is good for your skin and if eaten regularly it can help to prevent wrinkles as you age.
9. Lard may contain between 500 to 1000 I.U. of vitamin D if the lard is from farm raised pigs that were allowed to spend part of the day in the sun because the sun's vitamin D collects in the fat under the skin of the pig. Lard available in a grocery store does not contain any vitamin D. Lard with vitamin D may be found at some Farmers' Markets. Ask the person selling the lard if they raised and butchered the pigs, and if so, then how much time did the pigs spend in the sun on an average day.

Shortening: Shortening is made by hydrogenating vegetable oil. It does not contain cholesterol. However, it may contain saturated fat depending on how it is made (read its nutrition label).

Measuring Butter, Margarine, Lard, and Shortening: Insert the end of a measuring spoon in some hot water for about 15 seconds to heat the end of the spoon before you scoop up the butter, margarine, lard, or shortening. The fat will more easily and completely slide off the end of a hot moist spoon.

Cheese and Cream Cheese

Cheese: Freshly shredded or grated cheese from a block of cheese will yield smoother sauces. Packaged shredded cheese is coated with anti-caking compounds, such as cornstarch, to help prevent the pieces of cheese from sticking together. This can cause a sauce made with pre-shredded cheese to be slightly gritty.

Cream Cheese: A soft fresh cheese with a mild pleasant taste that is made from equal parts of cream and whole milk.

Chicken

Chicken Breasts: Depending on the recipe, boneless skinless chicken breasts, or chicken tenders, or chicken breasts with the skin and bone may be specified. If the recipe specifies chicken breasts with the skin and bone then there is a reason. For traditional fried chicken both are required. For boiled chicken, the skin and the bone enhance the flavor of the boiled chicken meat, and the pot water may be strategically used in another part of the same recipe.

Velveting Chicken: Coat one pound of chicken pieces (except thighs) with 1 1/2 teaspoon of baking soda and let rest for 10 minutes. Then rinse the chicken well and pat dry with a paper towel.

Chicken thighs have more chicken flavor and are more tender than chicken breasts.

Cool Whip and Ready Wip

Cool Whip (plastic tub): Cool Whip was invented in 1966. Currently it contains light cream, skim milk, corn syrup, water, hydrogenated vegetable oil, and other ingredients. It needs to be stored in the freezer and thawed prior to use. It retains its shape on top of a dessert longer than Ready Wip. Cool Whip is the best selling whipped topping.

Ready Wip (metal can): Ready Wip was invented in 1948 and it was patented with its easy dispensing valve in 1955. It is gas propelled with nitrous oxide (laughing gas) and it "whips" as it exits through the valve. It contains real cream, non-fat milk, corn syrup, water, sugar, nitrous oxide, and other ingredients. It should be stored in the refrigerator and it needs to be eaten soon after it has been sprayed out of the can because it will gradually flatten into a thin white layer on top of a dessert.

Corn, Cornmeal, and Cornstarch

Types of Corn: When **dent** corn is dried a small depression or dent appears in each kernel of corn. Most cornmeal is made from **dent** corn. When **flint** corn is heated the kernel explodes into popcorn. **Sweet** corn is table corn and it is most frequently eaten as corn on the cob.

Color: White corn has the mildest flavor, it is the most popular, and it is most frequently used to make cookies, breads, and for coating baking surfaces to prevent sticking, and as a thickener in soups. Yellow corn has the most vitamin A. Blue corn has more antioxidants and protein.

Grind: Stone-ground (sometimes called water ground) corn still contains its germ which means it is a whole grain, and therefore it has more vitamins, minerals, and fiber, and it contains some fat so it has a short shelf life and it should be stored in the refrigerator. Steel-ground cornmeal (fine, medium, coarse) removes the germ so the cornmeal will have a longer shelf life. Fine-ground (sometimes called corn flour) has the smallest particle size and it is recommended for muffins, pancakes, and for coating fried foods. (Note: If a British recipe specifies "corn flour" it actually means "cornstarch.") Medium-ground is a little more dense, and is recommended for cornbread, and it is usually what is in a package of cornmeal that does not specify the grind. Coarse-ground has the largest particle size and is almost the same thing as grits or polenta (which are more expensive), and it takes longer to cook and to soften.

Masa Harina: It means "dough flour." It is made from dried hominy cooked in limewater. It is used to make dough for tortillas and tamales.

Polenta: A porridge or mush that originated in northern Italy by slow cooking coarse-ground or medium-ground yellow cornmeal (made from a dent corn or a flint corn) into a thick creamy consistency and eaten hot, similar to American grits. Or it can be chilled until it solidifies and then sliced into bars and reheated and crisped on the outside.

Grits: Coarse-ground white or yellow cornmeal made from dent corn and usually a little denser than coarse-ground cornmeal. It is cooked into a porridge and it is very popular in the southern USA.

Cornstarch: A gluten-free white powder extracted from the endosperm of a corn kernel. Used to thicken sauces, gravies, soups, casseroles, and desserts. It has almost no flavor and it has **twice** the thickening power as flour. It should be added to a cool or room temperature liquid and stirred until it dissolves. It should not be added to a hot liquid because it will form clumps. Liquids that contain cornstarch should be heated to a boil after the cornstarch is added and before cooling to prevent the liquid from separating and to neutralize its starchy flavor. Sauces that contain cornstarch should not be frozen because freezing breaks down the molecules and the sauce will be thin when thawed. Cornstarch stored in an airtight container in a dark cool area will last indefinitely.

Self-Rising Cornmeal: Contains cornmeal, baking powder, and salt. If a recipe calls for it then you can make it by combining 1 cup cornmeal, 1/2 tablespoon baking powder, and 1/2 teaspoon iodized salt. Since it contains baking powder it has a short shelf life and you should only make the exact amount you need when you need it.

Storage: To maximize shelf life and retain flavor, store all cornmeal products, except cornstarch, in airtight containers in the refrigerator.

Eggs

Bad Egg Test: Check the quality of eggs by placing them in a bowl of cold water. If they float then they are **not** fresh and should **not** be used.

Whole Eggs (yolks and whites): Eggs are one of the best sources of high quality protein with few calories. Eggs contain choline which the human body needs but which most people do not get enough of. If you only eat the white of an egg then most people will normally crave something more to eat because their stomach will send a message to the brain that something critical is missing. The most recent unbiased scientific research reveals that eating up to 2 whole eggs per day actually improves a person's overall health profile, unless your personal physician has advised you to not eat eggs for a specific medical reason.

Cold Eggs are easier to separate into yolks and whites.

Yolks Only: Egg yolks contain most of the nutrition in an egg. Yolks contain about 43% of the protein in an egg and 100% of the vitamins A, D, E, and K. Over 90% of the calcium, iron, phosphorus, zinc, thiamin, B vitamins, folate, and carotenoids are in the yolks. When carotenoids are eaten with the fat in an egg they contribute to good eye health and reduce the chance of inflammation. Yolks contain the healthy fats and the healthy cholesterol that is necessary to maintain good health. Since egg yolks contain fat they will produce dough that is soft, pliable, and smooth, and the dough will retain its moisture.

Whites Only: Whites are fat-free and they contain about 57% of the protein in an egg. Egg whites lack flavor. Egg whites can result in a firmer drier dough which is sometimes desirable. However, using whole eggs with one or more extra egg yolks will usually produce a superior quality dough.

Meringue: Egg whites, without even a tiny speck of yolks, can be whipped into meringue. If the egg whites are allowed to come to room temperature then this will increase their volume when whipped.

Leftover Yolks or Whites: Leftover yolks or whites may be combined with whole eggs in scrambled eggs or egg omelets. Or whites can be frozen as they are. Yolks can be refrigerated for 2 days. For storage beyond 2 days, place 1 egg yolk into its own compartment in a ice cube tray, sprinkle with a pinch of iodized salt, and freeze overnight. When frozen transfer the yolks to a heavy-duty freezer bag or a plastic airtight freezer container. Write the date on the plastic bag because frozen yolks will remain stable for up to 3 months. When needed thaw in the refrigerator and then beat until smooth.

Flour

Hard wheat is high protein wheat (10 to 14 percent).

Soft wheat is low protein wheat (5 to 10 percent).

Protein and Gluten: More protein means more gluten which creates more elastic, firmer dough (holds its shape better), with more volume and a chewier texture. This is important for bread but is not desirable for pastries or cakes where softness is desired instead of firmness.

Cake Flour: A bleached flour that has a low protein content of 5 to 8 percent. It will make good cakes, muffins, scones, and biscuits.

Pastry Flour: Made from soft wheat. It has a protein content of 8 to 10 percent. It will make good piecrusts, cookies, brownies, and tarts. You can make your own pastry flour by mixing 2 parts all-purpose flour with 1 part cake flour.

Bread Flour: It has the highest protein content of 12 to 14 percent and it will make the best yeast bread. All-purpose flour is very close to bread flour and all-purpose flour can be used instead of bread flour to make good bread.

All-purpose Flour: A mixture of hard wheat and soft wheat and it has an average protein content of 8 to 12 percent. It is not appropriate for everything but it is good for bread, biscuits, and piecrusts.

Whole Wheat Flour: It has more fiber and nutrients, but less protein and less gluten. It is usually mixed with other flours in recipes. Store whole wheat flour in the refrigerator because it will become rancid.

Self-Rising Flour: It contains baking powder and salt. However, the baking powder has a short shelf life of six-months when it is fresh and it gradually looses its ability to make the bread rise. It is good for biscuits, pancakes, muffins, cakes, and pastries. If you need self-rising flour then you can make it by adding 1/2 tablespoon baking powder, and 1/2 teaspoon iodized salt, to 1 cup all-purpose flour. Do not add salt, baking powder, or yeast to a recipe if using self-rising flour. If you have self-rising flour that is more than six months old then you should add 1/2 tablespoon of fresh baking powder to each cup of flour.

Bleached Flour: Chemically treated with less protein than unbleached flour. It is good for piecrusts, waffles, pancakes, and cookies.

Unbleached Flour: Good for bread and pastries.

Shelf Life and Storage: Store in an airtight, moisture-proof container in a cool, dry area. During hot weather store in the refrigerator. Flour should be used within six months of when it was purchased. If the flour has a bad or unusual smell then discard it.

Advantages of Sifting Flour: If a recipe says that the flour and/or other ingredients should be sifted then you should follow the instructions and not omit this important procedure. Sifting does all the following:

1. Flour can easily get packed down during packaging and shipping and this increases the actual amount of flour per measured cup. This additional flour can adversely impact a sensitive recipe.
2. Sifting breaks up any lumps that may be present.
3. Any foreign particles that may have gotten into your flour will be caught in the sifting screen and you can easily discard them.
4. Sifting aerates the flour and makes it light and fluffy.
5. Sifting can produce very desirable results in a recipe, such as cakes that rise better and higher, cookies that have a lighter texture, and icings that are silky smooth.
6. Sifted flour more easily absorbs the moisture added to a recipe and this results in a dough that is easier to work with,

The following can benefit from sifting: flour, powdered sugar, baking soda, baking powder, cornstarch, and cocoa powder. If you sift cocoa powder then wash your sifter before sifting something else.

Pay attention to what the recipe says. If it says "1 cup of flour, sifted" then measure one cup of flour first and then sift it. If it says "1 cup of sifted flour" then sift the flour first and then measure one cup of it.

Even if you buy "pre-sifted" flour it will settle with the passage of time and it will need to be sifted again.

Pour flour into a measuring cup and do not dig into the flour with a measuring cup to fill the cup or you will pack the flour down.

After adding the flour and other dry ingredients together it is good practice to whisk the ingredients using a "whisk" in order to mix the ingredients, break up any small lumps, and aerate the mixture.

Opinion: In the USA "White Lily" brand flour is softer and lighter than most other brands of flour and it will normally yield the best possible results from any recipe.

Garlic

Garlic Whole: The garlic bulb is composed of several individual cloves that can be easily separated from one another. When the cloves are eaten their essential oils remain in the body a long time and those oils can impact a person's breath and skin odor. Purchase firm fresh bulbs and avoid shriveled or soft bulbs. Store at room temperature in an open container in a cool, dark area. Do not store in the refrigerator.

Garlic Cloves: Individual cloves will remain fresh for about 8 weeks if left attached to the main bulb. After a clove has been removed from the main bulb it will remain fresh for 3 to 10 days. Garlic cloves are not eaten whole. They are roasted, chopped, crushed, minced, pressed, or pureed. Garlic cloves may be used with pasta, beef, chicken, fish, lamb, pork, seafood, mushrooms, beans, potatoes, rice, and many vegetables.

Garlic Minced: Wear disposable kitchen gloves when mincing garlic to keep the fluids and the lingering odor off your hands. Use a sharp knife to cut a garlic clove into very tiny pieces. Mincing with a knife does not release as much fluid as other mincing methods and the tiny pieces are drier. Or a garlic press may be used but a garlic press will release more of the fluid and some of it will spray out of the garlic press so be prepared. Pressed garlic also has a more powerful flavor than knife minced garlic. Finally, minced garlic can be purchased in a jar with water in the herb and spice racks of a store. Some cooks will not use pre-minced garlic but some cooks use it regularly or it would not be available in a grocery store.

Garlic Powder: Garlic that has been dried, dehydrated, and ground. It provides some of the flavor of fresh garlic but not the texture. It mixes and disperses more evenly throughout liquids to create a more uniform flavor. It has a long shelf life and therefore it will usually be available when you don't have any fresh garlic. It is considered by many cooks as a better substitute than minced garlic in a jar. Some garlic powder is pure garlic (recommended) but some has other ingredients added (read the label). Garlic powder is a common ingredient in many recipes such as pizza, pasta, and a variety of salad dressings.

Garlic Salt: Finely ground garlic powder plus salt plus anti-caking ingredients. It is 1 teaspoon garlic powder plus 3 teaspoons salt.

Substitutions: 1 garlic clove = 1 teaspoon chopped garlic = 1/2 teaspoon minced garlic = 1/2 teaspoon garlic flakes = 1/4 teaspoon granulated garlic = 1/8 teaspoon garlic powder = 1/2 teaspoon garlic salt (and reduce the salt in the recipe).

Lemons and Limes

Lemons and Limes: Allow the fresh lemon (of lime) to come to room temperature. Then roll the lemon around on a table or countertop with the palm of your hand and press down on the lemon as you roll. Then slice and squeeze the lemon and you will get the maximum amount of lemon juice out of the lemon.

Lemon Juice: One medium fresh lemon will yield about 2 3/4 teaspoons of juice.

Lime Juice: One fresh lime will yield about 2 teaspoons of juice.

Milk, Cream, Half & Half, and Buttermilk

Milk: If your family drinks fresh milk then it will normally be available in your refrigerator when you need it for a recipe. However, if no one in your family drinks fresh milk then it would be more convenient to store dry powdered milk for recipe use, or evaporated milk in a can.

Whole Milk: Contains the normal 3.5 percent fat that is present in cow's milk. Most commercially available milk has been pasteurized to kill bacteria, and homogenized to prevent the milk fat (cream) from separating from the milk and rising to the top of the milk.

Low Fat Milk: Contains either 2 percent or 1 percent fat. Skim milk contains less than 1/2 percent fat. The removed fat is sold as cream.

Cream: The normal fat that is present in cow's milk. It will rise to the top of milk that has not been homogenized where it can be easily removed and used for other purposes.

1. **Sour Cream:** Contains 18 percent fat. It is used on potatoes, tacos, and in soups.

2. **Light Cream:** Contains between 16 to 29 percent fat. It is used in sauces and soups.

3. **Whipping Cream:** Contains 30 percent fat. When whipped it will thicken but not as much as heavy cream. It is only available in the USA.

4. **Heavy Cream:** Contains 36 to 40 percent fat. When whipped it will double in volume and it will hold firm peaks. If a recipe requires cream but does not specify what type of cream then use heavy cream. It will not curdle when heated and it does not form a skin on top.

Half & Half: Contains half milk and half light cream and has between 10 to 12 percent fat. Used to sweeten coffee because it adds sweetness without watering down the coffee. Also used in recipes that benefit from a mixture of milk and cream because half & half is homogenized and the milk and cream will not separate. However, overcooking half & half can cause it to curdle. It can also cause a food to become too rich and greasy. It will not thicken sauces. It cannot be used as a substitute for cream in recipes because it does not contain enough fat. To make half & half use the following amounts of milk and cream:

     1 part whole milk and 1 part light cream
     3 parts whole milk and 1 part whipping cream
     4 parts whole milk and 1 part heavy cream

Buttermilk: Originally a byproduct of churning butter but now it is called "traditional buttermilk." The buttermilk available today is made by adding lactic acid bacteria to skim milk to give it a thicker texture and a tangy flavor. Buttermilk is lower in fat and in calories than whole milk. If it is only needed occasionally in recipes, then buttermilk powder (longer shelf life than fresh buttermilk) can be purchased and mixed with water when buttermilk is needed in a recipe. Or you can make a buttermilk substitute following the instructions in chapter six.

Evaporated Milk: Canned milk with approximately 60 percent of the water removed. It has a long shelf life. It can be used to sweeten coffee. It is used in recipes for desserts, sauce, and soups. If it is mixed with an equal amount of water then it can be used as whole milk in a recipe.

Sweetened Condensed Milk: Canned milk that is made by heating milk mixed with sugar until the water evaporates to leave a sticky sweet thick liquid. It can be used to sweeten coffee. It is used in recipes for desserts and pie fillings, such as key lime pie.

Onions

Fresh or Dried Onions: Onions do more than just add their unique flavor to a recipe. When cooked with meat, fresh onions help to tenderize the meat and they can enhance the flavor of the meat. Cooked onions also have a unique flavor that cannot be replicated with dried onions. Therefore dried onions should not be substituted for fresh onions except in those recipes where the onion is not making a significant contribution to the final flavor of the recipe and its basic purpose is to simply add a little zest to the flavor of the recipe. For example, fresh diced onions are appropriate as a topping on a hotdog but dried onion powder could be used in a recipe that requires either 1/2 teaspoon of dried onion powder or 1 teaspoon of freshly minced onion.

Raw or Cooked Onions: There is a significant taste difference between raw onions and cooked onions. Raw onions have a sharp flavor, a distinctive odor, a crunchy texture, and you can't see through them. Cooked onions have a milder flavor, a different smell, a soft texture, and they are partly transparent (translucent). As an example a blindfolded person could easily detect whether raw onions or cooked onions were on a hamburger after just one or two bites. This same concept applies to recipes where onions play an important role in the final flavor and texture of the food. If a recipe specifies raw onions or cooked onions then you should follow the recipe recommendation if you want to experience the intended flavor of that recipe.

Dicing an Onion: Cut onion in half. Remove both ends and the thin outside layer of the onion for sanitary reasons. Lay the flat side of one-half onion against the cutting board. Cut into 1/8 inch thick slices but hold the slices together and be careful not to cut yourself. Rotate the sliced onion 90 degrees and slice again from one end to the other end in order to created diced onions. Repeat for the other half of the onion.

Peppers

Banana Pepper: Sweet mild flavor if allowed to ripen. Has a banana shape up to 6 inches long. Yellow when mature but red if allowed to fully ripen on the vine.

Bell Pepper: Mild to sweet flavor. May be eaten raw or cooked. Varieties differ in size, shape, thickness, and color. Usually green at maturity but they will turn red if allowed to fully ripen on the vine. They have their strongest flavor when mature and their flavor becomes milder and sweeter as they continue to ripen.

Chile (or Chili) Peppers: More than 200 varieties of different sizes, shapes, and flavors that range from mild to extremely hot. Generally the smaller the pepper the hotter it is. May be eaten raw or cooked. Wear kitchen gloves when handling chile peppers and be careful to not touch your eyes. Fresh peppers are best stored wrapped in a clean dry cloth inside a paper bag in the refrigerator but sun dried peppers are best stored in a cool dark dry area.

1. **Cayenne Peppers:** Very common chile pepper with a very hot taste that is often used in Cajun and chili recipes.
2. **Jalapeño Peppers:** One of the most popular chile peppers because of their spicy flavor and the ease with which their seeds can be removed. Green when harvested but will gradually turn red if allowed to ripen over a long period of time. Smoked and dried jalapeño peppers are called "Chipote Chiles" and they can be ground into a powder.
3. **Pepperoncini (or Tuscan) Peppers:** Mild, sweet, slightly hot flavor commonly added to Greek and Italian salads to add crunch.

How to Process Peppers: If processing hot peppers, wear disposable kitchen gloves and do not touch your eyes. Rinse the pepper. Remove and discard the stem. Cut pepper in half (or quarters) and use a thin sharp knife (or a spoon) to scrap out the ribs (or membrane) and the seeds and discard them. It may be left as a half pepper if it will be stuffed. Or it can be cut into thin slices, or diced into small pieces.

Sugar

All sucrose sugar is made from sugar cane or sugar beets.

White granulated sugar, or table sugar, has medium-size white crystals (granules) that do not stick together. It is good for cooking and baking. It will yield cookies that are thin, tender, and crisp. When heated it can caramelize and become brown in color.

White confectioners' powdered sugar is white granulated sugar that is ground into a smooth powder, sifted, with 3% cornstarch added to prevent caking. It is used for confections, icings, and whipping cream.

Light brown sugar is granulated sugar with some molasses added to give it a brown color and unique flavor. Used in sauces and baking.

Dark brown sugar is granulated sugar with more molasses for a richer flavor. It is used with gingerbread, baked beans, and for barbequing.

Brown sugar is not healthier than white sugar just because it contains a trivial amount of molasses. Brown sugars contain more moisture than granulated sugar and they help baked goods retain their moisture and stay soft and chewy. If brown sugar is used with baking soda then they will combine to create carbon dioxide and this will yield cookies that are soft, thick, and fluffy, but not crisp.

Tomatoes and Ketchup

Tomato: A fruit (not a vegetable) that has a pleasant taste. Fresh tomatoes may be sliced, chopped, or diced and eaten raw or added to salads or sandwiches. Tomatoes contain a lot of water and can easily be cooked into a fluid consistency that is used to thicken sauces without having to add flour or cornmeal. After cooked tomato sauces have cooled they should be refrigerated if not used immediately.

Tomato Sauce: A thin sauce that includes tomatoes, water, olive oil, and salt. Some brands include other spices and ingredients. It has a flavor that is normally associated with Italian dishes.

Tomato Puree: A thicker liquid made from tomatoes that have been briefly boiled and strained. It has less acidic flavor than a fresh tomato and less of the sweet flavor of tomato paste. Tomato puree adds color and thickness to sauces and soups without overpowering them with tomato flavor. It is commonly used in Indian and Greek dishes.

Tomato Paste: The thickest tomato concentrate with very little water because the water has been removed during a long boiling process.

Can of Tomato Paste: Open both ends of a can of tomato paste. Push the top end up just a bit and then slide the top lid off. Push the bottom lid up through and then out of the top of the can. Wipe both lids clean of tomato paste and use a flat-sided butter knife to scrape the inside of the can clean.

Tomatoes: Available fresh and in the following canned varieties:
1. Whole Tomatoes: tomatoes that have not been sliced or diced.
2. Stewed Tomatoes: cooked and they contain large pieces of tomato.
3. Diced Tomatoes: diced into normal size pieces.
4. Petite Diced Tomatoes: diced into very small pieces.
5. Diced Italian Tomatoes with basil, garlic, and oregano.
6. Diced Mexican Tomatoes with jalapeños, or with hutch green chilies, or with green chilies and chipotle peppers, or with lime juice and cilantro.
7. Diced Tomatoes with green peppers, celery, and onions.
8. Diced Tomatoes Chili Ready for making homemade chili.

Sugar and Tomatoes: If a recipe requires some type of tomatoes (or sauce) and some type of sugar, then the sugar is usually being added to help offset the tartness of the tomatoes in that specific recipe. Light brown sugar, instead of white sugar, will do a better job of reducing the tartness of the tomatoes in the recipe.

Ketchup (Catsup): An extremely thick sauce that contains tomatoes, sugar, vinegar, and spices. It is usually a condiment that is eaten at room temperature (or cold) with food. In the United Kingdom ketchup is called tomato sauce. The word ketchup comes from the Malaysian word "kechap" which means sauce.

Vanilla Extract

Pure vanilla extract contains 13.35 ounces (100 grams) of vanilla beans per gallon of liquid that contains at least 35% ethyl alcohol by volume. The rest of the liquid is usually water. The alcohol permits the maximum amount of vanillin to be extracted from the beans. Once extracted it is sold as pure vanilla extract and it will contain 35% alcohol (or 70 proof). When cooked the alcohol will rapidly evaporate to yield an alcohol free dish that has a vanilla flavor.

Imitation vanilla extract is not the same thing. It should not be used.

Vinegar

Vinegar is from the French words "vin aigre" which mean "sour wine."

Apple Cider Vinegar: It has a more balanced flavor than red or white wine vinegar. Add it to barbecue sauce and to coleslaw. When added to salads it helps the lettuce stay fresh and crisp longer.

Balsamic Vinegar: Excellent on salads. May also be added to vegetables when roasting them.

Distilled White Vinegar: Used to tenderize meat. Can also be used to remove the smell of onions from your hands.

Wine, Rice Wine, Sherry, and Other Alcohol

A wine labeled as "Cooking Wine" is usually not acceptable as a beverage and most good cooks will not use it for cooking because a poor quality wine can only add its poor qualities to a dish. Instead if a recipe specifies wine or alcohol most good cooks will use an alcoholic beverage that is acceptable for drinking because it will add is flavor to the dish. And the alcohol will rapidly evaporate when cooked to yield an alcohol free dish that has the desired flavor and aroma.

Red Wine: Instead of red wine, red wine vinegar can be used in sauces. Chicken, beef, or vegetable stock can be used in stews.

White Wine: Dry vermouth is a good substitute for white wine because it has a shelf life of about 6 months after it is opened and then stored in the refrigerator. Instead of white wine, white wine vinegar, lemon juice, chicken stock, or vegetable stock can be used.

Rice Wine: Adds a unique flavor to Asian dishes. Chinese (Taiwanese) rice wine (35% alcohol) adds acidity to stir-fried foods. Japanese rice wine, such as Mirin (8 - 12% alcohol), is salty and sweet and is added to sauces and glazes.

Zest of Lemon, Lime, or Orange

Zest is the finely grated exterior rind of a lemon, lime, or orange. Below the exterior rind is the white pith and it has a bitter taste so do not get any pith in the zest.

Chapter Five
Cooking Objectives,
Cooking Methods, and Cooking Times

Gourmet Cook Objectives

It is very important that a gourmet cook understand the concepts in this chapter. The reason is because the reputation of a gourmet cook depends not only on the appearance, aroma, and taste of the food, but also on how easily the food can be digested, and on how long the food satisfies a person's hunger before they feel the need to eat again. If a person gets indigestion, or gets really hungry just one-hour after eating a gourmet meal, then the person will not desire to eat that same meal again, or eat other meals prepared by that same cook. If a person's health gradually deteriorates with the passage of time because of vitamin deprivation, then that also adversely reflects on the person who has been cooking the meals. Therefore a culinary miracle needs to be prepared in a way that retains as much of the original nutrition that was present in the food before it was cooked.

Salt and Black Pepper

Many of the recipes in this cookbook include iodized salt and fine grind black pepper. Black pepper is a significant aid to digestion and it helps to facilitate normal bowel movements and long-term good health.

Many people in the USA consume too much sodium but not enough potassium or iodine, and this imbalance contributes to weight control problems and health problems. **Morton's® Lite iodized salt** can help correct this nutritional problem because it contains half the sodium of regular salt and it contains potassium and iodine.

Fresh, Frozen, and Canned

Fresh is best. Frozen is very good. Canned is good but some people do not enjoy the flavor of canned food because of the additives.

Vitamins and Nutrients in Vegetables

More than half the vitamins in vegetables are water-soluble. These vitamins will be leeched out of the vegetables the longer the vegetables are allowed to make contact with water. Decreasing the amount of water will minimize the loss of these vitamins. If fresh vegetables need to be soaked then do so before slicing in order to retain as much of their nutritional value as possible.

If boiling more than one type of vegetable, then boil them separately, each for the minimum amount of time for that vegetable, to preserve the maximum amount of its vitamins. Then combine the vegetables in your recipe. Or add the vegetables to the boiling water at different times so each type of vegetable only boils for the minimum amount of time that it requires. Save the vitamin enriched water that was used to boil vegetables, in an airtight container in the refrigerator, for future use when making soup or stew.

Vitamins B1, B5, C and folate are destroyed by heat and they will be lost the longer the vegetables are cooked.

However, cooking some vegetables enhances their antioxidants, such as carrots and tomatoes. Although available when eaten raw, cooking releases the antioxidants trapped in the fibers of these vegetable so that between 3 to 4 times more antioxidants are available during the normal digestive process. Expose to any type of heat, including boiling, steaming, stir-frying, and microwaving, will release these antioxidants.

Therefore the best way to minimize nutrient loss is to cook vegetables using a method that does not soak the vegetables in water, such as steaming, stir-frying, and microwaving. Steaming results in a softer vegetable. Stir-frying results in a crisper vegetable, and it helps to display the combination of natural colors in a dish without covering them with sauces or gravies, and it takes less time to cook a complete meal. Baking is also a healthy way to cook food because it does not require oil or liquids, it cooks using dry heat, and therefore it helps food retain their natural nutrients.

How to Cook Vegetables

Canned Vegetables: Canned vegetables are already fully cooked. However, they should be heated until their internal temperature reaches at least 200°F in order to neutralize any harmful microorganisms that might be in the vegetables.

Fresh Vegetables: Rinse all fresh vegetables under cool faucet water before using for sanitary reasons and to remove foreign particles. When possible, use fresh vegetables within a few days of when they were first purchased for optimal flavor, firmness, and texture.

How to Boil Fresh Vegetables

1. In a saucepan, add just enough water to cover the sliced or chopped vegetables. Use more water for large whole vegetables. Use less water for finely diced vegetables.
2. If desired, add 1/2 teaspoon of iodized salt per pound of vegetables.
3. If the vegetable grew underground then add it to the cold water in the pot and then bring the water to a boil.
4. If the vegetable grew above ground, then bring the water to a boil and then add the vegetable, and do cover the pot while boiling.
5. When the vegetables are in the pot, and the water starts to boil, then immediately reduce heat to low.

6. The boiling time begins when the water first begins to boil with the vegetables in the pot.

7. If necessary, add a little **hot** water while the vegetables cook to replace water that boils away.

8. Boil for the **minimum** recommended time and then check to see if the vegetables are tender and done. If necessary, boil a little longer.

9. Drain the vegetables and, if desired, save the water to make soup.

How to Steam Fresh Vegetables

1. Place a steamer basket, or a foldout steamer insert, into a saucepan.

2. Add water to the saucepan up to the bottom of the steamer basket but no water should be in the bottom of the steamer basket.

3. Bring to a boil over medium-high heat. When the water begins to steam, carefully add the vegetables to the steamer basket.

4. Immediately reduce heat to medium-low and put a cover on the pot.

5. The steaming time begins when the vegetables are first exposed to the steam.

6. Steam for the **minimum** recommended time and then check to see if the vegetables are tender and done. If necessary, steam a little longer.

How to Stir-Fry Fresh Vegetables

1. Rinse and prepare the vegetables and meat before you begin. Cut everything into small bite-size pieces that are all approximately the same size, so everything will cook quickly and evenly when exposed to high heat.

2. Use an oil with a high smoking point because the oil will be subjected to high heat. The best choices are olive oil, peanut oil, and rice bran oil. Extra light olive oil has the highest smoking point of any cooking oil. Do not use butter because it will burn.

3. Use just barely enough fresh clean oil to coat the pan and the ingredients in order to prevent a greasy taste in the cooked food

4. After putting a little oil in a wok, or a large deep skillet or frying pan, lift and tilt the wok in different directions to evenly distribute the oil over the interior surface of the pan.

5. Heat the oil in the wok over medium-high heat until the oil is hot.

6. Add one piece of vegetable. If it sizzles then the oil is hot enough.

7. Add the food to the wok but do not add too much food or it will not cook properly. If you put too much food in the wok then the food will pile up and it will begin to steam instead of frying, and this defeats the purpose of using the wok.

8   Continuously toss and stir the food so it does not burn or stick to the pan. Stir-fry for the **minimum** recommended time and then check to see if the vegetables are tender and done. If necessary, stir-fry a little longer.

9. Serve the food immediately after it is cooked or the ingredients will begin to lose their vitality.

How to Microwave Fresh Vegetables

Some cooks use the microwave whenever it is feasible. Other cooks will not use the microwave except to reheat food that has already been cooked. The recipes in this cookbook rarely mention the use of the microwave for cooking food. Each cook will need to make their own decision on whether or not they wish to use the microwave. The microwave information in this chapter is for those cooks who decide that microwaving is a reasonable option. The information in this chapter is not intended to be an endorsement or a recommendation for microwave cooking.

1. Different vegetables may require different cooking times so you may need to cook each vegetable in the microwave by itself.

2. Some vegetables will not require any extra water for microwaving, except for their natural water content, and the rinse water that is still clinging to them.

3. Put the vegetables in a microwave safe dish.

4. If appropriate, add 2 tablespoons of water (or more if necessary).

5. If desired, add a little optional salt, up to 1/2 teaspoon of iodized salt per pound of vegetables.

6. Cover the dish.

7. Microwave for one-half of the **minimum** recommended time shown in the following chart.

8. Remove the cover, stir the vegetables to rearrange them in the dish, and replace the cover.

9. Microwave for the remaining one-half of the **minimum** time shown in the following chart. Check to see if the vegetables are tender and done. If necessary, microwave a little longer.

10. Let the vegetables remain uncovered in the microwave dish for 2 minutes so they can finish cooking after removing them from the microwave.

Cooking Time Chart for
Different Methods of Cooking Vegetables

The cooking times in the following chart are in minutes. A range of times is given for each cooking method because of differences in the size of whole vegetables, and in the thickness of cut or sliced vegetables, and in the ripeness of vegetables. A vegetable is done when it is tender, but not mushy, and it still has a crisp bite.

<u>Vegetable</u>	<u>Boil</u>	<u>Steam</u>	<u>Stir-Fry</u>	<u>Microwave</u>
Artichoke, Whole	22 to 35	25 to 40	-	6 to 8
Artichoke, Hearts	8 to 12	10 to 15	-	5 to 7
Asparagus	6 to 10	5 to 8	4 to 5	4 to 6
Beans, Green	14 to 22	11 to 16	-	7 to 12
Beans, Lima	20 to 26	-	-	7 to 12
Beets	30 to 40	42 to 56	-	11 to 15
Broccoli, Spears	6 to 9	8 to 14	3 to 4	5 to 8
Broccoli, Florets	4 to 5	5 to 6	3 to 4	4 to 5
Brussels Sprouts	9 to 13	8 to 13	3 to 4	5 to 7
Cabbage, Wedges	10 to 14	8 to 11	-	10 to 12
Cabbage, Shredded	5 to 9	7 to 10	3 to 4	8 to 10
Carrots, Whole	17 to 21	10 to 15	-	8 to 10
Carrots, Sliced	6 to 10	6 to 9	3 to 5	5 to 8
Cauliflower, Whole	9 to 14	10 to 15	-	8 to 11
Cauliflower, Florets	6 to 9	7 to 10	3 to 4	3 to 4
Celery, Sliced	6 to 9	7 to 10	3 to 4	3 to 4
Corn, On Cob	5 to 8	5 to 9	3 to 4	3 to 4
Corn, Kernels	4 to 6	4 to 6	2 to 4	2 to 4
Eggplant, Whole	10 to 15	15 to 20	-	7 to 10
Eggplant, Diced	5 to 8	5 to 7	-	6 to 8
Fennel, Quartered	7 to 10	9 to 12	-	5 to 7
Kohlrabi	15 to 25	20 to 25	-	11 to 16
Leeks	10 to 12	10 to 12	2 to 4	4 to 6
Mushrooms	-	4 to 5	4 to 5	3 to 6
Okra	9 to 11	6 to 8	-	5 to 7
Onions, Cut	10 to 15	13 to 18	2 to 3	5 to 7
Parsnips	7 to 11	8 to 11	-	4 to 6
Peas	8 to 12	13 to 17	2 to 3	4 to 6

Vegetable	Boil	Steam	Stir-Fry	Microwave
Peppers, Bell	5 to 6	4 to 6	2 to 3	3 to 5
Potatoes, Whole	22 to 30	22 to 30	-	7 to 9
Potatoes, Cut	15 to 20	14 to 17	-	6 to 8
Potatoes, Sweet, Whole	26 to 32	20 to 25	-	10 to 13
Rutabagas	19 to 22	19 to 22	-	12 to 14
Spinach	2 to 5	4 to 6	3 to 4	3 to 4
Squash, Sliced	6 to 11	6 to 11	-	3 to 6
Turnips, Whole	18 to 23	15 to 20	-	8 to 11
Turnips, Cubed	5 to 8	12 to 16	2 to 3	6 to 8
Zucchini	4 to 7	4 to 8	3 to 4	4 to 6

Chapter Six
Abbreviations, Temperatures, Substitutions, and Recipes for Homemade Items

Abbreviations Used in All the Recipes

tsp. = teaspoon   c. = cup   lb.= pound   opt. = optional
T. = tablespoon   oz. = ounce   pkg. = package

Quantity Conversion Table

1 tsp. = 1/3 T.   1 cup = 8 ounces   1 quart = 2 pints
1 T. = 1/2 ounce   1 pint = 2 cups   1 gallon = 4 quarts

Cooking Temperature Conversion Chart
Degrees Fahrenheit (°F) to Degrees Centigrade (°C)
Centigrade is also called Celsius

Equation: $°C = (°F - 32°) \times (5/9)$

100°F	=	37.8°C	300°F	=	148.9°C
125°F	=	51.7°C	325°F	=	162.8°C
150°F	=	65.6°C	350°F	=	176.7°C
175°F	=	79.4°C	375°F	=	190.6°C
200°F	=	93.3°C	400°F	=	204.4°C
225°F	=	107.2°C	425°F	=	218.3°C
250°F	=	121.1°C	450°F	=	232.2°C
275°F	=	135.0°C	475°F	=	246.1°C

Useful Substitutions

1 cup butter = 1 cup shortening + 1/2 tsp. iodized salt

1 cup buttermilk = 1 cup milk + 1 T. vinegar (or lemon juice)

1 cup corn syrup (for use in a recipe) = 1 cup honey = 1 cup sugar + 1/2 cup of the liquid used in the recipe

1 cup corn syrup = 1 cup sugar + 1/3 cup water, boil until syrupy

1 cup milk (nonfat) = 1/3 cup nonfat dry milk + 1 cup water

1 cup milk (whole) = 1/3 cup nonfat dry milk + 1 cup water + 2 T. melted butter

1 cup milk (whole) = 1/2 cup evaporated milk + 1/2 cup water

1 T. oil = 1 T. melted shortening (or lard)

1 cup sugar = 1 cup corn syrup (decrease recipe liquid by 1/4 cup)

1 cup sugar = 1 cup honey (decrease recipe liquid by 1/4 cup)

1 oz. unsweetened chocolate = 3 T. cocoa + 1 T. shortening

1 garlic clove = 1 tsp. chopped garlic = 1/2 tsp. minced garlic = 1/2 tsp. garlic flakes = 1/4 tsp. granulated garlic = 1/8 tsp. garlic powder = 1/2 tsp. garlic salt (and reduce the salt in the recipe).

Recipes to Make Some of the Items You Normally Buy

Baking Powder
(from McCormick's® Cream of Tartar Label)

1/2 tsp. cream of tartar   1/4 tsp. cornstarch
1/4 tsp. baking soda

(Note: If you do **not** have cornstarch then increase the baking soda to 1/3 teaspoon.)

Mix the cream of tartar, baking soda, and cornstarch together. Use exactly like baking powder and use the amount specified in the recipe.

When the cream of tartar is combined with the baking soda a slow chemical reaction begins and the shelf life of the resulting baking powder is only a few months. Therefore make just enough baking powder each time you need it so it will always be fresh and active.

Breadcrumbs

2 to 8 slices bread, your choice

Bread: The bread will have a significant impact on the flavor of the breadcrumbs when used in a recipe. Therefore do **not** use old stale bread. Good choices are white bread, whole wheat bread, French bread, sourdough bread, herbed bread, or a combination of breads.

Seasonings: Plain breadcrumbs are suitable for almost any recipe that specifies breadcrumbs because you can add the appropriate seasonings to the recipe. However, if you prefer you may lightly sprinkle a little dry seasoning on each cube of bread before you bake it. Examples would be Italian seasoning, garlic powder, or onion powder.

Crust: End pieces, or bread crusts, will yield coarser breadcrumbs. Trim off the crusts and keep them separate. The rest of the bread will yield breadcrumbs with a finer texture and they should be kept separate.

Instructions: Use a sharp knife to cut the bread into 1/2 inch cubes. Cut a piece of parchment paper so it fits in the bottom of a baking sheet. Place the bread cubes on the parchment paper and bake in a preheated 250°F oven for about 15 to 20 minutes. Remove from oven, turn the bread cubes over, and then bake for another 15 to 20 minutes or until the cubes are golden brown and hard. Transfer to a wire rack to cool. Crumble the cubes into a large bowl until they are fine crumbs of bread. Or put in a zipper plastic freezer bag, and crush with a rolling pin. Or use a food processor and convert into fine breadcrumbs. Use immediately of save in an airtight container in the freezer until needed.

Homemade Bisquick™ Biscuit Mix (about 1 Cup)

1 c. all-purpose flour
1 tsp. baking powder
1 1/3 tsp. granulated sugar

1/3 tsp. iodized salt
2 1/2 T. Crisco® shortening

Mix the flour, baking powder, sugar, and salt. Cut in the shortening.
May be used in any recipe that specifies Bisquick™ Biscuit Mix.

Self-Rising Flour (about 1 Cup)

1 c. all-purpose flour
1/2 T. baking powder

1/2 tsp. iodized salt

Combine flour, baking powder, and salt together. May be used in any
recipe that specifies self-rising flour.

Half & Half

1 part whole milk and 1 part light cream, or
3 parts whole milk and 1 part whipping cream, or
4 parts whole milk and 1 part heavy cream.

Combine the whole milk and the cream, stir, and refrigerate until
needed. If you only need half & half occasionally then you can buy
heavy cream and pour it into an ice cube tray and freeze it. Then put
the frozen ice cube tray of heavy cream inside a heavy-duty zipper
freezer bag to protect the cream from moisture loss during your
freezer's defrosting cycles. When you need half & half remove as
many heavy cream ice cubes as required and allow them to come to
room temperature inside a cup.

Sweetened Condensed Milk (equal to one 14 oz. can)

1/3 c. boiling water
1 c. instant nonfat dry milk
2/3 c. granulated sugar

4 T. butter, room temperature
1/2 tsp. pure vanilla extract

Bring water to a boil and then remove from heat. Wait one minute and
then add the dry milk powder and stir until all the milk powder is
dissolved. Stir in the sugar and butter. Wait for the mixture to cool
and then stir in the vanilla extract until well blended. This milk may be
stored in an airtight container in the refrigerator for up to 7 days.

Smooth Peanut Butter (about 3/4 cup)

1 c. roasted shelled peanuts   1/4 tsp. iodized salt
1 1/2 tsp. oil

Note: Omit the salt if you are using salted peanuts.

Note: The oil may be peanut oil, or olive oil, or vegetable oil. The flavor of the oil will be present in the finished peanut butter.

Note: If you have fresh unroasted peanuts then remove the peanuts from their shells, rub off and discard the paper thin pink skins, place the peanuts on a cookie sheet and roast in a preheated 300°F oven for 12 minutes. Allow the peanuts to cool before using.

Directions: Place the roasted peanuts, oil, and salt in a blender and secure the lid. Blend until the mixture becomes spreadable. If necessary, add a few more drops of oil. If necessary, stop the blender and scrape the mixture off the sides of the blender to the bottom of the blender, and then continue blending. Use the peanut butter immediately or store it in an airtight container in the refrigerator. If the oil separates during storage and rises to the top of the mixture then stir it back into the peanut butter before using.

Option: For **crunchy** peanut butter, stir in 1/8 cup of finely chopped roasted peanuts after blending.

Chapter Seven
Appetizers

Assorted Fruit and Cheese Kabobs

apples
bananas
cantaloupe
honeydew
kiwi

maraschino cherries
oranges
pineapple
seedless grapes, red or green
strawberries

Cheese: Select one or more flavors of cheese that would taste good with fruit, such as mozzarella, muenster, Monterrey Jack, pepper jack, Swiss, or any other cheese that you enjoy.

Fruit: Either fresh or canned fruit may be used. If canned fruit is used then drain the fruit before placing on the kabob.

Instructions: Select at least 4 of the above fruits or cheese. Consider how the flavors would taste and the colors (appearance) of the finished kabob. If the fruit or cheese is not already precut then slice the fruit and cheese into 1 inch cubes. Stick a wood or metal skewer through the center of each item, with approximately 4 to 6 items on a skewer, and place the kabob on a tray for serving. Consider putting a different selection of items on different skewers. This would enhance the appearance and variety of the finished tray of kabobs. Refrigerate until ready to serve. If desired, place one or more dips beside the kabobs.

Bacon Cheeseburger Balls (24 Balls)

12 oz. lean ground beef
4 slices bacon, cooked, crumbled
opt. 1/4 c. onions, finely diced

2 c. Bisquick^{TM} Baking Mix
1/4 c. whole milk
2 c. shredded cheese, your choice

Type of Cheese: Medium cheddar cheese is normally used to make a bacon cheeseburger. However, you may use Colby-Jack, Monterrey Jack, or 4 Cheese Mexican, or something different if you prefer.

Instructions: Crumble ground beef into small pieces and fry in a skillet over medium heat until done, stirring frequently. Drain off grease. Transfer cooked beef into a large bowl. Add crumbled crispy cooked bacon and diced onions and stir. Add Bisquick^{TM} and milk and stir. Add cheese and stir until everything is well blended. The mixture will be crumbly. Do **not** add more milk. Instead wet your hands with water and form the mixture into 1.5 inch round balls and place them 1.5 inches apart on a nonstick cookie sheet. Keep your hands wet so the mixture

---

does not stick to your hands. The water on your hands will be absorbed into the crumbly dough mixture and the ball will hold together nicely in your hands. Bake in preheated 400°F oven 12 to 16 minutes.

Chicken Salad, or Egg Salad, or Ham Salad, or Tuna Salad, or Turkey Salad (2 Servings)

meat, eggs, or tuna - see below	1 T. sweet pickle relish
2 1/2 T. mayonnaise	1/4 c. celery, finely diced

Chicken Salad: Use 3/4 cup chopped cooked chicken.

Egg Salad: Use 3 hard boiled eggs, finely diced.

Ham Salad: Use 3/4 cup chopped cooked ham. Add 1/2 teaspoon yellow mustard to the above ingredients.

Tuna Salad: Use 1 (5 ounce) can solid albacore water-packed tuna and not oil-packed tuna. The water does not add an oily flavor to the tuna and it has fewer calories. Drain the water from the tuna before using. Add 1 teaspoon lemon juice and 1 hard boiled finely diced egg to the above ingredients.

Turkey Salad: Use 3/4 cup chopped cooked turkey.

Mayonnaise: Binds the ingredients together and adds its unique flavor.

Pickle Relish: Adds color and enhances the flavor of the salad.

Celery: Dice the celery into small pieces, or about 1/4 inch cubes. Celery adds a pleasant chewy crunch to the salad.

Onions and Tomatoes: Do not include diced onion or diced tomatoes inside the salad. Instead slice them and serve them beside the salad as an option.

Salad Instructions: Put your choice of meat, or eggs, or tuna into a mixing bowl. Add the mayonnaise, pickle relish, and celery. Stir well so that all the ingredients are nicely blended.

Serving Suggestions: The salad may be used as a dip using your favorite crackers. Or the salad may be placed on a layer of lettuce with some sliced tomatoes and eaten as a salad. Or the salad may be put on a bun and eaten as a sandwich (see chapter twenty-eight).

Deviled Eggs (12 Halves)

6 eggs	opt. 1 tsp. granulated sugar
2 or 3 T. mayonnaise	opt. 1/8 tsp. iodized salt
1 tsp. yellow mustard	opt. dash fine grind black pepper
opt. 1 1/2 T. sweet pickle relish	opt. paprika, sprinkle as a garnish

Trivia: Deviled eggs appear in ancient Roman recipes. However, they were not called "deviled" until the 1700s in England. The implication was that they are now so delicious it is almost sinful. In my opinion, instead of "deviled eggs" or "devil's food chocolate" a better name would have been "heavenly" to imply a taste good enough for angels.

Instructions: Boil the eggs and remove their shells (instructions in chapter twelve). Slice each egg lengthwise from end to end and carefully remove the yolks with a spoon. Put the yolks in a bowl. Put the egg white on a plate.

Mash the yolks with a spoon. Add 2 tablespoons mayonnaise if you omit the pickle relish but add 3 tablespoons mayonnaise if you include pickle relish. Add the mustard and stir until smooth. All the other ingredients are optional and you may add them or omit them based on your taste preferences.

Optional Sweet Pickle Relish: The pickle relish adds color, texture, a mild tangy flavor, and a minor chewy crunch to the deviled eggs. If you add the pickle relish then do **not** add the optional sugar or the optional salt. The pickle relish already contains salt. And the sugar will offset the tangy taste of the pickle relish which is why it is added.

Optional Granulated Sugar: People who do not like pickle relish may prefer a slightly sweeter deviled egg.

Optional Salt: Salt adds flavor to the deviled eggs and it helps to extend their shelf life if there are any leftover eggs. Before adding salt taste a very small sample of the filling to see if it needs more salt. If you added the pickle relish then the filling already contains salt.

Optional Black Pepper: A small dash of fine grind black pepper in the filling will not be noticed by most people if the filling contains pickle relish. Black pepper helps the body to metabolize and digest food and it can help to prevent gas. However, black pepper upsets the stomach of some people. If in doubt, do not add black pepper to the filling but put a shaker of black pepper beside the deviled eggs so each person can sprinkle black pepper on their eggs if they wish.

After adding the optional items of your choice, stir the yolk mixture to uniformly blend the items. Scoop the mixture into each egg white so it is evenly distributed among all the eggs and all the filling is used.

If desired, sprinkle the tops of the deviled eggs with paprika. If in doubt, place the paprika shaker beside the deviled eggs so each person can sprinkle paprika on their eggs if they wish.

Some people prefer room temperature deviled eggs and some people prefer chilled deviled eggs. Serve the deviled eggs as you think best. Store any leftover eggs in an airtight container in the refrigerator.

Mini Corn Dogs (40 Corn Dogs)

2/3 c. all-purpose flour
2/3 c. self-rising cornmeal
1/4 tsp. iodized salt
1 large egg, beaten

3/4 c. whole milk
16 oz. miniature smoked sausages
oil for frying
ketchup or mustard for dipping

Cornmeal: If you do not have self-rising cornmeal then you can use regular yellow cornmeal and add 1 teaspoon baking powder.
Meat: I recommend miniature smoked sausages. Select the flavor your family enjoys. Or use 100% beef hotdogs and cut each hotdog into 2 or 3 pieces crosswise. Or you may use Vienna sausages.
Instructions: Put flour, cornmeal, and salt in a bowl and mix well. In a separate bowl beat the egg. Add milk and stir until well blended. Add egg mixture to the flour bowl and stir until the flour is well moistened.
Heat 3 inches of oil in a pan or deep fryer to 375°F. Put 4 sausages into the batter and thoroughly coat with batter. Allow excess to drip back into the bowl. Immediately put them in the hot oil. Fry for 2 to 3 minutes until the batter is golden brown. Place on paper towel to drain. Serve with small individual cups of ketchup and mustard for dipping.

Mozzarella Cheese Sticks (Baked or Fried)
(12 to 14 Sticks - 4 inches long by 1/2 inch by 1/2 inch)

1/4 c. all-purpose flour
2 eggs, beaten
1 T. water or milk
1 c. Panko bread crumbs
1/8 c. cornstarch
2 T. Italian seasoning

1/2 tsp. garlic powder
1/2 tsp. iodized salt
1/8 tsp. fine grind black pepper
8 oz. block mozzarella cheese
2 T. butter, melted
1 c. marinara sauce, heated

Bread Crumbs: If Italian seasoned bread crumbs are used instead of regular bread crumbs then omit the Italian seasoning.
Sauce: Marinara, spaghetti, or pizza sauce may be used.
Instructions: Put the flour in a medium bowl by itself.
In a different medium bowl beat the two eggs. Stir in the water.
In a different medium bowl mix the bread crumbs, cornstarch, Italian seasoning, garlic powder, salt, and black pepper until well blended.
Slice the block of mozzarella cheese into sticks about 4 inches long and between 3/8 inch to 1/2 inch square on the sides.
Gently press a cheese stick into the flour and use your fingers to gently press the flour onto all the surfaces of the cheese stick. Dip the coated

Grandpappy's Gourmet Cookbook

cheese stick into the egg mixture. Allow any excess egg to drip back into the egg bowl. Gently press the egg coated cheese stick into the bread crumb mixture and use your fingers to gently press the bread crumbs onto the surface of the cheese stick. Dip the cheese stick into the egg bowl again and allow any excess egg to drip back into the egg bowl. Gently press the coated cheese stick into the bread crumb mixture again and gently press the bread crumbs onto the cheese stick. Place the coated cheese stick on parchment paper. Repeat for the remaining cheese sticks and leave about 1/2 inch between the coated cheese sticks on the paper. Freeze the coated cheese sticks for at least one hour.

Bake Option: Preheat oven to 425°F. Place the parchment paper containing the cheese sticks on a baking sheet. Bake uncovered for 5 minutes and then reduce the oven temperature to 175°F. Continue to bake uncovered for another 5 minutes. Remove from oven and allow to cool for 5 minutes.

Fry Option: Preheat one inch of oil in a saucepan to 350°F. Put the frozen cheese sticks into the hot oil in batches. Cook between 30 to 60 seconds. When a cheese stick floats to the top of the oil it is done. Use tongs to transfer the cheese stick onto a paper towel. Allow to drain and cool for 5 minutes.

Serve: Drizzle melted butter over cheese sticks. Serve with small individual cups of heated marinara sauce as an optional dip.

Sausage and Cheese Balls (24 Balls)
Sausage and Cream Cheese Balls (24 Balls)
Sausage and Cream Cheese Muffins (24 Muffins)

Sausage and Cheese Balls:
1 lb. Jimmy Dean® regular sausage   3/16 c. water
2 c. Bisquick™ Baking Mix   2 c. shredded cheese, your choice

Sausage and Cream Cheese Balls (or Muffins):
1 lb. Jimmy Dean® regular sausage   3/16 c. water
2 c. Bisquick™ Baking Mix   1 c. shredded cheese, your choice
1 (8 oz.) pkg. cream cheese, room temperature

Type of Cheese: Experiment with mild, medium, and sharp cheddar cheese, and with 4 Cheese Mexican, to discover the flavor you like best.

Sausage and Cheese Balls Instructions:
Crumble the sausage into very small pieces and fry in a skillet over medium heat until done, stirring frequently. Do not drain. (Note: Jimmy Dean® sausage has very little grease.) In a large mixing bowl combine the Bisquick™ and the water and stir. Add the shredded cheese and stir. Add the cooked sausage and stir until everything is well blended.

The mixture will be very crumbly. Do **not** add more water. Instead wet your hands with water and form the mixture into 1.25 inch round balls and place them 1 inch apart on a nonstick cookie sheet. Keep your hands wet so the mixture does not stick to your hands. The water on your hands will be absorbed into the crumbly dough mixture and the ball will hold together very nicely in your hands. Makes approximately 24 to 30 balls.

Bake in a preheated 400°F oven for 12 to 14 minutes.

Sausage and Cream Cheese Balls Instructions:
Follow the above instructions but add the room temperature cream cheese at the same time you add the shredded cheese. (Note: Half of the shredded cheese is replaced with cream cheese.)

Bake in a preheated 400°F oven for 12 to 14 minutes.

Sausage and Cream Cheese Muffins Instructions:
Follow the above instructions but instead of forming the mixture into cheese balls, spoon the mixture into cupcake papers inside a cupcake pan until each cupcake paper is approximately 2/3 full. If necessary, add just a little more water to the mixture so the muffin dough will spread out to the sides of the cupcake papers.

Bake in a preheated 400°F oven for 12 to 14 minutes until done, or until a toothpick inserted into one of the center muffins comes out dry.

Turkey Meatballs

1 egg	4 T. parmesan cheese, shredded
1 tsp. onion powder	1/2 c. breadcrumbs
1 tsp. garlic powder	1 lb. ground turkey
1/2 tsp. iodized salt	3 T. canola oil, for frying
1/8 tsp. fine grind black pepper	1 c. spaghetti sauce

Beat egg in a medium bowl until smooth. Add onion, garlic, salt, and black pepper and stir until well blended. Mix in parmesan cheese. Stir in breadcrumbs. Mix in ground turkey until well blended. Form into meatballs about 1 inch in diameter. Heat oil over medium heat in a large nonstick skillet until hot. Add the meatballs in one layer and cook on bottom for 3 minutes or until brown. Turn over without piercing, and cook other side for 2 minutes or until brown. Add spaghetti sauce, reduce heat to low, roll meatballs in sauce until coated, cover the skillet, and cook over low heat for 10 to 15 minutes, stirring occasionally, until the meatballs are done, or until the internal temperature of the meatballs is 165°F. Serve over pasta (with another cup of spaghetti sauce) or serve as appetizers with a toothpick in each meatball.

Chapter Eight
Asian-American Recipes

Bean Sprouts

Bean sprouts are a common ingredient is some recipes in many parts of the world, especially in eastern Asia. The most common type of bean sprouts are mung bean sprouts. It takes about 1 week for the sprout to grow to its normal size under humid conditions, and these conditions are perfect for the growth of bacteria. Since 1996 there have been 30 outbreaks of food related illnesses that have been traced to "salmonella" and "e. coli" bacteria on bean sprouts. These bacteria can be neutralized by thoroughly and completely cooking the sprouts. The government organization at "https://www.foodsafety.gov/keep/types/fruits/sprouts. html" recommends that sprouts be avoided by "children, the elderly, pregnant women, and persons with weakened immune systems."

Because of the potential serious health problems that may occur with bean sprouts. I have not included mung bean sprouts in any of the recipes in this cookbook. Most of the Asian recipes in this chapter include a wide assortment of other safe vegetables and the omission of bean sprouts should not significantly impact the flavor of the final dish. However, you may use your own judgment on whether or not you wish to avoid mung bean sprouts.

Asian Baked Salmon (4 Servings)

1 1/2 lb. salmon
2 T. extra light olive oil
3 T. soy sauce
1 T. light brown sugar
1/4 tsp. garlic powder

1/2 tsp. iodized salt
1/4 tsp. fine grind black pepper
1 lime, squeezed
opt. 1/3 tsp. ground dill weed

Preheat oven to 425°F. Rinse the salmon in water and pat dry with a paper towel. Cut salmon into 4 equal pieces. Place the salmon with its skin side down on a nonstick baking pan. In a bowl mix the olive oil, soy sauce, brown sugar, garlic powder, salt, and black pepper. Squeeze the juice of one lime into the bowl. Stir to mix all the ingredients together. Pour half of the marinade mixture over the salmon and allow it to rest for 10 minutes. If desired, sprinkle evenly with dill weed.

Cook uncovered in a preheated 425°F oven for 15 to 25 minutes depending on the thickness of the salmon and the desired degree of doneness. Remove from oven and pour the remaining room temperature marinade over the salmon and let it rest for 5 minutes. Transfer skin side down to individual serving plates.

Asian Meatballs (about 36 Meatballs)

Meatballs:

1 egg

1 tsp. soy sauce

1/2 onion, minced

1 clove garlic, minced

1/4 tsp. iodized salt

1/2 lb. 80% lean ground beef

1/2 lb. ground turkey

1/4 c. Panko breadcrumbs, crushed

Sauce:

2 T. soy sauce

1/2 c. tomato paste

1/2 tsp. garlic powder

2 tsp. dark brown sugar

1/4 tsp. iodized salt

Each Asian country has its own unique version of "Asian" meatballs. This recipe is a blend of several Asian recipes and it was designed for people who enjoy international cuisine but who do not have a strong preference for the food of one specific Asian nation.

Meatballs: Beat egg in a medium bowl. Add the soy sauce, onion, garlic, and salt, and stir to combine the ingredients.

In a large bowl crumble the beef and turkey together. Use your hands and thoroughly mix the two meats together. Crush the breadcrumbs into fine pieces. Mix the crushed breadcrumbs with the meat using your hands. Add the egg mixture and use your hands to mix all the ingredients together. Moisten your bare hands with some water and form the meat mixture into small individual meatballs about 1 inch round. Make about 36 meatballs. Place each meatball 1 inch apart on a broiler pan (one that allows the grease to drip into a different pan below the top pan). Bake in a preheated 350°F oven for 20 to 25 minutes. While the meatballs are cooking make the sauce.

Sauce: Add the soy sauce and tomato paste to a large nonstick skillet, stir and simmer over low heat for 5 minutes. Add the garlic powder, brown sugar, and salt, and stir to blend the ingredients together. Continue to simmer over low heat for 5 minutes. Add the meatballs and stir to coat the meatballs with the sauce. Simmer over low heat for 10 minutes to allow the sauce to moisten and add flavor the meatballs.

Serve: May be eaten as an appetizer with a toothpick in each meatball. Or it may be served with 10 ounces of pasta such as fettuccini or linguine. Vegetables such as snow peas and carrot slivers can be added to the sauce at the same time as the garlic if the meatballs will be served with pasta as a main dish.

Chow Mein Noodles (2 Servings)

Trivia: "Mein" or "mian" is the English spelling of the Chinese word that means "noodles." "Chow" is the English spelling of the Chinese word that means "stir-fried." Together "chow mein" means "stir-fried noodles." "Lo" is the English spelling of the Chinese word that means "tossed" or "stirred." Therefore "lo mein" means "tossed noodles" or "stirred noodles" but not fried. However, in the USA the terms are frequently used interchangeable and they can mean whatever the Chinese-American restaurant wants them to mean. There are two types of noodles: (1) "chow mein" noodles that have a soft texture and they are usually served with soy sauce, and (2) crispy "chow mein" noodles (also called "Hong Kong style") that are fried crispy like hash browns, or like the ones in a can, and they are usually served with a thick brown sauce.

There are differences between Asian recipes on the West Coast and the East Coast of the USA. People who are accustomed to eating in one area are sometimes disappointed when ordering the same food at an "authentic" Chinese-American restaurant on the opposite coast of the USA. It may help to remember that China is an extremely large nation and there are significant differences in the same food prepared in the different regions of China. Even within one region of China, the restaurants prepare food differently.

Chow mein noodles are the most popular stir-fried noodles in the world, and they are made using thousands upon thousands of different recipes.

The following chow mein noodle recipe was **not** created to match the recipe of any one restaurant. Instead it was designed to blend a variety of different restaurant cuisines into a single recipe that would appeal to the largest number of people. However, it will not appeal to everyone because some people are accustomed to the flavor of the noodles of a specific restaurant.

6 oz. soft chow mein noodles	1/2 tsp. garlic powder
2 1/2 tsp. oil	1/2 tsp. ginger
1/2 c. celery, sliced	1/4 tsp. iodized salt
1/4 c. onions, sliced	1/8 tsp. fine grind black pepper
2 T. carrots, shredded	1 1/2 T. Asian sauce (sauce chapter)
2 c. cabbage, shredded	

Optional Ingredients: The celery, onions, carrots, and cabbage, are all optional ingredients. If your favorite Asian restaurant does not include one or more of these items then you may omit them from this recipe.

However, if you wish to experience a recipe that is popular at a lot of different Asian restaurants, all across the USA, then you should include all four optional ingredients. Because this recipe contains a good quantity and mixture of vegetables, it is very nutritious and it can be a complete meal all by itself. However, in the USA it is common to add some type of meat and those meat recipes follow this noodle recipe in this chapter.

Noodles: Stir-fried or steamed soft chow mein noodles are recommended. You may use Yakisoba noodles, Pad See Ew noodles, Pad Thai noodles, or Singapore noodles, or Chinese egg noodles. Soft chow mein noodles are usually in the refrigerator section of a store.

Oil: There is no agreement among Asian restaurants on which oil is best. Each restaurant strongly supports the oil they use. The most popular options are: canola oil, peanut oil, and olive oil, in that order. You may use the type of oil you prefer.

Celery: Rinse and pat dry one stalk of celery. Cut across the narrow width of the celery on a diagonal about 3/8 inch between slices until you have enough.

Onion: Remove and discard the paper thin layer around the outside of the onion. Cut the onion into 1/4 inch thick slices until you have enough. Separate into onion rings. Cut each onion ring into pieces about 1/2 inch long.

Carrot: Rinse and peel the carrot. The carrot should be julienne cut on a diagonal. This is the traditional method because labor was cheap and equipment was expensive. The same exact cut can be achieved by shredding the carrots using the largest opening on a shredder, and holding the carrot at a 45 degree angle to the shredder to make the longest possible pieces. The carrots will taste exactly the same, and they will look the same, regardless of which method you use.

Cabbage: The cabbage needs to be in small pieces. About half the restaurants slice and chop the cabbage, and about half the restaurants grate the cabbage using the largest opening in a shredder.

Instructions: Cook noodles according to the package directions. Drain and set aside. In a wok, or large skillet, heat the oil over medium-high heat until the oil is hot. Add the celery, onions, and carrots. Stir and cook for 1 minute. Reduce heat to medium, and continue to stir and cook for 3 to 4 minutes until the onions have turned a golden caramel color and the celery is soft when pierced with a fork. Add the cabbage, garlic powder, ginger, salt, and black pepper. Stir and fry for 1 to 2 minutes or until the cabbage is just starting to wilt. Add the Asian sauce and the cooked noodles and stir to evenly coat everything. Stir and fry for about 2 minutes until the noodles are thoroughly heated. Serve immediately.

Beef Chow Mein (2 Servings)

1/2 lb. raw lean beef	1/2 c. beef stock
2 T. oil	2 T. water
2 T. Asian sauce	opt. 1/2 c. mushrooms, drained

Serve On: White rice, brown rice, egg noodles, or chow mein noodles (recipe this chapter). Prepare following the directions on the package.

If you are using rice or egg noodles, and you **not** using the chow mein noodle recipe in the chapter, then add the following to this recipe:

1/2 c. celery, sliced	2 T. carrots, shredded
1/4 c. shallots, sliced	2 c. cabbage, shredded

Beef: Sirloin or other lean tender steak about 3/4 inch thick. Trim off all the fat. Rinse steak under cold faucet water. Cut steak into 1/4 inch thick slices across the grain. Cut each slice into 1 1/4 inch long pieces with the grain.

Cooking: Heat oil in wok or large nonstick skillet over medium-high heat. When the oil is hot, add the beef and stir "occasionally" for 3 to 5 minutes, or until the beef is done based on how done you prefer your beef. If you overcook the beef then it will become tough and chewy. Remove the beef from the pan.

Optional Vegetables (only if you are **not** using the chow mein noodles in this chapter): Add the optional celery, shallots, carrots, and cabbage.

Optional Mushrooms: If desired, add the optional mushrooms.

Continue Cooking: Add Asian sauce, beef stock, and water. Stir constantly for 1 minute, or until the vegetables are done.

Optional Noodles: If using egg noodles or chow mein noodles, add the fully cooked warm noodles at this time. Stir to mix the noodles with the other items in the pan

Continue Cooking: Reduce heat to medium. Return the fully cooked beef to the pan. Stir constantly for 1 more minute.

Finish Cooking: Remove from heat and serve immediately.

Optional Rice: If serving with rice instead of noodles then pour over the cooked warm rice and serve.

Chicken Chow Mein (2 Servings)

1/2 lb. raw chicken, cut up	1 garlic clove, finely chopped
opt. 1/2 tsp. baking soda	opt. 1/2 c. mushrooms, drained
3 T. Asian sauce	opt. 1/2 c. water chestnuts
1 1/2 T. canola oil	3 T. water

Serve On: White rice, brown rice, egg noodles, or chow mein noodles (recipe this chapter). Prepare following the directions on the package.

If you are using rice or egg noodles, and you **not** using the chow mein noodle recipe in the chapter, then add the following to this recipe:

1/2 c. celery, sliced	2 T. carrots, shredded
1/4 c. shallots, sliced	2 c. cabbage, shredded

Chicken: Thigh, or breast, or chicken tenders. Thigh meat is the most common choice because it has more chicken flavor than breast meat. Cut the chicken into bite size pieces.

Optional Velveting: If using thighs this step is not necessary. If using breasts or chicken tenders then this step will break down the chicken fibers to make it soft and tender like thigh meat. Put chicken pieces in a bowl. Sprinkle with 1/2 teaspoon of baking soda and then toss the chicken, and stir the chicken, to distribute the soda on all the chicken. Let it rest of 10 minutes. Thoroughly rinse the chicken under cold faucet water. Pat dry with a paper towel.

Marinating: Put the chicken pieces in a bowl and pour 1 tablespoon of Asian sauce over the chicken. Toss the chicken, and stir the chicken, to distribute the sauce on all the chicken. Let it rest for 10 minutes.

Cooking: Heat oil in wok or large nonstick skillet over medium-high heat. When the oil is hot, add garlic and stir constantly for 10 seconds, or until it begins to turn a golden brown. Add the cut up chicken pieces and stir constantly for 1 minute.

Optional Vegetables (only if you are **not** using the chow mein noodles in this chapter): Add the optional celery, shallots, carrots, and cabbage.

Continue Cooking: Stir constantly for 1 1/2 minutes and continue to cook the chicken (and the optional vegetables).

Optional Mushrooms and Water Chestnuts: If desired, add the optional mushrooms and/or water chestnuts.

Continue Cooking: Add 2 tablespoons of Asian sauce and the water. Stir to coat everything. Stir constantly for 1 minute, or until the chicken and the vegetables are done.

Optional Noodles: If using egg noodles or chow mein noodles, add the fully cooked warm noodles at this time. Stir to mix the noodles with the other items in the pan.

Continue Cooking: Reduce heat to medium and stir constantly for 1 more minute.

Finish Cooking: Remove from heat and serve immediately.

Optional Rice: If serving with rice instead of noodles then pour over the cooked warm rice and serve.

Shrimp Chow Mein (2 Servings)

---

20 small shrimp	2 T. Asian sauce
2 T. canola oil	2 T. water
1 garlic clove, finely chopped	

Serve On: White rice, brown rice, egg noodles, or chow mein noodles (recipe this chapter). Prepare following the directions on the package.

If you are using rice or egg noodles, and you **not** using the chow mein noodle recipe in the chapter, then add the following to this recipe:

1/2 c. celery, sliced	2 T. carrots, shredded
1/4 c. shallots, sliced	2 c. cabbage, shredded

Shrimp: Asian restaurants do not agree on the size of the shrimp, or on the amount of shrimp. The shrimp can be popcorn, small, or medium. Generally large and extra large shrimp are not used in this recipe because the flavor of the shrimp would overpower the other flavors in the recipe. When medium size shrimp are used the number of those shrimp can vary from 3 to 10 per person (per serving). Therefore you may use whatever size shrimp your favorite Asian restaurant uses, and you may use as many shrimp as you believe appropriate. A reasonable compromise is to plan for 10 small shrimp per person.

Shrimp Preparation: Use fresh or frozen shrimp. If using frozen shrimp then thaw the shrimp in the refrigerator. Remove the shell, devein, and cut off the hard tail piece (and the head if still attached).

Cooking: Heat oil in wok or large nonstick skillet over medium-high heat. When the oil is hot, add garlic and stir constantly for 10 seconds, or until it begins to turn a golden brown. Add the shrimp and stir constantly for 1 or 2 minutes or until the shrimp is done based on the size of the shrimp. Remove the shrimp from the pan.

Optional Vegetables (only if you are **not** using the chow mein noodles in this chapter): Add the optional celery, shallots, carrots, and cabbage.

Continue Cooking: Add 2 tablespoons of Asian sauce and the water. Stir to coat everything. Stir constantly for 1 minute, or until the vegetables are done.

Optional Noodles: If using egg noodles or chow mein noodles, add the fully cooked warm noodles at this time. Stir to mix the noodles with the other items in the pan

Continue Cooking: Reduce heat to medium. Return the fully cooked shrimp to the pan. Stir constantly and cook for 1 more minute.

Finish Cooking: Remove from heat and serve immediately.

Optional Rice: If serving with rice instead of noodles then pour over the cooked warm rice and serve.

Honey Walnut Shrimp (2 Servings)

Honey Sauce:

1 T. honey	1 1/2 tsp. sweetened condensed milk
2 T. mayonnaise	opt. 1/2 tsp. lemon juice

Candied Walnuts:

1/2 c. water	1/4 c. walnut halves
1/3 c. granulated sugar	

Shrimp:

1/2 lb. large shrimp	1/4 c. rice flour (or cornstarch)
1 egg white	1/2 c. canola oil (for frying)

Optional Items:

2 c. cooked white rice	2 T. scallions, sliced

In a medium bowl, combine the honey, mayonnaise, milk, and the optional lemon juice, and stir until well blended. Set aside for later.

In a small nonstick saucepan, add the water and the sugar. Stir until the sugar is completely dissolved in the water. Bring to a boil and then add the walnuts. Immediately reduce heat and boil for two minutes, stirring frequently. Transfer onto a clean plate. Separate the walnuts so they do not stick together. Let the walnuts dry. (Do not put on a paper towel because the walnuts will stick to a paper towel.)

Use fresh or frozen shrimp. If using frozen shrimp then thaw the shrimp in the refrigerator. Remove the shell, devein, and cut off the hard tail piece (and the head if still attached).

In a medium bowl, whip the egg white until foamy. Add the flour (or cornstarch) and stir into a batter. Dip the shrimp in the batter and set aside for 2 minutes to give the batter time to stick to the shrimp.

In a small nonstick saucepan, heat the oil over medium-high heat. When the oil is hot, add the shrimp and fry for about 5 minutes or until done. (Note: If using precooked shrimp only cook for 2 minutes to heat them.) Remove shrimp from pan and drain on a paper towel.

Put the drained shrimp in the bowl with the honey sauce, and stir gently to coat the shrimp. Transfer to two serving bowls. If desired put shrimp on top of the optional white rice.

Pour half the candied walnuts on the shrimp in each bowl. If desired, garnish with sliced scallions. Serve immediately.

Sweet & Sour Chicken (6 Servings)

1 egg, beaten	1 (15 oz.) can pineapple chunks
2 T. soy sauce	2 T. cornstarch
1/4 c. cornstarch	5 T. light brown sugar
1/4 tsp. garlic powder	1/3 c. ketchup
1/2 tsp. iodized salt	1/2 c. green bell pepper, chopped
1/4 tsp. fine grind black pepper	1/2 c. red bell pepper, chopped
1 lb. chicken tenders	1/2 c. sweet onion, chopped
1 1/2 T. canola oil	cooked white rice, for serving

Beat egg in a medium bowl until smooth. Add soy sauce and cornstarch and stir until the cornstarch is dissolved. Add garlic powder, salt, and black pepper, and stir until well blended.

Rinse chicken tenders under cold tap water. Remove and discard any pieces of fat. Cut chicken tenders into bite size pieces about 1/2 inch long and 1/2 inch wide. Put in bowl with egg mixture and coat thoroughly. Let stand at room temperature for 15 minutes.

Heat oil in a medium nonstick skillet over medium heat. When the oil is hot, add the chicken. Fry on bottom side for 1 minute until golden brown and then flip over and fry on other side until golden brown. Continue to rotate the chicken in the skillet until brown on all sides. Cut one piece of cooked chicken in half. If it is still pink on the inside, then cook longer. When done remove chicken and drain on paper towels.

Remove the pineapple chunks from the can and set aside. Pour the pineapple juice from the can into a measuring cup. Add enough water to make 1 cup of liquid. Transfer to a large nonstick skillet or wok and add 2 tablespoons cornstarch and stir until all the cornstarch is dissolved. Add brown sugar and ketchup and stir. Bring to boil over medium heat. Add the green bell peppers, red bell peppers, onions, and cook until the peppers and onions are tender. Add the pineapple chunks, and chicken, and stir. Cook and stir until everything is well heated.

Serve over rice. Or, if desired, serve over egg noodles.

Teriyaki Ribeye Steak (1 Steak)
(or T-bone, Filet Mignon, Sirloin, or New York Strip)

1 T. soy sauce	1/2 tsp. balsamic vinegar
1 T. water	1/4 tsp. coarse Kosher salt
1 1/2 tsp. granulated sugar	1/8 tsp. fine grind black pepper
3/4 tsp. Worcestershire sauce	1/8 tsp. garlic powder
3/4 tsp. honey	1/8 tsp. onion salt
1/2 tsp. extra virgin olive oil	1 (8 oz.) ribeye steak

In a medium bowl combine soy sauce, water, sugar, Worcestershire sauce, honey, olive oil, vinegar, salt, black pepper, garlic powder, and onion salt and stir until well blended to make the marinade.

Rinse ribeye steak under running water and pat dry. Use your fingers to press the marinade into both sides of the steak. Let the steak absorb the marinade inside a sealed plastic zipper bag for two hours at room temperature.

Heat a wok or nonstick skillet over medium heat. Fry the steak for the following number of minutes on each side based on how done you desire your steak. Turn the steak over with tongs. Do not poke holes in the steak with a fork or its juices will leak out. After frying both sides of the steak use an instant read meat thermometer to check the temperature in the middle of the steak to determine its degree of doneness. Remember that the internal steak temperature will increase by 5°F while it is cooling.

Degree of Doneness	Cooking Time per Side	Internal Meat Temperature
Rare	5.5 minutes	125°F (52°C)
Medium	7 minutes	145°F (63°C)
Well Done	8.5 minutes	165°F (74°C)

The above cooking time is based on a steak that is 1 inch thick cooked over medium heat. If the steak is thinner then decrease the time. If the steak if thicker then increase the time. The instant read meat thermometer will indicate the exact degree of doneness of your steak.

After the steak is cooked to the degree of doneness you like, then allow the steak to rest for 5 minutes on a plate so the juices inside the steak can cool down a little, and become less fluid, and infuse back into the meat. This will help more of the juices to stay inside the meat when you slice into it, and this will improve the flavor and moistness of the steak. (Note: This resting time will also help to kill bacteria that might still be present in the meat.)

Chapter Nine
Beef

Beef Pot Roast (8 to 10 Servings)

3 to 4 lb. beef roast
1 medium onion
1/2 lb. carrots
opt. 2 lb. red potatoes
4 T. extra light olive oil, divided
1 1/2 tsp. coarse Kosher salt

1/2 tsp. fine grind black pepper
1 (14 oz.) can beef broth
opt. 1/2 c. red wine
For Brown Gravy:
2 T. butter
2 T. all-purpose flour

Beef Roast: Boneless chuck roast, eye of round roast, bottom roast, or sirlon tip roast. Select roast based on price and amount of lean meat.

Onion: Remove paper thin outer layer. Cut off and discard the top and bottom. Cut onion into 1/3 inch thick slices. Cut each slice into 4 quarters. Separate the quartered slices into individual pieces.

Carrots: Baby carrots can be used without slicing. Regular carrots should be cut into 1/4 inch thick slices.

Optional Potatoes: Decide if you wish to cook potatoes with the pot roast or if you prefer mashed potatoes as a side dish. To cook the potatoes with the roast, peel and chop into pieces about 1 inch in size.

Intructions: Spread 2 tablespoons oil over the bottom of a Dutch oven or an oven-safe pot with a lid. Rub salt and pepper all over the roast. Put 2 tablespoons oil in a different cast iron skillet and heat over medium-high heat. Use tongs to handle the meat and do not poke holes in the meat with a fork. When the oil in the skillet is hot put the meat in the skillet and sear for 2 minutes on each side until the meat is browned on every side. Transfer meat to Dutch oven using tongs. Add onion pieces to the skillet with the hot oil and cook for 2 minutes or until a very light brown. Remove skillet from the heat. Transfer onions to the Dutch oven and put onions on top of and around the meat on all sides. Pour the beef broth and the red wine into the Dutch oven. Put lid on Dutch oven and put the Dutch oven in the middle of a preheated 300°F oven. If the meat is 3 pounds then bake for 3 hours; or 3 1/2 pounds bake for 3 1/2 hours; or 4 or more pounds bake for 4 hours. Add the optional potatoes 60 minutes before the meat is done. Add the carrots 30 minutes before the meat is done. Cook until the meat easily pulls off the roast with a fork and the vegetables are tender but not mushy.

Brown Gravy: Melt butter in a separate nonstick saucepan over medium heat. Add flour and cook 4 minutes while stirring. Add 1 cup of the liquid from the Dutch oven. Stir and cook until gravy thickens. Let each person add gravy to their meat and vegetables as desired.

Chili and Beans (10 Servings)

This Recipe won the First-Place Award at Three Different Chili
Cooking Contests and it was cooked by Three Different People.
The Judges at One Contest awarded it First Place by Unanimous Vote.
(This recipe is unique because it uses no garlic and it uses black beans.)

1 lb. lean ground beef	1/2 tsp. paprika (smoked if available)
2 onions, diced	1/2 tsp. cayenne pepper
1 green bell pepper, diced	1 T. jalapeño pepper, finely chopped
1 c. water	1 (14 oz.) can Mexican style tomatoes
2 T. chili powder	2 (8 oz.) cans tomato sauce
2 T. ground cumin	1 (14 oz.) can red kidney beans
1 tsp. iodized salt	1 (14 oz.) can black beans

Suggested Toppings: Sour cream, cheddar cheese, green onions.

In a Dutch oven, crumble the ground beef. Use the edge of the stirring spoon to help break up the pieces. Add the diced onions and diced green bell pepper. Cook over medium heat, stirring occasionally, until the meat is done. Drain off the grease.

In a separate bowl combine the water, chili powder, cumin, salt, paprika, cayenne pepper, and jalapeño, and stir until well blended. Add to the meat in the Dutch oven. Stir to coat the meat with the mixture. Add the Mexican style tomatoes (such as Rotel) and the tomato sauce. Bring to a boil over medium heat. Then reduce heat to very low.

Drain and rinse the two types of beans. Add the beans to the Dutch Oven, stir, cover, and simmer over very low heat for 1 to 2 hours. Stir occasionally until most of the water is gone but the meat is still moist.

Serve in soup bowls with the toppings listed above.

Grandpappy Comment: Allow each person to add their choice of optional toppings. Other optional toppings include the following, either by themselves or combined:

A. 1 scoop (3 tablespoons) of sour cream on top of one bowl of chili.

B. 1 tablespoon diced raw onions sprinkled on top of one bowl of chili.

C. 1 handful of shredded cheese on top of one bowl of chili.

D. 1 handful of Fritos corn chips on top of one bowl of chili.

E. 1 handful of crushed tortilla chips on top of one bowl of chili.

F. A few saltine crackers (or oyster crackers) on top of a bowl of chili.

Chili, Macaroni, and Cheese - Baked or Stovetop

Before you begin you need to decide the following:

1. Do you want to include beans or not?
2. Do you want to include tomatoes or not?
3. Do you want to include chili powder or just ground beef?
4. Do you want to use the oven or just the stovetop?

If you want to include beans then you can use the chili recipe in this chapter and combine the cooked chili with the Macaroni and Cheese Recipe in chapter thirty. Add the cooked chili at the same time that you add the cooked macaroni near the end of the Macaroni and Cheese Recipe in chapter thirty but use a 4 inch deep casserole dish.

If you do not want to include beans then follow the recipe below and only include the optional ingredients you desire.

1 lb. lean ground beef	opt. 1 tsp. chili powder
1/4 c. onions, diced	opt. 2 T. water
opt. 1 can (14 oz.) diced tomatotes	

Instructions: Crumble the ground beef into a skillet. Use the edge of the stirring spoon to help break up the pieces. Add the diced onions. Cook over medium heat, stirring occasionally, until the meat is done. Drain off the grease.

Tomatoes: If desired, add the diced tomatoes to the skillet.

Chili Powder: If desired, dissolve the chili powder in the water and then add to the skillet.

Instructions Continued: Stir to mix the new ingredients with the cooked beef and onions and continue to stir and cook over medium heat to give all the flavors a chance to blend together.

Now follow the Macaroni and Cheese Recipe in chapter thirty. Add the cooked beef at the same time you add the cooked macaroni near the end of the Macaroni and Cheese Recipe in chapter thirty.

Country Fried Steak (4 Steaks)
(sometimes called Chicken Fried Steak)

Steaks:

2 eggs   1/8 tsp. paprika
3/4 c. all-purpose flour   4 (4 oz. each) cubed steaks 1/4" thick
3/4 tsp. iodized salt   1/4 c. lard, or shortening, for frying
1/4 tsp. fine grind black pepper

Gravy:

1 c. chicken broth   1/8 tsp. dried thyme
1/8 tsp. fine grind black pepper   3/4 c. whole milk

Beat the eggs in a bowl until smooth and pour into a cake pan.

In a different cake pan add flour, salt, black pepper, and paprika, and stir until well blended.

Dredge the steaks in the flour mixture until coated with flour on both sides. Then press the flour into the steaks with your fingers. Now dip both sides of the steaks in the egg. Finally dredge both sides of the steaks in the flour mixture a second time until well coated with flour. Press the flour into the steaks with your fingers. Place the floured steaks in the refrigerator for 15 minutes to help the flour mixture stick to the steaks when fried. Save 1 tablespoon of the leftover flour from the dredging pan.

Melt the lard in a large nonstick skillet over medium high heat. Cook each side of each steak for about 5 or 6 minutes, or until golden brown. Turn off the heat. Put the cooked steaks on a paper towel to soak up the excess grease. Pat the top of the steaks with another paper towel to remove the grease. Put the steaks on a pan in a warm oven to keep the steaks warm while you make the gravy.

Put 1 tablespoon of the leftover flour from dredging into the skillet with the pan drippings and set the heat to medium. Cook the flour, stirring frequently, until the flour turns a medium brown and the mixture begins to bubble. Add the chicken broth, black pepper, and thyme, and whisk constantly until the mixture boils and begins to thicken. Slowly add 1/4 cup of milk and stir constantly for 1 minute. Add 1/4 cup of milk and stir constantly for 1 minute. Add the last 1/4 cup of milk and stir constantly for 1 minute. Bring to a boil again and then immediately reduce the heat to low, and simmer for 5 to 10 minutes, stirring frequently, until the gravy thickens. Transfer the steaks to plates and pour the pan gravy on top of the steaks so each steak receives the same amount of gravy.

Ground Beef , Noodle, and Cheese Casserole

3 c. wide pasta noodles	1/2 tsp. iodized salt
1 lb. lean ground beef	1/8 tsp. fine grind black pepper
1/2 c. onions, diced	opt. 1 (4 oz.) can sliced mushrooms
1 (15 oz.) can tomato sauce	1 c. sour cream
1/2 tsp. garlic salt	1 c. cottage cheese, or ricotta
3/4 tsp. granulated sugar	3/4 c. sharp cheddar cheese, shredded

Cook pasta "al dente" following package directions but for 2 minutes less time than recommended. Drain and set aside.

Crumble ground beef into a medium nonstick skillet and break up the larger pieces with the edge of a stirring spoon. Add the onions and cook over medium heat, stirring frequently, until the beef is done. Drain the grease. Immediately reduce heat to low. Stir in tomato sauce, garlic salt, sugar, salt, and black pepper. If desired, add the optional mushrooms. Simmer for 3 minutes, stirring occasionally, until slightly thickened.

In a large bowl, stir the sour cream and the cottage cheese together until well blended. Add the cooked pasta and stir until the pasta is evenly coated with the cheese mixture.

Lightly grease a 3-quart (13-inch by 9-inch) casserole dish. Spoon half of the pasta mixture into the bottom of the dish. Spread half of the meat mixture evenly over the pasta. Sprinkle half of the shredded cheddar cheese evenly over the meat. Add a layer of pasta, a layer of meat, and finish with a layer of cheddar cheese.

Bake in a preheated 350°F oven for 30 minutes or until the cheese is thoroughly melted.

Hamburger, White Rice, and Scrambled Eggs

1 lb. white rice
1 lb. lean ground beef
opt. 1/4 c. diced onions
opt. 3/8 c. diced tomatoes

opt. 3/8 c. diced green peppers
6 eggs
6 T. shredded cheddar cheese,
  medium or sharp

Cook the white rice, ground beef, and eggs at the same time but in different pots or skillets.

White Rice: Do not rinse the white rice. Boil the rice in twice the volume of water with a pinch of salt. Trickle the white rice into the water so the water does not stop boiling. Cover the pot and let it simmer for 15 to 18 minutes over very low heat until all the water is absorbed. Do not stir while simmering. Stirring causes the grains of rice to stick together. Do not lift the lid until the rice is almost done or you will release essential steam and moisture. When done, remove the pot from the heat and fluff the rice with a fork. Cover and let stand another 5 minutes. The rice will continue to steam and absorb flavors.

Lean Ground Beef: Crumble the raw ground beef into very small pieces into a skillet and then add the optional diced onions. Cook over medium heat and stir continuously while cooking. Just before the ground beef is done add the optional diced tomatoes and the optional diced green peppers and continue stirring until done. Drain off the grease.

Scrambled Eggs: Break the eggs into a different nonstick skillet. Add the cheese (1 heaping tablespoon per egg). Stir the eggs and cheese together in the skillet. Then cook over low or medium low heat. Continuously stir the eggs while they are cooking. Do not let the eggs stick to the bottom of the skillet and burn. The most important thing is to continuously stir the eggs while they are cooking. Continuous stirring is not intermittent stirring. The scrambled eggs should be completely done in 5 to 7 minutes.

Combine: When the rice, ground beef, and scrambled eggs are all done then thoroughly mix them all together in a large serving bowl, or in the largest pot or skillet that was used to cook the three items. Serve immediately.

Salisbury Steak (4 Servings)

Steak Patties:

1 egg	1/8 tsp. fine grind black pepper
1 lb. lean ground beef	1/3 c. fine dry breadcrumbs
2 T. onions, finely diced	1 T. canola oil, for frying
1/2 tsp. iodized salt	

Gravy:
1 1/2 c. brown gravy (sauce chapter)   1 (4 oz.) can sliced mushrooms

Trivia: In 1897 "Salisbury Steak" was named after a USA physician named James H. Salisbury (1823-1905) because he told his patients to eat lots of beef to improve their health and to help cure their illnesses.

Instructions: In a medium bowl beat egg until smooth. Add ground beef and mix well. Add onions, salt, and black pepper and mix until well blended. Add breadcrumbs and toss until well blended. Shape into four oval patties about 3/4 inch thick.

Heat oil in large nonstick skillet over medium heat. Reduce heat to medium low and put patties in skillet. Brown on one side and then flip over. Brown the other side of the patties for 2 minutes. Reduce heat to very low. Add gravy and the drained mushrooms to skillet. Cover skillet and simmer for 20 minutes.

Serve: Serve with mashed potatoes, or rice, or steamed vegetables.

Salisbury Steak Meatballs (4 Servings)

Salisbury Steak Meatballs (see instructions below)

Brown Gravy (see instructions below)

Other Ingredients:
1 (4 oz.) can sliced mushrooms   8 oz. pkg. egg noodles

Salisbury Steak Meatballs: Follow Salisbury Steak Recipe at the top of this page. However, instead of shaping into four steak patties, form into 1.5 inch round balls and place 1.5 inches apart on a nonstick cookie sheet. Bake in preheated 400°F oven 12 to 16 minutes.

Brown Gravy: Follow the instructions for the Brown Gravy Recipe in the sauces chapter. However, after adding the beef broth immediately add the above drained mushrooms and cooked meatballs. Then continue to follow the instructions in the Brown Gravy Recipe.

Egg Noodles: Cook noodles following the instructions on the package.

Serve: Serve gravy and meatballs over the cooked noodles.

Steak, Broiled (One Steak), or
Imitation "Outback Steakhouse" Victoria's Filet, or
Imitation "Longhorn Steakhouse" Outlaw Ribeye, or
Imitation "Longhorn Steakhouse" Renegade Sirloin

1 steak, 8 to 16 ounces, at least 1 inch thick

Imitation Outback Steakhouse Seasoning, and
Imitation Longhorn Steakhouse Seasoning:

2 tsp. extra light olive oil	1/4 tsp. garlic powder
1 tsp. coarse Kosher salt	1/16 tsp. coriander, freshly ground
3/4 tsp. paprika	1/16 tsp. turmeric
1/2 tsp. fine grind black pepper	opt. 1/16 tsp. cayenne pepper
1/4 tsp. onion powder	

This recipe can transfer almost any steak into a culinary masterpiece similar to what you would be served at an Outback Steakhouse, or at a Longhorn Steakhouse. The amount of seasoning is the same for one steak. Bigger steaks will simply have the seasoning spread in a thinner layer over a larger surface area than a smaller steak. But the seasoning will still penetrate the same depth into each steak based on the amount of time the seasoning is left on the steak before it is cooked. Any extra seasoning will simply come off the steak as it cooks on the grill surface.

Type of Steak: Between 1 inch to 1 1/2 inch thick. Filet mignon, ribeye, porterhouse, T-bone, club, sirloin, New York strip, and London broil are good steak choices, depending on your budget. Filet mignon is the best steak. Ribeye is a very good steak. Porterhouse, T-bone, and club steaks are the same type of steak except for the size of the fillet. The fillet is the smaller side of the steak and it is more tender and flavorful than the meat on the other side of the bone. A club steak has no or almost no fillet, and it is the same as a New York strip steak but it has a bone. A T-bone steak has a fillet that is about 1/4 the size of the entire steak, or about 1/3 the size of the piece of meat on the other side of the bone. A porterhouse steak has a fillet that is about 1/3 the size of the entire steak, or about 1/2 the size of the piece of meat on the other side of the bone. A porterhouse steak is a filet mignon plus a New York strip steak with a bone between them. Do not rely on how the butcher classifies the steak. Instead use your eyes to determine how much fillet is on the steak and decide what you would call it based on the size of the fillet. But do not argue with the butcher. Make your steak choice based on the steaks available, the amount of lean meat on the steak compared to the amount of fat and grizzle, and whether or not a steak is on sale. If possible, cook the steak the day you purchase it.

Prepare the Steak: Do not pierce the steak with a fork. Allow the steak to come to room temperature. Rinse the steak under cold faucet water for sanitary reasons, and to remove any tiny bone chips that may be on the steak. Pat dry with a paper towel. If desired, trim off any extra fat you do not want on the steak.

Prepare the Seasoning: Combine the extra light olive oil, salt, paprika, black pepper, onion powder, garlic powder, coriander, turmeric, and the optional cayenne pepper in a small bowl and stir until well blended. (Extra light olive oil is recommended because it has a higher smoking point than most other cooking oils.) Rub one side of the steak with half of the marinade seasoning. Rub the seasoning into the meat with your fingers. Repeat with the other side of the steak. Season generously, but reasonably, because some of the seasoning will come off the steak when it is cooked. Cover the steak with another plate to protect it from contamination. Let the steak absorb the seasoning for about 1 hour at room temperature. (Note: This would be a good time to bake a potato.)

Prepare the Cast Iron Griddle (or cast iron skillet): Place a cast iron griddle on the top oven shelf, about 6 inches below the top broiler in an oven. If your favorite steakhouse cooks their steaks on a flat grill, similar to Waffle House, then you may be accustomed to steaks with no grill marks. If you do not want grill marks on your steak, then put the flat side of the grill face up in the oven. If you prefer grill marks on your steak, then put the ridged surface of the grill face up in your oven. The ribbed surface will put "imitation" grill marks on the steak. If you will be serving the steak to a guest then you can ask your guest what they prefer. I recommend grill marks, even though they are "imitation" grill marks, because appearance has a significant impact on how the mind perceives the food, and the mind can significantly influence how the tongue perceives the taste of the food. Set the oven to "bake" at 500°F and allow it to preheat for 20 minutes.

Cook the Steak: Change the oven from "bake" to "broil" and allow the broiler to heat for 2 minutes. Pull out the top oven shelf and carefully lay the steak on the extremely hot griddle being very careful to not burn yourself. The meat will sizzle and pop when it touches the hot griddle. If cooking more than one steak then allow a little space between the steaks so the outside edges of the steaks can cook properly. After placing a steak on the hot griddle do not adjust it or move it -- leave it alone. Push the oven shelf back into the oven and sear the bottom side of the steak, and simultaneously broil the top side of the steak, for 3 minutes. Pull out the oven shelf and use a spatula or tongs to turn the steak over. Do not pierce the steak with a fork or its juices will run out. Push the shelf back into the oven and sear and broil the steak for 3 more minutes. Switch the oven from "broil" to "bake" and set the baking temperature at 450°F. Bake for the total number of additional minutes shown in the table below. If the additional cooking time is 3 minutes or longer then, if you wish, you may turn the steak over using tongs or a spatula halfway through the additional cooking time.

Additional Total Cooking Time Based on the Desired
Degree of Doneness and the Thickness of the Steak

Doneness Middle of Steak	Meat Temp.	Steak Thickness		
		1 inch	1.25 inch	1.5 inch
Rare	125°F	1.5 min.	2.5 min.	3.5 min.
Medium Rare	135°F	2.5 min.	3.5 min.	4.5 min.
Medium	145°F	3.5 min.	4.5 min.	5.5 min.
Medium Well	155°F	4.5 min.	5.5 min.	6.5 min.
Well Done	165°F	5.5 min.	6.5 min.	7.5 min.

Different ovens cook differently based on the size of the oven, the type of heat, and the design of the broiler element. Therefore, remove the steak early and use an instant-read meat-thermometer to check the meat temperature inside the center of the steak. If the steak is too rare then cook the steak a little longer.

(Note 1: The internal steak temperature will increase by approximately 5°F while it is resting for 5 minutes after removing it from the oven.)

(Note 2: The USDA recommends that beef be cooked until its internal temperature reaches 145°F and then let it rest for at least 3 minutes.)

(Note 3: A steak loses more of its natural juices the longer it is cooked and it becomes drier, chewier, and tougher. A steak cooked for less time is moister, easier to chew, and more tender. However, some people cannot eat beef unless it is well done, or almost burnt.)

(Note 4: A gourmet cook respects other people. Other people have the right to enjoy their steak the way they want it cooked. Master chefs at the best steakhouses in America cook steaks exactly the way their customers order their steaks, and they do not lecture their customers on how they think beef should be cooked.)

After the steak is cooked then allow it to rest for 5 minutes so the juices inside the steak can cool down a little, and become less fluid, and infuse back into the meat. This will help more of the juices to stay inside the meat when you slice into it, and this will improve the flavor and moistness of the steak. (Note: This resting time will also help to kill bacteria that might still be present in the meat.)

Serve with your favorite bread and room temperature butter, and with a baked potato, or mashed potatoes with gravy, or corn on the cob, or broccoli with cheese sauce, or a vegetable medley, or whatever you wish. Steak may also be served as part of a "Surf and Turf" meal.

Chapter Ten
Beverages

Electrolyte Beverage (Gatorade, Pedialyte) (One Quart)

1 quart water
8 tsp. granulated sugar
1/2 tsp. baking soda

1 tsp. Morton's Lite Salt
opt. 1 pkg. Kool-Aid Drink Mix

Combine water and sugar and stir until the sugar is dissolved. Add the baking soda and the Lite salt and stir well. If desired, add 1 package of your favorite favor of Kool-Aid drink mix and stir until well blended. This beverage will replace lost electrolytes due to dehydration (diarrhea, vomiting, excessive sweating, etc.).

Milkshake (One Serving)

4 c. vanilla ice cream
1 c. milk

1 tsp. pure vanilla extract
opt. other flavorings

Vanilla Milkshake: Put the ice cream, milk, and vanilla extract in a blender and blend until smooth. Pour into a big glass and drink with a straw.

Note: The above recipe, including the vanilla ice cream and vanilla extract, can be used to make the following milkshake flavors.

Chocolate Milkshake: Add 4 teaspoons chocolate syrup to the blender. Note: If you substitute chocolate ice cream for the vanilla ice cream (and even if you don't use any chocolate syrup), you may discover the chocolate flavor of the milkshake is too strong for you.

Strawberry Milkshake: Dice 3 strawberries and add to the blender. Or use strawberry ice cream instead of vanilla ice cream.

Peanut Butter Milkshake: Add 3 tablespoons peanut butter to the blender.

Peanut Butter Banana Smoothie (One Serving)

1 banana, frozen	1 T. pure honey
1 c. very cold whole milk	1/4 tsp. pure vanilla extract
1 T. peanut butter, smooth	opt. 1/2 c. crushed ice

Banana: Before a banana becomes too ripe you need to make a decision: (1) eat the banana now, or (2) freeze the banana, or (3) wait until the banana becomes really, really ripe and make some banana bread. If you freeze the banana then you will be able to preserve it for a future smoothie beverage. Peel the banana, cut it into 1/2 inch slices, put into a zipper plastic sandwich bag, put that bag inside a heavy-duty zipper freezer bag, and put it in the freezer. Later when you are in the mood for a smoothie, follow the instructions below:

Smoothie Instructions: Put one cup of whole milk in a glass and put it in the freezer for about 30 minutes but remove it before it starts to freeze. Remove the frozen banana slices from the freezer at the same time. Put the milk, banana slices, peanut butter, honey, and vanilla extract into a blender and blend until smooth. Taste a small sample of the smoothie.

Milder Flavor and Thicker Smoothie: If you wish the flavor to be milder and the smoothie to be thicker, then add the optional crushed ice, and blend again until smooth.

More Flavor: If you want more peanut butter flavor, then put a little more peanut butter in the blender and blend again until smooth. Continue to add a little more peanut butter until the flavor is acceptable to you.

Serve immediately.

Strawberry Limeade (One Serving)

2 T. strawberry juice	1 (12 oz.) can Sprite soft drink
1 tsp. lime juice, freshly squeezed	opt. garnish, 1 slice of fresh lime

Put the strawberry juice and the lime juice in a 16 ounce glass and stir. Slowly pour the chilled 12 ounce can of Sprite down the side of the glass and then stir. Add ice cubes and a straw.

Optional Garnish: 1 thin slice of fresh lime, cut 1/2 way through, and pushed down on the top edge of the glass. If you made the strawberry juice fresh in a blender, then put 1 thin slice of strawberry on top of the ice inside the glass.

Chapter Eleven
Bread

A Few Suggestions for Baking Bread

Greasing Baking Pans: If available, use lard or shortening to grease baking pans. If you use butter, margarine, or oils then they will be absorbed into the dough more quickly.

Flour Shaker: Purchase a new clear glass pepper shaker and fill it with all-purpose flour. Use your new "flour shaker" whenever you need to dust a rolling surface, or a rolling pin, or the top of your bread dough.

Oven Water: If you have a problem with a bread recipe producing a crust that is too hard or too brown, then place a shallow pan containing about 1/2 inch of water on the bottom shelf of the oven. The water will help keep the exterior crust of the bread from becoming too dry as it bakes.

Optional Crust Variations for All Breads: Just before putting the bread dough into the oven, use a pastry brush to carefully and very gently paint the top of the dough if you desire any of the following results:

1. Cold water brushed or sprayed on the bread dough will yield a crisp, chewy crust.
2. Oil or melted butter will yield a soft crust.
3. 1 tbsp. honey with 2 tbsp. water yields a sweet, glossy finish.
4. 1 tbsp. lemon juice with 2 tbsp. sugar gives a fruity, sweet flavor.
5. 1 egg white beaten with 1 tbsp. water gives a shiny, crisp crust.
6. 1 egg white beaten with 1 tbsp. milk gives a shiny, softer crust.
7. 1 whole egg with 2 tbsp. water gives a shiny, rich, dark crust.

Optional Liquid Substitutions in Bread Recipes:

1. **Water:** Yields a chewy texture with more of the original flour flavor.
2. **Milk:** Bread will rise higher and have a finer texture and it will keep longer. Heat fresh milk until it almost boils to kill the enzymes that can interfere with the yeast action in the bread. Do not heat canned milk or instant milk. Milk also adds nutritional value to the finished bread.
3. **Buttermilk:** Bread will be more tender. Heat the buttermilk until it almost boils to kill the enzymes in the milk. Do not use too much or it will make the bread too tender and it will fall apart.
4. **Potato Water:** The water left over after boiling potatoes. It will cause the bread to rise higher and it will add a coarser texture and moistness. Do not substitute more than 1/2 potato water for the normal water required in the recipe.

5. **Oils or Butter:** Adds tenderness and improves elasticity of bread. Increases bulk and helps bread brown more evenly. However, too much oil will make the bread crumbly. Use a maximum of 1 tablespoon oil, or lard, or shortening, or butter per 1 cup of flour.
6. **Wheat Berry Sprouting Water:** Adds nutrition, texture, and a flavor enhancement to the bread.

Miscellaneous Optional Recipe Ingredients:
1. **Eggs:** Adds protein, color, and bulk. Eggs help to extend the shelf life of the bread. For each egg used, deduct 1/4 cup of the other liquid in the recipe. Use no more than 2 eggs per loaf of bread.
2. **Honey:** Maximum of 1 tablespoon per 1 cup of flour. Adds flavor and moistness and helps to feed the yeast and increases the shelf life of the bread.
3. **Iodized Salt:** Maximum of 1/2 teaspoon per 1 cup of flour. Controls the yeast process. Improves flavor and increases the shelf life of the bread. A bread made with no salt will taste flat. Do **not** add salt to the yeast water or it will inhibit the initial yeast process.

Amish Sweet White Bread (One Loaf)

1 c. warm water	3/4 tsp. iodized salt
1 pkg. yeast	2 T. extra light olive oil
2 3/4 to 3 c. bread flour	1 T. butter, unsalted, melted
1/3 c. granulated sugar	

Crumble yeast into 1/4 cup warm water with a pinch of sugar. Stir yeast to mix with water. Good yeast will become foamy in 10 to 12 minutes.

Sift flour, sugar, and salt into large bowl and stir. Add oil, the foaming yeast solution, and the rest of the warm water, and stir until well blended. The dough should pull away from the sides of the bowl. If necessary, add a little more flour. Knead by hand for at least 5 minutes.

Cover the bowl and let it rise in a warm place (such as inside your oven with the oven light on) for about 60 minutes or until doubled in size.

Punch the dough down and knead it by hand for at least 5 minutes. Shape dough into a loaf and put it into a lightly greased 9x5-inch loaf pan. Cover and let rise 30 minutes in a warm place.

Bake in a preheated 350°F oven for 30 minutes. The bread is done when a toothpick inserted into the center of the loaf comes out clean.

When you remove from oven immediately brush melted butter on top of loaf. Cover with a towel and allow to cool to produce a soft top crust.

Variation: Reduce sugar to 2 tablespoons to produce a loaf bread that is less sweet, lighter, and fluffier. However, it will not be Amish bread.

Banana Nut Bread (One Loaf)

1 stick (8 T.) butter, unsalted
2 T. whole milk, or buttermilk
2 eggs, beaten
2 c. all-purpose flour
1 tsp. baking soda
1/2 tsp. iodized salt

1/2 c. light brown sugar
1/2 c. granulated sugar
1 tsp. pure vanilla extract
3 overripe bananas (black peels)
opt. 1/2 c. pecans or walnuts, pieces

Remove the butter, milk, and eggs from the refrigerator, measure the quantity you need, and allow them to come to room temperature.

Very lightly grease only the bottom of a 9-inch by 5-inch loaf pan with some lard or shortening.

Adjust the shelves in the oven so the middle of the empty loaf pan is a little above the middle of the oven. Remove the empty loaf pan from the oven.

Preheat oven to 325°F.

In a large bowl combine the flour, baking soda, and salt and stir to blend the dry ingredients together.

In a different bowl cream the two sugars and the softened butter together. Add the beaten eggs and stir. Add the milk and the vanilla extract and stir until well blended.

Remove and discard the black peels from the overripe bananas, mash the bananas, and add the mashed bananas to the sugar mixture and stir. Add the optional nuts and stir.

Add the banana and sugar mixture to the large bowl with the flour and stir just enough to moisten the flour. Do not stir too much or the finished bread will be dense and dry.

Pour the batter into the bread loaf pan.

Bake at 325°F for 50 to 70 minutes. After 50 minutes insert a toothpick into three different spots in the top center of the bread to test for doneness. If done the toothpick will come out clean in 2 of the 3 spots (allows for toothpick contact with a tiny piece of banana). If not done, continue baking and test every 5 minutes until it is done. Allow the bread to cool inside the loaf pan for 12 minutes and then invert the bread onto a wire rack and allow the bread to cool for at least two hours before slicing. If there is any leftover bread then wrap it in some plastic wrap, or put it in an airtight container, and save it in the refrigerator. It will last about 10 days in the refrigerator (if nobody eats it).

Biscuits (12 Biscuits)

2 c. all-purpose flour, sifted
1 T. baking powder
1 T. granulated sugar
3/4 tsp. iodized salt

3/4 c. whole milk
1/3 c. lard, or shortening
6 tsp. butter, cold

Remove the milk and the lard from the refrigerator, measure the amount you need, and allow them to come to room temperature.

Combine flour, baking powder, sugar, and salt and stir. Gradually add the milk and stir until the mixture pulls away from the side of the bowl. Cut in the warm lard and stir until well blended. Knead dough for about 10 minutes. Cover and let stand 30 minutes. Transfer dough onto a piece of wax paper or a floured surface. Pat the dough flat, or roll with a rolling pin, until it is about 3/4 inch thick. Use a 2 1/2 inch round cookie cutter, or glass, to cut biscuits from the dough. Put each biscuit on an ungreased nonstick baking sheet about 2 inches apart. Gather the leftover dough pieces together, form into a ball, and flatten to about 3/4 inch thick. Use the cookie cutter to cut out 1 or 2 more biscuits. Gather the leftover dough pieces together, form into a ball, and then form into the shape of a biscuit and add it to the baking sheet. Use your thumb to make an indentation in the top center of each biscuit and put a thin slice (1/2 tsp.) of chilled butter in the spot. Bake in a preheated 425°F for 13 to 15 minutes or until lightly browned.

Biscuits, Red Lobster Cheddar Biscuits (12 Biscuits)

Biscuits:
2 c. Bisquick™ baking mix
2/3 c. whole milk, cold

1/2 c. sharp cheddar cheese, shredded

Brush on Top:
4 T. butter
1/4 tsp. garlic powder

1/2 tsp. dried parsley

Combine Bisquick™ and whole milk in a large bowl and stir until well blend. Add cheese and stir to mix the cheese evenly throughout the dough. Drop large spoonfuls of dough onto an ungreased nonstick baking sheet about 2 inches apart. Bake in a preheated 450°F oven for 8 to 10 minutes or until golden brown.

While the biscuits are baking, melt the butter in a small nonstick saucepan. Add the garlic powder and parsley and stir. When you remove the biscuits from the oven, use a pastry brush to coat the tops of the biscuits with the butter mixture. Serve biscuits warm.

Broccoli Rolls (8 Rolls)

pastry dough, fresh or packaged
5 oz. broccoli florets, chopped
1 T. olive oil
1/2 tsp. iodized salt

1/8 tsp. fine grind black pepper
8 tsp. cheddar cheese, shredded
4 tsp. butter

Pastry Dough: Homemade pastry dough, or piecrust dough, or 2 packaged piecrusts. Roll out the dough into two 9-inch squares about 1/4 inch thick. Cut the 9-inches in half to make a rectangle 4 1/2 inches by 9-inches long. Cut each 9-inch side in half to make two 4 1/2 inch squares. Repeat for the other 9-inch square. This should yield 8 dough squares. They will not be perfect squares but each square should have sides somewhere between 4 to 4 1/2 inches. Put the dough squares on parchment paper on a baking sheet and bake in a preheated 400°F oven for 4 minutes. Remove from oven and cool to room temperature.

Broccoli Florets: Either fresh or frozen. If fresh then chop the florets into small pieces. If frozen then unthaw and drain off the water. Place on a paper towel and gently press on the unthawed broccoli pieces to press out as much water as possible.

Instructions: Heat oil in a wok or nonstick skillet over medium-high heat until hot. Add the salt, black pepper, and chopped broccoli florets and stir constantly for 4 minutes or until the broccoli is tender but still crisp. Use a soup spoon to transfer a heaping soup spoon full of cooked broccoli onto the center of each dough square. Add 1 teaspoon of shredded cheddar cheese and 1/2 teaspoon butter on top of the broccoli in each dough square. Moisten the top and bottom of all four corners of each square with a little water on your fingertip and thumb. Fold one corner of a square up and over the broccoli near the top center of the dough. Hold the corner in position with the left forefinger and thumb. Use the right hand to fold the opposite corner of the dough square up to overlap the first corner just a little and press the two ends together using water moistened fingers. Fold the third and fourth sides of the square up until they overlap a little in the center and press them together using water moistened fingers. Use your left forefinger that is still inside the roll where all four corners meet, and press the dough firmly with your left thumb to seal all four corners together. If the four corners are not sealed they will open up during baking. Pull the four open sides of the roll together and seal gently with a little moisture and pressure. You will not be able to seal the side your forefinger was in but you can bring the edges more closely together.

Bake in a preheated 400°F oven for 8 to 9 minutes or until the rolls are light brown and done.

Cornbread or Cornbread Muffins

1/2 c. granulated sugar
2 tsp. baking powder
3/4 tsp. iodized salt
1 c. cornmeal, white or yellow
1 c. all-purpose flour

5 T. butter
1 egg, beaten
1 c. whole milk, or buttermilk
1 T. lard, or shortening

Trivia: Cornbread enthusiasts insist that cornbread should only be baked in an 8-inch or 9-inch round cast iron skillet in the oven.

Instructions: Preheat oven to 400°F.

In a large mixing bowl combine sugar, baking powder, and salt, and stir until well blended. Add cornmeal and flour and stir until well blended.

Melt butter in a small saucepan over low heat until just barely melted.

Beat egg in a different bowl until smooth. Add barely melted butter and milk and stir until well blended.

Pour the egg mixture into the large bowl with the dry ingredients. Stir until the dry ingredients are well moistened but still a little bit lumpy.

Cornbread Option: Very lightly grease an 8-inch or 9-inch round or square nonstick baking pan with lard or shortening. Pour the batter into the lightly greased baking pan.

Cornbread Muffin Option: Put paper baking cups into the individual openings of a cupcake pan, or very lightly grease each opening. Fill each about 3/4 full with batter.

Baking Instructions: Bake in preheated 400°F oven for 20 to 25 minutes or until a toothpick inserted into the middle of the cornbread, or a cornbread muffin, comes out without any batter clinging to the toothpick.

Cornbread Dressing (or Stuffing) - Baked (4 Servings)

4 c. cornbread, crumbled
3 T. butter
1/2 c. sweet onion, diced
1/2 c. celery, diced
1 c. chicken stock
1 tsp. dried thyme

1 tsp. sage (or poultry seasoning)
opt. 1/2 c. shredded cooked meat
2 large eggs, beaten
1/2 tsp. iodized salt
1/2 tsp. fine grind black pepper
opt. 2 eggs, boiled, chopped

Buy cornbread at the store or make your own (recipe above).

Melt butter in large nonstick saucepan over medium heat. Add diced onions and diced celery and cook for about 4 minutes or until the onions become soft and translucent. Add chicken stock, thyme, and sage. If desired, add shredded cooked meat, such as chicken, ham, bacon, turkey, or sausage, depending on what you will be serving with the dressing. Stir to blend all the ingredients. Bring to a boil. Remove the saucepan from the heat. Allow to cool for 5 minutes.

In a large bowl, beat eggs until smooth. Add salt and black pepper and mix well. Add warm liquid from saucepan and stir until well blended. Add crumbled cornbread and stir until the cornbread is moist but not soggy. If desired, stir in the chopped boiled eggs. Transfer to a lightly greased 9x13-inch (3 quart) baking dish. Bake in a preheated 400°F oven for about 40 to 50 minutes, or until the top is a golden brown and the dressing is done in the middle.

French Bread (One Loaf)

1 pkg. yeast	1/2 T. granulated sugar
3/4 c. warm water	3/4 tsp. iodized salt
2 1/4 c. bread flour	2 tsp. canola oil

Crumble the yeast into 1/4 cup warm water with a pinch of sugar added and stir until the yeast is mixed with the water. Good yeast will become foamy and creamy in about 10 to 12 minutes.

In a large bowl mix bread flour, sugar, and salt until well blended. Then sift the flour mixture to mix the ingredients more evenly and to break up any small pieces. Add the oil, and the foaming yeast solution, and the rest of the warm water, and stir until well blended. The dough should pull away from the sides of the bowl. If necessary, add a little more flour. Knead by hand for at least 5 minutes.

Cover the bowl and let it rise in a warm place (such as inside your oven with the oven light on) for about 60 minutes or until doubled in size.

Punch the dough down and knead it by hand for at least 5 minutes. Form the dough into a long slender loaf about 15-inches long. Grease a nonstick baking sheet and sprinkle lightly with cornmeal. Put the loaf of bread on the baking sheet. Use a sharp knife to cut diagonal slashes about 1/4 inch deep, about 1/2 the distance across of the top of the loaf, and about 3-inches apart. Cover and let rise 20 minutes in a warm place.

Bake in a preheated 375°F oven for 25 to 30 minutes, or until the loaf sounds hollow when thumped on the top center of the loaf. Transfer loaf to a wire cooling rack and cool for at least 30 minutes.

Different crust options are discussed at the beginning of this chapter.

Honey Whole Wheat Bread (One Loaf)

2 T. butter, room temperature
1 pkg. yeast
1 c. warm water
1 1/2 c. bread flour

1 c. whole wheat flour
1 tsp. iodized salt
3 T. pure honey

Remove the butter from the refrigerator, measure the amount you need, and allow the butter to come to room temperature.

Crumble the yeast into 1/4 cup warm water with a pinch of sugar added and stir until the yeast is mixed with the water. Good yeast will become foamy and creamy in about 10 to 12 minutes.

In a large bowl mix bread flour, whole wheat flour, and salt until well blended. Then sift the flour and salt to mix them more evenly and to break up any small pieces. Add the warm soft butter and honey and stir until well blended. Add the foaming yeast solution and the rest of the warm water and stir until well blended. The dough should pull away from the sides of the bowl. If necessary, add a little more flour. Knead by hand for at least 5 minutes.

Cover the bowl and let it rise in a warm place (such as inside your oven with the oven light on) for about 60 minutes or until doubled in size.

Punch the dough down and knead it by hand for at least 5 minutes.

If you wish to make a round loaf of bread then form the dough into a round ball and press down on the ball to spread out the dough and flatten the ball on the bottom. Place on a greased baking sheet.

If you wish to make a loaf of bread the put the dough in a lightly greased loaf pan.

Cover and let rise 20 minutes in a warm place.

If you are making a round loaf of bread then use a sharp knife to cut an "X" shape in the top of the loaf about 1/2 inch deep and 3/4 of the distance across the top of the loaf.

For a round loaf of bread and for a loaf pan of bread, bake in a preheated 375°F oven for 20 minutes.

If you are baking a round loaf of bread then thump the top center of the loaf and if it sounds hollow then it is done. If not then bake a few minutes longer.

If you are baking a loaf of bread in a loaf pan then reduce the oven heat to 350°F and bake for an additional 10 to 15 minutes or until a toothpick inserted into the center of the loaf comes out clean without any batter sticking to the toothpick. Baking for the minimum amount of time until done yields a loaf of bread with more moisture in it. Cool for at least 30 minutes.

Imitation Little Caesar's Crazy Bread (8 Pieces)

1 pizza dough, fresh or canned
2 1/2 T. butter

3/4 tsp. garlic salt
2 1/2 T. Parmesan cheese, grated

Dipping Sauce:
1/3 c. marinara sauce

Pizza Dough: There are 3 options: homemade pizza dough following the recipe in the Italian chapter of this cookbook, or a Pillsbury canned pizza crust, or a Wewalka rolled up pizza crust in a plastic package. The Pillsbury and Wewalka pizza crusts are available near the canned biscuits in a grocery store. Buy a thick crust package.

Instructions: Roll out the pizza dough into a rectangle about 9-inches by 16-inches and about 1/4 inch thick. Cut the 9-inches in half to make 4 1/2 inches by 16-inches. Cut the 16-inches into 4 equal pieces about 4-inches long. This should yield 8 dough pieces. Roll each piece of dough until it is about 6-inches long and round in the center. Place each piece of long dough on a piece of parchment paper on a baking sheet and bake in a preheated 425°F oven for 6 to 8 minutes, or until they just begin to turn a very light brown. While the bread sticks are baking, melt the butter in a nonstick saucepan over medium heat (or in a bowl in a microwave). Add the garlic salt to the hot melted butter and stir until it completely dissolves. When the bread sticks are done, remove them from the oven and immediately use a pastry brush to coat each bread stick with the garlic butter. While the garlic butter is still hot, sprinkle freshly grated Parmesan cheese generously on top of each bread stick. Serve hot.

Yeast Dinner Rolls (12 Rolls)

Recipe of my Granny Mary Ingle Johnson-Nickels.
Ingredients in Mary's own handwriting dated 3/23/46 (March 23, 1946).
The instructions below were added to match the ingredients.

3/4 c. buttermilk
opt. 6 tsp. salted butter, softened
1 pkg. dry yeast
1/4 c. warm water for dry yeast
2 1/4 c. all-purpose flour, sifted

1/2 tsp. baking soda
1/2 tsp. baking powder
1 tsp. salt (iodized recommended)
4 T. granulated sugar
3 T. lard (or shortening)

Lard Substitution: Until the mid-1900s lard was commonly used in recipes but it was gradually replaced with Crisco® vegetable shortening. Adjust the shelves in the oven so the top of a cookie sheet is a little above the middle of the oven. Remove the cookie sheet from the oven.

Heat the buttermilk in a saucepan and stir until it almost boils and then allow it to cool to room temperature. Heating fresh milk, or buttermilk, until it almost boils kills the enzymes that can interfere with the yeast action in the bread.

Remove the optional butter from the refrigerator, measure the amount you need and allow it to come to room temperature.

Crumble the yeast into 1/4 cup warm water with a pinch of sugar added and stir until the yeast is mixed with the water. Good yeast will become foamy and creamy in about 10 to 12 minutes.

In a large bowl mix exactly 2 cups of flour with the baking soda, baking powder, salt, and sugar. Stir until the dry ingredients are blended together. Then sift the dry ingredients to mix them more evenly and to break up any small pieces. Pour the room temperature buttermilk into the bowl and stir to mix the buttermilk throughout the flour. Add the foaming yeast solution and stir. Cut in the lard (or shortening) and stir until well blended. Then knead by hand for at least 5 minutes. Cover the bowl and let it rise in a warm place (such as inside your oven with the oven light on) for about 60 minutes or until doubled in size.

Punch the dough down and then add the remaining 1/4 cup of flour to make a smooth non-sticky dough and knead it by hand for at least 5 minutes. Cover and let it rise 20 minutes in a warm place.

Divide the dough in half. Roll half the dough on a floured surface, or on a piece of wax paper, until it is 1/4 inch thick. Then cut into circles with a round cookie cutter (about 3 inches in diameter). Use the end of your finger to push down and flatten each roll just a little from side to side across its center where it will be folded in half. If desired, add about 1/2 teaspoon butter in the center of the roll and then fold the roll in half. Pinch together the middle of the two outside edges of the folded roll so the roll will stay folded while baking. If you don't pinch the edges of the roll together then the top of the roll will rise while cooking and it will pop open and lay flat. Place the rolls about 1.5 inches apart on a nonstick cookie sheet.

Repeat with the other half of the dough.

Preheat oven to 400°F.

Cover the rolls on the cookie sheet with a clean kitchen towel and let the rolls rise for 10 to 15 minutes.

Bake at 400°F for 8 to 10 minutes until very light brown but still soft.

Chapter Twelve
Breakfast

Bacon - Baked or Fried
---

1 lb. of lean bacon (mostly red meat with minimal white fat)

Bacon Grease: Regardless of how you cook the bacon, after the bacon is done and before the bacon grease hardens, pour the warm bacon grease into a suitable storage container with a lid. Later you may use the bacon grease as needed in other recipes. For example, add a little bacon grease to your beans when you cook them to give them a unique flavor.

Paper Towel: Regardless of how you cook the bacon, place the cooked bacon strips on a clean paper towel and pat the top of the bacon with another clean paper towel to remove the grease clinging to the bacon.

Oven Method: Place strips of bacon on a two-piece broiler pan so the bacon grease can collect in the lower half of the pan. Bake at 450°F in the center of the oven. Turn the bacon over after 10 minutes. The bacon will be crisp in about 15 to 20 minutes. The thickness of the bacon determines the time required to cook the bacon, so you must check the bacon as it cooks to avoid burning it. Remove each strip of bacon when it is done.

Skillet Method: Layer the bacon in a room temperature skillet so the slices are barely touching. Turn on the heat to medium-high. The bacon will gradually provide its own grease to keep it from sticking to the pan. As the bacon shrinks in size adjust the position of the bacon slices towards the center of the pan. Before the bacon is half done turn it over so the other side can cook. When the other side is done turn the bacon over again so the first side can finish cooking. Remove each slice of bacon from the pan when it is done.

Sausage - Baked or Fried
---

1 lb. pork sausage (see below)

Ground Sausage and Link Sausage: Ground pork sausage may be sliced into patties about 1/4 inch thick and cooked similar to a hamburger patty, or crumbled into small pieces and cooked similar to crumbled hamburger. Link sausages are usually cooked whole and then either served whole or sliced into pieces and added to a recipe.

Oven Method (Patties or Links): Place a piece of nonstick aluminum foil or parchment paper in the bottom of a baking pan. Place the patties or links in the baking pan so they do not touch. Bake at 450°F in the

---

center of the oven. Turn the sausages over after 8 minutes. Cook another for 10 to 14 minutes, or until the sausages are done, but turn the sausages every three minutes to prevent them from burning on one side.

Skillet Method Crumbled Sausage: Crumble the sausage into a nonstick skillet. Turn on the heat to medium. Stir the sausage as it cooks and use the edge of the stirring spoon to break larger pieces into smaller pieces. The sausage will gradually provide its own grease to keep it from sticking to the pan. Cook until completely done. Drain the grease off the cooked crumbled sausage before serving.

Skillet Method for Patties or Links: Place patties or links in a room temperature skillet so they are barely touching. Turn on the heat to medium. The sausages will gradually provide their own grease to keep them from sticking to the pan. Patties and links should be turned over before they are half done so the other side can cook. When the other side is done turn over again so the first side can finish cooking. Put patties and links on a paper towel and use another paper towel to remove as much grease as possible before serving.

Eggs, Fried (One Egg)

1 egg   3/4 T. butter

Put butter in a nonstick skillet with gently curved sides. Melt the butter over medium heat. Crack the egg and use both hands to open the egg shell so the egg gently falls a very short distance into a small shallow saucer plate without breaking the yolk. Remove any shell fragments. Gently slide the egg out of the saucer onto the melted butter in the skillet. Immediately reduce the heat to low. (If the heat is too high the egg will become tough and rubbery.) Cook uncovered about 5 or 6 minutes or until the egg white is "white" and it is no longer transparent and the white is set and not runny, and the yolk has begun to thicken. Now you must decide how you wish to serve the egg:

Sunny Side Up with Very Runny Yolk: Slide the egg out of the skillet onto the serving plate.

Fried Egg Over Easy with Slightly Runny Yolk: Use a spatula or turner that is big enough to get under the entire egg and gently flip it over in the skillet without breaking the yolk. Allow the egg to cook on the other side for 2 minutes. Slide the egg out of the skillet onto the serving plate.

Fried Egg Over Hard with Firm Yolk: Use a spatula or turner that is big enough to get under the entire egg and gently flip it over in the skillet without breaking the yolk. Allow the egg to cook on the other side for 4 minutes. Slide egg out of the skillet onto the serving plate.

Eggs, Hard Boiled (2 Eggs)

2 eggs   opt. 1 tsp. baking soda

Hard boiled eggs are much easier to peel if you will remove the number of eggs you require from the refrigerator and allow the eggs to come to room temperature for at least four hours or overnight. (Note: Adding salt or baking soda to the boiling water has no or very minimal benefits.)

Instructions: Put eggs in a saucepan and cover with cool water. Bring the water to a boil. After the water starts to boil, wait at least seven minutes. Turn off the heat and put a lid on the pot but leave the eggs in the hot water for another five minutes. Use tongs to transfer the eggs into a bowl of ice cold water. Wait four minutes. Crack the egg shell by gently hitting it against a hard surface at lots of different places all over the exterior of the egg. The more cracks you put in the shell the easier the shell will separate from the egg. Starting at the large end of the egg peel off the egg shell using the thin inner membrane that has separated from the boiled egg and is now between the egg and the exterior shell, and the shell should easily come off the egg. However, if the shell is sticking to the egg and it is difficult to remove, then put the eggs back into ice cold water and wait two minutes for the ice cold water to make its way between the exterior cracked shell and the hard boiled egg inside the shell. The eggs may now be a little easier to peel.

Eggs, Omelet (One Omelet)

2 eggs   1/16 tsp. fine grind black pepper
1 T. whole milk   2 T. butter, for frying
1/4 tsp. iodized salt   optional fillings below

Prepare any optional filling and set it aside. A list of optional fillings is at the end of this recipe.
Crack the eggs into a medium bowl. Remove any shell fragments. Beat eggs until smooth. Add milk, salt, and pepper, and stir to blend the ingredients. Whisk the egg mixture for 2 minutes in order to add as much air as possible into the eggs.
Put butter in a nonstick skillet with gently curved sides. Melt the butter over medium heat. Gently slide the egg mixture from the bowl onto the butter in the skillet. Immediately reduce the heat to medium low. Cook eggs for about 3 minutes or until the eggs are firm on the bottom but there is still some raw egg on top. If desired, spread optional fillings

evenly on one-half of the egg. Use a spatula or turner to separate the other half of the omelet from the skillet and fold the omelet over onto the filling half of the omelet. When the bottom of the omelet begins to turn a very light golden brown gently flip the omelet over in the skillet and cook the other side of the omelet for about 30 seconds or until it turns a very light golden brown. Do not brown the omelet. Slide the omelet out of the skillet onto a plate.

Optional Fillings: The most popular filling is 1/4 cup of shredded cheddar cheese. Other fillings include precooked ham or precooked turkey diced into small pieces, cooked crisp bacon crumbled into pieces, diced tomatoes, diced raw onions, diced green bell pepper, and sliced mushrooms. In order to maintain a reasonable ratio of filling to eggs, the maximum amount of all fillings combined should be between 1/4 to 1/3 cup per 2 egg omelet. Except for the cheese, sauté the other fillings in a separate saucepan with 1 teaspoon of butter until they are warm (or depending on the filling until done), and then set them aside until they are needed in the omelet.

Eggs, Scrambled (One Serving)

2 eggs   opt. 1 tsp. whole milk per egg
opt. 1 heaping T. shredded cheese per egg (mild, sharp, or blended)

Break the eggs by hitting them gently against the inside flat bottom of a nonstick skillet. Discard the egg shells (or add the crushed egg shells to your compost pile or put them in your sink garbage disposal unit). Thoroughly mix the yokes and egg whites together using a long plastic fork or a long plastic forked spoon. (If desired, add 1 heaping tablespoon shredded cheese per egg to the skillet. Or add 1 teaspoon whole milk per egg to the skillet. You may add either cheese or milk but not both. Mix the cheese or the milk with the eggs in the skillet.) Turn on the heat below the skillet to low or medium-low. Continuously stir the eggs while they are cooking. As the eggs cook you should scrape the eggs off the bottom of the skillet and mix them with the rest of the eggs in the skillet. Do not let the eggs stick to the bottom of the skillet and burn. The most important thing is to continuously stir the eggs while they are cooking. Continuous stirring is not intermittent stirring. The eggs should be completely done in about 5 to 7 minutes. If the eggs are done sooner than 5 minutes then you are using too much heat and you need to reduce the heat next time. If the eggs take longer than 7 minutes then you will need to increase the heat a little the next time you scramble eggs.

Breakfast Pizza (8 Slices)

1 lb. sausage, or bacon, or ham	1 pizza dough, fresh or canned
4 eggs	1 c. pizza sauce, fresh or canned
4 T. shredded cheddar cheese	1 c. mozzarella cheese, shredded
1/2 tsp. iodized salt	1 c. tomatoes, diced
1/4 tsp. fine grind black pepper	opt. 4 oz. can mushrooms, sliced

Pizza Dough: There are three options: a homemade pizza crust following the instructions in the Italian chapter in this cookbook, or a Pillsbury canned pizza crust, or a Wewalka rolled up pizza crust in a plastic package. The Pillsbury and Wewalka pizza crusts are available near the canned biscuits in a grocery store.

Instructions: Cook the sausage, or bacon, or ham. If sausage then crumble the sausage and use the edge of the stirring spoon to break up the sausage pieces as they cook until done. If bacon, then cook the bacon, and crumble the cooked crisp bacon into smaller pieces. If ham, then cook the ham and dice the cooked ham into small chunks. Set the cooked meat aside.

Scramble the eggs with the shredded cheddar cheese following the instructions in this chapter. Add the salt and black pepper while scrambling the eggs. Stop cooking the scrambled eggs while they are still moist and not quite fully cooked. Set the eggs aside.

Unroll the pizza dough, or unthaw the pizza crust. Place the pizza dough or crust on the appropriate size of baking pan so that the outside edge of the crust is a little higher than the rest of the crust. Bake the pizza crust for 6 minutes at 400°F or at the temperature specified in the instructions for the pizza crust. Remove the pizza crust from the oven.

Spread the pizza sauce evenly over the pizza crust to within 1/2 inch of the outside edge. Sprinkle the shredded mozzarella cheese evenly on top of the pizza sauce. Sprinkle the cooked meat, the diced tomatoes, and the optional sliced mushrooms over the cheese.

Bake for another 5 minutes and then remove from the oven. Sprinkle the cooked scrambled eggs evenly over the top of the pizza and put the pizza back in the oven and bake for another 3 to 5 minutes, or until the total time specified on the pizza dough package. Allow to cool for 3 minutes and then slice and serve.

Buttermilk Pancakes (or Waffles) (6 to 12 Each)

2 c. all-purpose flour
2 tsp. baking powder
2 T. granulated sugar
1/2 tsp. iodized salt

3 T. lard, shortening, butter, or oil
2 eggs
2 c. buttermilk
serve with butter, syrup, or honey

Good Cook Strategy: Remove the butter, eggs, and buttermilk from the refrigerator, measure the amount you need, and allow the measured ingredients to sit for one hour until they come to room temperature.

Waffle Option: Reduce buttermilk to 1.5 cup and add an additional 1/3 cup of vegetable oil to the batter. If desired, add chopped pecans to the waffle after you pour the batter on the waffle iron. Cook in a waffle iron until the steam stops rising around the outside edges of the waffle iron.

Fruit Option: Whole blueberries, or the diced fruit of your choice, may be dropped into each pancake immediately **after** pouring the wet batter into the skillet. Or sprinkle the fresh fruit on the cooked pancakes.

Instructions: In a large bowl mix the flour, baking powder, granulated sugar, and salt. Cut in the warm lard (or shortening or butter or oil).

In another bowl beat the eggs and then add the buttermilk and stir.

Mix eggs and buttermilk with the dry ingredients in the large bowl. Stir until well blended but there should be a few small lumps in the batter. Let the batter stand for 30 minutes before heating the skillet.

Heat skillet or griddle over medium-low heat until a drop of water beads up and sizzles on the surface. Grease bottom of skillet with a little lard, shortening, butter, or oil. Ladle between 1/4 to 1/2 cup of batter onto the hot skillet. (If necessary use the bottom of the ladle to spread the batter into a smooth round circle between 4 to 6 inches in diameter.) Cook between 3 to 6 minutes until the top of the pancakes are covered with tiny bubbles and the edges look cooked and the batter is set. Flip pancakes and cook the other side for 2 to 4 minutes or until the bottom is golden brown. Serve hot with butter or syrup or honey.

Elvis Option (Chocolate and/or Peanut Butter and/or Banana):
Chocolate: Drop 6 to 9 chocolate chips into each pancake **after** pouring the batter on the skillet. Or drop chocolate chips and/or drizzle some chocolate syrup on top of the stack of pancakes instead of syrup.
Peanut Butter: Spread a thin layer of peanut butter on top of each cooked pancake. Or heat 1/4 cup of peanut butter in a microwave for 60 seconds and mix the peanut butter into the batter just before cooking.
Banana: Add banana slices on top of the stack of pancakes. Or mash one banana and mix the banana into the batter just before cooking.

English Muffins (about 16 to 20 Muffins)

1 egg, gently beaten
4 T. butter, room temperature
1 pkg. yeast
1/4 c. water, warm
1 3/4 c. whole milk

4 1/2 c. bread flour
2 T. granulated sugar
1 1/2 tsp. iodized salt
1/2 c. cornmeal

Remove the egg and butter from the refrigerator, measure the quantity you need, and allow them to come to room temperature.

Crumble the yeast into 1/4 cup warm water with a pinch of sugar added and stir until the yeast is mixed with the water. Good yeast will become foamy and creamy in about 10 to 12 minutes.

Heat the milk in a saucepan and stir until it almost boils and then allow it to cool to room temperature. Heating fresh milk until it almost boils kills the enzymes that can interfere with the yeast action in the bread.

In a large bowl mix flour, sugar, and salt. Stir until the ingredients are blended together. Add the room temperature milk and stir to mix the milk throughout the flour. Add the foaming yeast solution and stir. Add the egg and butter and stir until well blended. Then knead by hand for at least 5 minutes. The dough should pull away from the sides of the bowl. If necessary, add a little more flour. Cover the bowl and let it rise in a warm place (such as inside your oven with the oven light on) for about 90 minutes or until doubled in size.

Punch the dough down. Gently knead it by hand for 30 seconds and no longer, or you will drive out the air bubbles in the dough that form the nooks and crannies.

Option 1: Divide the dough into 2 large balls. Roll one ball between 2 pieces of wax paper to a thickness of 1/2 inch. Use a 3 inch, or a 3 1/2 inch, round biscuit cutter, or a glass, or the metal ring of a wide-mouth canning jar, to cut out muffins. Repeat for the other ball.

Option 2: Instead of rolling the dough, form small balls about 3 inches in diameter. Press the balls down flat into muffins about 1/2 inch thick.

Put the cornmeal on a plate. Gently press the bottom and the top of each muffin into the cornmeal and then place the muffin on the flat side of a room temperature cast iron griddle, or cast iron skillet, or nonstick skillet, with about 1 inch between the muffins. If you have too many muffins then put the extra muffins on a piece of wax paper.

Cover and let rise for 45 minutes. Gradually heat the griddle or skillet over low heat. Do not move the muffins. Cook the bottom side of the muffins until they are a light brown and then turn the muffins over.

Cook the other side of the muffins for 5 to 10 minutes, or until they are a light brown and they are done in the center. Transfer to a wire cooling rack. If you have more muffins than needed then you can freeze the extra muffins for up to 2 months.

When ready to serve, push the tines of a fork into the entire outside edge of the muffin where it will be split and pull it apart with your fingers. Do not use a knife to split the muffins because a knife will not create the small holes and crannies that are customary in an English muffin. Toast and then serve hot with the desired topping.

English Muffins with Sausage, Egg, and Cheese (4)

4 English muffins	4 eggs
4 slices cheese, your choice	2 T. butter
1/2 lb. Jimmy Dean regular sausage	salt and pepper as desired

If necessary, cook the English muffins according to the package directions.

Use a round cookie cutter, or a glass, that is about the same size as one English muffin, and cut the centers out of four slices of your favorite type of cheese. Save the small leftover pieces of cheese in a plastic zipper bag in the refrigerator for use in another recipe.

Slice 4 sausage patties, each about 5/8 inch thick, from a roll of Jimmy Dean sausage. Flatten the patties to 1/4 inch thick. Fry the sausage patties in a nonstick skillet over medium low heat until both sides are done, turning the patties as necessary to prevent burning on either side.

Beat 2 eggs in a bowl and pour into a preheated nonstick skillet that contains one tablespoon of melted butter. Cook over medium low heat as one long omelet with a width that approximately matches the size of one English muffin. Turn over once and cook the other side of the omelet until done. Transfer the omelet to a plate and use the other 2 eggs to make another omelet the same way. Use the same round cookie cutter, or glass, that you used on the cheese and cut round egg shapes out of the omelets, or one egg per muffin. Save the small pieces of leftover eggs in a plastic zipper bag in the refrigerator for use in another recipe.

Place a sausage patty, a round egg, and a round slice of cheese on each English muffin. Bake in a preheated 350°F oven for 3 minutes or until the cheese is slightly melted. Serve immediately and allow each person to add salt and pepper as desired.

French Toast (6 Slices of Bread)

6 tsp. butter, unsalted	3/4 tsp. cinnamon
2 eggs	2 tsp. granulated sugar
1/2 c. whole milk, or half & half	6 slices of bread, fresh preferred
1 tsp. pure vanilla extract	maple syrup or sugar for topping

Remove the butter, eggs, and milk from the refrigerator, measure the quantity you need, and allow them to come to room temperature.

In a wide shallow bowl (or baking pan) beat the two eggs. Add the milk, vanilla extract, cinnamon, and sugar and stir well.

Preheat a skillet over medium heat. Dunk 1 slice of bread in the egg mixture for 5 seconds and coat 1 side of the bread and then turn the bread over and coat the other side of the bread for 5 seconds so the egg mixture completely and evenly covers both sides of the bread. Shake off any excess egg mixture back into the bowl. Put 1 teaspoon of butter in the hot skillet and use a spatula to spread the butter over the bottom of the skillet. Place one slice of coated bread in the skillet and cook until the bottom side turns a golden brown. Turn the bread over using a spatula and cook until the other side turns a golden brown. Remove from skillet.

Repeat for the other slices of bread. Coat each slice of bread with the egg mixture just before you put it in the skillet. Always put 1 teaspoon of butter in the bottom of the skillet before cooking each slice of bread.

If desired place each slice of French toast in a warm oven (200°F) to keep the French toast warm until you have cooked all the French toast. Then you can serve all the French toast at the same time.

If you do not eat all the French toast at one meal then you can freeze the leftover slices (with no syrup on them). Put the cooked slices of French toast on a cookie sheet and place in the freezer for one hour. Then remove the cookie sheet from the freezer and transfer the slices of French toast to a zipper plastic freezer bag with the date written on the bag. Return the bagged French toast to the freezer and the French toast will last for up to two months. Reheat in a toaster or in a skillet.

If desired the French toast can be served with maple syrup, or the top of each slice of bread can be lightly dusted with powdered sugar.

Grandpappy's Hash Browns (4 servings)

2 c. potatoes, shredded   2 c. ice cold water
8 tsp. butter, for frying   1/2 tsp. iodized salt

Spatula: A turning spatula with a soft flexible flat solid end that is 6 inches long and 4 inches wide is very useful for cooking hash browns. This type of spatula can be purchased for about $6 at Walmart.

Potatoes: Red skin potatoes or baking potatoes, such as Idaho or Russet, may be used. I personally prefer red skin potatoes for hash browns because they have a slightly better flavor after frying in butter. One medium red skin potato will yield about 1 cup of shredded potatoes. One large baking potato will yield about 2 cups of shredded potatoes.

Butter or Oil: Frying in a little butter will enhance the flavor of the hash browns. And butter will help to provide the desirable golden brown color that is associated with properly cooked crispy hash browns. However, if you prefer you may use canola oil instead.

Crispness: This recipe will create hash browns with a crispy top layer, and a crispy bottom layer, and a very thin inner layer of cooked potatoes that are not crispy. This yields the eating and chewing texture and flavor that most people enjoy. However, if you prefer all the hash browns to be crispy then use a little less potatoes per skillet or spread the potatoes in a thinner layer on the skillet.

Instructions: Put 2 cups cold water in a large bowl, add 1/2 teaspoon salt, and stir. Put the bowl of water in the freezer for about 30 minutes, or until a very, very thin layer of ice just begins to form against the inside edge of the bowl, and/or on top of the water. Salt is added to the water to lower its freezing temperature just a little and to make the water "denser" so it does not easily saturate **into** the potatoes, but the water can still leech the starch **out of** the potatoes.

Rinse the whole potato under cold faucet water to remove any impurities. Dry the potato with a paper towel. Peel the potato and discard the peelings. Shred the potato using the largest holes in a grater (be very careful so you don't hurt yourself). One large baking potato will yield about 2 cups of shredded potatoes. Remove water from freezer, add shredded potatoes to the ice-cold water, and stir gently. Put the bowl of potatoes in the refrigerator for 30 to 60 minutes. The ice-cold water will extract most of the starch from the potatoes because the starch is what causes the potatoes to stick to the skillet. The potatoes will not absorb very much water because the water is so very cold. This yields potatoes that are very low in starch and with very little extra water. The potatoes need to soak in ice-cold water for at least 30 minutes but no more than 60 minutes to avoid saturating the potatoes with water. If you have the time then 60 minutes is recommended. When you remove the potatoes from the water you will notice the water is darker and a small pool of milky white starch in the bottom of the bowl.

Rinse 1/2 cup of shredded potatoes in a strainer under cold tap water for about 12 seconds to rinse off the starch that is clinging to the outside of the potatoes. Then rinse another 1/2 cup of shredded potatoes, and so on. Rinsing in small batches helps to get more of the starch off the outside of the potatoes quicker with the use of less water.

Put a total of 1 cup of shredded potatoes lengthwise down the center on a clean dishtowel. Roll the towel up around the potatoes and firmly twist both ends of the towel to help squeeze some of the water out of the potatoes and into the dishtowel.

Put a piece of parchment paper, or nonstick aluminum foil, on a baking sheet. Put 1 cup of shredded potatoes on the parchment paper in one thin layer with a little space between the potatoes at random spots. Heat for 3 minutes in a preheated 250°F oven to help dry the potatoes for frying.

Heat a large nonstick skillet with a gently curved outer edge over medium heat. Melt 1 teaspoon of butter (a thin slice) in the skillet and collect it into the center of the skillet with the end of your spatula. Spread 1/2 cup of shredded potatoes on top of the end of your spatula. Do not try to fry more than 1/2 cup in one stack or the stack will be too long or too wide to flip properly, or if the stack is the right size then it will be too thick for the potatoes in the center of the stack to cook properly. Allow the shredded potatoes to slide off the spatula into the butter in the middle of the skillet. Use the end of the spatula to form the potatoes into a long rectangle about 6-inches long and 4-inches wide (or the size of your spatula). Use the end of the spatula to gently level out the potatoes so they will cook evenly, especially in the middle. Do not press the potatoes firmly against the skillet. Sprinkle the top of the potatoes with a very small amount of iodized salt. Fry for about 11 to 13 minutes over medium heat until the bottom side is a light golden brown. Do not stir or adjust the potatoes after they start frying -- just leave them alone. Medium heat, or just a little below medium, is recommended so the center of the hash browns will cook correctly and the bottom of the hash browns will brown lightly without burning. About 1 minute before you flip the potatoes, put 1 teaspoon of butter in the skillet near its outside edge so it will melt. Use the end of the spatula to slide the potatoes to one side of the skillet and then use the end of the spatula to slide the melted butter into the middle of the skillet. Slide the spatula under the potatoes and flip them over onto the new pool of melted butter. Gather any loose potatoes back with the rest of them, and if necessary, form into a 6-inch by 4-inch rectangle. Use the end of the spatula to gently level out the potatoes. Fry for about 8 to 11 minutes over medium heat, or until the other side is a light golden brown. If you flipped the potatoes just a little too soon then fry just a little longer on the other side to make sure the inside of the potatoes are done. When done tilt the skillet and allow the hash browns to slide over the edge of the skillet onto a plate. Serve immediately.

Imitation McDonald's Hash Browns (6 Patties)

4 baking potatoes	2 T. butter, softened
1 egg, beaten	1 tsp. iodized salt
5 T. all-purpose flour	1/8 tsp. fine grind black pepper
2 T. dry instant milk powder	4 T. canola oil, for frying

Peel the potatoes and discard the peelings. Grate potatoes through the largest opening in a grater. Squeeze out as much water (starch) as possible between two paper towels. Melt 1 teaspoon butter in a nonstick skillet over medium low heat and sauté the potatoes for 5 to 7 minutes, stirring frequently, or until they are about half done. Remove from the skillet and allow them to cool.

Beat egg in a large bowl until smooth. Add the flour, milk powder, 1 tablespoon softened room temperature butter, and stir until well blended. Add the salt and black pepper and stir. Add the grated potatoes and mix until well blended. Form into six patties in the shape of a long oval about 4 1/2 inches long and 2 1/4 inches wide and 1/2 inch thick. Press and gently compact the patties to firm them up and to help them hold together.

Heat oil in a large nonstick skillet over medium-high heat until the oil is hot. Fry patties on bottom side for about 3 minutes or until crispy and golden brown. Flip patties over and fry other side for about 3 minutes or until crispy and golden brown. Serve immediately.

Sausage and Cheese Biscuits (10 to 12 Biscuits)

1 1/2 c. Bisquick™ Baking Mix	1 c. shredded cheese
1/2 c. water	1/2 lb. Jimmy Dean® regular sausage

Type of Cheese: Experiment with mild, medium, and sharp cheddar cheese, and with 4 Cheese Mexican, to discover the flavor you like best.

Instructions: Preheat oven to 400°F.

Combine the Bisquick™ and the water in a large bowl and stir into a thick biscuit dough. Add the shredded cheese and stir until the cheese is well blended throughout the dough. Set the dough aside until after the sausage has been cooked.

Crumble the sausage into very small pieces into a nonstick skillet and cook over medium heat until done, stirring frequently and using the edge of the stirring spoon to break the larger sausage pieces into smaller pieces. Do not drain. (Note: Jimmy Dean® sausage has very little grease.) Gradually add the cooked sausage to the dough inside the bowl and stir until everything is well blended. Transfer a large spoonful of the dough onto a nonstick cookie sheet and use the spoon to form a round biscuit about 1/2 inch thick in the middle. Place biscuits 1.5 inches apart on the nonstick cookie sheet.

Bake on the middle shelf of a preheated 400°F oven for 11 to 14 minutes until the exposed pieces of cheese on top of the biscuits turn a golden brown. Remove from the oven and immediately transfer the biscuits to a serving plate to prevent the bottom of the biscuits from overcooking. Let the biscuits cool for about 2 minutes but serve while still hot.

Sausage Gravy and Biscuits (4 Servings)

1 lb. Jimmy Dean regular sausage	1/2 tsp. iodized salt
4 T. all-purpose flour	1/4 tsp. fine grind black pepper
2 1/2 c. whole milk	1 (16 oz.) can jumbo biscuits

Biscuits: Bake the biscuits following the package instructions.

Sausage Gravy: Crumble the sausage into a nonstick skillet and cook over medium heat stirring constantly and using the edge of the stirring spoon to break the larger pieces of sausage into smaller pieces. When the sausage is almost done, gradually add the flour, 1 tablespoon at a time, and stir after adding each tablespoon of flour. Gradually stir in the milk 1/2 cup at a time and cook for 30 seconds before adding more milk. Add the salt and black pepper and continue stirring until the gravy thickens. If the gravy becomes too thick then add just a little more milk to thin the gravy.

Serve: Split each baked biscuits in half, place two biscuits (4 halves) on each individual serving plate, and cover the warm biscuits with the sausage gravy.

Sausage, Hash Browns, and Cheese Casserole

1 lb. Jimmy Dean® Sausage
1/3 c. onions, diced
opt. 1/3 c. green bell peppers, diced
4 c. frozen hash browns
8 eggs, beaten

1/2 tsp. iodized salt
1/4 tsp. fine grind black pepper
1 c. cottage cheese, small curd
2 c. cheddar cheese, shredded

Sausage Substitute: Instead of pork sausage you may use lean ground beef. If you wish to enhance the neutral flavor of the ground beef then cook the beef with 2 teaspoons of sage and 2 teaspoons of ginger.

Sausage: The sausage adds its distinctive flavor to the casserole. Some options are: regular, mild, hot, sage, and maple. Using different sausage flavors will add variety to this basic recipe each type you make it.

Hash Browns: Frozen hash browns are recommended. If you shred your own potatoes then extract the starch using the method described in the Hash Browns recipe in this chapter. Or frozen French fries may be used instead. Chop the French fries and use them like hash browns.

Cottage Cheese: Milk, or half & half, may be used instead.

Shredded Cheese: Sharp cheddar cheese is recommended. However, any cheese that blends well with sausage may be used, such as Colby Jack, Monterrey Jack, or 4 Cheese Mexican.

Instructions: Crumble sausage into a nonstick skillet with the diced onions, and optional bell peppers, and cook over medium heat, stirring frequently and breaking up the larger pieces with the edge of the stirring spoon, until the sausage is no longer pink but it is not completely done. Drain off the grease.

Use the sausage grease (on a double folded paper towel), or shortening, to lightly grease the bottom and sides of a 9-inch by 13-inch baking pan. Spread the hash browns evenly over the bottom of the pan and bake on the bottom rack in a preheated 350°F oven for 5 minutes.

Beat eggs in a large bowl until smooth. Add the salt and pepper and stir until well blended. Add the cottage cheese and stir until well blended. Add one-half of the shredded cheese and stir until well blended. Add one-half the cooked sausage and stir until well blended. Pour mixture evenly over the hash browns.

Sprinkle the rest of the cooked sausage evenly on top. Sprinkle the rest of the shredded cheese evenly on top of the sausage.

Cover the top of the baking pan with aluminum foil.

Bake on the center shelf of preheated 350°F oven for 30 minutes. Remove aluminum foil and bake for another 10 to 20 minutes, or until a toothpick inserted in the center comes out clean. Allow to cool for 5 minutes before slicing and serving.

Chapter Thirteen
Cakes, Cupcakes, and Frostings

Cake Pedestal and Refrigeration: Cakes should be put on a covered cake pedestal to keep the cake moist. If any cake is left over after the second day, it should be put in the refrigerator. If the cake contains cream cheese, or fresh fruit, or custard, then it should be refrigerated the same day. If the frosting contains cream cheese, whipped cream, or fresh fruit, then it should be refrigerated the same day.

Cakes: Cakes can be baked as a single layer cake in a 9-inch by 13-inch casserole dish. The cake can be frosted in the dish and cut into slices from the dish. Or a cake can have two layers with half the batter baked in each of two round 9-inch cake pans. Or a cake can have three layers with one-third of the batter baked in each of three round 8-inch cake pans. The same amount of frosting is normally used on a single layer cake and a two-layer cake. However, about 25% more frosting is used on a three-layer cake. Approximate baking times are as follows:

Type of Cake	Temp.	Baking Time
One layer - 9-inch x 13-inch	350°F	30-35 minutes
Two layer - two 9-inch round	350°F	25-30 minutes
Three layer - three 8-inch round	350°F	30-35 minutes
Bundt cake or Angel food cake	350°F	35-60 minutes
Cupcakes - 30 cupcakes	350°F	16-21 minutes

Temperature Adjustment: The above temperatures are for a shiny metal baking pan. If you use dark nonstick pans, or glass pans, then reduce the above temperature by 25°F to 325°F.

Multiple Pans: If you have two or more pans in the oven at the same time, then put them on the same oven shelf, but leave a little air space between the pans, and do not let the pans touch one another because where they touch will create a hot spot on each pan at that location.

Greasing the Pans: All cake pans should be lightly greased with lard or shortening, and then lightly dusted with flour, before adding the batter into the pan.

Parchment Paper (recommended): Cut a piece of parchment paper in a round circle to match the inside bottom of each cake pan. Lightly grease the bottom of each cake pan, put a round parchment paper in the bottom of each pan, and then lightly grease and then lightly dust the paper with flour (or use nonstick spray). Then add the cake batter.

Leveling the Batter in the Pans: After pouring the cake batter into the cake pans, wait 2 minutes for the batter to settle and then gently tap each cake pan on the counter three times to help level out the batter in each cake pan.

Cooling: Allow hot pans to cool, and allow cakes to cool on wire racks, away from any drafts. When you invert the cake onto the wire rack allow it to remain with the top curved side down because it will help to flatten some of the curve.

Two-Layer Cake: For a two-layer cake put the bottom layer with its round side down and its flat side up. Add frosting. Then put the top layer with its flat side down and its round side up and finish frosting.

Three-Layer Cake: Look at the three cakes and select the one with the least rise in the middle. After it has finished baking and it has cooled in the pan for 2 minutes, put a clean kitchen towel on top of the cake and gently push down on the center of the cake. This will be the center layer of the three-layer cake. Now invert all three cakes onto wire cooling racks. Put the bottom cake layer rounded side down and flat side up. Add frosting onto the top of the bottom layer. Put the center layer flat side down and rounded side up. If the center-layer of cake still has too much rise after you place it on the bottom layer, then use a very sharp knife to slice off some of the center rise to help flatten the cake. Add frosting on the top of the center layer, and then put the third layer flat side down and rounded side up. Finish frosting the cake.

Modified Poke Cake: To add frosting inside a cake, insert a table knife through the top of the cake to the bottom of the cake, and hold the cake open just a little, and pour warm frosting into the hole. Then remove the knife. Repeat several more times. Then finish frosting the cake as usual.

Cupcakes: Instead of using a knife or spoon to spread the frosting on a cupcake, it is usually easier and more visually appealing to wait until the cupcakes cool to room temperature and then dip each cupcake into the frosting, very slowly twirl it, and then lift and remove it as you are still twirling.

Chocolate Cake or Cupcakes

1 3/4 c. all-purpose flour	2 eggs, beaten
2 c. granulated sugar	1 c. whole milk
1 1/2 tsp. baking powder	1/2 c. canola oil
1 1/2 tsp. baking soda	1 1/2 tsp. vanilla extract
1 tsp. iodized salt	1 c. hot coffee, or boiling water
3/4 c. cocoa powder, unsweetened	frosting of your choice

Remove the milk and eggs from the refrigerator. Measure the amount you need and allow them to come to room temperature.

Lightly grease the bottom of two 9-inch diameter cake pans with shortening, and then light dust with a little flour. If available, also use round parchment paper. A cupcake option is at the end of this recipe.

Adjust the shelves in the oven so the middle shelf is just a little below the middle of the oven.

Your choice of hot coffee will impact the flavor of the cake. Therefore select a neutral flavor of coffee instead of a coffee with a distinctive unusual flavor.

Preheat oven to 350°F (or 325°F if using glass or dark pans).

Sift the flour, sugar, baking powder, baking soda, and salt together into a large bowl. Stir the contents inside the bowl to thoroughly mix the dry ingredients. Add the cocoa powder and stir until well blended with the other dry ingredients.

In a different large bowl beat the eggs until smooth. Add the milk, oil, and vanilla extract and stir until well blended. Gradually add the flour mixture and stir until the dry ingredients are moistened. Do not over mix or the cake will go flat.

Gradually add the hot coffee (or boiling water) and stir until the hot liquid is just blended throughout the batter, and be sure to scrap the bottom and sides of the bowl to include that batter with the rest of the batter. The batter will be very thin after adding the hot liquid and this is normal.

Divide batter equally between the two cake pans. Wait 2 minutes for the batter to settle and then gently tap each cake pan on the counter three times to help level out the batter in each cake pan.

Put both cake pans on the middle shelf of a preheated 350°F (or 325°F) oven and bake for 25 to 30 minutes until the middle of the cake has risen slightly. Do not open the oven door while baking. Use the oven light to check on the cakes. A toothpick inserted into the middle of the cake should come out clean. If necessary bake a few minutes longer until done. Remove both cake pans from the oven and cool for 30 minutes inside the cake pans. Invert the cake pans onto wire racks and allow the cakes to cool completely.

When cool transfer one layer to a cake pedestal, with the flat side facing up, and the round side down, and use a knife to cover the top flat side of the cake with your choice of frosting. Place the second layer on the first, with the flat side down and the rounded side facing up, and cover the top and sides evenly with frosting.

Cupcake Option: Fill about 30 cupcake tins (or papers) about 2/3 full of batter. Bake in a preheated 350°F oven for 18 to 23 minutes until a toothpick inserted in one of the center cupcakes comes out clean. Wait for the cupcakes to cool completely before icing.

Strawberry Cake

1 box (16.25 oz.) white cake mix	1 c. water
1 box (3 oz.) strawberry gelatin	1/2 c. canola oil
3 whole eggs, beaten	1 c. strawberries crushed (or jam)

Strawberries: Frozen or fresh strawberries may be used. Thaw frozen strawberries and drain off the excess water. Remove the tops of fresh strawberries. Slice the strawberries and then either crush them with a fork or put them in a blender on a low setting. If you don't have strawberries then you may use strawberry jam or preserves.

Cake Instructions: In a large bowl combine the cake mix and gelatin and stir until well blended. In a separate bowl beat the eggs until smooth. Add the water and the oil to the eggs and stir until well blended. Pour the egg mixture into the cake bowl and stir until the cake mix is evenly moistened and the batter is smooth. Then add the crushed strawberries and stir until the strawberries are evenly distributed in the batter. Pour the batter into one large rectangular cake pan, or two 9-inch cake pans, or three 8-inch cake pans depending on whether you want a one, two, or three layer cake. Bake in 350°F oven for 25 to 35 minutes or until a toothpick inserted into the center of the cake comes out clean. Cool in the pans for 10 minutes and then transfer to wire racks to cool.

Frosting Instructions: Use the strawberry frosting recipe or one of the vanilla frosting recipes at the end of this chapter to frost the cake.

Yellow Cake or Cupcakes

1 1/4 c. buttermilk	2 tsp. baking powder
1 c. (2 sticks) butter, softened	3/4 tsp. iodized salt
3 eggs (yolks and whites)	2 c. granulated sugar
3 egg yolks	2 tsp. vanilla extract
2 1/2 c. all-purpose flour	frosting of your choice

Remove the buttermilk, butter, and 6 eggs from the refrigerator. Measure the amount you need and allow to come to room temperature. Allow the butter to become soft like mush.

Lightly grease the bottom of two 9-inch diameter cake pans with shortening, and then lightly dust with a little flour. If available, also use round parchment paper. A cupcake option is at the end of this recipe.

Adjust the shelves in the oven so the middle shelf is just a little below the middle of the oven.

Preheat oven to 350°F (or 325°F if using glass or dark pans).

Instructions: Sift the flour, baking powder, and salt together into a large bowl. Stir the contents inside the bowl to thoroughly mix the dry ingredients.

If a different large bowl cream the soft butter and the sugar together for at least 3 minutes. Beat in each whole egg (yolk and white) one at a time and stir for 1 minute before adding the next egg. Beat in the egg yolks one at time and stir thoroughly for 1 minute before adding the next egg yolk. Add the vanilla extract and stir. Add 1/3 of the flour mixture and 1/3 of the buttermilk and stir until just blended. Add another 1/3 of the flour mixture and 1/3 of the buttermilk and stir until just blended. Add the final 1/3 of the flour mixture and the final 1/3 of the buttermilk and stir until just blended. Do not stir too much or the cake will go flat.

Divide batter equally between the two cake pans. Wait 2 minutes for the batter to settle and then gently tap each cake pan on the counter three times to help level out the batter in each cake pan.

Put both cake pans on the middle shelf of a preheated 350°F (or 325°F) oven and bake for 25 to 30 minutes until the middle of the cake has risen slightly. Do not open the oven door while baking. Use the oven light to check on the cakes. The top of the cake should spring back when lightly tapped. A toothpick inserted into the middle of the cake should come out clean. If necessary bake a few minutes longer until done. Remove both cake pans from the oven and cool for 30 minutes inside the cake pans. Invert the cake pans onto wire racks and allow the cakes to cool completely.

When cool transfer one layer to a cake pedestal, with the flat side facing up, and the round side down, and use a knife to cover the top flat side of the cake with your choice of frosting. Place the second layer on the first, with the flat side down and the rounded side facing up, and cover the top and sides evenly with frosting.

Cupcake Option: Fill about 30 cupcake tins (or papers) about 2/3 full of batter. Bake in a preheated 350°F oven for 18 to 23 minutes until a toothpick inserted in one of the center cupcakes comes out clean. Wait for the cupcakes to cool completely before icing.

Chocolate Frosting

4 T. butter, softened
1 (8 oz.) pkg. cream cheese

1/2 c. cocoa powder, unsweetened
3 c. powdered sugar

Remove the butter and cream cheese from the refrigerator, measure the quantity you need, and allow them to come to room temperature.

Stir the butter and cream cheese together in a large bowl until smooth. Add cocoa powder and stir until blended. Put 1 cup sugar in the bowl and stir until smooth. Continue to add 1 cup sugar to the bowl and stir until all the sugar has been added and the mixture is smooth and creamy.

Milk Chocolate Frosting

12 T. butter, softened
7 T. cocoa powder, unsweetened
3 T. whole milk

1/2 tsp. pure vanilla extract
1 (16 oz.) pkg. powdered sugar

Remove the butter from the refrigerator, measure the quantity you need, and allow it to come to room temperature until it becomes soft as mush.

Stir the butter and cocoa powder together in a large bowl until smooth. Add milk and vanilla extract and stir. Put 1 cup sugar in the bowl and stir until smooth. Continue to add 1 cup sugar to the bowl and stir until all the sugar has been added and the mixture is smooth and creamy. If the frosting is too thick then add a little more milk and stir.

Red Velvet Frosting

12 T. butter, softened
4 drops red food coloring
1 (8 oz.) pkg. cream cheese
1 tsp. pure vanilla extract

3 T. whole milk
2 tsp. cocoa powder
1 (16 oz.) pkg. powdered sugar

Remove the butter and cream cheese from the refrigerator, measure the quantity you need, and allow them to come to room temperature.

Put the butter and the red food coloring in a large bowl and stir together. Add the cream cheese and vanilla extract and stir until well mixed. Add the milk and cocoa powder and stir until blended. Put 1 cup sugar in the bowl and stir until smooth. Continue to add 1 cup sugar to the bowl and stir until all the sugar has been added. If desired, add more red food coloring to increase the color of the frosting.

Strawberry Frosting I

1 stick (8 T.) butter, warm
1/2 tsp. pure vanilla extract
opt. 2 drops red food coloring

1/2 c. strawberries crushed (or jam)
5 c. powdered sugar

Strawberries: Frozen or fresh strawberries may be used. Thaw frozen strawberries and drain off the excess water. Remove the tops of fresh strawberries. Slice the strawberries and then either crush them with a fork or put them in a blender on a low setting. If you don't have strawberries then you may use strawberry jam or preserves.

Frosting Instructions: In a large bowl mix the room temperature butter, vanilla extract, and food coloring. Add crushed strawberries and stir until well blended. Gradually add powdered sugar and stir until frosting reaches the desired consistency.

Strawberry Frosting II

6 T. butter, room temperature
1/2 tsp. pure vanilla extract
opt. 2 drops red food coloring

8 oz. cream cheese, softened
1/2 c. strawberries crushed (or jam)
5 1/2 c. powdered sugar

Strawberries: Frozen or fresh strawberries may be used. Thaw frozen strawberries and drain off the excess water. Remove the tops of fresh strawberries. Slice the strawberries and then either crush them with a fork or put them in a blender on a low setting. If you don't have strawberries then you may use strawberry jam or preserves.

Frosting Instructions: In a large bowl mix the warm butter, vanilla extract, and food coloring. Stir in the room temperature cream cheese. Add crushed strawberries and stir until well blended. Gradually add powdered sugar and stir until frosting reaches the desired consistency.

Vanilla Frosting

2 T. butter, room temperature
2 T. whole milk
2 c. powdered sugar

1/2 tsp. pure vanilla extract
opt. food coloring of your choice

Put the milk in a bowl. Put 1/2 cup sugar in the bowl and stir until smooth. Continue to add 1/2 cup sugar to the bowl and stir until all the sugar has been added. Add butter and vanilla extract. If desired, add 1 or 2 drops of your choice of food coloring. Stir until the frosting is smooth.

Vanilla Buttery Frosting

1 1/2 stick (12 T.) butter, softened   3 T. whole milk
1/4 c. lard, or shortening   opt. food coloring of your choice
1 tsp. pure vanilla extract   1 (16 oz.) pkg. powdered sugar

Remove the butter from the refrigerator and allow it to come to room temperature until it becomes soft as mush.

In a large bowl cream the butter and lard together. Add vanilla extract and milk. If desired, add 1 or 2 drops of your choice of food coloring. Stir until well mixed. Add 1 cup sugar to the bowl and stir until smooth. Continue to add 1 cup sugar and stir until all the sugar has been added.

Vanilla Buttery Cream Cheese Frosting

1 stick (8 T.) butter, softened   opt. food coloring of your choice
1 (8 oz.) pkg. cream cheese   2 1/2 c. powdered sugar
1 tsp. pure vanilla extract

Remove the butter and cream cheese from the refrigerator and allow them to come to room temperature.

Put the butter, cream cheese, and vanilla extract in a bowl. If desired, add 1 or 2 drops of your choice of food coloring. Stir until well mixed. Put 1/2 cup sugar in the bowl and stir until smooth. Continue to add 1/2 cup sugar and stir until all the sugar has been added.

Vanilla Cream Cheese Frosting

4 T. butter, softened   opt. food coloring of your choice
1 (8 oz.) pkg. cream cheese   1 (16 oz.) pkg. powdered sugar
1 tsp. pure vanilla extract

Remove the butter and cream cheese from the refrigerator, measure the quantity you need, and allow them to come to room temperature.

Put the butter, cream cheese, and vanilla extract in a bowl. If desired, add 1 or 2 drops of your choice of food coloring. Stir until well mixed. Put 1 cup sugar in the bowl and stir until smooth. Continue to add 1 cup sugar to the bowl and stir until all the sugar has been added.

Chapter Fourteen
Candy and Fudge

Parchment paper provides a good nonstick surface for candy cooling and storage. Wax paper does not work well for hot or warm candy.

Dark Chocolate Candy

1/2 c. coconut oil
1/2 c. cocoa powder
2 1/2 T. honey (or maple syrup)

1/2 tsp. pure vanilla extract
1/8 tsp. iodized salt
opt. 1/2 c. chopped nuts

Melt coconut oil in saucepan over medium-low heat. Add cocoa and honey and stir until cocoa completely dissolves. Remove from heat and stir in vanilla extract and salt. If desired, stir in optional nuts. Pour into a foil lined pan and refrigerate 2 hours. Slice into pieces and serve. Store uneaten candy in an airtight container in the refrigerator.

Fantastic Fudge

1 stick (8 T.) butter
1/4 c. milk
2 tsp. pure vanilla extract
1 (16 oz.) box powdered sugar

1/2 c. cocoa powder
1/8 tsp. iodized salt
opt. 1/2 c. chopped nuts

Melt butter in large nonstick saucepan over medium-low heat. Then stir in milk. Add vanilla extract, powdered sugar, cocoa powder, and salt and stir well. Continue to cook over medium-low heat for 6 minutes stirring continuously. Remove from heat and cool for 2 minutes. (If desired, add the optional nuts and stir throughout the mixture.) Pour into a buttered 8-inch or 9-inch cake or pie pan and spread fudge evenly to the edges of the pan. Chill in refrigerator for 2 hours. Slice into pieces about 1.5 inches square and transfer to a serving dish.

Peanut Butter Fudge

1/2 c. whole milk, or half & half
2 c. granulated sugar

1 tsp. pure vanilla extract
1 c. peanut butter, creamy or crunchy

Put milk and sugar in large nonstick saucepan and stir. Bring to a boil over medium-low heat and boil 2 minutes stirring constantly. Remove from heat. Add vanilla extract and peanut butter and stir until smooth. Pour into a buttered 8-inch or 9-inch cake or pie pan and spread fudge evenly to the edges of the pan. Chill in refrigerator for 2 hours. Slice into pieces about 1.5 inches square and transfer to a serving dish.

Chocolate Caramel Pecan Clusters
(also known as Millionaires or Billionaires)

1 (14 oz.) bag caramels
3 T. evaporated milk (or water)
2 c. pecans, chopped

opt. 1 c. crispy rice cereal
2 tsp. lard, or shortening
3 c. milk chocolate chips

Amount of Pecans: If using the optional crispy rice cereal then reduce the pecans to 1 1/2 cups.

Instructions: Put caramels and evaporated milk in a heavy nonstick saucepan. Stir and cook over low heat until smooth.

Remove from heat and add chopped pecans. If desired, add the optional crispy rice cereal.

Stir until pecans (and cereal) are well coated. Work quickly. Drop by spoonfuls onto parchment paper. Work quickly.

Allow to cool for 10 minutes and then refrigerate for 30 minutes.

Size of Caramel Pecan Cluster Centers:

1. Smaller flatter spoonfuls will have thinner caramel pecan centers with the same thickness of chocolate on the outside and therefore more chocolate per piece of candy and less caramel pecan cluster at the center.

2. Bigger thicker spoonfuls will have thicker caramel pecan centers with the same thickness of chocolate on the outside and therefore less chocolate per piece of candy and more caramel pecan cluster at the center.

In a clean nonstick saucepan add the lard (or shortening) and the chocolate chips. Stir and cook over low heat until melted and smooth. Do not overcook or the chocolate will burn. Remove from heat. Use a spoon to pick up each caramel cluster and then dip it and roll it in the melted chocolate until the cluster is well coated with chocolate on all sides. Use the spoon to transfer the chocolate coated cluster on parchment paper. (If the chocolate begins to harden before you finish coating all the pecan clusters, then reheat the chocolate briefly to soften the chocolate.) Refrigerate clusters for at least 30 minutes.

Store uneaten chocolate caramel pecan clusters in an airtight container in the refrigerator.

Oatmeal Candy Balls

1 c. granulated sugar	1 tsp. pure vanilla extract
8 T. butter, room temperature	2 1/2 c. quick oats
2 T. warm water	

In a large bowl mix the sugar, warm butter, warm water, and vanilla extract. Add 1/2 cup of quick oats and stir until the oats are coated. Continue to add 1/2 cup of quick oats, stirring until blended, until all the oats have been added. Roll into balls about 1 1/2 inches in diameter and place in a plastic storage container with a lid. Leave a little space between the candy balls so they do not touch. Refrigerate for one hour before serving. Return any leftover candy balls to the refrigerator and store in the airtight plastic container.

Peanut Butter Candy Balls (about 20 to 26 balls), and Imitation Reece's Peanut Butter Cups

1 c. peanut butter, creamy	2 c. powdered sugar
4 T. butter, softened	opt. 1 1/2 c. crispy rice cereal, crushed
2 T. pure honey	opt. 1 c. milk chocolate chips
1/2 tsp. pure vanilla extract	opt. 24 Hershey's® chocolate kisses

Instructions: In a large bowl combine the peanut butter, softened butter, honey, and vanilla extract. Stir until well blended. Add 1/4 cup sugar and stir until well blended. Add another 1/4 cup sugar and stir until well blended. Continue to gradually add sugar but stop when the mixture pulls away from the sides of the bowl and stays together in a large ball. The mixture contains enough powdered sugar when it can be formed into a ball without sticking to your hands.

Options: There are 3 basic options: crispy rice cereal, mini chocolate chips, or chocolate kisses. None of the options are necessary. The candy tastes delicious without any of the optional ingredients. Or you may use each option by itself. Or you may combine the crispy rice cereal option and the chocolate chip option at the same time. However, the chocolate kisses option should not be combined with the crispy rice cereal or chocolate chips. This gives you the flexibility to produce eight different versions of this candy as follows: (1) Candy with no options, (2) Candy with Crispy Rice Cereal, (3) Candy with Chocolate Chips inside, (4) Candy with Crispy Rice Cereal and Chocolate Chips inside, (5) Candy coated with melted Chocolate, (6) Imitation Reece's Peanut Butter Cups, (7) Candy with Crispy Rice Cereal coated with melted Chocolate, or (8) Candy with Hershey's® Chocolate Kisses inside.

Crispy Rice Cereal Option: Gently crush the crispy rice cereal with a rolling pin before adding it to the mixture. Do not flatten the cereal. Just break the cereal into smaller pieces. Then stir the cereal into the mixture until it is well blended throughout the mixture.

Chocolate Chips Option: Stir the chocolate chips into the mixture until they are well blended throughout the mixture.

Hershey's® Chocolate Kisses Option: Push your thumb into one ball and put one chocolate kiss (with the tip cut off or with the tip melted flat) in the center of the ball and cover with candy so it cannot be seen. This makes the chocolate a "surprise." Serve at room temperature or the chocolate kiss with be too hard to bite into.

Instructions Continued: Shape the mixture into 7/8 inch round balls. Place the balls about 1/4 inch apart in a single layer on a serving plate.

Imitation Reece's Peanut Butter Cups (no crispy rice): Press each 7/8 inch round ball down into a 1/4 inch flat circle about 1 3/8 inches in diameter with a slightly tapered side. Dip in chocolate.

Balls (or Cups) Coated with Melted Chocolate: Refrigerate the balls (or cups) for 30 minutes before dipping in chocolate. Melt 1 teaspoon lard and the milk chocolate chips in a nonstick saucepan over low heat until the chocolate is melted (do not overcook or the chocolate will burn). Use a spoon to dip and roll the balls in the melted chocolate. Put on parchment paper to cool. Refrigerate for 30 minutes before serving.

Storage: Eat the candy the same day it is made. Or save uneaten candy in an airtight plastic storage container in the refrigerator.

Peanut Butter Candy Roll

Recipe of my Mother Olene Dare Nickels-Atkins.

4 T. butter, room temperature	opt. 4 drops food coloring
2 T. whole milk	2 c. powdered sugar
opt. 1/2 tsp. pure vanilla extract	3/4 c. peanut butter, creamy

Remove the butter and milk from the refrigerator, measure the quantity you need, and allow them to come to room temperature.

Put the milk and vanilla extract in a medium bowl and stir. If desired, add the optional food coloring of your choice and stir.

Add soft butter and stir. Add sugar and stir to the consistency of pie dough. Divide dough into 2 portions. Chill dough in the refrigerator to make it less sticky. Roll each portion separately between sheets of wax paper. Spread each portion with creamy peanut butter and roll up like a jelly roll. Chill in the refrigerator for 2 to 3 hours. Cut into 1/2 or 3/4-inch slices. Store uneaten candy in refrigerator in an airtight container.

Chapter Fifteen
Chicken

Bacon Wrapped Chicken Tenders (2 or 3 Servings)
---

6 boneless skinless chicken tenders
6 slices of bacon
1/3 tsp. garlic salt

1/8 tsp. fine grind black pepper
2/3 tsp. light brown sugar

Select chicken tenders that are about 4 inches long.

Place each slice of bacon on a broiler pan that allows for the grease to drain into a separate pan below the top pan. Bake in a preheated 450°F oven for 8 minutes until bacon is about half done. Transfer the bacon onto a paper towel and pat dry with another paper towel to remove as much bacon grease as possible. Drain the bacon grease from the bottom broiler pan. Reduce the oven heat to 400°F.

Rinse the chicken tenders under cold tap water and remove any pieces of fat. Pat dry with a paper towel. Sprinkle a little garlic salt, and a little black pepper, and a little brown sugar on each tender. Place a slice of partially cooked bacon on a plate. Put the small end of one chicken tender at a slight angle on one end of one slice of the bacon. Roll the chicken and pull the bacon tight against the chicken so the bacon does not overlap itself and there is a small space between the bacon as you wrap the bacon around the chicken tender from one end to the other. Place the chicken tender on the broiler pan with the loose end of the bacon under the chicken tender so it will be held in place while baking.

Bake in a preheated 400°F oven for 20 minutes. Flip the chicken tenders over so the other side of the bacon is up. Bake for another 10 to 15 minutes, or until the chicken is done in the middle. (Note: The bacon wrapped chicken needs to be cooked on a broiler pan so the bacon grease can drain off the bacon and the bacon can finish cooking properly.)

Recommended Side Dishes: Pasta, or mashed potatoes with gravy, or sliced tomatoes.

Baked Honey Mustard Drumsticks (4 Servings)
---

16 drumsticks (see below)
1/2 c. honey
1/4 c. Dijon mustard
1/4 c. yellow mustard
1/2 tsp. poultry seasoning

1/2 tsp. paprika
1/2 tsp. garlic powder
1/4 tsp. dried rosemary
1/2 tsp. iodized salt
1/4 tsp. fine grind black pepper

Chicken Drumsticks: Instead of 16 drumsticks, you may use 8 thighs, 16 wings, 4 breasts, or 12 tenders. The chicken may contain skin and bones, or it can be boneless and skinless. Drumsticks, thighs, and wings cook better if still on their bones with their skin. Rinse chicken under running water and pat dry with paper towels. Put in a large bowl.

Honey Mustard Sauce: In a different bowl combine honey, mustard, poultry seasoning, paprika, garlic powder, rosemary, salt, and black pepper, and stir until well blended. Pour the honey mustard sauce over the chicken in the bowl. Toss pieces in the sauce until all pieces are equally covered in sauce. Cover bowl and refrigerate for 1 to 24 hours.

Instructions: Select a size of baking pan that allows the chicken pieces to just barely touch one another, but not the sides of the pan, and there is not much empty space near the edges of the pan. The helps keeps the sauce on the chicken. If cooking breasts with the skin, then put skin side up and bone side down.

Pour the honey mustard sauce from the bowl over the chicken. Bake in a preheated 350°F oven for 25 minutes. Turn pieces over. Spoon sauce over chicken. Bake another 10 minutes. Remove wings if done. Turn pieces over, spoon sauce over chicken, bake another 10 to 15 minutes. Cook chicken until an instant read meat thermometer reads 175°F when inserted into the thickest part of the meat, or until the juices run clear and not bloody when pierced with a fork.

Transfer chicken to a serving plate and spoon the honey mustard sauce from the baking pan over the chicken. However, if the sauce is too thin because it has absorbed moisture or grease from the chicken then heat the sauce in the oven until it thickens to the consistency you prefer.

Chicken and Dumplings

1 1/2 lb. uncooked chicken	opt. 1 c. carrots, peeled, sliced
water to cover the chicken	opt. 3/4 c. celery, chopped
2 1/4 c. biscuit dough	opt. 1/2 c. onion, chopped
1 can (10 3/4 oz.) cream of chicken soup	

Chicken: The best chicken for this recipe is chicken breasts with their skin and bones. When boiled the skin and bones add a subtle but distinctive chicken flavor to the boiled chicken and to the broth in the cook pot. However, chicken thighs with their skin and bones may be used instead. (Note: If you have leftover turkey after Thanksgiving or Christmas then you can substitute the cooked shredded turkey white meat for the cooked chicken and skip to the dumpling step.)

Biscuit Dough: The biscuit dough needs to be prepared before you cook the chicken. There are three options:

1. Make your own homemade biscuit dough using the biscuit recipe in the bread chapter of this cookbook.

2. Combine 2 1/4 cups of Bisquick™ baking mix with 2/3 cup whole milk in a large bowl and stir until it becomes a biscuit dough.

3. Purchase 2 cans (16.3 oz each) of Pillsbury™ Grands!™ refrigerated biscuits.

Chicken Cooking Instructions: In a Dutch oven, add the chicken still on the bone with the skin. Add enough water to cover the chicken in the pot. Bring to a boil over medium-high heat. Then reduce heat to low, cover the pot, and simmer for 60 minutes, stirring occasionally, or until the chicken is done. (Note: Thighs are smaller and cook a little faster than breasts.) When the chicken is done, turn off the heat, carefully remove the chicken from the pot and allow the chicken to cool. Leave all the newly formed chicken broth in the pot because you will need it later. Use two forks to pull the skin off the chicken. Use one fork to hold the chicken steady and use the other fork to pull the chicken off the bone. Discard the skins and bones or save them in a plastic zipper bag in the refrigerator for use in another recipe. Use the two forks to separate the larger chicken pieces into smaller thin strips of chicken.

Dumpling Instructions: Prepare the biscuit dough. Place the dough on a floured flat surface. (Note: Later the extra flour will add thickness to the chicken broth in the cook pot.) Press the dough flat with your hands, or roll the dough flat with a rolling pin, until it is about 1/8 thick. (Or flatten each "can biscuit" using your hands.) Use a sharp knife, or a rolling pizza cutter, and cut the dough into 5/8 inch wide strips about 1 1/4 inches long. Place the dough strips on wax paper and allow the strips to rest for at least 30 minutes to firm them up for boiling.

Pot Instructions: Add the cream of chicken soup to the pot with the freshly made chicken broth and stir until well blended. Return the chicken pieces to the pot. Turn on the heat to medium. Heat for 10 minutes or until the broth just starts to boil. Drop dough strips, one at a time, into the boiling pot with the chicken, until there is one layer of dough strips floating on top of the broth. Wait one minute and then push the dumplings down into the broth. Add another layer of dumplings, one at a time, and repeat until all the dumplings are in the pot. If desired, add the optional carrots, celery, and/or onions. (Note: Traditional southern chicken & dumplings do not contain any vegetables. Instead vegetables are served as a side dish because this provides more different options for a side dish.) Reduce heat to low. Cover the pot, and simmer 15 to 20 minutes (or longer), stirring occasionally, until the broth has thickened to the consistency you desire.

Chicken Cordon Blue (2 Servings)

2 boneless skinless chicken breasts   3/4 c. breadcrumbs, or cornflakes
1 egg, beaten   4 slices cooked deli ham
2 T. butter, melted   4 slices cheese, Swiss or provolone
1/4 tsp. iodized salt   4 tsp. butter, for topping
1/16 tsp. fine grind black pepper   1/4 tsp. paprika

Trivia: In French the words "cordon bleu" literally mean "ribbon blue." In the 1700s during the reign of the Bourbon Kings it referred to the sky blue ribbon that was worn as an Emblem by the Knights of the Holy Ghost, the highest order of Knighthood in France. Later it was used to describe a cook that adhered to the highest standards of cookery. Today it is used to describe a dish of either veal or chicken, rolled, filled with cheese and either ham or bacon, breaded, and then either fried or baked.

Instructions: Ask your store butcher to slice each boneless skinless chicken breast in half to reduce the thickness of each breast. If necessary, place each half breast between two pieces of wax paper and gently pound with the flat end of a meat mallet until approximately 1/4 inch thick. Rinse the chicken under cold tap water and remove any pieces of fat.

Beat egg in a medium bowl until smooth. Add the melted butter and stir. Add the salt and pepper and stir until well blended.

Put breadcrumbs, or crushed cornflake cereal, in a flat baking pan.

Cut the cooked ham and the cheese to the same width as the chicken.

Dip one chicken piece in the egg mixture and coat all sides of the chicken. Place the chicken on the breadcrumbs. Fold the two small ends of the chicken breast over onto the main chicken breast. Put one layer of ham on the chicken and put one layer of cheese on the ham. Tightly roll the chicken up in the breadcrumbs into the shape of a jelly roll. Gently squeeze the chicken roll to help seal it into a roll shape. Secure with a toothpick. Repeat with the other pieces of chicken. Place the chicken in a lightly greased baking dish. Sprinkle a little paprika on top of each piece of chicken. Put 1 teaspoon (a thin slice) of butter on the top center of each piece of chicken. Bake in a preheated 350°F oven for 25 to 35 minutes, based on the thickness of the chicken roll, or until brown and done in the center. Remove toothpicks. If desired, slice into pinwheels about 3/4 inch thick. Serve immediately.

Recommended Side Dishes: Rice, steamed vegetables, hot buttered rolls.

Chicken Nuggets - Baked or Fried (4 Servings)

1 lb. chicken tenders, boneless
1 egg, beaten
1/2 c. whole milk
1 c. all-purpose flour
1/2 tsp. garlic powder
1/2 tsp. paprika

1 tsp. iodized salt
1/2 tsp. fine grind black pepper
1 1/2 c. Panko breadcrumbs
opt. canola or peanut oil for frying
opt. 1 c. dill pickle juice
opt. 2 T. powdered sugar

Baked or Fried: The above quantities are for frying. If you wish to bake the chicken nuggets in an oven then only use 1/2 cup flour and 3/4 cup breadcrumbs. The reason is because some of the coating comes off if the chicken is fried in hot oil, but it does not come off when baked.

Instructions: Rinse the boneless, skinless, chicken tenders under cold tap water and remove any pieces of skin or fat. Use a sharp knife to cut the chicken into cubes between 1 inch to 1 1/2 inch in size. The smaller you cut the chicken, the faster the chicken pieces will cook. However, do not cut them too small or you will have a nice crust on a small piece of chicken inside the crust. If you cut them too big then you will have less crust and more chicken in each bite. Chicken nuggets should be the correct ratio of crust to chicken.

Imitation Chick-fil-A Chicken Nuggets: Cut the chicken into 1 inch nuggets and then marinate in a bowl with 1 cup of dill pickle juice in the refrigerator for 4 hours. Drain the chicken. Also add 2 tablespoons powdered sugar to the flour mixture. (Note: Fry the nuggets instead of baking them.)

Instructions Continued: Beat egg in a medium bowl until smooth. Add milk and stir until well blended.

Put flour, garlic powder, paprika, salt, and black pepper in a flat baking pan. Stir until well blended.

Spread out the breadcrumbs on a plate.

Put one piece of chicken in the flour mixture and evenly coat it with a thin layer of flour and remove any lumps of flour sticking to the chicken. Then dip in the egg mixture and coat all sides with some egg mixture. Put chicken in the breadcrumbs and coat it evenly on all sides. Gently press the breadcrumbs into the chicken to help them stick to the chicken.

Put chicken on a piece of wax paper, or parchment paper, or nonstick aluminum foil. Continue until all the pieces are coated and on the paper, but with a little space between the pieces. Let the chicken sit for 15 minutes.

Baking Instructions: Put an *oven-safe* wire rack on top of a baking sheet. This is the type of wire rack used for cooling cookies. Put the chicken nuggets on the wire rack with a little space between each nugget. Bake in a preheated 400°F for 10 minutes. Flip the nuggets over so the other side is up. Bake for another 5 to 10 minutes, or until golden brown. Do not bake too long or the nuggets will taste dry.

Frying Instructions: Add enough lard (or oil) to a large cast iron frying skillet, or a nonstick skillet, until it is about 2 inches deep. Heat over medium heat until the temperature of the melted lard (or oil) is approximately 355°F. Carefully place the chicken in the skillet with a little space between the pieces. If necessary, fry the chicken in 2 or more batches. Cook on each side for between 1 to 2 minutes, or until done. Remove one nugget from the skillet, cut it open and if it is not pink in the center then it is done. Drain on a paper towel covered plate. If desired, sprinkle lightly with salt while still hot.

Serving Suggestions: Serve with honey mustard dipping sauce, or the type of sauce that you prefer, or with ketchup.

Chicken Pot Pie or Chicken Cupcakes

2 1/2 c. cooked chicken, cubed	3/4 c. whole milk
3/4 c. frozen carrots, diced	3/4 tsp. iodized salt
1/2 c. green peas	1/4 tsp. fine grind black pepper
1/2 c. frozen sweet corn	1 3/4 c. chicken broth
1/4 c. onion, finely diced	bottom and top piecrust
1/3 c. butter	opt. 1 egg white, beaten
1/3 c. all-purpose flour	

Chicken: There are three options:
1. One boneless skinless chicken breast you cook yourself.
2. One deli-cooked rotisserie chicken. Remove and discard the skin and then carve off 1/4 inch thick slices of breast meat.
3. Two cans (10 ounces each) premium white meat chicken breast.
Cut the chicken into 1/4 inch bite-size cubes.

Vegetables: Individual bags of frozen vegetables, or one bag of mixed frozen vegetables that have carrots, peas, and corn. Or use canned vegetables such as canned peas & carrots, and canned sweet corn. Smaller vegetable pieces will spread out more evening in the filling.

Piecrusts: Either make the piecrusts yourself, or purchase frozen or refrigerated piecrusts for the bottom and top of the pie.

Instructions: In a large nonstick saucepan, add the carrots, peas, and corn, and onion. If frozen then cover with water. If canned then put the can water in the saucepan. Add the cooked cubed chicken and heat over medium heat for 4 minutes until warm. Remove from heat, drain, and set aside.

Sauce: In the same nonstick saucepan (now empty), melt the butter over medium heat. Add flour and cook for 4 minutes stirring constantly. Gradually add the milk and stir to break up any clumps. Stir constantly to prevent burning the milk, and bring to a boil. Then reduce the heat to low, add the salt and black pepper and stir. Add the chicken broth and stir. Simmer over low heat until the mixture thickens, stirring occasionally.

Put a baking sheet on the middle shelf of an oven and preheat the oven to 425°F with the baking sheet in the oven.

Now decide if you wish to follow the instructions below for one large Pot Pie in a piecrust, or for individual Pot Pies the shape of cupcakes.

Chicken Pot Pie in Piecrust: Beat an egg white in a separate bowl. Brush the inside of the bottom piecrust with the egg white. Put the piecrust in a preheated 425°F oven on the baking sheet and prebake for 5 minutes. Remove the piecrust from the oven. Spread the chicken and vegetable mix over the bottom of the piecrust. Pour the warm sauce mixture over the chicken and vegetables. Cover with a top piecrust, trim off any excess top crust, fold the edge of the top crust under the outside edge of the bottom crust, crimp the edges of the top and bottom crusts together to seal, and cut several slits in the top crust to allow steam to escape. (Flute the edges if desired.) Brush the top of the piecrust with any leftover egg white that remains in the egg bowl. Bake in a preheated 425°F oven on the preheated baking sheet for 35 to 40 minutes, or until the top crust is a golden brown. Remove from the oven and allow to cool for 8 minutes.

Chicken Cupcakes: Reduce the oven temperature to 400°F. Combine the chicken and vegetables with the sauce and stir to blend evenly. Lightly grease the inside of the openings in a cupcake pan. Spread out the piecrust on a cutting board and use a 3 inch round cookie cutter, or a glass, to cut out little round piecrusts. Place one little piecrust in each cupcake opening and use your fingers to mold, stretch, and smooth out the dough so it fits in the bottom and up the sides of the opening. If needed, form the leftover pieces of dough into a ball and flatten by hand into a circle of the right size and put in an empty cupcake opening. Spoon the combined chicken, vegetables, and sauce mixture into each opening. The piecrust dough will expand when baked so do not fill each cupcake to the top of the pan. Do **not** put a top crust on each cupcake. Bake in a preheated 400°F oven on the preheated baking sheet for 15 minutes. Remove from the oven and allow to cool for 3 minutes.

Chicken, Rice, and Broccoli Casserole (4 servings)

1 lb. chicken (or beef) (see below) 3/4 c. onion, diced
2 T. to 4 T. oil   opt. 1 tsp. garlic powder
1 c. white rice, uncooked   opt. 1 tsp. dried thyme
2 c. chicken broth (or beef broth)   opt. 1 (4 oz.) can sliced mushrooms
16 oz. broccoli florets, chopped

Cheese Sauce:
1 T. butter   1 c. whole milk (or half & half)
1 T. all-purpose flour   1/2 c. sour cream
1/4 tsp. iodized salt   1 1/4 cup cheese (see below)

Remove milk, sour cream, and cheese from the refrigerator and allow to come to room temperature.

Beef: 1 pound ground beef or beef tips may be used instead of chicken.

Chicken: 1 pound chicken thighs. Or 1 pound boneless, skinless, chicken tenders or chicken breasts. Or a pre-cooked rotisserie chicken.

Pre-cooked Rotisserie Chicken: Thighs or breasts may be used. Remove and discard skin. Shred the cooked chicken by hand into thin pieces until you have 1 1/2 cups of shredded chicken.

Raw Chicken: If necessary, remove and discard skin. Cut chicken into small bite size pieces. Heat 2 tablespoons oil in skillet over medium-high heat. Add chicken pieces, stir, and cook until done in the center.

Rice: Either long grain or medium grain white rice. Short grain rice is too sticky for this casserole. Heat the chicken (or beef) broth in a large saucepan until it begins to boil. Add rice, reduce heat, cover pan, and cook for 15 to 18 minutes following the instructions in the rice chapter.

Broccoli Florets: Either fresh or frozen. If fresh then chop florets into small pieces. If frozen then unthaw and drain off water. Place on paper towel and gently press on unthawed broccoli to press out as much water as possible. Heat 2 tablespoons oil in a wok or skillet over medium-high heat until hot. Add chopped broccoli and diced onion and stir continually for 4 minutes or until broccoli is tender but still crisp. If desired, add the optional garlic, thyme, and/or mushrooms and stir.

Cheese: Any type of cheese that melts easily may be used. This includes cheddar, mozzarella, parmesan, or Havarti. Or you may use a blend of two or more cheeses. The cheese may be shredded or grated.

Sauce Instructions: Melt butter in a saucepan over medium heat. Add flour and salt and stir continually for about 2 minutes or until the sauce darkens slightly. Add 2 tablespoons of milk and stir until sauce is smooth. Gradually add milk 2 tablespoons at a time, and stir until the sauce is smooth, until all the milk is in the sauce. Gradually add the sour cream and stir continually until the sour cream is well blended into the sauce. Gradually add the cheese and stir continually until the cheese is melted and well blended into the sauce.

Casserole Instructions: Grease the bottom and sides of a casserole dish with lard or shortening. Mix the chicken (or beef) with the rice until well blended. Stir in the broccoli until well blended. Pour mixture into the greased casserole dish. Cover with the sauce. Bake uncovered in preheated 350°F oven for 30 minutes. Cool for 5 minutes and serve.

Chicken Spaghetti Casserole

2 chicken breasts with skin & bone 3/4 tsp. iodized salt
12 oz. thin spaghetti noodles   1/4 tsp. fine grind black pepper
1/4 tsp. garlic powder   2 c. sharp cheddar cheese
2 (10 3/4 oz.) cans cream of mushroom soup
1 (10 oz.) can diced tomatoes with green peppers, celery, and onions

Bring a large pot of water that contains 1/4 teaspoon salt to boil over medium-high heat and then add the two chicken breasts with the skin and bone still attached. Boil for 5 minutes and then reduce the heat to low and simmer for 35 to 45 minutes depending on the size of the chicken breasts. Remove the chicken and save the pot water (broth). Allow the chicken to cool a little and then use a fork to pull off the skins and discard the skins (or use the skins to make chicken broth). Use a fork to pull the chicken off the bones and discard the bones (or use the bones to make chicken broth). Use a fork to tear the bigger pieces of chicken into thin short pieces so the chicken can be more evenly distributed throughout the casserole.

Bring the pot of leftover chicken water to a boil. Grasp the center of a handful of noodles with the left hand and break off the top and the bottom of the noodles with the right hand. Drop the broken noodles into the pot that has the boiling chicken water. Cook the thin noodles for 7 minutes until "al dente" but do not cook the noodles until they are done. Transfer 1 1/2 cups of the water from the pot into a 13-inch by 9-inch casserole baking dish. Drain the spaghetti and set it aside. Add the garlic powder, mushroom soup, tomatoes, 1/2 teaspoon salt, pepper, and 1 cup of the shredded cheese to the casserole dish and stir until well blended. Add the cooked chicken pieces and stir until well blended. Add the cooked spaghetti and stir until well blended. Evenly spread the remaining 1 cup of shredded cheese over the top of the casserole.

Bake uncovered in a preheated 350°F oven for 30 to 35 minutes until the cheese on top is browned. If the cheese browns too quickly then cover the top of the casserole with a piece of nonstick aluminum foil. Cool for 5 minutes before serving.

Imitation Hooter's Buffalo Hot Wings (3 or 4 Servings)

Chicken Wings:
10 to 12 whole chicken wings
1/2 c. all-purpose flour
1/4 tsp. cayenne pepper
1/4 tsp. paprika
1/4 tsp. iodized salt
oil for frying

Buffalo Sauce:
4 T. butter, unsalted
4 T. hot sauce, such as Tabasco
1/8 tsp. garlic powder
1/2 tsp. fine grind black pepper

Rinse wings in cold water. Separate wings into two pieces at large joint. Tear off and discard the thin almost meatless end piece of each wing.

Mix flour, cayenne pepper, paprika, and salt together in a large mixing bowl. Add the wing pieces and toss to thoroughly and evenly coat the wing pieces with the seasoning. Chill in refrigerator for 90 minutes.

Buffalo Sauce: Equal amounts of butter and hot sauce will yield a medium hot sauce. Increasing butter and decreasing hot sauce, each by 2 tablespoons, will yield a mild hot sauce. Decreasing butter and increasing hot sauce, each by 2 tablespoons, will yield a very hot sauce. Combine butter, hot sauce, garlic powder, and black pepper in a saucepan over low heat until butter is melted and sauce is well blended. Turn heat down to very low and keep sauce warm until it is needed.

Frying: Heat about 1 inch of oil in a sauce pan or deep fryer to 375°F. Fry wing pieces completely covered in hot oil for 10 to 15 minutes until the meat begins to turn brown. Transfer wings to a serving platter. Pour the warm buffalo sauce over the wings and thoroughly coat the wing pieces with the sauce.

Serving Options: May be served with celery sticks, blue cheese dip, or ranch dip, or hot dipping sauce (recipe in sauce chapter).

Imitation KFC Popcorn Chicken (3 or 4 Servings)

1 lb. boneless skinless chicken
2 eggs, beaten (see below)
1 1/2 all-purpose flour
1 tsp. Cajun seasoning
1 tsp. paprika
1 tsp. garlic powder
1/2 tsp. iodized salt
1/4 tsp. fine grind black pepper
oil for frying

Eggs: Instead of eggs you may use 1/2 cup buttermilk, or half & half, or whole milk. Or you may use 1/4 cup milk plus 1 beaten egg.

Instructions: Chicken tenders or breasts may be used. Rinse chicken under running water and pat dry with paper towels. Use a sharp knife to cut chicken into 1/2-inch to 3/4-inch bite size cubes or pieces. It is okay if some of pieces are a little bigger or a little smaller.

In a large food plastic zipper bag, combine Cajun seasoning, paprika, garlic powder, salt, and black pepper. Shake to blend ingredients. Put chicken pieces in bag and shake well to coat pieces with seasonings. Let the chicken absorb the seasonings inside the bag for at least 30 minutes.

In a medium bowl beat the two eggs until smooth.

Put the flour in a different medium bowl.

Roll a chicken piece in the flour. Then dip it in the egg bowl and let the excess egg drip off. Roll the chicken in the flour again. Now put it on a wire rack. Continue to coat the chicken pieces and place on a wire rack. Allow the coated chicken to rest on the wire rack for 10 minutes.

Heat about 1 1/2 inches of oil in a saucepan or deep fryer to 350°F. Drop a small bit of the moist flour mixture from the flour bowl into the oil and if it sizzles the oil is hot enough. Deep fry in batches, without crowding the pan, for 3 to 5 minutes or until golden light brown. Use a slotted spoon to transfer onto paper towels to drain. Immediately sprinkle a tiny bit of iodized salt on the hot chicken. Repeat for the next batch of chicken. Serve with your favorite dipping sauce.

Parmesan Crusted Oven Baked Chicken Tenders
(2 or 3 Servings)

6 chicken tenders, 1/2 inch thick	1/4 tsp. garlic powder
3/4 c. breadcrumbs, plain	1/2 c. whole milk
1/2 c. Parmesan cheese, grated	1 T. butter, melted

Rinse chicken tenders under cold tap water. Inspect each tender and remove and discard any white strips of fat.

In a shallow dish combine breadcrumbs, Parmesan cheese, and garlic powder. Mix until well blended.

Pour milk into a different shallow dish. Add melted butter and stir until well blended.

Drench a chicken tender in the milk and butter. Then press the chicken in the breadcrumb mixture until evenly coated on all sides. Gently press the breadcrumb mixture into the chicken to help it stick to the chicken. Place the breaded chicken tender in a lightly greased baking dish. Continue until all the chicken tenders have been breaded and placed in the baking dish.

Bake for 20 minutes in a preheated 400°F oven or until the Parmesan crust is a golden brown.

Serve with a baked potato, or pasta, or rice, or broccoli.

Southern Fried Chicken (4 to 6 Servings)

1 (3 lb.) chicken, whole or cut up
4 c. very cold water, for soaking
2 tsp. iodized salt
3 eggs, beaten

1 c. buttermilk, or whole milk
1 tsp. fine grind black pepper
1 2/3 c. all-purpose flour
lard, shortening, or oil, for frying

If you purchase a whole chicken then cut it into 8 pieces: 2 breasts, 2 wings, 2 legs, and 2 thighs.

Put very cold water and salt in a large bowl and stir to mix the salt in the water. Add the chicken pieces, 1 at a time, with the biggest pieces on the bottom of the bowl. Put into the refrigerator for 2 hours.

Beat eggs in a large bowl until smooth. Add buttermilk and black pepper and stir until well blended. Put flour in a flat baking pan.

Remove chicken from refrigerator and drain off water. Allow water to drain for 2 minutes, or pat each piece dry with a paper towel.

Very lightly coat a piece of chicken with just enough flour to help the egg stick to the chicken. Then dip it in the egg and lightly coat all sides with egg. Put chicken in flour again and now coat it good with flour, but remove any flour lumps. Put chicken on a piece of wax paper, parchment paper, or nonstick foil. Continue until all pieces are coated but with a little space between them. Let chicken rest for 15 minutes.

Add 1/2 inch of lard (or oil) to a large cast iron frying skillet or nonstick skillet and heat over medium-high heat until the temperature is about 355°F. Carefully place chicken in skillet with a little space between pieces. If necessary, fry chicken in 2 or more batches. Cover skillet and cook 3 minutes. Turn chicken over, replace cover, and cook another 3 minutes. Remove cover and cook another 5 to 10 minutes or until done. Turn chicken pieces over every 2 minutes so the bottom does not overcook and get too dark. Cook chicken until it is a golden brown. The wings will be done first because they are smaller. Test for doneness by piercing the thickest part of a piece of chicken to the bone with a fork -- if the juices run clear and not bloody then that piece is done. Remove each piece from the skillet when it is done and place it on a paper towel to drain. Let it cool for at least 10 minutes so the crust can dry and get crispy. This also prevents someone from biting into a piece of hot chicken and getting a grease burn.

Notes: The reason the skillet is covered for the first 6 minutes is to retain the heat in the skillet so the inside of each chicken piece can start cooking. The cover is then removed so the chicken will cook evenly and the crust will become a crispy golden brown. If the flour comes off the chicken while frying then your cooking oil is not hot enough.

Chapter Sixteen
Cookies and Icing
and Protein Energy Bars

A Few Suggestions for Baking Cookies

Sticky Dough: If your recipe yields a "sticky" cookie dough, then refrigerate the dough for about 30 minutes. This will reduce the "stickiness" of the dough and eliminate the need to add more flour to the dough. The addition of too much extra flour can sometimes make the finished cookie hard and brittle.

Rolled Dough: If your recipe requires the cookie dough to be rolled, then sprinkle some flour on your rolling surface and on your rolling pin. Divide your cookie dough into several small balls about four inches round. Smaller balls of dough are easier to roll than one huge batch of dough. Press the small ball down with your hands to form a thick round flat circle. Then use the rolling pin to flatten out the dough to the desired thickness.

Wax Paper: A piece of wax paper below your ball of dough and another piece of wax paper above your ball of dough will allow the dough to be rolled more easily into the desired thickness without the dough sticking to your rolling surface or to your rolling pin.

Cookie Cutters: Before cutting each cookie, press the cookie cutter into some flour, or powdered sugar (or cocoa powder if making chocolate cookies) and shake off the excess before cutting each cookie. The cookie will slide easily out of the cookie cutter and retain its desired shape.

Number of Cookie Sheets: Only bake one pan of cookies at a time in the oven.

Oven Shelf: Cookies normally turn out better if the cookie pan is placed on an oven shelf that is about two-thirds of the distance above the bottom of the oven (or a little higher than the middle of the oven). This prevents the bottom of the cookie pan from getting too hot and burning the bottom of the cookies, and it also reflects a little more heat off the top of the oven onto the top of the individual cookies, and therefore each cookie cooks at a more uniform temperature throughout the cookie.

Burnt Cookie Edges: A few minutes before the recipe says that the cookies will be done, look at the outside edges of the cookies. If the outside edges of the cookies are turning brown then you may need to remove the cookies from the oven before the recipe recommends in order to avoid a batch of cookies with burned edges. This doesn't mean there is anything wrong with your cookie recipe. It may simple mean that your oven is cooking at a little higher temperature than you think it is. The next time you use that same cookie recipe you should decrease your oven temperature just a little bit.

Sugar Dusted Cookies: Buy a new clear glass pepper shaker and fill it with granulated sugar. Only use this pepper shaker for granulated sugar. Use it when you need to sprinkle sugar on the top of cookies. Your new "sugar shaker" will distribute the sugar easily, quickly, and evenly over a big batch of cookies.

Brownies: Cook in glass or shiny metal pans. Dark pans and nonstick pans will usually result in soggy flat brownies.

Protein Energy Bars

---

1 c. quick oats	1/4 c. wheat germ
1/2 c. natural peanut butter	2 T. pure vanilla extract
1/2 c. honey	1/4 c. sweetened coconut, shredded
1/2 c. cocoa powder	opt. 1/4 c. finely crushed nuts

In a large bowl add the oats, peanut butter, and honey and stir until well blended. Add the cocoa power, wheat germ, and vanilla extract and stir until well blended. If desired, stir in the optional finely crushed nuts (peanuts, pecans, or walnuts). Chill in the refrigerator for 30 minutes.

Moisten your hands with a little water and roll some of the mixture into a roll about 2 inches long and 3/4 inch round. Flatten the roll into a rectangular bar about 1/2 thick. Gently press all sides of the bar into the shredded coconut. The coconut will enhance the appearance of the bar and the coconut will make the surface of the bar non-sticky so it can be easily picked up and eaten without it sticking to your fingers. Chill the bars for at least 30 minutes before serving. Store uneaten bars in an airtight container in the refrigerator.

Chocolate Chip Cookies (about 30 Cookies)

1 egg, room temperature	3/4 c. light brown sugar, packed
1 egg yolk, room temperature	1/2 c. granulated sugar
2 c. all-purpose flour	1 T. pure vanilla extract
1/2 tsp. baking soda	1/2 c. semisweet chocolate chips
1/2 tsp. iodized salt	1/2 c. milk chocolate chips
1 1/2 sticks (12 T.) butter, melted	opt. 1/2 c. walnuts, chopped

Remove 1 egg from the refrigerator and allow the egg to come to room temperature. Remove another egg from the refrigerator and while it is still cold separate the yolk from the white. Allow the yolk to come to room temperature. Use a nonstick cookie sheet or lightly grease a cookie sheet with lard or shortening.

Instructions: In a large bowl combine flour, baking soda, and salt, and stir. Then sift the dry ingredients to mix them more evenly and to break up any large pieces.

Melt the butter over low heat in a small saucepan. Allow the butter to cool but do not let it harden.

In a medium bowl cream the butter and the two sugars together until smooth. Add the vanilla extract and beat the egg and egg yolk into the mixture until creamy. Add the flour mixture and stir until just blended.

There are two options for adding the chocolate chips. You can add them to the batter now and stir by hand to evenly distribute them in the batter. Or you can wait until after the cookie batter has been dropped as cookies on the cookie sheet and then randomly drop an equal number of each type of chocolate chip on top of each cookie.

If desired, add the optional chopped walnuts and stir by hand to mix the walnut pieces throughout the batter.

Refrigerate the cookie batter for between one to two hours (mandatory).

Drop the batter by large spoonfuls onto the cookie sheet with the cookies about 3 inches apart. You should have 18 big cookies or about 36 smaller cookies (3 1/2 inch diameters).

Bake in a preheated 325°F oven for 15 to 20 minutes until the outside edges of the cookies become golden brown and the tops are still soft. Remove from oven and allow the cookies to cool on the cookie sheet for 5 minutes and then transfer them to wire racks to finish cooling. If you eat them too soon they will be gooey in the center. (Note: If the cookies are not done after cooling then simply put them back on a cookie sheet and cook them another 5 minutes in a preheated 325°F oven.) If you want moist cookies then store them in a container with a lid. If you want crunchy cookies then store them on an open air platter.

Oatmeal Cookies (about 36 Cookies)
or Oatmeal Raisin Cookies
or Walnuts, or Pecans, or Chocolate Chips, or Coconut

8 T. (1 stick) butter, softened
1/2 c. granulated sugar
1/2 c. light brown sugar, packed
1 egg
1/2 tsp. pure vanilla extract

1 c. all-purpose flour
1/2 tsp. baking soda
1/2 tsp. iodized salt
1/2 tsp. ground cinnamon
1 1/2 c. uncooked dry oats

Oats: Either quick oats or old fashioned oats work well and they both produce the same taste in the finished oatmeal cookies.

Options: Omit the cinnamon and add 1/2 cup of any one of the following: raisins, or chopped walnuts, or chopped pecans, or chocolate chips, or butterscotch chips, or peanut butter chips, or grated coconut.

Instructions: Remove the butter and the egg from the refrigerator, measure the quantity you need, and allow them to come to room temperature.

In a large bowl mix the butter and the two sugars.

In a different small bowl beat the egg and add the vanilla extract. Pour the egg mixture into the first bowl and stir well.

In another bowl combine the flour, baking soda, salt, and cinnamon and stir to thoroughly blend the dry ingredients. Then add the dry ingredients to the first bowl and stir.

Finally, add the oats and stir well. If desired, add any one of the optional ingredients and stir to evenly mix everything together.

Preheat oven to 375°F. Drop the dough by rounded spoonfuls 2 inches apart on an ungreased cookie sheet.

Chewy Cookies: Do not flatten the cookies. Bake for 8 to 9 minutes.

Crispy Cookies: Flatten the center of each cookie using the round end of your spoon and then bake for 10 to 11 minutes or until a light golden brown.

Allow cookies to cool on the cookie sheet for about 2 minutes and then transfer the cookies onto wire racks to finish cooling. If stored in an airtight container these cookies will remain fresh and soft for several days.

Peanut Butter Cookies (about 42 Cookies)

1 1/3 c. all-purpose flour   1/2 c. light brown sugar
1 tsp. baking soda   1/2 c. smooth peanut butter
1/2 tsp. salt   1 egg
1/2 c. lard, or shortening   1 tsp. pure vanilla extract
1/2 c. granulated sugar   opt. a few small chocolate chips

Remove egg from refrigerator and let egg come to room temperature.

Combine the flour, baking soda, and salt in a large bowl and stir. Stir in the lard. Stir in the granulated sugar and the light brown sugar. Stir in the peanut butter. In a separate bowl beat the egg and vanilla extract together. Then pour the egg mixture into the flour mixture in the large bowl. Stir until everything is evenly blended together. Pinch off walnut sized pieces of the dough and roll into 1 1/2 inch round balls. Roll the balls in a little granulated sugar and place the balls one inch apart on an ungreased cookie sheet. Use a wet fork to press the balls flat and then press in the opposite direction to form a crisscross pattern on the top of each cookie.

Bake at 350°F for 11 to 13 minutes. Transfer to wire racks to cool.

If desired, press between one to four small chocolate chips into the top of each cookie after they have been transferred to the wire racks and before they are allowed to cool. (A different option is to gently press one Hershey's® chocolate kiss into the top center of each cookie.)

Peanut Butter Cookies (only three ingredients) (about 14 Cookies)

1 large egg   1 c. smooth peanut butter
1 c. granulated sugar

Remove egg from refrigerator and let egg come to room temperature.

Beat egg in large bowl. Whisk the sugar into the egg until well blended. Then add the peanut butter and stir until smooth. Chill dough in refrigerator for 10 minutes. Pinch off walnut sized pieces of the dough and roll into 1 1/2 inch round balls. Roll the balls in a little granulated sugar and place balls one inch apart on an ungreased cookie sheet. Use a wet fork to press the balls flat and form a crisscross pattern on top of each cookie.

Bake at 350°F for 14 to 18 minutes. Transfer to wire racks to cool.

Snickerdoodle Cookies (about 15 Cookies)

4 T. butter, room temperature
4 T. lard, or shortening
3/4 c. granulated white sugar
1 egg, medium or large

3/4 tsp. cream of tartar
1/2 tsp. baking soda
1/4 tsp. iodized salt
1 1/2 c. all-purpose flour

Cinnamon and Brown Sugar Coating:
1 1/2 tsp. ground cinnamon   2 T. light brown sugar

Cream of Tartar Trivia: Cream of tartar gives the cookie a tangy flavor, and helps the cookie rise and become fluffy in the center, and it makes the cookie chewy by preventing the sugar in the cookie from crystallizing. If you do not have cream of tartar then you may substitute 1 1/2 teaspoon lemon juice (or vinegar) for 3/4 teaspoon cream of tartar to create the tangy flavor these cookies are famous far.

Remove the butter, lard, and egg from the refrigerator, measure the quantity needed, and allow to come to room temperature.

All ingredients should be mixed by hand. If you use an electric mixer then you will not achieve a perfect gourmet baked cookie.

Cream the soft room temperature butter and lard together in a large bowl. Add the white sugar and stir until well blended.

In a small bowl beat the egg until smooth. Add the beaten egg to the sugar mixture and stir until well blended.

In a separate bowl mix the cream of tartar, baking soda, and salt, and stir until well blended. Add the flour and stir until well blended. Gradually add the flour mixture to the egg and sugar mixture, and stir until well blended but do not over stir.

In a separate small bowl mix the cinnamon and brown sugar together.

Trim a piece of parchment paper so that it covers the bottom of your cookie sheet and place it on the cookie sheet.

Keep your hands moist with water and roll the dough into balls about 1 inch in diameter, and then roll the ball in the cinnamon and brown sugar mixture until the entire surface of the ball is extremely well coated. Place the coated ball on the parchment paper and gently press down on the ball to flatten it just a little. Place the balls about 2 inches apart on the parchment paper.

Bake in a preheated 375°F oven for 9 to 10 minutes, or until the edges of the cookies are firm but the centers are still soft. Remove the cookies from the oven when the cookies look like they need to cook just a little longer in the center. They will firm up while cooling. Allow the cookies to cool on the parchment paper for 3 minutes and then transfer to wire cooling racks.

Sugar Cookies (about 36 Cookies)

10 T. butter, soft as mush
1 egg
2 c. all-purpose flour
1/2 tsp. baking soda
1/2 tsp. baking powder

1/2 tsp. iodized salt
1 c. granulated sugar
1/2 c. lard, or shortening
1 tsp. pure vanilla extract

Remove the butter and the egg from the refrigerator, measure the quantity you need, and allow the butter and egg to come to room temperature. You must allow the butter to become as soft as mush.

Use a nonstick cookie sheet or very lightly grease the bottom of a cookie sheet with some lard or shortening.

Instructions: Combine the flour, baking soda, baking powder, and salt, and stir to thoroughly mix all the dry ingredients.

In another bowl, cream the sugar and lard. Stir in the butter. Beat in the egg. Blend in the vanilla extract. Gradually blend in the dry ingredients.

You can now make either of the following two kinds of cookies:

Basic Round Cookies: Moisten your hands with just a little water and use your bare hands to roll pieces of the dough into 1.5 inch round balls. Roll each ball in some granulated sugar and place 2 inches apart on a cookie sheet. If desired, flatten each ball with the bottom of a glass dipped in water and then in granulated sugar. Bake in a preheated 375°F oven for 8 to 10 minutes. Let cool on the cookie sheet for 2 minutes and then transfer the cookies to wire racks to cool.

Cookie Cutter Shaped Cookies: Put the dough in an airtight container and refrigerate the dough for at least one hour or overnight. Coat a flat surface with powdered sugar to roll the dough on. Roll the dough to a thickness between 1/4 inch (crunchy cookie) up to 1/2 inch (soft chewy cookie). Use your favorite cookie cutter shapes to cut out cookies. (Note: Or you can roll pieces of the dough into ropes and make rings, twists, or braids.) Place cookies 1.5 inches apart on a cookie sheet. Bake in a preheated 375°F oven for 8 to 10 minutes. Let cool on the cookie sheet for 2 minutes and then transfer the cookies to wire racks to cool.

Soft Chewy Cookie: Make thicker cookies and bake for 8 or 9 minutes.

Crunchy Cookie: Make thinner cookies and bake for 9 or 10 minutes.

Variations: Substitute almond extract or any other flavoring extract for the vanilla extract. Or add nuts or raisins to the dough at the end.

Icing for Sugar Cookies I

1 T. whole milk
1 c. powdered sugar
2 tsp. light corn syrup

1/4 tsp. pure vanilla extract
opt. food coloring of your choice

Put the milk in a bowl. Put 1/4 cup sugar in the bowl and stir until smooth. Continue to add 1/4 cup sugar to the bowl and stir until all the sugar has been added. Add the corn syrup and vanilla extract and stir until the icing is smooth. Divide into two or three bowls and add the food coloring of your choice to each bowl and stir. Dip cookies in the icing or use a pastry brush to spread the icing on top of each cookie. The icing will be dry enough on a cookie in about 20 minutes to allow the addition of a second color of icing on that same cookie without the colors bleeding together. The icing will dry hard in about 90 minutes so the icing must be used immediately after it is made.

Variations: Instead of vanilla extract you can substitute a different flavor to enhance the cookie, such as almond extract or lemon extract.

Icing for Sugar Cookies II

2 T. whole milk
1 c. powdered sugar

1/2 tsp. pure vanilla extract
opt. food coloring of your choice

Put the milk in a bowl. Put 1/4 cup sugar in the bowl and stir until smooth. Continue to add 1/4 cup sugar to the bowl and stir until all the sugar has been added. Add the vanilla extract and stir until the icing is smooth. Divide into two or three bowls and add the food coloring of your choice to each bowl and stir. Dip cookies in the icing or use a pastry brush to spread the icing on top of each cookie. The icing will be dry enough on a cookie in about 20 minutes to allow the addition of a second color of icing on that same cookie without the colors bleeding together. The icing will dry hard in about 90 minutes so the icing must be used immediately after it is made.

Variations: Instead of vanilla extract you can substitute a different flavor to enhance the cookie, such as almond extract or lemon extract.

Chapter Seventeen
Desserts

Ambrosia (6 Servings)

opt. 3/4 c. nuts (see below)
1 (8 oz.) can mandarin oranges
1 (8 oz.) can pineapple chunks
1 (4 oz.) jar maraschino cherries

1 c. coconut, shredded
1/2 c. (4 oz.) sour cream
1 (8 oz.) container Cool Whip
3 c. mini marshmallows, colored

Optional Nuts: Either pecan pieces or walnut pieces may be used. Or you may use half pecans and half walnuts if you like the taste of both.

Fruit: Drain the oranges, pineapple, and cherries. Remove the stems from the cherries and cut each cherry in half.

Instructions: In a large bowl, mix the sour cream with the Cool Whip. Add the oranges, pineapple, cherries, and coconut and stir until well blended. If desired, add the optional nuts and stir.

Add the marshmallows and stir gently. Refrigerate for at least one hour but not more than 4 hours. Serve chilled.

Apple Dumplings (4 Servings)

1 baking apple, large (see below)
1/2 c. butter, melted
1/2 c. light brown sugar
1/4 tsp. ground cinnamon

1/2 tsp. pure vanilla extract
1/2 cup liquid (see below)
1 (8 oz.) can crescent rolls
opt. vanilla ice cream

Baking Apples: Examples are Fuji, Golden Delicious, Granny Smith, Honeycrisp, Jonagold, Pink Lady, Winesap. Remove and discard peel. Slice apple into 8 equal pieces. Remove and discard core and seeds.

Sauce: Melt butter in saucepan over very, very low heat. Add brown sugar, cinnamon, and vanilla extract and stir until well blended.

Liquid: Pour water, or apple cider, or carbonated beverage (Sprite, Mountain Dew, Ginger Ale, or Dr. Pepper), in bottom of a baking pan.

Instructions: Separate the crescent rolls into 8 triangles. Place an apple slice on the shortest side of a triangle and roll to the other side. Place seam side down in liquid in baking pan to hold the roll tightly against the apple slice. When all the wrapped apples are in the baking pan then pour the warm sauce evenly over the top of the wrapped apples.

Bake at 350°F for 30 to 35 minutes or until done. Cool for 15 minutes.

Serve: Spoon sauce from pan over dumplings when served. If desired, add a scoop of vanilla ice cream on top of each apple dumpling.

Variation: Instead of apples use canned sliced peaches and use the peach syrup from the can as the liquid.

Banana Pudding (No Bake)

8 oz. cream cheese, warm, soft	5 oz. pkg. instant vanilla pudding
1/2 c. sweetened condensed milk	1 (8 oz.) container Cool Whip
3 c. cold whole milk (or half & half)	25 to 50 cookies
1 tsp. pure vanilla extract	3 or 4 bananas

Cookies: Nilla wafers are the traditional choice. Or you may use Nutter Butter cookies, or Vienna Fingers Cream Filled cookies instead. Break the Nutter Butter or Vienna Finger Cookies into 3 pieces.

Instructions: Remove cream cheese from refrigerator and allow it to come to room temperature. If it is not soft then it will be lumpy in the pudding mix.

In a medium bowl beat the room temperature cream cheese and the condensed milk until fluffy.

In a separate large bowl add **cold** milk, vanilla extract, and pudding mix and stir until well blended. Add beaten cream cheese and stir well. Add 4 ounces (half) of the Cool Whip and stir until well blended.

Instructions for a 8 1/2 inch Square Casserole Dish: Completely cover the bottom of the casserole dish with one flat layer of Nilla wafers. Cut bananas into 1/8 inch thick slices. Place layer of sliced bananas on top of the Nilla wafers. Spread the pudding mixture evenly over the top of the bananas. Put 4 ounces (the remaining half) of the Cool Whip on top of the pudding mixture. If desired, just before serving crumble a few Nilla wafers into very small pieces and sprinkle them evenly over the top layer of Cool Whip.

Instructions for a Large 2 Quart Bowl: Cover the bottom of the bowl with a thin layer of pudding. Add a layer of Nilla wafers on top of the pudding and position Nilla wafers up the side of the bowl so the curved surface of the Nilla wafer is facing the bowl and continue all the way around the inside of the bowl. Cut bananas into 1/8 inch thick slices. Place a layer of sliced bananas on top of the Nilla wafers. Cover the bananas with 1/2 of the remaining pudding. Add a layer of Nilla wafers, sliced bananas, and then the remainder of the pudding. Put 4 ounces (the remaining half) of the Cool Whip on top of the pudding. If desired, just before serving crumble a few Nilla wafers into very small pieces and sprinkle them evenly over the top layer of Cool Whip.

Serve: Serve immediately or chill in the refrigerator for 2 hours. Best if eaten within 6 hours after it is made. Even if stored in the refrigerator overnight, the cookies will become soggy and mushy and the consistency of the pudding will no longer be acceptable to most people.

Grandpappy's Ice Cream (One Serving)
An Ice Cream Churn is Not Needed

Vanilla Ice Cream Recipe

1 c. whole milk, cold   3 T. sugar, granulated or powdered
1 tsp. pure vanilla extract   1/4 tsp. iodized salt

Instant Dry Milk Option: If you do not have whole milk then you can use instant dry milk. Mix 1/3 cup instant nonfat dry milk with 1 cup hot water and then put it in the refrigerator overnight to give the milk powder time to completely dissolve.

Instructions: In a small bowl combine the cold milk, vanilla extract, sugar, and salt, and mix well. Put it in the freezer and allow it to chill. Stir the mixture every 30 minutes. Do **not** let the ice cream freeze solid. It is ready to eat when it is the consistency of soft-serve ice cream. Depending on the temperature of your freezer and how full your freezer is, the freezing process normally takes between 2 to 3 hours.

Recipes for Other Ice Cream Flavors

Chocolate Ice Cream: Add 1 tablespoon cocoa powder **or** 1 tablespoon chocolate syrup at the same time the vanilla extract is added. Mix well so the chocolate is blended consistently throughout the mixture.

Fruit or Berry Ice Cream: After putting the ice cream mixture in the freezer, wait 90 minutes. Then add finely chopped/diced fresh peaches or strawberries or whole fresh blueberries to the freezer mixture just **before** it begins to harden. Stir well and then return the mixture to the freezer. This will help keep the fruit crisp tasting and prevent the fruit from becoming soggy.

Walnut or Pecan Ice Cream: After putting the ice cream mixture in the freezer, wait 90 minutes. Then add chopped/crushed walnuts or pecans to the freezer mixture just **before** it begins to harden. Stir well and then return the mixture to the freezer. This will help keep the nuts chewy and prevent them from becoming soggy.

Optional Ice Cream Churn: If you have an Ice Cream Churn, crushed ice, and rock salt, then follow the directions for making ice cream that accompany your churn. You will need to increase the above quantities in order to more fully utilize the capacity of your ice cream churn.

Blackberry Cobbler

1 c. self-rising flour	2 c. blackberries, fresh or frozen
1 1/3 c. granulated sugar	4 T + 2 T. butter, unsalted, melted
1 c. whole milk	

Trivia: A cobbler has a pastry crust that begins under the fruit but while baking it separates and floats to the top of the fruit. When done it has no bottom or side crust. Therefore it is not a pie. A "buckler" has the flour mixed in with the fruit and it does not have a separate crust.

Instructions: Rinse fresh blackberries. Or thaw frozen blackberries. Remove any foreign particles. Pat blackberries dry with a paper towel. In a medium bowl combine blackberries and 1/4 cup sugar and stir to distribute the sugar throughout the blackberries. Let stand for about 20 minutes so that fruit syrup can form.

In a medium bowl mix flour and 1 cup sugar until well blended. Add the milk and 4 tablespoons melted butter and stir until well blended. Pour batter into the bottom of a greased 9-inch baking pan or 3-quart baking dish.

Pour blackberries over batter. Bake in preheated 350°F oven for 45 to 50 minutes or until dough has risen to the top. Sprinkle 2 tablespoons sugar on top of cobbler and bake another 10 minutes. Allow to cool.

Serving Options: May be topped with Cool Whip or vanilla ice cream.

Variations: Instead of blackberries you may use cooked apples or cooked peaches.

Blueberry Muffins (12 or 18 Muffins)

This recipe was used in the famous dining room on the top floor
of the Jordan Marsh Department Store in Boston
before it became Macy's in the mid-1990s

1 stick (8 T.) butter, softened	2 c. all-purpose flour
1/2 c. whole milk	2 tsp. baking powder
1 1/8 c. granulated sugar	1/2 tsp. iodized salt
2 eggs	2 1/8 c. blueberries, fresh
1 tsp. pure vanilla extract	12 tsp. sugar for topping

There is some disagreement over the exact quantities of two of the ingredients in the original Jordan Marsh recipe and the above quantities are the average of the disputed quantities for those two ingredients (sugar and blueberries).

The original muffins were cooked in a pan designed for large muffins. If you do not have a pan for big muffins then you may use a normal size cupcake pan. This recipe will yield 12 big muffins or 18 smaller cupcake size muffins.

Muffin Instructions: Remove the butter, milk, and eggs from the refrigerator, measure the quantity you need, and allow them to come to room temperature.

Very lightly grease the inside of the individual muffin compartments in a muffin pan with some shortening. Or place a muffin size paper baking cup inside each compartment.

Adjust the oven shelf so the top of the muffin pan is a little above the middle of the oven. Remove the empty muffin pan from the oven.

Preheat oven to 375°F (big muffins) or 400°F (cupcake size muffins).

In a large bowl cream 1 1/8 cup of sugar and the softened butter together. Add one egg and beat it thoroughly into the mixture for two minutes. Add the second egg and beat it thoroughly into the mixture for two minutes. Add the milk and the vanilla extract and mix well.

In a different bowl combine the flour, baking powder, and salt and stir to blend the dry ingredients together. Add 1/4 of the flour mixture to the milk and sugar mixture in the large bowl and stir just enough to mix the ingredients. Add another 1/4 of the flour mixture to the milk and sugar bowl and stir just enough to mix the ingredients. Add another 1/4 of the flour mixture to the milk and sugar bowl and stir just enough to mix the ingredients. Add the final 1/4 of the flour mixture to the milk and sugar bowl and stir just enough to mix the ingredients.

In a separate bowl mash half of the blueberries with a fork. Add the mashed blueberries and the whole blueberries to the batter and stir just enough to evenly distribute them throughout the batter. Do not stir too much or the finished muffins will be dense and dry.

Scoop or ladle the batter into the individual muffin compartments so each one is about 2/3 full. Sprinkle 1 teaspoon of granulated sugar on top of each individual muffin.

Bake large muffins at 375°F for about 30 to 35 minutes, or until the muffins are golden brown on top and a toothpick stuck into the top center of one of the middle muffins comes out clean. Bake cupcake size muffins at 400°F for about 18 to 25 minutes, or until done.

Remove the muffins from the oven. Allow to cool for 5 minutes and then transfer the muffins to wire racks to cool. Allow the muffins to cool uncovered for 30 minutes before serving.

Blonde Brownies (about 18 brownies)

6 T. butter, softened
1 egg
1 c. all-purpose flour
3/4 tsp. baking powder
1/2 tsp. iodized salt

1 c. light brown sugar, packed
2 tsp. pure vanilla extract
1/2 c. semisweet chocolate chips
opt. 1/2 c. walnuts, chopped

Remove the butter and egg from the refrigerator, measure the quantity you need, and allow the butter and egg to come to room temperature.

Use a nonstick 9-inch square baking pan, or very lightly grease a 9-inch square baking pan with some lard or shortening.

Adjust the shelves in the oven so the middle of the baking pan is a little above the middle of the oven. Remove the empty baking pan from the oven.

Preheat oven to 350°F.

In a large bowl combine flour, baking powder, and salt, and stir. Then sift the dry ingredients to mix them more evenly and to break up any large pieces.

In another bowl cream the butter and the light brown sugar together. Add the vanilla extract and beat the egg into the mixture. Add 1/3 of the flour mixture and stir until smooth. Add another 1/3 of the flour mixture and stir until smooth. Add the last 1/3 of the flour mixture and stir until smooth.

There are two options for adding the chocolate chips. You can add them to the batter now and stir by hand to evenly distribute them in the batter. Or you can wait until after the batter has been poured into the baking pan and sprinkle them on top of the batter in the baking pan.

If desired, add the optional chopped walnuts and stir by hand to mix the walnut pieces throughout the batter.

Pour the batter into a 9-inch square baking pan and smooth out the batter to all four sides of the pan.

Bake at 350°F for 20 to 28 minutes or until a toothpick inserted in the center of the brownies comes out clean. Remove from oven and allow the brownies to cool inside the pan. Cut into squares.

Chocolate Brownies (about 18 brownies)

12 T. butter, unsalted, melted   3/4 c. cocoa powder
3/4 c. granulated sugar   3/4 c. all-purpose flour
3/4 c. light brown sugar   1/2 tsp. baking powder
3 eggs   1/4 tsp. iodized salt
1 tsp. pure vanilla extract   opt. 3/4 c. walnuts or pecans, pieces

Grease a 9-inch square baking pan with shortening.

Adjust the oven shelf so the top of the baking pan is a little above the middle of the oven. Remove the baking pan from the oven.

Preheat oven to 350°F

Melt butter is a saucepan. In a medium bowl blend the two sugars and the melted butter. Add one egg and beat it thoroughly into the mixture for two minutes. Add the second egg and beat it thoroughly into the mixture for two minutes. Add the third egg and beat it thoroughly into the mixture for two minutes. Add the vanilla extract and mix well. Add the cocoa powder and mix until well blended.

In a separate bowl, combine the flour, baking powder, and salt, and stir to blend all the dry ingredients. Add the dry ingredients to the batter and beat well for at least 2 minutes. If desired, add the optional nut pieces and stir to distribute the nuts throughout the batter. Pour the batter into the greased pan.

Bake at 350°F for 30 to 35 minutes, or until the brownies pull away from the sides of the pan. Remove from oven and allow to cool inside the baking pan. If desired, after the brownies are cool you may cover the tops of the brownies with a Creamy Brownie Frosting (recipe below).

Creamy Brownie Frosting (Hershey's® Recipe)

6 T. butter, unsalted, softened   1 tsp. pure vanilla extract
6 T. Hershey's® cocoa powder   2 c. granulated sugar
2 T. honey or light corn syrup   3 T. whole milk

In a small bowl beat the butter, cocoa powder, honey, and vanilla extract until well blended. Add the sugar and the milk to the bowl and beat until it reaches spreading consistency. Makes 1 2/3 cups of frosting

Chocolate and Oreo Truffles (18 Truffles)

14 Oreo cookies (see below)
3 oz. cream cheese, softened

1 tsp. lard or shortening
1 c. (6 oz.) chocolate (see below)

Oreo Cookies: Regular Oreo cookies do well but the "Double Stuff" cookies contain too much cream and they do **not** make good truffles.

Chocolate: Semi-sweet baker's chocolate, or almond bark, or candy melts. Regular chocolate or white chocolate may be used.

Instructions: Drop 2 or 3 cookies into a blender and pulse on and off. Continue to add cookies until mixture is relatively smooth and uniform.

In a large bowl beat the room temperature cream cheese until smooth. Add crushed Oreo cookies and stir until well blended. Chill 15 minutes. Roll dough into 1 inch round balls and place about one-half inch apart in a single layer on a piece of wax paper. Chill 30 minutes.

Melt 1 teaspoon lard in nonstick saucepan over low heat. Add chocolate and stir until chocolate is melted (do not overcook or the chocolate will burn). Use two spoons to roll the Oreo balls in the chocolate. Return balls to the wax paper. Refrigerate.

If desired, serve truffles in mini cupcake or bon-bon foil or paper cups.

Optional Coatings: If desired, before refrigerating, roll truffles in finely crushed nuts (peanuts, pecans, or walnuts), or cookie crumbs, or in tiny candy sprinkles. A very light coating is recommended. Or you can put a different color of melted chocolate in a plastic bag, cut a small tip off one corner of the bag, and drizzle thin stripes of color on and around the truffle after the first layer of chocolate has cooled.

Cinnamon Buns (12 Buns)

Buns:
3/4 c. whole milk
5 T. butter, softened
2 eggs, room temperature
1 pkg. yeast

1/4 c. warm water
1/2 c. granulated sugar
1 tsp. iodized salt
4 1/4 c. bread flour, or all-purpose

Filling:
5 T. butter, softened
1/2 c. light brown sugar

4 tsp. ground cinnamon
opt. 1/2 c. pecans, crushed

Icing:
6 T. butter, softened
1/2 tsp. pure vanilla extract
1/8 tsp. iodized salt

1/4 c. cream cheese, softened
1 1/2 c. powdered sugar

Trivia: The cinnamon bun originated in Sweden. In 1999 they officially dedicated October 4 as "Cinnamon Bun Day" in honor of the cinnamon bun. In Sweden the average person eats approximately 316 cinnamon buns every year.

Flour: Bread flour is recommended because it will yield a lighter bun. However, all-purpose flour may be used instead.

Bun Instructions: Heat 3/4 cup of milk in a nonstick saucepan and stir until it almost boils and then allow it to cool to room temperature. Remove 2 sticks of butter and 2 eggs from the refrigerator and allow them to come to room temperature.

Crumble yeast into 1/4 cup warm water with a pinch of sugar and stir to mix yeast in water. Good yeast will become foamy in about 12 minutes.

In a large bowl beat 2 eggs until smooth. Add milk and stir. Add 5 tablespoons warm butter, 1/2 cup granulated sugar, and 1 teaspoon salt and stir until well blended. Gradually add flour and stir until well blended. Knead dough by hand at least 5 minutes. Cover bowl and let rise in a warm place (such as in your oven with the oven light on) for 60 minutes or until doubled in size. Punch dough down and knead by hand at least 5 minutes. Cover and let rise 20 minutes in a warm place.

Roll the dough on a floured surface, or on a piece of wax paper, into a rectangle that is about 14-inches by 21-inches, and about 1/4 inch thick.

Filling Instructions: Spread 5 tablespoons of warm butter evenly over the top of the dough. Sprinkle brown sugar evenly over butter. Sprinkle cinnamon evenly over brown sugar. If desired, sprinkle 1/2 cup of crushed pecans evenly over cinnamon. Grasp the 21-inch long side of the dough and roll dough up over the filling (like a jelly roll). Cut the 21-inch long roll of dough into 12 pieces with each piece about 1 3/4 inches thick. Cover a 9x13-inch baking pan with a piece of parchment paper. Place the 12 rolls flat on the paper about 1 inch apart. Cover and let rise in a warm place for 30 minutes, or until doubled in size.

Bake rolls in preheated 400°F oven for 15 to 20 minutes, or until a light golden brown. While the rolls are baking make the icing as follows:

Icing Instructions: In a medium bowl add warm butter, vanilla extract, and salt, and stir until well blended. Add room temperature cream cheese and stir. Add powdered sugar and stir until well blended.

Cinnamon Bun Instructions: Immediately after you remove the rolls from the oven, put a new piece of parchment paper over the top of the rolls. Then turn the baking pan over onto a flat surface. This allows the hot cinnamon drippings to fall off the original piece of parchment paper onto the rolls on the new piece of parchment paper. Allow the rolls to cool for 30 seconds and then cover the warm rolls with the icing. Cinnamon buns taste best if eaten while they are still warm.

Rice Pudding (6 Servings)

3 c. whole milk
5 T. granulated sugar
1/2 tsp. iodized salt

1 1/2 c. white rice
1 tsp. pure vanilla extract
opt. 1/3 c. raisins

In a medium-size nonstick saucepan, add the milk, sugar, and salt and bring to a low boil over medium heat. Trickle the rice into the boiling milk solution slowly over a period of about 30 seconds, stirring continually. Bring to a low boil again and then immediately reduce the heat to low. Cook uncovered about 20 minutes, stirring occasionally, until the rice absorbs the milk, and the rice becomes tender, and the mixture thickens. Remove from heat and stir in the vanilla extract. If desired, stir in the optional raisins.

The rice pudding may be served warm, or refrigerated and served cold. Leftover pudding should be refrigerated in an airtight plastic container.

Strawberry Pudding and Strawberry Banana Pudding

1/2 c. granulated sugar
2 c. strawberries, sliced
3 c. cold whole milk
1 (5.1 oz.) box instant vanilla pudding

1/2 (4 oz.) tub of Cool Whip
2 c. mini Nilla wafers
opt. 1 cup bananas, sliced

Sprinkle the sugar on the sliced strawberries, toss until the strawberries are coated, and put in the refrigerator while making the pudding.

In a large bowl add the **cold** milk and the pudding mix and stir until well blended and smooth. Add 4 ounces (half a tub) of Cool Whip and stir until well blended.

Line the bottom of an 8 1/2 inch square baking dish (glass if available) with mini Nilla wafers. Cover the Nilla wafers with 1/2 of the pudding mixture. Add a layer of sliced strawberries. Add a layer of Nilla wafers.

If desired, add one layer of optional sliced bananas on top of the Nilla wafers to make "Strawberry Banana Pudding." The bananas are a secondary fruit flavor and there are less bananas than strawberries.

Add a layer of 1/2 of the pudding mixture, and a layer of sliced strawberries.

Serve immediately or chill for 3 hours. Best if eaten within 6 hours after it is made. If refrigerated overnight, the Nilla wafers will become soggy and mushy, and the pudding will not be acceptable to most people.

Chapter Eighteen
European Recipes

Beef Stroganoff (5 or 6 servings)

1 lb. ground beef or sirloin steak
3 T. butter
3/4 c. onion, finely diced
1 T. Worcestershire sauce
1 1/2 c. beef broth
1/2 tsp. iodized salt

1/4 tsp. fine grind black pepper
opt. 1 tsp. garlic powder
opt. 1 can sliced mushrooms, drained
3/4 c. sour cream, room temperature
16 oz. egg noodles

Trivia: In 1891 a French chef named Charles Briere won a cooking contest in St. Petersburg, Russia with his creation "Beef Stroganov." The Stroganovs were a prominent and wealthy Russian family.

Beef: Use lean ground beef, ground sirloin, or sirloin steak. Ground sirloin is recommended because it is the perfect compromise between ground beef and sirloin steak, it is easier to cook than steak, it more completely absorbs the flavors of the ingredients, it yields a more dependable consistent flavor, and it is easier for most people to digest.

Pasta Noodles: Fettuccine or egg noodles. If using long noodles then grasp the center of a small handful of noodles with the left hand and break off the top and the bottom of the noodles with the right hand. Or spiral noodles will provide a nice twist (joke) to an old recipe.

Instructions: Cook the beef using the appropriate instructions below:
1. **Ground Beef:** Cook the ground beef and onions in a large nonstick skillet over medium heat until done. Drain fat. Add butter and stir.
2. **Sirloin Steak:** Trim off all the fat and any thick sinews inside the steak. Slice into thin strips. Cut the strips into 1 inch long pieces. Melt butter in a large nonstick skillet over medium heat. Add the beef strips in a single flat layer. Add the onions. Cook for 4 minutes and then flip the meat over and cook the other side for 3 minutes.

Beef Stroganoff: Reduce heat to low. Add Worcestershire sauce, beef broth, salt, and black pepper to the beef in the skillet. If desired, add the optional garlic powder and optional mushrooms. Stir and simmer for 7 minutes. Add the sour cream and stir for about 30 to 45 seconds to heat the sour cream. Do not cook the sour cream.

Pasta Noodles: While the beef stroganoff is simmering, cook the noodles following the package directions. Drain.

Serve: Pour the beef stroganoff on top of the noodles, or combine the beef stroganoff with the noodles and toss to coat the noodles with the stroganoff gravy.

British (or Irish) Shepherd's Pie (Lamb) or Cottage Pie (Beef) (4 to 6 servings)

1 1/2 lb. potatoes, mashed	opt. 3/4 c. carrots, thin sliced
4 T. butter, room temperature	3/4 c. sweet corn
opt. 4 oz. sour cream, softened	opt. 3/4 c. green peas
1 T. canola oil	1 tsp. iodized salt
1/3 c. onions, diced	1/4 tsp. fine grind black pepper
1 lb. beef, or lamb, or mutton	opt. 3/4 c. cheese, shredded
1 c. brown gravy (or 10.5 oz. can)	opt. 1/4 tsp. paprika, garnish

Trivia: Traditionally these pies were made with minced meat and they had a topping of mashed potatoes. The meat was cooked in gravy with onions. Other vegetables, such as carrots and/or peas, were included depending on what was available. The "cottage pie" (beef pie) was created in 1791 when potatoes were first introduced in England as an affordable, dependable, easy to grow vegetable for the country's poor rural workers who lived in cottages. In 1854 "shepherd's pie" was created by substituting lamb or mutton for the beef. More recently, a thin layer of grated or shredded cheese was added to the top of both pies to enhance their flavor and nutritional value.opt.

Baking Pan: A 9-inch by 13-inch casserole dish, or a large cast iron skillet, may be used. If a cast iron skillet is used then the meat and vegetables can be cooked in the skillet, and then the mashed potatoes can be layered on the meat and vegetables, and the optional cheese added, and then the food can be baked inside the cast iron skillet in the oven. This reduces the number of pots that will need to be cleaned.

Potatoes: Red potatoes or baking potatoes (Idaho, Russet) may be used.

Meat: The meat may be minced, ground, or diced into small pieces, so the meat will cook quickly and thoroughly, and the meat can better absorb the flavor and tenderizing effect of the onions. Use very lean ground meat, or trim the fat off the meat, to minimize grease in the pie.

Gravy: A package of brown gravy dry mix may be used instead of a can of brown gravy. Prepare following the directions on the package.

Cheese: Mild, medium, or sharp cheddar, or Colby Jack, or Monterey Jack, or whatever cheese you prefer when you eat potatoes.

Instructions: Lightly grease a 9-inch by 13-inch casserole dish with lard or shortening, or use a nonstick cast iron skillet.

Peel the potatoes, cut into pieces about 1 inch in size. Place in a nonstick saucepan and just barely cover the potatoes with water. Add 1/4 teaspoon salt to the water. Bring to a boil over medium heat, reduce heat to medium-low, slightly cover pan with a lid at a slight angle, and boil between 15 to 20 minutes, or until the potatoes are soft and will easily break apart when pierced with a fork. Drain water and mash the potatoes. Add butter and stir until well blended and smooth. If desired, add the optional sour cream and stir until well blended and smooth.

While the potatoes are boiling, heat oil in a skillet over medium-high heat. When the oil is hot, add onions and stir constantly for 1 minute. Add the meat and stir until the meat is separated and no large clumps of meat remain. Cook for 2 minutes and stir occasionally.

If necessary, drain off the grease.

If desired, add the optional carrots.

Cook for 1 minute, stirring occasionally

If desired, add the optional corn and/or the optional green peas.

Cook for 1 minute, stirring occasionally.

Reduce heat to medium. Add the gravy, salt, and black pepper. Cook for 1 minute and stir until everything in the skillet is evenly coated with the gravy.

Pour the meat and vegetable mixture into the bottom of a lightly greased casserole dish. Let the meat and vegetables cool for 5 minutes.

Spoon the mashed potatoes evenly over the top of the meat and vegetable mixture. If desired, sprinkle the optional cheese evenly over the top of the potatoes.

Bake in a preheated 375°F oven for 20 minutes.

Remove from oven and, if desired, sprinkle the optional paprika over the casserole.

Let stand for 5 minutes and then serve.

Swedish Meatballs (4 to 6 servings)

Meatballs:

3 slices white bread
1/2 c. half & half, or milk
1 egg
1 medium onion, minced
1/4 tsp. All Spice powder

1/4 tsp. ground nutmeg
1/2 tsp. iodized salt
1/4 tsp. fine grind black pepper
1/2 lb. 90% lean ground beef
1/2 lb. ground pork

Gravy:

3 T. butter
3 T. all-purpose flour

2 c. beef broth
1/3 c. heavy cream

Beef and Pork Ratio: The ratio of beef and pork can be changed to suit your taste, such as all beef and no pork, or 3/4 beef and 1/4 pork, or 2/3 beef and 1/3 pork. Also ground turkey can be substituted for the pork.

Meatball Instructions: Remove the bread crust from the bread slices. Cut the bread into 1/2 inch cubes. Pour the half & half into a small bowl. Drop one bread cube into the half & half for about 2 seconds and immediately remove. The bread cube should be moist but not soggy mushy wet. Continue until all the bread cubes are wet. Put any leftover half & half in the egg bowl.

Beat egg in medium bowl. Add onion, All Spice, nutmeg, salt, black pepper, and stir to combine ingredients. Add wet bread cubes and stir.

In a large bowl crumble the beef and pork together. Use your hands and thoroughly mix the two meats together. Add the egg mixture and use your hands to mix all the ingredients together. Moisten your bare hands with some water and form the meat mixture into small individual meatballs about 1 inch round. Makes 35 to 40 meatballs. Place each meatball 1 inch apart on a broiler pan (one that allows the grease to drip into a different pan below the top pan). Bake in a preheated 350°F oven for 20 to 25 minutes. While the meatballs are cooking make the gravy.

Gravy: Add butter to a large nonstick skillet and melt over medium heat. Add flour and stir and cook for 1 minute. Add 1/2 of the beef broth and stir. Reduce heat to simmer and add the rest of the beef broth and stir until lump free. Add the cooked meatballs and increase heat to medium-low. Cook and stir for 8 to 10 minutes until the liquid thickens into a thin gravy. Reduce heat to low and add the cream and stir for 2 minutes. If you want the gravy to have a lighter color then add a little more cream and stir. Remove from stove.

Serve: May be eaten as an appetizer with a toothpick in each meatball. Or it may be served with your favorite pasta, or with boiled potatoes, or with a baked potato, or with mashed potatoes.

Chapter Nineteen
Fish and Seafood

Baked Catfish (2 Servings)

2 (6 to 8 oz.) catfish fillets
2 tsp. canola oil
1 tsp. lemon juice
1 tsp. paprika

1/2 tsp. dried thyme
1/2 tsp. Cajun seasoning
1/4 tsp. iodized salt
1/4 tsp. fine grind black pepper

Rinse each fillet under cold faucet water. Pat dry with a paper towel.

In a small bowl combine the oil, lemon juice, paprika, thyme, Cajun seasoning, salt, and black pepper and mix until well blended. Rub on both side of the fillets.

Place fillets on parchment paper on a rimmed baking sheet. Bake uncovered in a preheated 400°F oven for 10 to 16 minutes (depending on the thickness of the fillets), or until the fish flakes easily with a fork.

Baked Trout Amandine (2 Servings)

2 (6 oz.) trout fillets
2 T. lemon juice
1/4 tsp. iodized salt
1/16 tsp. fine grind black pepper

1 tsp. dried parsley flakes
2 T. butter
1/4 c. almonds, sliced

TRIVIA: Amandine is a French term that means "garnished with almonds." In the USA it is usually misspelled as "almondine" when associated with trout.

Trout: Rainbow trout are recommended if you can find them.

Rinse each fillet under cold faucet water. Pat dry with a paper towel.

Place trout on a lightly greased baking dish with their skin side down. Gently rub lemon juice onto trout. Sprinkle with salt, black pepper, and parsley flakes.

In a nonstick saucepan melt the butter over medium heat. Add the sliced almonds and stir until some of the almonds start to turn brown. Pour the buttered almonds over the trout and spread the almonds into an even layer on top of the fillets.

Bake in a preheated 450°F oven for 8 to 12 minutes (depending on the thickness of the fillets), or until the trout flakes easily with a fork.

Bass (Baked or Fried) (2 Servings)

2 bass filets (6 ounces each)
2 T. Cajun seasoning

1/2 c. cornmeal
1/4 c. oil

Basting Sauce for Baking:

2 tsp. lemon juice, or lime juice
2 T. melted butter

1 tsp. Worcestershire sauce

Rinse each filet under cold tap water. Pat dry with a paper towel. Coat meat side of each filet with Cajun seasoning. Gently press the seasoning into each filet. However, the more seasoning you use, the more spicy hot the filets will taste. Allow to sit at room temperature for 15 to 30 minutes. Dredge filets in cornmeal. Shake off excess cornmeal.

Fry Option: Heat oil in nonstick skillet. Fry until golden brown or about 3 or 4 minutes per side. Transfer skin side down onto a plate. Squeeze 1 teaspoon lemon juice, or lime juice, over each fillet. Serve immediately.

Bake Option: Put oil in bottom of a baking pan. Place the filets skin side down in the oil. Pour 1/2 of the basting sauce on top of the filets. Bake uncovered in 400°F oven for 20 to 25 minutes or until golden brown and done. Do not turn filets over. Transfer skin side down onto a plate. Pour remaining basting sauce over each fillet. Serve immediately.

Blackened Tilapia (or Grouper) (2 Servings)

4 tilapia filets
4 T. Cajun seasoning

3 T. butter
4 tsp. lemon juice, or lime juice

Rinse each filet under cold tap water. Pat dry with a paper towel. Thoroughly coat both sides of each filet with the Cajun seasoning. Gently press the seasoning into each side of each filet. Remember that the more seasoning you use, the more spicy hot the filets will taste. Allow to sit at room temperature for 15 to 30 minutes.

Melt butter in a large nonstick skillet over medium-high heat until the butter sizzles. Place filets in skillet and fry for about 3 minutes on bottom side, or until blackened. Turn filets over and fry for about 3 minutes on the other side or until the fish is blackened and can be flaked with a fork. Transfer to plates and pour the juices from the skillet over the fillets. Squeeze 1 teaspoon lemon juice, or lime juice, over each fillet. Serve immediately.

Suggested Side Dishes: Potato salad, or Mexican rice, or brown rice cooked with diced onions, sliced mushrooms, and sweet green peas.

Crab Cakes
(or Salmon, or Jack Mackerel, or Catfish, or Tuna)

1 egg	1 lb. lump crabmeat
1/4 c. mayonnaise	1 c. breadcrumbs (or crackers)
1 1/2 tsp. mustard	opt. 1 T. fresh parsley, chopped
3/4 tsp. Old Bay® seasoning	opt. 1/4 c. onion, finely diced
1 tsp. Worcestershire sauce	opt. 1/4 c. celery, finely diced
1/8 tsp. fine grind black pepper	

Mustard: Dijon mustard, or Grey Poupon mustard, or yellow mustard.

Old Bay Seasoning: This is the traditional seasoning used in crab cakes. However, it can be replaced with Italian seasoning if you wish.

Crabmeat: Fresh, or imitation (from seafood deli of grocery store), or three 6-ounce cans of Premium Lump Crabmeat.

Breadcrumbs: Dry breadcrumbs, or saltine crackers crumbled, or Ritz crackers crumbled, or 2 slices torn white bread without the crust.

Optional Items: A traditional crab cake does not include parsley, onion, or celery. However, a small amount of parsley enhances the taste of seafood. A small amount of onion adds its flavor and a little crunch to the crab cake. Celery adds a little crunch.

Instructions: Beat egg in a bowl. Add mayonnaise, mustard, Old Bay seasoning, Worcestershire sauce, and black pepper, and stir. If desired, add parsley, and/or onion, and/or celery, and stir.

Inspect the crabmeat and remove any tiny pieces of shell or cartilage. If using canned crabmeat then drain off all the water, separate the crab meat into flakes, and then place on a paper towel and gently press on the top of the crabmeat with a different paper towel to remove as much water as possible. In a separate bowl use your fingers to gently mix the crabmeat and the breadcrumbs without breaking up too many of the crabmeat lumps because a traditional crab cake is a little lumpy. Add the mayonnaise mixture to the crabmeat and use your fingers to gently blend the ingredients. Do not over mix. Use your hands and form the mixture into 4 large patties (3 inch diameters), or 6 average patties (2.5 inch diameters), or 8 smaller patties (2 inch diameters), or 16 patties for appetizers (1.5 inch diameters). Each patty should be between 1/2 inch to 3/4 inch thick.

Optional Bread Crumb Crust: Finely crush some breadcrumbs and put them on a plate. Gently press both sides of each crab cake into the breadcrumbs to coat both sides of each crab cake with a very thin layer of breadcrumbs.

Refrigerate: Put in the refrigerator for 60 minutes to firm the crab cakes so they will stay together as they cook.

Cooking Options: Choose one of the following cooking options. Do not overcook or the crab cake will be tough and chewy.

1. **Broil:** Preheat oven broiler and then broil for 3 to 4 minutes on top. Then turn crab cake over and broil 3 to 4 minutes on other side.

2. **Bake:** Place crab cakes on a lightly greased baking pan and bake in a preheated 400°F oven for 15 minutes. Then turn crab cakes over and bake for another 10 minutes until golden brown.

3. **Fry:** Spread 1 tablespoon of canola oil over the bottom of a large skillet. Heat over medium heat until the oil is hot. Add the crab cakes to the skillet and cook 4 to 5 minutes until golden brown on the bottom and then turn over with a spatula and cook 3 to 4 minutes until golden brown on the other side.

Serving Options: One crab cake per person as a side dish or two crab cakes per person as a main dish. May be served with saltine crackers, or on a bed of lettuce with one or two slices of tomato and with a little of your favorite salad dressing, or with a wedge of lemon, or with cocktail sauce, or with tartar sauce. Or crab cakes may be eaten as a sandwich on a bun, or on two toasted slices of bread. If desired, add a little Russian dressing or Thousand Island dressing on the sandwich.

For Young Children: Sponge Bob's Krusty Krabs' Krabby Patty: (This secret recipe needs to be carefully protected so the evil Plankton does not steal it.) Serve the crab cake "Krabby Patty" on a hamburger bun (sesame seeds on top) with your child's choice of any (or none) of the following "traditional" toppings from the Sponge Bob TV show: slice of cheese, ketchup, mustard, lettuce, tomato, pickle, and/or onion. However, in the TV show there are many episodes with references that say the Krabby Patty is made with "imitation crab meat" or hamburger.

Imitation Longhorn Steakhouse Wild West Shrimp

1 (12 oz) pkg. popcorn shrimp 1/4 c. cherry peppers, sliced
6 T. butter   2 tsp. Prairie Dust (sauce chapter)
2 tsp. lemon juice   opt. ranch dressing, for dipping

Purchase one 12 ounce package of frozen "SeaPak" popcorn shrimp. Fry shrimp following the instructions on the package. Drain on a paper towel covered plate and pat dry with another paper towel.

Melt butter in a large nonstick skillet over medium-low heat. Add lemon juice and stir. Add cooked shrimp, cherry peppers, and "Prairie Dust" seasoning, and stir. Reduce heat to low and cook 5 minutes, stirring frequently. Serve with ranch dressing for dipping, or serve with the dipping sauce of your choice.

Lobster Tails (2 Servings)

2 lobster tails, 6 to 8 ounces each
8 T. butter, unsalted

Marinade:

2 T. brown butter (sauce chapter)	1/2 tsp. iodized salt
1 tsp. lemon juice	1/2 tsp. white pepper
1/2 tsp. garlic powder	1/4 tsp. paprika

Lobster Tails: The lobster tails must be completely thawed and not frozen. Thaw frozen tails in the refrigerator for two days before cooking. If needed immediately then put frozen tails into 2 quarts of cold water with 1 tablespoon of salt stirred in, and wait until the tails are thawed.

Lobster Shells: Depending on when the lobster was caught during its normal molting cycle (shedding its old hard shell for a new soft shell), its shell may be thick and hard to cut, or thin and easy to cut.

Marinade Sauce: In a small bowl combine 2 tablespoons brown butter with the lemon juice, garlic powder, salt, white pepper, and paprika. Stir until well blended. Set aside for later.

Preparation Instructions: Rinse the lobster tail under cool faucet water and wipe clean with a paper towel. Use sharp kitchen shears to carefully cut through the top of the shell lengthwise from the open end to the tip of the tail. Cut through the top portion of the meat as you cut the shell.

Flip the tail over onto its back and squeeze the shell to crack the ribs in the center. This will make it easier to open the shell. Flip the tail back over and pull the shell halves about 1 or 2 inches apart.

How to Prepare Maine Lobster (meat stays inside the shell): (Note: This is how **Red Lobster** prepares lobster tails at their restaurant. However, if you wish you may prepare a Maine Lobster following the instructions for a Rock Lobster below. **Red Lobster** restaurant also does not use brown butter in their marinade but instead uses 4 tablespoons melted unsalted butter per tail.) Separate the meat under the shell with a spoon so it will be easy to eat after it is cooked, but leave the meat inside the shell. The shell is sharp so be careful. If present, remove the vein. If you did not cut through the center of the meat when you cut the shell, then cut through the meat from end to end to expose the colored part of the meat. Spread the tail meat apart inside the shell so it can receive the brown butter marinade.

How to Prepare Rock Lobster (meat fully exposed on top of shell):
Carefully loosen the meat from the shell with a spoon. The shell is sharp so be careful. If present, remove the vein. Carefully pull the meat up through the split, and let it rest it on top of the shell, but leave the meat connected to the tip of the tail. Press the shell halves back towards one another so that most of the meat is on top of the shell. If you did not cut through the meat when you cut the shell, then slice the tail meat lengthwise from near the tip of the tail up to the opening of the tail about half way through the tail meat but not all the way through, in order to expose the colored part of the meat.

Optional Rock Lobster Additional Cuts: Slice lengthwise again about half the distance from the original center cut to the right side of the meat. Slice lengthwise again on the left side of the meat. These three long cuts will allow the tail meat to lay partially open over the sides of the shell, from end to end, so the meat can more easily absorb the brown butter marinade.

Cooking Instructions: Preheat the broiler for at least 5 minutes before putting the lobster tails in the oven.

Pour the marinade sauce over the tail meat from end to end. Place the lobster tails on a foil lined broiling pan and place the broiling pan on a shelf near the center of the oven so the top of the meat is at least 6-inches below the broiler in the top of the oven.

Broil the lobster tails based on the weight of one lobster tail, and not based on the total number of lobster tails. Broil for one minute for each one pound of lobster tail. In other words, broil 4 ounce tails for 4 minutes, and broil 10 ounce tails for 10 minutes.

Broil until the shell turns a bright red. The tail meat is done when an instant read meat thermometer inserted into the meat shows 145°F.

May be served with some additional brown butter as a dipping sauce. May also be served with steak as part of a "Surf and Turf" meal similar to the meals you enjoy at your favorite steakhouse restaurant. Steak recipes are in the beef chapter of this gourmet cookbook.

Red Snapper - Broiled or Stovetop (2 Servings)

2 (6 to 8 oz.) red snapper fillets   2 T. canola oil
2 T. butter   opt. 1/8 tsp. iodized salt
1/2 tsp. lemon juice   opt. 1/16 tsp. fine grind black pepper
1/16 tsp. garlic powder   opt. 1 T. parsley flakes

Instructions: Rinse red snapper fillets under cold faucet water. Pat dry with a paper towel.

Butter Sauce: Cut butter into 1 tablespoon slices and put in a small nonstick saucepan. Melt butter over low heat. Add lemon juice and garlic powder and stir until well blended.

Stovetop Option: Heat oil in a different nonstick skillet over medium-high heat. Add red snapper fillets to hot skillet so they do not touch and cook for 3 minutes on each side, or until done.

Broiler Option: Brush oil on both sides of each fillet. Place red snapper fillets on a broiler pan. Broil about 6 inches below the heating element for 4 minutes. Turn the fillets over and broil for another 4 minutes, or until done.

Serve: Transfer cooked red snapper fillets to serving plates and pour the warm butter sauce on the fillets. Season with salt, black pepper, and/or parsley as desired. Serve immediately.

Rice, Shrimp, and Crab Casserole (6 Servings)

1 (6.4 oz.) box wild rice pilaf   2 (6 oz.) cans crabmeat, lump
1/2 tsp. Old Bay seasoning   1/3 c. celery, diced
1/2 tsp. iodized salt   1/3 c. onions, diced
1/8 tsp. fine grind black pepper   1/2 c. Ritz crackers, crushed
12 oz. frozen shrimp, cooked   2 T. butter, unsalted, melted

Cook rice following the box instructions. When the rice is done, add the Old Bay seasoning, salt, and black pepper and stir to distribute the seasonings throughout the rice.

Thaw shrimp (peeled, deveined, cooked). In a large bowl, gently mix shrimp, crabmeat, celery, and onions. Add cooked rice and toss until well blended. Spread mixture over bottom of greased 3 quart casserole dish. Sprinkle crushed crackers on top of casserole. Drizzle melted butter over crackers.

Bake in a preheated 350°F oven for 25 to 30 minutes. Allow to cool for 5 minutes and serve.

Scallops - Broiled or Stovetop (3 Servings)

1/2 lb. scallops (see below)
4 T. butter
1 tsp. lemon juice
1/8 tsp. garlic powder
1/16 tsp. paprika

opt. 1/8 tsp. iodized salt
opt. 1/16 tsp. fine grind black pepper
opt. 1 tsp. Parmesan cheese, grated
opt. 5 slices bacon (sea scallops only)

Scallop Diameter: Bay scallops are about 1/2 inch in diameter and there are about 80 per pound and they should be cooked for 3 minutes, or 1 1/2 minutes per side, or until done. Sea scallops are about 1 1/2 inch in diameter and there are about 20 per pound and they should be cooked for 4 minutes, or 2 minutes per side, or until done.

Scallop Thickness: If some of the scallops are thicker than 1 inch then slice them in half so all the scallops will be done at approximately the same time. Or cook the thicker scallops longer until they are done.

Optional Bacon for Sea Scallops: 1/2 slice bacon per sea scallop. To prepare bacon wrapped scallops fry the strips of bacon in a separate nonstick skillet until bacon is more than half done but still flexible and not crisp. Transfer to a paper towel and pat with another paper towel to remove as much grease as possible. Cut each slice of bacon in half. After coating the scallops in the butter sauce wrap one half piece of bacon around each scallop and secure with a toothpick through the bacon and scallop. Follow broiler instructions below and remove toothpick when done.

Instructions: Rinse scallops under cold faucet water. Pat dry with a paper towel.

Butter Sauce: Cut butter into 1 tablespoon slices and put in nonstick saucepan. Melt butter over low heat. Add lemon juice, garlic powder, and paprika, and stir until well blended.

Stovetop Option: Increase heat under the butter skillet to medium-high. Add scallops to hot skillet so they do not touch and cook the scallops for 1 1/2 to 2 minutes on each side, or until done.

Broiler Option: Place scallops on a broiler pan. Broil about 4 to 6 inches below the heating element for 1 1/2 or 2 minutes. Turn all the scallops over and broil for another 1 1/2 to 2 minutes, or until done.

Serve: Transfer cooked scallops to serving plates and pour the rest of the warm butter sauce in the skillet on the scallops. Season with salt, pepper, and/or grated Parmesan cheese if desired. Serve immediately.

Serving Options: Serve as a main dish with Rice Pilaf, Rice-A-Roni, or your favorite pasta.

Shrimp Scampi

1 lb. frozen shrimp, deveined	1/4 tsp. fine grind black pepper
1 lb. pasta	1/3 c. dry white wine, or chicken broth
3 T. butter	1 T. lemon juice
3 T. extra light olive oil	2 tsp. parsley flakes
2 garlic cloves, minced	opt. 1 tsp. Italian seasoning
1/2 tsp. iodized salt	opt. 1/2 c. Parmesan cheese, grated

Shrimp: Frozen medium or large shrimp. Make sure the frozen shrimp are fully cooked and they have been deveined. Thaw the frozen shrimp before cooking the pasta. Remove and discard the shells and the small hard tail end piece. The shrimp should have a fresh sea smell. If they smell like ammonia they are spoiled and must be discarded.

Pasta: You may use your favorite pasta. The most commonly used pastas are angel hair or linguine.

Instructions: Cook the pasta following the instructions on the pasta package, stirring to make sure the pasta separates. Drain when done.

While the pasta is cooking, heat the butter and olive oil in a large nonstick skillet over medium-low heat. Add the minced garlic, salt, and black pepper, and stir. Cook for 1 minute. Add dry white wine (or chicken broth), and cook for 3 minutes. Add the shrimp, reduce heat to low, and cook for 2 to 3 minutes, depending on the size of the shrimp, or until they turn pink. Add the lemon juice and simmer for 1 minute to allow the flavors to meld. Do not overcook the shrimp or they will become tough.

Mix the shrimp with the warm pasta and the parsley in a large bowl. Serve immediately.

Imitation Red Lobster Shrimp Scampi: Add the optional Italian seasoning at the same time as the shrimp. Also garnish with Parmesan cheese when serving.

Tuna Casserole - Baked or Stovetop

4 oz. (2 1/2 cups) pasta noodles   1 (10.5 oz.) can cream mushroom soup
2 T. butter   1 can sliced mushrooms, drained
1/4 c. onion, diced   2 (5 oz.) cans solid white tuna, drained
1 c. whole milk   1 c. cheddar cheese, fine shredded
1/2 tsp. iodized salt   1/2 c. Parmesan cheese, fine shredded
1/4 tsp. fine grind black pepper   opt. 3/4 c. crackers, crushed
1 (10.5 oz.) can cream of celery soup

Crackers: Butter crackers or cheese crackers, crushed.

Pasta Noodles: Fettuccine or egg noodles. If using long noodles then grasp the center of a small handful of noodles with the left hand and break off the top and the bottom of the noodles with the right hand. Or spiral noodles will provide a nice twist (joke) to an old recipe. Or use special shape noodles such as bowties or sea shells.

Instructions: Cook the pasta noodles in a medium nonstick saucepan following the instructions on the package. Drain off the water. Set the pasta aside.

In the same pot (now empty) melt the butter over medium heat. Add the onion, stir constantly, and cook until the onions are tender. Gradually add the milk and stir to break up any clumps. Stir constantly to prevent burning the milk, and bring to a boil. Then reduce the heat to low, add the salt and black pepper and stir. Add the celery soup, the mushroom soup, and the sliced mushrooms and stir. Simmer over low heat until well blended and smooth, stirring constantly. Add drained tuna, cheddar cheese, and Parmesan cheese, and stir constantly until the cheese melts. Add the noodles and toss to coat the pasta with the cheese mixture.

Now decide if you wish to follow the instructions below for Stovetop Tuna Casserole, or for Baked Tuna Casserole.

Stovetop Tuna Casserole: Simmer over low heat while stirring occasionally, until the pasta has warmed up. Serve.

Baked Tuna Casserole: Put a baking sheet on the middle shelf of an oven and preheat the oven to 375°F with the baking sheet in the oven. Transfer the tuna and pasta mixture to a casserole dish and bake in a preheated 375°F oven for 10 minutes. Remove from oven, evenly cover the top of the casserole with crushed cheese crackers, return to the oven, and bake for another 5 minutes to heat and crisp the crackers.

Chapter Twenty
Ham, Pork, and Sausage

Ham, Oven Baked

1 ham (weight below)
opt. 1/2 c. whole cloves
opt. 1 lb. light brown sugar
opt. 1/2 c. yellow mustard

opt. 1 (15 oz.) can pineapple slices
opt. 1 (4 oz). jar maraschino cherries
4 c. water or as needed

Weight of Ham: If you want leftovers then buy a bigger ham.
1. **Bone In:** Plan for at least 1/2 pound of ham per person (includes the fat weight and bone weight even though the bone is not eaten)
2. **Boneless:** Plan for at least 1/3 pound of ham per person (includes the fat weight but no bone weight).

Type of Ham: Both types of ham taste the same when cooked properly.
1. **Butt:** Has more meat and more fat. It has a hip bone and a pelvic bone and this makes it more challenging to slice.
2. **Shank:** Has less meat and less fat. It only has a leg bone and this makes it easier to slice. It has a slightly sweeter flavor. A shank ham is recommended.

Center Cut Slice: The best 1/2 inch thick slice of ham at the lean end.
1, **Half Ham:** The best end slice has **not** been cut off.
2. **Portion Ham:** The best end slice has been cut off.

Instructions: Remove the ham from the refrigerator and allow the ham to come to room temperature for about 2 hours (while it is still wrapped) so the entire ham can cook more evenly while baking.

Preheat oven to 325°F. Place a long piece of 18-inch wide heavy-duty aluminum foil in the bottom of the pan so the foil extends a few inches beyond the ends of the pan and up the sides of the pan. The foil will catch the drippings and make it easier to save the drippings, and it will make it easier to clean the pan. Place ham on the aluminum foil in the roasting pan. If your ham is not spiral sliced or pre-basted, then slash the fat on top of the ham in a diamond pattern with the slashes about 1 1/2 inches apart and about 3/8 inch deep into the fat but do not cut into the lean meat. The cross-hatch pattern helps the ham capture and retain as much glaze as possible.

Optional Whole Cloves: Stick whole cloves into the fat at the intersections of the diamond slashes.

Optional Basting Glaze (Use on a ham that has not been pre-basted or spiral sliced): Put brown sugar and yellow mustard in a bowl. Stir until well blended into a thick paste. Use a pastry brush to spread the brown sugar glaze over the top of the ham. Try to get some of the glaze down into the knife scores in the fat of the ham. The glaze will melt down the sides of the ham while baking so most of the glaze should be spread on top of the ham.

Optional Pineapple Slices: If desired, position pineapple rings 1.5 inches apart on the fat on top of the ham.

Optional Maraschino Cherries: If desired, place a maraschino cherry, with its stem removed, in the center of each pineapple ring. Use a toothpick pushed through the cherry to hold the cherry in the center of the pineapple ring and this will also hold the pineapple ring in position.

Instructions Continued: If the ham does not have any added water, then add water inside the aluminum foil in the bottom of the roasting pan to a depth of 1 inch. However, if the ham is pre-saturated with water then do not put any water in the bottom of the pan. Place the lid tightly on the pan. If you do not have a lid then put more aluminum foil around the ham and fold and crimp all the foil edges together to form a steam seal.

Bake in a preheated 325°F oven for the amount of time specified in the instructions that came with the ham. If there were no instructions then use the following guidelines. Do not allow the "instant read" meat thermometer to touch the bone when checking the temperature.

Baking Time For:
1. **Uncooked Ham:** 18 to 20 minutes per pound. For all uncooked hams bake until the internal temperature of the ham reaches 160°F.
2. **Fully Cooked Ham or Ready to Eat Ham:** 15 to 18 minutes per pound. For all precooked hams bake until the internal temperature of the ham reaches a minimum of 140°F.

When done, remove from oven and let the ham rest, still covered, for at least 30 minutes. This allows the flavor of the glaze to meld deeper into the ham and the ham will be easier to carve into smooth, uniform slices.

If cloves or toothpicks were used then remove all the cloves and all the toothpicks from the ham.

Slicing Options: Select the slicing option that appeals to you.
1. Stand the ham on its flat wide end so the small end of the ham is sticking up. Slice down the outside edge of the ham parallel to the bone with the first short slice being closer to the bottom wide end of the ham. Continue to move closer to the center bone with each slice. This puts a thin piece of the glazed fat on the end of each slice of ham.
2. Stand the ham on its flat wide end so the small end of the ham is sticking up. Cut the ham in half next to the bone. Place the

boneless half of the ham with its long flat side down. Slice from one end to the other end so a small piece of the glazed fat is on the outside around each slice of ham. Then slice the ham from the bone half of the ham in the same way by cutting around the bone.

As you slice the ham put each slice on a serving platter.

Ham Bone: Save the ham bone in a zipper plastic heavy-duty freezer bag in the refrigerator for use in a future soup recipe.

Pork Chops with Parmesan Crust

1 egg, beaten
1 tsp. coarse Kosher salt
1/4 tsp. fine grind black pepper
1/3 c. Italian style breadcrumbs

1/2 cup Parmesan cheese, grated
4 pork loin chops, boneless, 5/8"
3 T. oil, vegetable or olive oil

Beat the egg in a bowl with the salt and black pepper and pour the egg onto a bread plate with a raised edge. Put the breadcrumbs on a second plate. Place the freshly grated Parmesan cheese on a third plate. Cut off and discard all the fat on the outside of each pork loin chop. Rinse the pork chops under cold faucet water and pat dry with a paper towel. Press both sides of each pork chop into the cheese and pat the cheese so it sticks to the pork chop. Briefly dip both sides of each pork chop in the egg and then immediately press both sides of each pork chop into the breadcrumbs and pat the breadcrumbs so they stick to the pork chop.

Heat 3 tablespoons of oil in a large nonstick skillet over medium heat. Add pork chops and cook 5 minutes on each side. Transfer pork chops to a nonstick baking pan or baking sheet so the pork chops do not touch. Bake in a preheated 350°F oven for 12 to 18 minutes, depending on the thickness of the pork chops. 1/2 inch thick chops cook faster and 3/4 inch thick chops take more time.

Sausage, Spinach, Pasta, and Cheese (4 servings)

1 lb. Jimmy Dean® regular sausage
1/4 c. onions, diced
1 (14.5 oz.) can diced tomatoes
8 oz. pasta

10 oz. frozen spinach, chopped
1/4 tsp. iodized salt
1/4 tsp. black pepper
1 c. mozzarella cheese, shredded

Sausage: Regular pork sausage is recommended. However, you may use mild, sage, or hot sausage if you prefer. Or use smoked sausage cut into slices. Or use turkey or chicken sausage. Or use ground beef.

Diced Tomatoes: Italian diced tomatoes that contain basil, garlic, and oregano, are recommended. However, if you prefer you may use Mexican diced tomatoes. Or use diced tomatoes with green peppers, celery, and onions (but do not omit the fresh diced onions in the recipe). If you use canned diced tomatoes without garlic then add 1/8 teaspoon of garlic powder to the recipe when you add the diced tomatoes.

Pasta: Spiral, tube, wheels, or bowties may be used. By changing the shape of the pasta you change the visual appearance of the dish.

Spinach: Frozen spinach is recommended. If you wish to use fresh spinach then steam it separately and chop it into small pieces. Then add it instead of the thawed frozen spinach in the following recipe.

Instructions: Crumble the sausage into very small pieces in a nonstick skillet. Add the diced onions. Cook over medium heat until no longer pink, stirring frequently and using the edge of the stirring spoon to break the larger sausage pieces into smaller pieces. Do not drain. (Note: Jimmy Dean® sausage has very little grease.) Add can of diced tomatoes. Bring to a boil and then immediately reduce heat to low. Cook uncovered while the pasta is cooking.

Cook pasta according to package directions.

While the pasta is cooking add the thawed spinach, salt, and black pepper to the sausage skillet and cook until the spinach is hot.

Add the drained cooked pasta to the sausage skillet. Stir to mix the pasta with the sausage.

One Skillet Option: Sprinkle the cheese on top. If desired, wait for the cheese to melt as a top layer and serve. Or stir the cheese into the sausage and pasta until everything is mixed together and serve.

Casserole Baking Option: If desired, pour the sausage and pasta mixture into a lightly greased casserole dish. Then sprinkle the cheese on top. Bake in a preheated 350°F oven for 10 to 15 minutes, or until the cheese is bubbly. Remove from oven, allow to cool for 5 minutes, and then serve.

Chapter Twenty-One
Italian-American Recipes

There is a difference between Italian recipes prepared by cooks who currently live in Italy when compared to recipes prepared by Italian cooks who were born in the USA and who are descended from good Italian cooks who were born in Italy. The reason is because over the years "Italian-American" cooks have had access to a broader assortment of recipe ingredients and they could invest a little more money in one recipe. Therefore good Italian cooks in the USA have been influenced by several generations of their Italian ancestors who lived their entire lives in the USA, and they have adopted the slightly modified Italian recipes of their USA ancestors as being authentic Italian recipes.

The recipes in this chapter more closely match "Italian-American" recipes when compared to an Italian recipe that is currently popular in Italy because most people in the USA today are very familiar with the taste of "Italian-American" recipes and those recipe flavors are what they enjoy and what they expect in "authentic" Italian food.

(Note: Even today in Italy, most good Italian cooks do not agree on exactly what should be included in an "authentic" Italian recipe, or the quantities that should be used, or how that recipe should be prepared.)

Baked Spaghetti (13-inch x 9-inch x 2-inch Pan)

24 oz. spaghetti sauce   2 c. mozzarella cheese, shredded
16 oz. spaghetti noodles   1/2 c. Parmesan cheese, grated
16 oz. meat (lean ground beef, or pork sausage, or Italian sausage)

Spaghetti Sauce or Marinara Sauce: Use your favorite brand of sauce or make your own sauce following the recipe in the sauce chapter.
Spaghetti Noodles: Regular, thin, or angel hair noodles may be used. Break noodles into thirds. Cook until almost done (al dente) following the package instructions.
Lean Ground Beef or Pork Sausage Option: Crumble ground beef or sausage into a skillet and cook over medium heat until done. Drain.
Sweet Italian Sausage Option: Cut sausage into small chunks. Cook over medium heat until done. Drain.
Instructions: Set aside 1/2 cup of meat. Stir the rest of the meat into the sauce until well mixed. Stir in the cooked noodles until well coated with sauce. Pour into greased casserole pan. Bake uncovered in 350°F oven for 20 minutes. Then cover with mozzarella cheese. Sprinkle the 1/2 cup of meat over the cheese. Sprinkle Parmesan cheese on top. Bake in 350°F oven for 8 minutes. Cool for 10 minutes. Slice and serve.

Eggplant Parmesan

2 1/4 lb. eggplants
1 tsp. iodized salt, for eggplant
3 egg whites, beaten
3/4 tsp. iodized salt, for egg whites
1/4 tsp. fine grind black pepper
3/4 c. all-purpose flour

2 1/2 c. Panko breadcrumbs
1/4 c. extra light olive oil
24 oz. pasta sauce
16 oz. mozzarella cheese, sliced
3/4 c. Parmesan cheese, grated
1 tsp. dried basil

Rinse the eggplants for sanitary reasons and to remove any foreign particles. If desired, peel the eggplants.

Cut the eggplants into 1/4 inch thick slices. Lightly sprinkle both sides of each slice with salt and place slices in a colander in the sink and allow to rest (sweat) for 60 minutes. Rinse each slice under cold faucet water and pat dry with a paper towel. Remove as much water as possible from the slices.

Separate the cold egg whites from the cold egg yolks. Save the yolks for use in another recipe. Beat egg whites in a medium bowl until smooth. Add salt and black pepper to the beaten egg whites and stir.

Put flour in the bottom of a flat baking pan.

Put Panko breadcrumbs in the bottom of a different baking pan.

Dip both sides of each eggplant slice in flour and then in the egg whites. Then dip both sides of the eggplant in the breadcrumbs. Place on a piece of parchment paper on a baking sheet. After all the eggplant slices have been coated and are on the parchment paper, lightly sprinkle the slices with a little olive oil. Bake the slices in a preheated 425°F oven for 8 minutes, remove, turn each slice over, lightly sprinkle with a little olive oil, return to the oven and bake another 8 minutes. Remove from oven and use a spatula to transfer the slices to a wire cooling rack and allow to cool until they can be safely picked up by hand.

Pour 1/3 of the pasta sauce in the bottom of a lightly greased 9-inch by 13-inch baking dish. Add one layer of eggplant slices and a layer of mozzarella cheese. Sprinkle with 1/3 of the Parmesan cheese. Add a layer of 1/3 of the pasta sauce, a layer of eggplant slices, and a layer of sliced mozzarella. Sprinkle with 1/3 of the Parmesan cheese. Add the remainder of the pasta sauce, a layer of eggplant slices, and a layer of sliced mozzarella. Sprinkle with the remainder of the Parmesan cheese. Sprinkle the basil evenly on top of the cheese.

Bake in a preheated 350°F for 35 minutes. Remove from oven and allow to cool for 10 minutes before serving.

Serve with your choice of pasta.

Fettuccini Alfredo with Meat (4 Servings)

12 to 16 oz. meat (see below)   Fettuccini Alfredo (see page 263)

Meat: Chicken, ground pork sausage, Italian sausage, or shrimp may be used to create a main dish meal using a side dish entrée as one of the two basic ingredients.

Chicken: 16 ounces of boneless, skinless, chicken breast or chicken tenders. Rinse the chicken under cold water and pat dry with a paper towel. Cut chicken into strips 1/4 inch wide and 1 inch long. Sprinkle with 1/2 teaspoon iodized salt and 1/8 teaspoon fine grind black pepper. Heat 1 tablespoon canola oil in a large skillet over medium heat. Add one layer of chicken and cook until lightly brown on bottom side. Flip chicken pieces over and cook other side until lightly brown and the chicken is completely done.

Ground Pork Sausage or Sweet Italian Sausage: 16 ounces of sausage. Crumble ground pork sausage or cut sweet Italian sausage into bite size pieces. Heat 1 tablespoon of canola oil in a large skillet over medium heat. Cook the sausage in the skillet until done. Drain the grease.

Shrimp: 12 to 16 ounces of frozen shrimp, peeled, deveined and fully cooked. Allow the frozen shrimp to come to room temperature. Then heat the thawed shrimp in a skillet over low heat stirring frequently.

Instructions: Prepare the fettuccini Alfredo following the instructions on page 263. Mix the cooked meat into the fettuccini Alfredo and serve immediately.

Italian Lasagna (13-inch x 9-inch x 4-inch Pan)

1 lb. Italian sausage, sweet or mild
1 lb. 90% lean ground beef
1/2 c. onions, diced
2 garlic cloves, minced
2 (14.5 oz.) cans tomatoes
2 (6 oz.) cans tomato paste
2 T. light brown sugar
1 T. dried basil
4 T. fresh parsley, chopped
10 to 12 lasagna noodles
1 egg
24 oz. ricotta cheese
1/2 tsp. iodized salt
1/4 tsp. fine grind black pepper
1 lb. mozzarella cheese, grated
3/4 c. Parmesan cheese, grated

Sausage: Pork sausage is recommended but turkey sausage is okay.

Sausage and Beef Ratio: The ratio of sausage and beef can be changed to suit your taste, such as all beef and no sausage, or 3/4 beef and 1/4 sausage, or 2/3 beef and 1/3 sausage, or 1/3 beef and 2/3 sausage.

Fennel Seed: This recipe does not include fennel seed because fennel is already included in the Italian sausage.

Tomatoes: The canned tomatoes can be crushed or diced, or one of each. Italian seasoned diced tomatoes are recommended for at least one can of tomatoes.

Noodles: You will need enough noodles for two layers of noodles in your baking pan. Experiment to determine the best way to lay the noodles in your baking pan so they cover the pan from side to side and from end to end, and they do not overlap. Later after the noodles are moist, you can use a sharp knife to slice a limp noodle into 2 or 3 pieces to get good coverage without overlapping.

Sugar: The sugar helps to neutralize the acidity in the tomatoes and it does not make the lasagna "sweet."

Ricotta Cheese: Ricotta cheese is recommended but cottage cheese may be used instead.

Mozzarella and Parmesan Cheese: Both should be freshly grated.

Instructions: Put the noodles in a big pan and completely cover them with very hot tap water and allow them to soak for 30 minutes and then drain. (Note: The noodles will cook inside the lasagna after it has been placed in the oven and there is no need to boil the noodles "al dente.")

Crumble sausage and ground beef in a large nonstick skillet and use a stirring spoon to break the meat into smaller pieces. Add onions and cook over medium heat, stirring frequently, for 5 minutes. Drain off the grease. Add garlic, tomatoes, and tomato paste and stir until blended. Add sugar and basil and stir. Only add 2 tablespoons of the fresh chopped parsley and stir. Simmer uncovered for 60 minutes.

Beat the egg in a large bowl. Add the ricotta cheese, salt, black pepper, and the rest of the chopped parsley, and stir until well blended.

Preheat oven to 375°F.

Lightly grease a 13-inch by 9-inch by 4-inch deep baking pan. (Note: A 3-inch deep baking pan may not contain all the ingredients without bubbling over inside the oven while cooking.)

Fill the baking pan with layers from bottom to top as follows: 1/3 of the meat sauce on the bottom, 1/2 of the noodles, 1/2 of the ricotta cheese mixture, 1/2 of the mozzarella cheese, 1/2 of the Parmesan cheese, 1/3 of the meat sauce, 1/2 of the noodles, 1/2 of the ricotta cheese, 1/2 of the mozzarella cheese, 1/3 of the meat sauce, and finally 1/2 of the Parmesan cheese.

Cover the top of the baking pan with nonstick aluminum foil (or spray the foil with some nonstick spray). Bake at 375°F for 25 minutes. Remove from the oven and carefully remove the foil. Put back in the oven and bake at 375°F for another 20 to 25 minutes, or until the top cheese layer is melted and brown but not burnt. Cool 15 minutes and serve.

Italian Meatloaf

2 eggs	1 tsp. garlic powder
3/4 c. Italian breadcrumbs crushed	1 tsp. iodized salt
1/2 c. onion, diced	1/2 tsp. fine grind black pepper
3/4 tsp. Italian seasoning	1/2 c. Parmesan cheese, grated
3/4 tsp. dried basil	1 1/2 lb. 90% lean ground beef

Topping:

1 c. ketchup	1/3 c. dark brown sugar
1T. yellow mustard	1 tsp. Worcestershire sauce

Meatloaf: Beat eggs in large bowl. Add crushed breadcrumbs, diced onion, Italian seasoning, basil, garlic powder, salt, black pepper, Parmesan cheese, and stir. Add ground beef and mix well using your hands. Shape into an oiled loaf pan (about 9-inches by 5-inches).

Topping: In a separate bowl combine the ketchup, mustard, brown sugar, and Worcestershire sauce, and stir until well mixed. Pour 3/4 cup of topping evenly over the top of the meatloaf and reserve the rest of the topping for later.

Bake: Bake in a preheated 350°F oven for 60 to 65 minutes. Let stand for 10 minutes. Slice and serve. Let each person spoon more topping on their slice of meatloaf if they wish.

Italian Meatballs

1/2 c. whole milk
2 eggs
3 slices white bread
1.5 T. extra light olive oil
1 tsp. Italian seasoning
1 T. parsley flakes
1 tsp. onion powder

1 tsp. garlic powder
1 tsp. iodized salt
1/2 tsp. fine grind black pepper
6 T. fresh Parmesan cheese, grated
1 lb. 80% lean ground beef
1/2 lb. ground pork sausage

Remove the milk and eggs from the refrigerator, measure the quantity you need, and allow them to come to room temperature.

Adjust the shelves in the oven so the shelf that will be used for baking is a little below the middle of the oven. This will prevent the top of the meatballs from overcooking.

Preheat oven to 375°F.

Remove the bread crust from the bread slices. Cut the bread into 1/2 inch cubes. Pour the milk into a small bowl. Drop one bread cube into the milk for about 2 seconds and immediately remove. The bread cube should be moist but not soggy mushy wet. Continue until all the bread cubes are wet with milk. Put any leftover milk in the egg bowl.

Beat the eggs in a medium bowl. Add the oil, Italian seasoning, parsley, onion, garlic, salt, and black pepper and stir to combine the ingredients. Add the cheese and stir. Add the wet bread cubes and stir.

In a large bowl crumble the beef and sausage together. Use your hands and thoroughly mix the two meats together. Add the egg mixture and use your hands to mix all the ingredients together. Moisten your bare hands with some water and form the meat mixture into individual meatballs about 1.25 inches round. Place each meatball 1.25 inches apart on a broiler pan (one that allows the grease to drip into a different pan below the top pan).

Bake at 375°F for 20 minutes if the meatballs are going to be added to a sauce mixture and cooked on the stove for awhile longer.

Bake at 375°F for 25 to 30 minutes or until done if the meatballs are going to be eaten without any additional cooking.

Pasta Primavera (4 Servings)

Pasta (select one):
8 oz. fettuccine, **or** linguine, **or** angel hair, **or** spaghetti, **or** bowtie pasta

Cheese (select one):
1/4 c. Parmesan cheese, freshly grated, and 1 c. half & half (or milk)
or 1 1/4 c. Alfredo sauce (sauce chapter)

Seasonings and Oil (use salt, pepper, and oil):
1/2 tsp. iodized salt   3 T. canola oil, for frying
1/8 tsp. fine grind black pepper

Vegetables: (Select 5 or 6 vegetables with at least 1 from each group):

Group One
3/4 c. broccoli florets   1/2 c. green peas
1/4 c. asparagus, chopped   1 green bell pepper, diced

Group Two
3/4 c. cauliflower florets   3/4 c. zucchini, sliced
3/4 c. carrots, shredded   1/4 c. onion, chopped

Group Three
1 c. cherry tomatoes, quartered   1 red bell pepper, diced

Trivia: Primavera is the Italian word that means "spring." A dish called "à la primavera" will usually contain fresh vegetables. Pasta primavera is one of the most popular "primavera" dishes and it contains pasta, cheese, salt and pepper, and fresh vegetables. It does not contain meat or tomato sauce (but cherry tomatoes are optional).

Pasta Primavera: This is a very flexible dish and there are hundreds of different recipes for this Italian favorite. Most of these recipes contain some type of pasta, some type of cheese, salt and pepper, and at least 5 or 6 different vegetables. Therefore you can create your own "pasta primavera" based on the fresh vegetables you have available. However, it is important to consider nutrition, flavor, and visual appeal, so at least one vegetable should be selected from each of the above groups of vegetables until you have at least 5 or 6 different vegetables.

Instructions: Rinse the vegetables under cool faucet water. Prepare the vegetables as suggested above (chopped, sliced, or diced).

Read the cooking directions on the pasta package and note how long the pasta needs to cook. Start the pasta boiling so it will be done at approximately the same time as the vegetables. When the pasta is done, drain off the water, and then add the hot pasta to the cooked vegetables and cheese sauce as explained below.

While the pasta is cooking, heat a large nonstick skillet (or wok), and add the vegetables when indicated below, and cook for the time indicated after adding the vegetables.

Heat a large nonstick skillet (or wok) over medium-high heat.

Add the oil and wait for the oil to get hot.

Add optional asparagus.

Add optional carrots.

Stir constantly for 1 minute (only if asparagus or carrots were added).

Add optional broccoli.

Add optional cauliflower.

Add optional zucchini.

Stir constantly for 1 minute (even if more vegetables were not added).

Add optional peas.

Add optional bell peppers.

Stir constantly for 2 minutes (even if more vegetables were not added).

Reduce heat to medium.

Add half & half and Parmesan cheese, or add the Alfredo sauce.

Add salt and white pepper.

Stir slowly for 1 minute, or until vegetables are crisp and tender, and the cheese or sauce is well heated.

Remove from heat and transfer to a large serving bowl.

Add optional tomatoes.

Add optional onions.

Add cooked hot pasta.

Toss gently and serve while hot.

Note: The optional tomatoes and onions were added at the end, and they were not cooked, in order to add their crisp fresh flavor to the dish so there would be a combination of cooked and raw vegetables. However, if you prefer, you may add the tomatoes, and/or the onions, earlier in the recipe, so that they will be cooked to the degree of doneness you prefer.

Pizza Crust (One 12-inch or 14-inch Pizza) or One Deep Dish Pan Pizza

Instructions for a Deep Dish Pan Pizza

Follow the instructions below for a "Deep Dish" crust, and for a 12-inch pizza, but instead of using a round pizza pan, use a 10-inch to 12-inch diameter cast iron skillet. Use 1 teaspoon of canola oil to grease the bottom of the skillet and 1/2 inch up the sides of the skillet (do not use any cornmeal). Lay the rolled dough (after the first rise) completely across the bottom of the skillet until it touches the sides of the skillet, but do not press it up the sides of the skillet. Then follow the instructions below except bake the final pizza in the cast iron skillet. When the pizza is done, let it cool 4 minutes inside the skillet and then slide it out of the skillet onto a cutting board before slicing the pizza.

Instructions for a Traditional Round Pizza

	Thin	Medium	Thick	Deep Dish
Crust Thickness (pre-rise)	3/16 inch	1/4 inch	3/8 inch	1/2 inch
Crust Ingredients:				
yeast (not instant rise)	1 pkg.	1 pkg.	1 pkg.	1 pkg.
warm water, 110°F	1/2 c.	3/4 c.	1 c.	1 c.
bread flour	1 1/2 c.	2 1/4 c.	3 c.	3 1/4 c.
granulated sugar	2 1/4 tsp.	3 tsp.	3 3/4 tsp.	4 tsp.
iodized salt	1/2 tsp.	3/4 tsp.	1 tsp.	1 tsp.
vegetable oil	3 tsp.	4 tsp.	5 tsp.	5 1/3 tsp.
Baking Information:				
cornmeal, for dusting pan	1 1/2 T.	2 T.	2 1/2 T.	None
oven temperature	450°F	450°F	450°F	500°F
minutes pre-bake crust	2	3	4	5
minutes baking pizza	10 - 12	12 - 15	13 - 16	12 - 14

Pizza Pan Data:	**10-inch**	**12-inch**	**14-inch**	**16-inch**
square inches	78.5 in^2	113.1 in^2	153.9 in^2	201.1 in^2
number of slices	6 slices	8 slices	12 slices	16 slices
square inches / slice	13.1 in^2	14.1 in^2	12.8 in^2	12.6 in^2

Toppings:				
Pizza Sauce	1 c.	1 1/2 c.	2 1/8 c.	3 c.
Shredded Cheese	2 c.	3 c.	4 1/4 c.	6 c.

Pizza Crust Thickness: There is no standard for the final thickness of a pizza crust. Pizza crust thickness depends on how the dough is kneaded, and how long the dough is allowed to rise at each step in the process, and how the dough ball is made into a flat pizza crust (machine rollers, hand rolling pin, hand flattening, or tossing in the air). Medium thickness pizza crusts made by different restaurants will **not** be of the same exact average thickness and the thickness of those crusts can vary by as much as 25% from one restaurant to the next. However, this thickness is usually not visually obvious because the average medium pre-rise crust is 0.25 inches thick with a range between 0.20 inches to 0.30 inches. The above recipe will make a 12-inch pizza crust that will be about 15% thicker than the *average* restaurant pizza crust of the corresponding thickness. It will make a 14-inch pizza crust that will be about 15% thinner than the *average* restaurant pizza crust of the corresponding thickness.

The above recipe will yield one **medium** 12-inch crust or one **medium** 14-inch crust. Or the dough can be divided in half to yield two **medium** 10-inch crusts. Or the dough can be spread thinner to yield one **thin** 16-inch crust.

Pizza Crust Options:
1. **Grandpappy's Gourmet Pizza Crust:** Use the above quantities of all the ingredients and follow the instructions below.
2. **Domino's Imitation Pizza Crust:** For a medium crust pizza, increase the sugar to 3 1/2 teaspoons, and use cornmeal to dust the kneading surface.
3. **Little Caesar's Imitation Pizza Crust:** For a medium crust pizza, increase the sugar to 5 teaspoons, and increase the salt to 1 1/2 teaspoons, and use cornmeal to dust the pizza pan.
4. **Papa John's Imitation Pizza Crust:** For a medium crust pizza, increase the sugar to 4 1/4 teaspoons.
5. **Pizza Hut Imitation Pizza Crust:** For a medium crust pizza, decrease the sugar to 1 teaspoon and use "Buttered Flavored Pam" spray to coat the top of the pizza crust to add flavor and to keep the edges of the crust from becoming too dry during baking. Thoroughly grease the pizza pan with oil instead of using cornmeal because the oil contributes to the "greasy" flavor of this pizza that Pizza Hut customers prefer.

Bread Flour: 100% bread flour is recommended. Bread flour will yield a crisper crust. If you use all-purpose flour then the crust will be chewier. If you desire a cornmeal crust then 1/4 of the bread flour may be replaced with cornmeal. If you desire a whole wheat crust then 1/2 of the bread flour may be replaced with whole wheat flour.

Rising: If you do not allow the raw dough to rise on the pizza pan before baking then huge air bubbles may form in the dough during baking and they will appear on the top crust of the pizza. Using a fork to prick the crust after rising and before baking can also help to minimize the problem of big air pockets on top of the cooked pizza.

Oil: Vegetable oil is normally used to make a pizza with a taste that is popular in the USA. However, extra light olive oil can be used instead.

Pizza Sauce (sauce chapter): The above recommended amounts of sauce are based on the diameter of the pizza and those amounts will yield a layer of sauce about 1/16 inch thick over the crust of the pizza to within 1/2 inch of its edge. The 1/2 inch edge provides a place to pick up the pizza with the hands without getting pizza sauce on the hands.

Cheese Topping: The type and amount of cheese is entirely a matter of personal preference. Some restaurants use a cheese blend ratio of between 1/2 to 2/3 finely shredded mozzarella cheese along with 1/2 to 1/3 finely shredded muenster cheese. A small amount of grated Parmesan cheese may also be added. The type of cheese and the amount of cheese is up to you. The above recommended amounts of shredded cheese are based on the diameter of the pizza and those amounts will yield a layer of melted cheese about 1/16 inch thick on the crust to within 1/2 inch of its edge. This is approximately the thickness of one slice of cheese. You may double the recommended amount if you prefer "double cheese" on your pizza and this will be a thickness of about two slices of cheese. (Note: Double cheese is usually used on deep dish pan pizzas.)

Other Toppings: Meat toppings should be cooked separately before putting them on the pizza. The amount of each topping will depend on the total number of toppings on the pizza. The toppings should not be piled up on top of the pizza. The toppings should be evenly mixed on top of the pizza and you should be able to see the cheese between some of the toppings. This allows the pizza, the cheese, and the toppings to cook evenly. Some optional other toppings include pepperoni, sausage, ground beef, ham, bacon, Canadian bacon, mushrooms, bell peppers, jalapeños, onions, tomatoes, olives (green or black), pineapple, or whatever appeals to you.

Pizza Pan: A round pan or a rectangular pan may be used. A perforated pan is recommended because it allows the oven heat to cook the bottom surface of the pizza.

Instructions: Crumble the yeast into 1/4 cup warm water with a pinch of sugar added and stir until the yeast is mixed with the water. Good yeast will become foamy and creamy in about 10 to 12 minutes. (Note: Some pizza crust recipes simply mix the yeast and the water with the flour and they omit the step of activating, or proofing, the yeast in warm water. A gourmet cook will not omit activating the yeast.)

In a large bowl mix one-half of the flour with all the sugar and the salt. Stir until the dry ingredients are blended together. Add the rest of the water, the oil, and the foaming yeast solution. Stir for at least 5 minutes. Gradually add more flour and stir until the dough pulls away from the sides of the bowl. Transfer to a flat floured (or cornmeal) dusted surface, or onto wax paper. Gradually add flour and knead by hand until the dough is smooth and elastic and it does not stick to your fingers. Put in a bowl, cover, and let rise in a warm place (such as inside your oven with the oven light on) for about 60 minutes or until doubled in size.

(Note: Instead of kneading the dough some pizza crust recipes recommend slapping the dough. Put the dough ball in your left hand and use your right hand to slap down on the dough. Turn your hands over while holding the dough and take control of the dough ball with your right hand and use your left hand to slap the dough. Repeat many, many times, on both sides of the dough, holding the dough in one hand and slapping with the other hand.)

(Note: Some pizza crust recipes recommend putting the dough in an airtight container in the refrigerator for between 1 to 3 days before proceeding to the next step.)

Punch the dough down. Use a rolling pin and flatten the dough on a floured (or cornmeal) dusted surface, or on a piece of wax paper, until it is 1/4 inch thick (more or less depending on the thickness of crust you like) and the approximate size of your pizza pan. Lightly dust the pizza pan with cornmeal (or oil the pan for a "greasier" pizza). Transfer the dough to the pizza pan and adjust its size by hand until it covers the pizza pan. Form a slightly raised outer edge all around the crust to help keep the sauce and toppings on the crust. Cover the pizza pan and let the dough rise 30 minutes in a warm place. After the dough has risen brush the top of the crust lightly with oil. Prick the dough every 1/2 inch with a fork to help prevent air bubbles.

Bake in a preheated 450°F oven for the number of minutes shown in the table at the beginning of this recipe. The crust should turn a light tan color. Pre-baking, or par-baking, helps the dough to set and it helps prevent the sauce from soaking into the dough which can result in an unevenly baked crust.

Remove the crust from the oven and spread pizza sauce evenly to within 1/2 inch of the outside edge of the dough. Then add the cheese evenly over the sauce. Finally add the other toppings that you like.

Bake in a preheated 450°F oven for the number of minutes shown in the table or until the cheese is melted and turns a golden brown. Remove from oven and cool for 3 to 5 minutes and then cut into slices with a rolling wheel pizza cutter. (Note: If you do not allow the pizza to cool for a few minutes before cutting and eating then you may cause pizza burns on the roof of your mouth.)

Chapter Twenty-Two
Mexican-American (Hispanic) Recipes

The title of this chapter is not "Mexican Recipes" because it contains recipes that evolved during the 1800s and 1900s in California, Arizona, New Mexico, and Texas, which are states close to the Mexican border. The "Mexican-American" Hispanic recipes in this chapter were gradually developed by cooks from many different Latin American countries and these recipes are extremely popular today in homes and in restaurants throughout the entire USA.

Lard is used more often in traditional Mexican restaurants than butter, shortening, or oil.

Guacamole Dip

1 avocado, ripe, peeled, mashed	1 T. lemon juice, or lime juice
1/4 cup finely shredded white onion	1/4 tsp. garlic salt
2 T. cilantro, chopped	1/4 tsp. ground black pepper
1 Roma tomato, finely diced	opt. 1 T. canola oil

Trivia: The word guacamole comes from two Aztec words: ahuacatl (avocado) and molli (sauce).

Guacamole Dip: The only necessary ingredients are an avocado, some onion, and some lemon juice.

Avocados: Gently press on the avocado. If it gives it is ripe. If it does not give it is not yet ripe. If it gives a lot then it is too ripe and it should not be used. If you are uncertain then taste before using.

Juice: Either lemon juice or lime juice works well. The acid in the juice helps to offset the rich flavor of the avocado. The acid will also help delay the avocado from turning brown.

Instructions: Cut the avocado in half around the pit. Grab one half of the avocado in each hand and twist in opposite directions and pull apart. Remove the pit with a spoon or a knife. Scoop out the inside flesh with a spoon and put in a bowl. Mash the avocado with a fork until creamy but with a few very small chunks still remaining. Use the smallest slots on a vegetable shredder and shred 1/4 of a white onion above the avocado bowl so the onion and its juices fall into the avocado bowl. Add the chopped cilantro, finely diced tomatoes, lemon juice, garlic salt, and pepper. If desired, add the optional oil. Stir until all the ingredients are well blended.

Store the dip in the refrigerator in an airtight container because the oxygen in the air will slowly turn the dip brown.

Sever the dip with the chips of your choice, or use as a dressing on a salad, or add a little to a taco or fajita.

Burritos (6 servings)

1 lb. cheese, shredded
1 lb. lean ground beef
1/4 c. onion, finely diced
1 pkg. taco seasoning mix
3/4 c. hot water

1 (16 oz.) can refried beans
6 (8-inch round) flour tortillas
opt. 1 T. canola oil
opt. sour cream, as desired
opt. hot sauce, or salsa, as desired

Cheese: Your choice of your favorite cheese, such as: 4 Cheese Mexican, or Colby Jack, or Monterrey Jack, or Cheddar Cheese.

Instructions: Crumble the ground beef into a large nonstick skillet. Use the edge of a stirring spoon to divide the bigger pieces into smaller pieces. Add the diced onions and stir. Cook over medium heat, stirring frequently, until the meat is no longer pink but it is not quite done. Drain the grease. In a small bowl mix the taco seasoning mix in hot water and stir until well blended. Pour onto the beef in the skillet and stir. Reduce heat to low and continue to cook, uncovered, and stir while the beans are heating.

In a separate nonstick skillet add the refried beans and stir. Cook over medium-low heat until the beans are very warm.

Lightly moisten the tortillas with just a little water on both sides and put them in a single layer on a nonstick baking pan in a preheated 250°F oven until very warm.

Put about 1/6 of the beans a little off center on a warm flat tortilla. Add about 1/6 of the cooked beef. Add about 1/6 of the cheese. Fold one end and both sides of the tortilla over onto the filling and then finish rolling up the tortilla.

Fry Option: If desired, heat oil in a large nonstick skillet over medium-high heat until hot. Place a filled tortilla in the skillet and lightly brown the bottom side in the oil. Use a spatula or turner to turn the tortilla over and lightly brown the other side.

Serve: Allow each person to top their burrito with the optional sour cream and/or the optional hot sauce, or salsa.

Burrito Pie (4 to 6 Servings)

1 1/2 c. cheese, shredded
1 c. cooked white rice
1 lb. lean ground beef
1/4 c. onions, finely diced
1 pkg. burrito seasoning mix
1/2 c. hot water
1/2 c. salsa, medium or hot
1 tsp. iodized salt
1/4 tsp. fine grind black pepper
1 (15 oz.) can refried beans
6 (8-inch round) flour tortillas

1 (15 oz.) can tomatoes, diced, with green chilies and chipotle peppers

Cheese: 4 Cheese Mexican, or Colby, or Colby Jack, or Monterey Jack, or Cheddar, or whatever you prefer.

Instructions: Lightly grease the bottom and sides of a 2-quart (8-inch square) glass baking dish with lard or shortening.

Prepare 1 cup of cooked white rice by boiling 1/3 cup uncooked white rice in 2/3 cup of water following the instructions in the rice chapter.

Crumble ground beef into a nonstick skillet and divide the bigger pieces with the edge of a stirring spoon. Add the onions and cook over medium heat, stirring frequently, until the ground beef is no longer pink. Drain off the grease. In a separate bowl mix the burrito seasoning mix in 1/2 cup hot water until well blended. Pour the burrito seasoning mixture into the skillet, stir, and heat to boiling. Immediately reduce heat to low and cook uncovered for about 3 minutes, stirring occasionally, until thickened. Reduce heat to very low. Stir in diced tomatoes, salsa, salt, and pepper, and cook for 10 minutes, stirring occasionally.

Briefly heat the refried beans in a different nonstick saucepan.

Pour 1/4 of the meat sauce mixture evenly over the bottom of the greased 8-inch square casserole dish.

Place one flour tortilla on a plate and spread 1/3 of the refried beans evenly over the entire top surface of the tortilla. Lift the tortilla off the plate and put it on top of the meat sauce in the casserole dish with the bean side facing up. (Note: There will be a small space between the round edge of the flour tortilla and the square edge of the casserole dish.) Sprinkle 1/3 of cooked white rice evenly on top of the beans. Sprinkle 1/4 of shredded cheese evenly on top of the rice. Put a flour tortilla on top of the cheese so that the beans, rice, and cheese are between two flat flour tortillas.

Pour 1/4 of the meat sauce on top of the flour tortilla in the casserole dish.

Place a flour tortilla on a plate and cover it with 1/3 of the refried beans. Put it on the meat sauce in the casserole dish with the bean side up. Sprinkle 1/3 of the rice on the beans and then sprinkle 1/4 of the cheese on the rice. Place a tortilla on top of the cheese.

Pour 1/4 of the meat sauce on top of the flour tortilla in the casserole dish.

Place a flour tortilla on a plate and cover it with the remaining 1/3 of the refried beans. Put it on the meat sauce in the casserole dish with the bean side up. Sprinkle the remaining 1/3 of the rice on the beans and then sprinkle 1/4 of the cheese on the rice. Place a tortilla on top of the cheese.

Pour the remaining 1/4 of the meat sauce on top of the flour tortilla in the casserole dish. Sprinkle the remaining 1/4 of the cheese on the meat sauce.

Bake in a preheated 350°F oven for 20 minutes. Remove from oven. Allow to cool for 2 minutes and then serve. (Note: This dish does not refrigerate and reheat well because the flour tortillas will gradually become soggy.)

Chicken Quesadillas (4 Servings)
or Cowboy Wild West Chicken Quesadillas (4 Servings)

1 1/2 c. cheese (see below)
flour tortillas (see below)
1 1/2 c. chicken (see below)
1 T. taco dry seasoning mix
1 or 2 T. canola oil

2 T. butter, room temperature
opt. 4 T. onions, finely diced
opt. 4 T. tomatoes, finely diced
opt. 4 tsp. jalapeños, finely diced
opt. 4 tsp. hot sauce

Traditional Chicken Quesadillas: A chicken quesadilla must include chicken and cheese inside either one or two tortilla shells. The chicken needs to be seasoned with at least one or more spices, such as cilantro, cumin, garlic, chili powder, paprika, cayenne pepper, or a combination of spices like the ones included in taco dry seasoning mix. Some Mexican restaurants add onions, or tomatoes, or jalapeños (or hot sauce), or some combination of these ingredients.

Cowboy Wild West Chicken Quesadilla: A Cowboy Quesadilla includes onions, tomatoes, and either jalapeños or hot sauce.

Cheese: Restaurants do not agree on which cheese is best. Some of the more common choices are Monterey Jack, Sharp Cheddar, Cheddar Jack, Colby Jack, Colby Monterey Jack, 4 Cheese Mexican, or a blend of two or more cheeses. Use the cheese you like best. Either shred or grate the cheese.

Flour Tortillas: Four 6-inch, or three 8-inch, or two 10-inch round flat flour tortillas. Restaurants do not agree on whether one quesadilla should consist of one tortilla shell or two tortilla shells. If one tortilla shell is used the cooking procedure is easier. If two tortilla shells are use to prepare a single quesadilla then more skill is required when the quesadilla has to be turned over on the grill to cook the top tortilla shell. This recipe uses one tortilla shell per quesadilla.

Chicken: Fresh chicken or fully cooked chicken may be used.

Fully Cooked Chicken: Canned chicken breasts chunks or Rotisserie chicken (pull chicken apart into small pieces). Sprinkle taco seasoning mix over the chicken pieces. Heat 1 tablespoon oil in a nonstick skillet over low heat. Add chicken pieces, stir, and heat until very warm.

Fresh Chicken: Boneless skinless chicken tenders are recommended. Rinse the chicken tenders under cold tap water and remove any pieces of skin or fat. Use a sharp knife to cut the chicken into cubes between 3/8 inch to 1/2 inch in size. Sprinkle taco dry seasoning mix over the chicken cubes. Heat 1 tablespoon oil in a nonstick skillet over medium-high heat until the oil is hot. Add chicken pieces, stir and toss and cook the chicken about 4 minutes, or until done.

Optional Onions, Tomatoes, and/or Jalapeños: If cooking fresh chicken then cook the optional items in the same skillet and at the same time as the chicken. If using precooked chicken then heat 1 tablespoon of oil in a nonstick skillet over medium-high heat until hot. Add the finely diced ingredients and stir and toss and cook for 3 to 4 minutes, or until tender.

Instructions: Heat a clean nonstick skillet (big enough to hold one flat tortilla shell) over medium heat. Spread room temperature butter evenly over one side of a tortilla shell. Place the buttered side down in the hot skillet.

Divide the chicken, the cheese, and the optional ingredients equally among the number of tortilla shells you will be cooking.

Sprinkle the appropriate amount of cheese over the entire surface of the tortilla. Add the appropriate amount of hot cooked chicken to one half of the tortilla.

If desired, add the cooked diced onions, tomatoes, and/or jalapeños.

Cook between 3 to 4 minutes, or until the cheese is melted and the tortilla shell is very lightly browned, and then use a spatula to fold the cheese half of the tortilla over onto the chicken half of the tortilla. Transfer to a serving plate. If desired, cut into wedges as follows:

> 6-inch diameter: Serve whole or cut into two equal halves.
> 8-inch diameter: Cut into three equal wedges.
> 10-inch diameter: Cut into four equal wedges.

Serve with your choice of sides, such as sour cream, guacamole, salsa, or whatever you prefer.

Fritos Casserole (or Tortilla Casserole) (8 Servings)

1 c. sour cream, softened
1 T. vegetable shortening
1 lb. lean ground beef
1/2 c. onions, diced
1 pkg. taco seasoning mix
2/3 c. hot water

1 (8 oz.) can tomato sauce
1 (15 oz.) can diced Mexican tomatoes
1 (15 oz.) can chili beans
5 c. Fritos corn chips
2 c. Four Cheese Mexican, shredded

Fritos: Instead of Fritos you can use crushed tortilla chips.

Remove the sour cream from the refrigerator, measure the amount needed, and allow it to come to room temperature.

Heat oven to 350°F.

Lightly grease the bottom and sides of a 3-quart (13-inch by 9-inch) glass baking dish with lard or shortening.

Crumble ground beef in a nonstick skillet and break up the bigger pieces with the edge of a stirring spoon. Add the onions and cook over medium heat, stirring frequently, until the ground beef is no longer pink. Drain off the grease. In a separate bowl mix the taco seasoning mix with the hot water until well blended. Pour the taco seasoning mixture into the skillet, stir, and heat to boiling. Immediately reduce heat to low and cook uncovered for about 3 minutes, stirring occasionally, until thickened. Stir in tomato sauce, diced Mexican tomatoes, and chili beans, and cook for 2 minutes, stirring occasionally.

Place a single layer of Fritos corn chips in the bottom of a lightly greased casserole dish and also up the sides of the dish. Pour the meat and bean mixture evenly over the corn chips. Spread the shredded cheese evenly over the meat.

Bake in a preheated 350°F oven for 15 minutes. Remove from oven and spread the room temperature cream cheese over the Mexican cheese in the casserole dish. Spread a layer of corn chips on top of the cream cheese. Return to oven and bake for 3 minutes. Remove from oven. Allow to cool for 2 minutes and then serve. (Note: This dish does not refrigerate and reheat well because the corn chips will gradually become soggy.)

Imitation Taco Bell®
Chili Cheese Burritos (6 Servings)

1 lb. lean ground beef
2 1/4 c. warm water
2 tsp. cornstarch
4 T. chili powder
1/3 tsp. cayenne pepper
1/2 tsp. iodized salt
2 T. jalapeño, finely diced
1/2 c. onion, finely diced

2 tsp. vinegar, white
1 (6 oz.) can tomato paste
1 (16 oz.) can refried beans
4 c. (1 lb.) cheddar cheese, shredded
6 (8-inch round) flour tortillas
opt. sour cream, as desired
opt. hot sauce, or salsa, as desired

Crumble ground beef into a large nonstick skillet. Use the edge of a stirring spoon to break the bigger pieces into smaller pieces. Cook over medium heat, stirring frequently, until the meat is no longer pink but it is not quite done. Turn off the heat. Drain the grease.

Put water in a different nonstick skillet and add cornstarch and stir until well blended. Add chili powder, cayenne pepper, and salt and stir until well blended. Add jalapeños and onions and stir. Add vinegar and tomato paste and stir to blend all the ingredients. Bring to a boil over medium heat while stirring. Immediately reduce heat to low and cook 3 minutes, stirring frequently.

Add the refried beans to the skillet with the cooked ground beef and stir. Add the sauce mixture and stir. Cook over low heat for 25 minutes, stirring frequently. Add one-half of the shredded cheese and stir. Cook over low heat, uncovered, for 5 minutes stirring frequently.

While the filling is cooking, lightly moisten the tortillas with just a little water on both sides and put them in a single layer on a nonstick baking pan in a preheated 250°F oven until very warm.

Put about 1/6 of the filling a little off center on a flat tortilla. Sprinkle 1/6 of the remaining cheese on top of the hot filling. Fold one end and both sides of the tortilla over onto the filling and then finish rolling up the tortilla.

Serve: Allow each person to top their burrito with the optional sour cream and/or the optional hot sauce, or salsa.

Mexican Rice (or Spanish Rice)
(Restaurant Style) (4 servings)

1 1/2 c. water, or chicken stock
2 T. canola oil, or olive oil
1/3 c. onions, chopped
1 c. uncooked long grain white rice
1 (10 oz.) can diced tomatoes with lime juice and cilantro
1/4 c. chopped jalapeño peppers, or green bell peppers, or half of each
1 garlic clove, minced (or 1/8 tsp. garlic powder)

1 tsp. taco seasoning dry mix
1/2 tsp. iodized salt
1/8 tsp. fine grind black pepper

Water or Chicken Stock: Some restaurants use chicken stock to enhance the rice with a zesty chicken flavor, and some restaurants use water instead. This is the major difference in how this rice is prepared. Usually if the rice is served with a chicken dish then chicken stock is added to the rice. If the rice is served with a beef dish then water is added to the rice. But you may use water or chicken stock as you prefer.
Instructions: Heat oil in a medium saucepan over medium heat. When the oil is hot then add the onions and stir for 3 to 4 minutes, or until the onions have a golden caramel color. Reduce heat to low. Add the rice and cook for about 3 minutes, or until the rice is brown, stirring constantly so the rice does not burn. Add the tomatoes and peppers, and cook for 2 minutes, stirring constantly. Add garlic, taco seasoning mix, salt, black pepper, and either the water or the chicken stock and increase heat to medium and bring to a boil, while stirring. As soon as the mixture boils, reduce heat to very low, cover the saucepan, and simmer over very low heat for 10 to 14 minutes, or until the liquid is absorbed and the rice is moist but done. (If cooked too long then add a little water so the rice is not sticky.) Remove from heat, fluff the rice with a fork, cover the saucepan, and allow to sit for 10 minutes so the rice can continue to absorb all the flavors, and then serve.

Refried Beans (6 Servings)

1/2 lb. pinto beans, dry
1 1/2 c. water, for soaking
water, for cooking
4 T. bacon grease, or lard
1/3 c. onions, minced

opt. 1 garlic clove, minced
1 tsp. iodized salt
1/4 tsp. fine grind black pepper
1 tsp. seasoning (see below)
opt. 1/2 c. cheese, shredded

Trivia: In the United Kingdom refried beans are called "Borlotti beans." In Mexico they are called "frijoles refritos" which means well-fried beans and not refried beans.

Beans: Pinto beans are the most popular choice for refried beans because they are tender, a little sweet, and they mash into a creamy consistency. Black beans are sometimes used for a different flavor but black beans are smaller, they are firmer even when fully cooked, and they are more challenging to mash by hand into a smooth consistency.

Dried Beans or Canned Beans: Mexican restaurants and good cooks use dried beans that they soak and cook themselves. However, precooked canned beans may be used if you enjoy their flavor.

Mash Consistency and Moisture: There is no agreement on how thoroughly the beans should be mashed, or on how moist the beans should be after cooking. Some people prefer a thick paste and some people prefer a soupy consistency. Some people like beans that are just barely mashed and that still contain small pieces of uncrushed beans, and some people prefer beans that are completely mashed into a very smooth consistency.

Fat: Canola oil and butter are rarely used. Lard is the most popular fat used to cook refried beans in Mexican restaurants and by Hispanic cooks. However, bacon grease is also extremely popular. Lard is rendered (melted) pork fat. Therefore lard and bacon grease are basically the same thing with the exception that bacon grease does have the flavor of bacon. If you have bacon grease (saved from when you cooked bacon for breakfast) then bacon grease is recommended.

Onions: Almost every refried bean recipe includes onions in one form or another. However, the type of onion, the amount, and the processing technique varies considerably. Either a sweet onion or a white onion is recommended. Finely minced onion is recommended.

Optional Garlic: About half of the recipes include garlic cloves and half the recipes do not add any type of garlic. You may add fresh garlic if you desire, or you may omit the garlic. If you wish to add garlic then 1/8 teaspoon garlic powder will add the taste of garlic without overpowering the natural flavor of the beans.

Seasoning: Most refried beans include some type of seasoning, such as cilantro, cumin, chili powder, epazote, or oregano. The seasoning adds flavor and aroma to the beans and it should **not** be omitted. Usually only one of these seasonings is used, but occasionally two are included. If you add two seasonings then only use half of each type seasoning.

Optional Cheese: About half of the recipes include a topping of cheese. Monterey Jack is the most popular choice. However, cheddar cheese is also sometimes used. My personal preference is Four Cheese Mexican. You may use the type of cheese you prefer or you may omit the cheese. If you add a garnish of cheese then the cheese may be shredded or the cheese may be melted. A very small amount of melted cheese poured on the top center of the refried beans is recommended.

Instructions: If using canned beans then skip the preparation instructions for dried beans.

How to Prepare Dried Beans: Look through the dry beans and remove any small foreign particles. Rinse the dry beans thoroughly and discard the rinse water. For 1/2 cup of dry beans add 1 1/2 cups of water and soak overnight in the refrigerator. Drain the beans and discard the soak water for health and safety reasons because although the soak water will contain some vitamins and nutrients, it may contain some undesirable chemicals. If the beans are not thoroughly cooked then they are more difficult to chew and digest, and they will generate more gas during the digestive process. In order to neutralize any minor amount of toxins that may still be in the beans, add the beans to the cook pot, cover with two inches of cold water, bring to a boil and boil for ten minutes. Then reduce the heat to very low. Put a lid or cover on the cook pot. The slower the beans are cooked the easier it is for the human body to digest them. Slowly cooking the beans over very low heat for between 3 to 8 hours is ideal. Check the beans every hour and add more hot water if necessary. Do not add cool water or cold water to the beans while they are cooking because the cool water shock will toughen the beans and they will require a longer cooking time and the beans will be a little harder to digest. Instead heat the extra water in a separate cook pot and then add the hot water to the bean pot. When the beans are soft and a bean can be easily mashed with a fork using just a little pressure, then the beans are done. Drain the water from the beans and reserve 1 cup of water for later. Mash the beans until they are the consistency you desire.

Refried Beans: Melt the bacon grease (or lard) in a large nonstick skillet over median-high heat. When the fat is hot add the onions. If desired, add the optional garlic.

Stir and cook for 3 or 4 minutes or until the onions have a golden caramel color. Reduce heat to medium. Add the salt and pepper. Add either one or two seasonings (your choice) and stir.

Add the mashed beans and stir until everything is well blended. Cook over medium heat, stirring, until the beans are hot. If the beans become too dry, then add some reserved bean water, one tablespoon at a time, and stir, until the desired amount of moisture is achieved.
Serve immediately. If desired, garnish with cheese.

Chapter Twenty-Three
Other Meats and Fowl

Deer Tenderloins, Bacon Wrapped (3 to 4 Servings)

1 lb. deer (venison) tenderloins
6 to 8 slices of bacon
1 tsp. coarse Kosher salt

1/4 tsp. fine grind black pepper
1/4 tsp. onion powder
1/4 tsp. rosemary

Gravy Sauce:
3 T. butter
1/4 c. sweet onions, diced
1 garlic clove, minced

1/4 c. mushrooms, sliced
2 T. all-purpose flour

Allow the deer tenderloins to come to room temperature.

Rinse the deer tenderloins under cold faucet water for sanitary reasons and to remove any tiny bone pieces. Pat dry with a paper towel. The thickness of the tenderloin will determine how you slice it as follows:

> 1/2 inch thick: slice into 1 1/2 inch widths.
> 3/4 inch thick: slice into 1 inch widths.
> 1 inch thick: slice into 3/4 inch widths.

Mix the salt, black pepper, onion powder, and rosemary together in a bowl. Roll each slice of meat in the mixture to coat all sides of the deer meat.

Use 1 slice of bacon for each piece of sliced deer meat. Place each slice of bacon on a broiler pan that allows for the grease to drain into a separate pan below the top pan. Bake in a preheated 450°F oven for 10 minutes, or until bacon is about half done. Transfer the bacon onto a paper towel and pat dry with another paper towel to remove as much bacon grease as possible. Drain the bacon grease out of the bottom broiler pan. Reduce the oven heat to 375°F.

Place a slice of partially cooked bacon on a plate. Put one slice of deer meat at a slight angle on one end of one slice of the bacon. Roll the deer meat and pull the bacon tight against the deer meat so the bacon does not overlap itself and there is a small space between the bacon as you wrap the bacon around the deer meat from one end to the other. Place the wrapped deer piece on the broiler pan with the loose end of the bacon under the piece of deer so it will be held in place while baking. (Note: The bacon wrapped deer needs to be cooked on a broiler pan so the bacon grease can drain off the bacon and the bacon can finish cooking properly.)

Bake in a preheated 375°F oven for 20 minutes.

While the meat is cooking in the oven prepare the gravy sauce but keep track of the meat cooking time (set the oven timer).

Gravy Sauce: Melt 1 tablespoon butter in a nonstick saucepan over medium heat. Add the onions and cook 2 minutes, stirring frequently. Add the minced garlic and cook 2 minutes, stirring frequently. Add the mushrooms and cook 10 minutes, stirring frequently. When the mushrooms are tender, add the rest of the butter and let the butter melt and mix with the vegetables in the pan. Reduce heat to low, add the flour and stir until it becomes a thick gravy sauce.

Flip the meat over so the other side of the bacon is up. Bake for another 10 to 20 minutes based on the thickness of your sliced deer meat, and based on how done you like your meat using an instant read meat thermometer inserted into the center of the deer meat.

135°F = medium rare
145°F = medium
155°F = medium well
165°F = well done

Remove from oven and let it sit for 8 to 10 minutes. Then pour the hot gravy sauce over the bacon wrapped deer tenderloins and serve.

Deer, Peppers, and Rice (3 to 4 Servings)

1 box (6.4 oz.) beef flavored rice mix
1 lb. deer (venison) chunks or strips
1 tsp. coarse Kosher salt
1/4 tsp. fine grind black pepper
1 green bell pepper
1 red bell pepper
1 medium onion
1 T. oil

Allow the deer meat to come to room temperature.

Rinse the deer meat under cold faucet water for sanitary reasons and to remove any tiny bone pieces. Pat dry with a paper towel. Slice the deer meat into 3/8 inch cubes, or slice the deep meat into strips about 3/8 wide thick, 1/4 inch wide, and 1.5 inches long. Sprinkle the salt and black pepper on the deer meat and toss to distribute it evenly.

Remove seeds from peppers and slice into strips about 1/4 inch wide and between 1.5 to 2 inches long. Slice ends off onion and discard. Slice onion into rings and then half rings. Separate the half rings.

Prepare rice in a pot by itself following the box instructions.

While the rice is cooking, heat oil and onion half rings in a skillet over medium heat. Add deer meat and cook until the meat is almost done on the inside. Add green pepper and red pepper. Continue to cook until the peppers are tender. Serve on a plate beside the rice, or serve on top of the rice. May be served with a salad and the bread of your choice.

Duck, Roasted

1 (5 to 5 1/2 lb.) whole duck   2 qt. water
4 c. chicken stock   1 T. iodized salt

Cavity Seasonings:
1/2 onion, cut into slices   1 lemon, cut into wedges

Skin Seasonings:
2 tsp. paprika   1 tsp. coarse Kosher salt
1 tsp. garlic powder   1 tsp. fine grind black pepper

Allow the duck to come to room temperature.

Rinse the duck under cold tap water for sanitary reasons and to remove any foreign particles. Also rinse out the cavity of the duck.

Prick the skin of the duck with the tines of a fork but not deep enough to piece the meat. Prick every two inches all over the duck. The tiny holes will allow fat to escape as the duck cooks.

Put the chicken stock into a pot that is big enough to hold the entire duck. Add the duck and then add enough water to completely cover the duck with about 3/4 inch of water. Remove the duck and set it aside. Stir 1 tablespoon salt into the liquid in the pot and bring to a boil over medium-high heat. Carefully lower the duck down into the boiling liquid. Bring to a boil again and then reduce heat to low. Cook the duck for 45 minutes.

Line a roasting pan with aluminum foil. Skim enough fat off the top of the liquid to just barely cover the foil in the roasting pan.

Carefully remove the duck from the pot and hold it over the pot so it can drain. Place the duck breast side up on the aluminum foil in the roasting pan. Carefully push the stuffing pieces into the cavity of the duck. The stuffing will help season the duck from the inside. Use paper towels to pat the moisture off the skin of the duck. Sprinkle paprika, garlic powder, salt, and black pepper on the outside of the duck. Allow the duck to sit at room temperature for 30 minutes so the skin will dry and absorb some of the seasonings.

Bake in a preheated 475°F oven for 30 minutes, or until an instant read meat thermometer inserted into the thickest part of the duck reads 160° F. Remove from oven and cover with an aluminum foil tent and allow to sit for 10 minutes. Remove and discard the stuffing.

Serve with brown rice or with the vegetables of your choice.

Lamb Loin Chops (2 to 3 Servings)

1 lb. lamb loin chops
1 tsp. coarse Kosher salt
1/4 tsp. fine grind black pepper
1 garlic clove, minced

2 tsp. rosemary
1/2 tsp. dried thyme
4 tsp. extra light olive oil

Lamb Loin Chops: Lamb is usually eaten rare or medium rare because of its unique pleasant flavor. However, you may cook your lamb to whatever degree of doneness you prefer.

Prepare the Chops: Do not pierce the chops with a fork. Allow the chops to come to room temperature. Rinse the chops under cold faucet water for sanitary reasons, and to remove any tiny bone chips that may be on the chops. Pat dry with a paper towel. If desired, trim off any extra fat you do not want on the chops.

Marinade: Combine the salt, black pepper, garlic, rosemary, thyme, and extra light olive oil in a small bowl and stir until well blended. (Extra light olive oil is recommended because it has a higher smoking point than almost all other cooking oils.) Rub one side of the chops with one-half of the marinade. Rub the marinade into the chops with your fingers. Repeat with the other side of the chops. Season generously, but reasonably, because some of the marinade seasoning will come off the chops when they are cooked. Cover the chops with another plate to protect them from contamination. Let the chops absorb the marinade for about 1 hour in the refrigerator if the chops are 1 inch thick or thinner, or for about 1 hour at room temperature if the chops are 1 1/4 thick or thicker.

Prepare the Cast Iron Skillet: Place a cast iron skillet on the top oven shelf, about 6 inches below the top broiler in an oven. Set the oven to "bake" at 500°F and allow the oven to preheat for 20 minutes.

Cook the Chops: Change the oven from "bake" to "broil" and allow the broiler to heat for 2 minutes. Pull out the top oven shelf and carefully lay the chops on the extremely hot skillet being very careful to not burn yourself. The skillet is hot and it will sizzle and pop when the meat touches it. Allow a little space between the chops so the outside edges of the chops can cook properly. After placing each chop on the hot skillet do not adjust it or move it -- leave it alone. Push the oven shelf back into the oven and sear the bottom side of the chops, and simultaneously broil the top side of the chops, for between 1 to 3 minutes per side based on the thickness of the chops as follows:

Chop

Thickness	Broiling Time per Side
1/2 inch	1 minute per side for rare, 2 minutes for medium
3/4 inch	1 1/2 minutes per side for rare, 3 minutes for medium
1 inch	1 1/2 minutes per side plus baking time in next chart
1 1/4 inch	2 minutes per side plus baking time in next chart
1 1/2 inch	2 1/2 minutes per side plus baking time in next chart
1 3/4 inch	3 minutes per side plus baking time in next chart

Pull out the oven shelf and use a spatula or tongs to turn the chops over. Do not pierce the chops with a fork or their juices will run out. Push the shelf back into the oven and sear and broil the chops for the same amount of time.

If the chops are one-inch or more thick, then switch the oven from "broil" to "bake" and set the baking temperature at 450°F. Bake for the total number of additional minutes shown in the table below. If the additional cooking time is 3 minutes or longer then, if you wish, you may turn the chops over using tongs or a spatula halfway through the additional cooking time.

Different ovens cook differently based on the size of the oven, the type of heat, and the design of the broiler element. Therefore, remove the chops a little early and use an instant-read meat-thermometer to check the meat temperature inside the center of a chop. If the inside of the chop is too rare then cook the chops a little longer in the hot oven until the center of the chops reach the temperature that represents the degree of doneness you prefer.

(Note: Please remember that the internal temperature of the chops will increase by approximately 5°F while they are resting for 10 minutes after removing them from the oven.)

Doneness Middle of Chop	Meat Temp.	. Chop Thickness .		
		1 inch	1.25 inch	1.5 inch
Rare	125°F	1.5 min.	2.5 min.	3.5 min.
Medium Rare	135°F	2.5 min.	3.5 min.	4.5 min.
Medium	145°F	3.5 min.	4.5 min.	5.5 min.
Medium Well	155°F	4.5 min.	5.5 min.	6.5 min.
Well Done	165°F	5.5 min.	6.5 min.	7.5 min.

Remove chops from oven, transfer chops to a plate, and cover with an aluminum foil tent to contain the heat (do not lay the foil on the chops). Let rest under the foil tent for 10 minutes.

While the chops are resting, enjoy a green garden salad as an appetizer. Then serve the chops with Brussels sprouts, or creamed spinach, or eggplant Parmesan, or mashed potatoes, or whatever you wish.

Quail (2 servings) (or Pheasant - 4 Servings)

4 (5 to 6 oz.) quail, or 1 (2 to 2 1/2 lb.) pheasant (adjust quantities)

1 tsp. fine grind black pepper	1/4 c. warm water
1 tsp. garlic powder	1/4 c. sour cream (or lemon juice)
8 T. butter, melted	

Brine:

1 qt. water	2 bay leaves
1/4 c. canning and pickling salt	

Allow the quail to come to room temperature.

If the feathers are still on the quail then do not scald the quail. Instead dry pluck the feathers off the quail. It will take about 10 or 15 minutes to pluck the feathers off one quail.

You may cook the quail whole, or you may cut the quail in half.

Brine: Prepare brine solution by mixing salt into water and add bay leaves. Bring the water to a boil and then remove from heat and allow to cool. Remove the bay leaves. Completely submerge the quail under the water and soak for 3 hours.

Line a large casserole dish or baking pan with nonstick aluminum foil.

Remove the quail from the brine solution and pat dry. Sprinkle black pepper and garlic powder on each quail. Melt butter in a large nonstick skillet over medium-high heat. Place one quail in the skillet and brown for 1 minute on each side, or until lightly browned. Place browned quail in the aluminum lined casserole dish. Brown each quail in the skillet and place in the casserole dish. Do not let the quail touch one another in the casserole dish. Pour 1/4 cup of warm water into the casserole dish with the quail and cover the dish with aluminum foil.

Bake in a preheated 450°F oven for approximately 15 to 18 minutes, or until an instant read meat thermometer reads 165°F when inserted into the thickest part of the thigh of one quail. Quail is similar to chicken and it will dry out quickly. Do not overcook the quail.

Melt 1/4 cup of sour cream in a nonstick saucepan and pour over the quail. Serve immediately.

(Note: If you do not have sour cream then you may drizzle room temperature lemon juice over the quail.)

Rabbit, Southern Fried (4 Servings)

1 1/2 lb. rabbit meat
water for soaking
1 T. iodized salt for soaking

1/2 c. all-purpose flour
1/8 tsp. fine grind black pepper
3 T. canola oil

Rabbit: A young rabbit is more tender than an older rabbit. Cut the rabbit into pieces similar to a chicken.

Tongs: Use cooking tongs to turn the rabbit pieces over in the skillet instead of a fork. A fork will punch holes in the rabbit pieces and their juices will leak out into the frying pan.

Instructions: Place the rabbit pieces in a bowl and completely cover the rabbit pieces with water that contains 1 tablespoon of salt. Put in the refrigerator for 12 hours or overnight. Remove the rabbit and discard the salted water.

Put the flour and black pepper in a large bowl and stir to mix together. Then put the rabbit pieces in the bowl and turn the pieces over several times to evenly coat the rabbit pieces with a thin layer of the flour mixture. Do not coat too heavily to avoid a dry hard crust on the fried rabbit pieces. Put the floured rabbit pieces in the refrigerator for 20 minutes and this will help the flour stick to the rabbit pieces.

Spread oil over the bottom of a nonstick skillet. Heat the oil on medium-high heat for 2 minutes and then turn the heat down to medium. Put the large meaty pieces of rabbit in the center of the skillet and cook for 10 minutes. Reduce the heat to low and turn the larger pieces over in the middle of the skillet and then add the other pieces of meat around the sides of the skillet. Cover the skillet. Cook for 30 minutes. Then remove the lid, turn all the rabbit pieces over, replace the lid, and cook another 15 minutes. Finally remove the lid and cook uncovered for another 10 minutes to put a crisp crust on the rabbit pieces.

Rock Cornish Hens Cordon Bleu (2 Hens or 4 Servings), or Imitation Rotisserie Chicken

2 frozen Rock Cornish Hens	2/3 c. chicken broth
3/4 c. Swiss cheese, 1/4 inch cubes	1/2 tsp. iodized salt
3/4 c. baked ham, 1/4 inch cubes	1/8 tsp. fine grind black pepper
2 T. butter	1/2 tsp. poultry seasoning

Trivia: Rock Cornish Hens are sometimes referred to as Rock Cornish, or as Cornish Hens, or as Cornish Game Hens. Mrs. Alphonsine Therese "Te" Makowsky mated White Plymouth Rock chickens with Cornish Game chickens on their family 200 acre "Idle Wild Farm" in Connecticut in the early 1950s and the result was the Rock Cornish Hen. The hens were plump and succulent with all white meat. Although they are called hens they may be either male or female.

Imitation Rotisserie Chicken: Omit the Swiss cheese and ham. For a traditional flavor use the poultry seasoning. For other flavors, omit the poultry seasoning and instead use Barbecue seasoning, or Cajun seasoning, or Italian seasoning, or Tex-Mex seasoning.

Instructions: Thaw frozen hens in refrigerator for at least one day before cooking. If present, remove the giblet package inside the hen after thawing. Rinse the inside and the outside of each hen under cold faucet water. Pat dry with a paper towel.

Mix half the Swiss cheese with half the ham and stuff it inside the cavity of one hen. Mix the rest of the Swiss cheese with the rest of the ham and stuff it inside the cavity of the other hen.

Use your index finger to gently lift up the skin on each side of the tail opening on each hen a little ways and insert 1 tablespoon of butter (in small slices) under the skin against the breast meat of each hen and push it towards the neck opening under the skin. Lower the skin back down onto the butter. Put hens breast side up on nonstick aluminum foil inside a roasting pan with the legs and wings trapped under the hens against the foil. Pour chicken broth evenly over both hens. Sprinkle salt, black pepper, and poultry seasoning on the outside of both hens. The hens should not touch so they will roast properly. Cover pan with its lid or with nonstick aluminum foil.

Hens 17 ounces of less should be baked a total of about 60 minutes.

Hens 18 ounces or more should be baked a total of about 75 minutes.

Bake for 30 minutes in a preheated 350°F oven. Remove lid and spoon the broth from the broiler pan back on top of the hens. Return to oven without the lid. Continue to baste every 15 minutes until done. During the last 10 minutes increase oven temperature to 400°F to brown the hens. Stick a knife into the thickest part of the thigh and if the juice runs clear it is done. Or use an instant read meat thermometer in the thickest part of the thigh and if it reads 180°F it is done.

Remove from oven and cover with lid or aluminum foil and let rest for 10 minutes. Cut in half down the breast from neck to tail and serve. Scoop the cheese and ham out of the cavity onto the serving plates. Enjoy the cheese and ham with the chicken.

Turkey, Oven Baked

1 turkey, whole or breast (weight below)   3 T. butter, slightly melted

Dry Brine Ingredients:

1 T. paprika, smoked or regular	1/2 tsp. dried oregano
1/2 T. onion powder	1/2 tsp. cayenne pepper
1/2 T. garlic powder	1 tsp. coarse Kosher salt
1 tsp. dried thyme	1 tsp. fine grind black pepper

Cavity Seasonings:

2 T. lemon juice	2 carrots, peeled, chopped
1/2 onion, cut into slices	2 celery tops, chopped

A turkey gravy recipe is in the sauces and gravy chapter. A dressing (stuffing) recipe is in the side dishes chapter.

Dressing or Stuffing: This recipe does not cook the dressing inside the turkey. The disadvantage of cooking the dressing separately is the turkey juices do not blend with the dressing. The advantages of cooking separately are:

1. It takes less total time to cook the turkey.
2. The turkey cooks more evenly from inside to outside.
3. The amount of dressing is not limited to what will fit inside the turkey.
4. The dressing cooks more evenly when cooked by itself.
5. The degree of doneness of the dressing is easier to control.
6. The texture of the dressing is more consistent and it does not contain dry spots or damp spots.

Whole Turkey or Turkey Breast: This choice depends on the preferences of the people who will be eating the turkey.

Weight of Turkey: Plan on about 1 pound of raw turkey (including the bones and giblet package) per person. Buy a larger turkey if you want leftovers.

Safety: Handle raw turkey carefully like raw chicken. Wash your hands after handling raw turkey, and wipe down any surface the raw turkey has made contact with.

Breast Side Down or Up when Baking:
Breast side down allows the juices to flow into the breasts of the turkey to make them more succulent. The thighs are more exposed and this is good because dark meat takes a little longer to cook than white meat. However, the skin on the breast will not brown and become crispy. However, there is enough brown crispy skin on the parts of the breasts that are exposed for those people who enjoy eating the skin of the turkey.

Normal Defrosting: Place a frozen turkey in a pan in the refrigerator for at least three days before you plan to cook it to give it a chance to defrost completely.

Quicker Defrosting: If you must defrost the turkey more quickly, then sanitize your kitchen sink, and put the turkey in some cool water in the sink basin. Drain and replace the water when the water gets very cold.

Giblet Package: Remove the paper wrapped giblet package from inside the main body cavity or the neck cavity. Put it in the refrigerator if you intend to use the neck and giblet parts (heart, gizzard, and liver) in another recipe, such as Turkey Giblet Gravy (recipe in sauces and gravy chapter). If not, then discard them.

Rinsing: Rinse the turkey thoroughly, inside and outside. Inspect the skin of the turkey and pluck out any tiny feathers you may find. Use paper towels to pat dry the turkey.

Plastic Tie on Drumsticks (Whole Turkey): Read the instructions that came with the turkey. Depending on the temperature you intend to bake the turkey, you may not need to remove those ties at this time.

Dry Brine Instructions: Mix the paprika, onion powder, garlic powder, thyme, oregano, cayenne pepper, salt, and black pepper in a bowl. Stir until well blended. Use your fingers to gently separate the skin from the turkey from the top center of the breast and then to the right and left, but do not take the skin off the turkey. Rub some of the brine on the turkey under its skin. Press the skin back into its original position. Evenly sprinkle the rest of the brine on top of the skin. Place the turkey in a roasting pan and cover with aluminum foil and put in the refrigerator overnight or for 1 day to allow the brine flavors to blend into the turkey.

Room Temperature Turkey: Remove the turkey from the refrigerator about 3 hours before you wish to cook it to give the turkey a chance to come to room temperature. This will allow the turkey to cook more evenly and more quickly.

Temperature: Preheat the oven to 400°F.

Cavity Seasonings: Rub lemon juice inside the turkey cavity. Put the onions, carrots, and celery inside the turkey cavity. These will aromatically flavor the turkey from the inside as it bakes.

Whole Turkey: Truss the turkey to keep the wings and legs close to the body while baking so they do not spread out and become overcooked. Use oven safe kitchen string to tie the legs together and to secure the wings.

Baking Instructions: Close the main body cavity opening with skewers or string. Place a large baking sheet with a raised outside edge under the roasting pan so it can catch any drippings from the roasting pan. This dissipates the heat around the roasting pan so that the bottom of the roasting pan does not get too hot and cooks the turkey unevenly.

Drizzle the barely melted butter evenly over the top of the turkey. It will gradually run down the sides of the turkey. Bake the turkey on the lowest rack in the oven for 13 to 14 minutes per pound, assuming the turkey was allowed to come to room temperature before putting it in the oven. Bake in a preheated 400°F oven for 20 minutes to brown the skin on the turkey. Then reduce the temperature to 325°F and bake for two hours. Then reduce the temperature to 225°F for the remaining time the turkey needs to cook based on its size. The temperature of the breast meat should be 160°F and the temperature of the thigh meat should be 165°F. The temperature of the meat will continue to increase by about 5 degrees after you remove the turkey from the oven. If you stick a sharp knife into the breast meat the juices should be clear and not pink. If you want to brown the breast then carefully turn the turkey over and set the oven to "broil" and put it back in the oven for 4 minutes. Set the turkey in a safe place and put a tent of aluminum foil over the turkey to keep it warm and allow it to rest for 30 minutes. This allows the flavors of the brine to meld deeper into the turkey and the turkey will be easier to carve into smooth, uniform slices.

Carve and serve the turkey.

Save the bones and carcass for turkey stock (this chapter) and turkey soup (soup chapter).

Turkey Stock

1 turkey carcass	1 bay leaf
10 c. cold water	1 tsp. iodized salt
1 onion, sliced	1/2 tsp. coarse ground black pepper

Cut or break the turkey carcass into 3 or 4 small pieces. Put the entire turkey carcass, including the bones and any leftover skin, and any leftover pan drippings from cooking the turkey, into a large stockpot. If not used in another recipe (such as turkey gravy), add the neck, gizzards, and heart to the pot. Completely cover the turkey parts with cold water by one inch. Add the onion slices and bay leaf. Stir. Bring to a boil over medium-high heat and then immediately reduce heat to very low or until the liquid just barely simmers. Skim off the foam and fat from the top of the pot and discard. Add salt and pepper. Place a cover on top of the pot so one edge of the cover is on top of the pot to allow some of the steam to escape. Simmer for four hours over very low heat and frequently skim off the fat, foam, and crud that floats to the top. Use tongs and/or a slotted spoon to remove the solid bones and vegetables from the pot and discard. Pour the stock through a fine mesh strainer. If your strainer is not fine mesh then line the inside of your strainer with paper towels and then strain the stock. You may use the stock immediately to make turkey soup (recipe in soup chapter). If you wish to save the stock to use later, then reduce the stock by about one-third by simmering very gently over very low heat in a partially covered stock pot until only two-thirds of the original stock remains. Cool and store in an airtight container in the refrigerator.

Chapter Twenty-Four
Pies and Piecrusts

A Few Suggestions for Baking Pies

Homemade Piecrusts: Recipes for a variety of different types of homemade piecrusts are at the end of this chapter.

Top Piecrust: If your pie recipe requires a top crust, then center the top crust on the pie and trim the outside edges of the top crust so that it is about 3/8 inch wider all the way around the bottom crust. Then fold the outside edge of the top crust over and under the outside edge of the bottom crust and then crimp the two crusts together. This will help to keep the contents inside the pie from bubbling up and over the top edges of the pie.

Soggy Bottom Piecrust: There are two methods that will help prevent a soggy bottom piecrust and you may do either or both of the following:

1. Use a pastry brush and coat the bottom piecrust with the beaten egg white from one egg.

2. Cook the piecrust for ten minutes before you add the ingredients to the piecrust.

Decorative Crust Edges: Use a spoon to create a scalloped edge. Use a fork to create a crisscross pattern.

Meringue: Before whipping egg whites into meringue, allow the egg whites to come to room temperature. This will increase their volume when whipped.

Apple Pie

3/4 c. granulated sugar
2 1/2 T. all-purpose flour
3/4 tsp. ground cinnamon
1/4 tsp. ground nutmeg
1/4 tsp. iodized salt
8 c. sliced tart apples

1 T. lemon juice
bottom and top 9-inch piecrusts
2 T. butter, unsalted
1 T. whole milk, to coat
1 T. granulated sugar, to sprinkle

Apples: Tart apples, such as Granny Smith, are good pie apples. Since apples grow to different sizes, the quantity needed to make an apple pie is stated in terms of cups of sliced apples. An apple pie will normally require somewhere between 4 very large apples to 7 smaller apples.

Instructions: In a small bowl, combine the sugar, flour, cinnamon, nutmeg, and salt, and stir to mix well. Set bowl aside.

Peel and slice the apples into consistent 3/16 inch thick slices so the apple slices will cook uniformly. Discard the peels, cores, and seeds. Put the lemon juice in a large bowl, add the sliced apples, and toss the apples to coat with lemon juice. Add the sugar mixture and toss the apples again to coat the apples with the sugar mixture. Put the apples into the bottom piecrust. Randomly put small very thin slices of butter on top of the apple filling.

Note: While the apples are baking they will lose moisture and shrink in size. Therefore pour the sliced apples all the way around the outside edge to the very top of the piecrust but pour the sliced apples higher in the center of the pie than the sides of the pie. This will allow the apples to cook and shrink and the apple pie will look full after baking.

Cut the other piecrust into 8 slices, each about 1 1/2 inches wide. Arrange the slices on top of the pie in an open weave interlocking lattice pattern (4 strips in one direction and the other 4 strips at 90 degrees to the first 4 strips) with small gaps in the weave for the moisture to escape while baking. Push the ends of each strip under the outside edge of the bottom crust and press together to seal. If desired, flute the outside edges of the crust.

Brush the top crust with a little milk and then sprinkle a little granulated sugar on top of the top crust.

Loosely cover the outside edge of the piecrust with a 2-inch wide strip of aluminum foil. Put the pie on a baking sheet in order to catch any spillovers during baking.

Bake at 375°F for 40 minutes and then remove the aluminum foil. Bake for an additional 10 to 15 minutes, or until the top crust is a golden brown and the apple filling is bubbly. Remove from the oven and cool inside the baking pan on top of a wire rack for 2 hours.

Cheesecake Pie

2 (8 oz.) pkgs. cream cheese   2 eggs
1/2 c. granulated sugar   1 graham cracker piecrust
1 tsp. vanilla extract

Remove cream cheese and eggs from the refrigerator and allow to come to room temperature.

Preheat oven to 325°F. Place a baking sheet in the oven so it can also preheat.

In a large bowl beat the cream cheese, sugar, and vanilla extract until well blended. In a separate small bowl beat the eggs until smooth. Add the eggs to the cream cheese mixture and stir until well blended. Pour into graham cracker piecrust. Place the pie on a baking pan and bake in a preheated 325°F oven for 35 to 40 minutes, or until center of pie is almost set. Allow to cool for 10 minutes and then cover the pie and refrigerate for at least 3 hours.

Optional Toppings: A lot of people prefer cheesecake without any toppings. On the other hand, some people enjoy the added flavor of certain toppings. If possible, allow each person to select the topping they prefer or no topping at all. For example, put one stemmed maraschino cherry on the top of a slice of pie when it is served. Or add a scoop of thawed Cool Whip, or strawberry preserves, or sliced fresh strawberries, or a little caramel syrup (the type used on ice cream), on top of a slice of pie when it is served. Or cover the entire top of the pie with a 20-ounce can of cherry pie filling.

Cherry Pie - First-Place Award Recipe

This Recipe won the First-Place Award in the
1999 American Pie Council's Pie Championship
in the Fruit and Berry Category

6 c. sour cherries, pitted   1 T. butter, unsalted
1 1/4 c. granulated sugar   1/4 tsp. almond extract
10 tsp. cornstarch   bottom and top 9-inch piecrusts

Piecrusts: The original recipe used the Shortening Piecrust recipe in this chapter.

Instructions: Preheat oven to 375°F. Place a baking sheet in the oven so it can also preheat.

Put the pitted sour cherries, sugar, and cornstarch in a medium nonstick saucepan and stir. Let the mixture stand for 10 minutes so the sugar can draw out the juices in the cherries. Then bring to a boil over medium heat while stirring constantly. Immediately reduce the heat to low and simmer for 1 minute or until the juices thicken in the saucepan and become transparent. Remove pan from heat and stir in the butter and almond extract. Allow the filling to cool to lukewarm and then pour into the bottom piecrust. Cover with a top piecrust, fold the edge of the top crust under the outside edge of the bottom crust, crimp the edges of the top and bottom crusts together to seal, and cut several slits in the top crust to allow steam to escape. If desired, flute the edges.

Bake in preheated 375°F oven on the preheated baking sheet for 45 to 55 minutes or until the top crust is a golden brown. Allow to cool inside the baking pan on a wire rack for 3 hours.

Chocolate Pie

1 piecrust, your choice	3 egg yolks
3/4 c. granulated sugar	1 3/4 c. half & half, or whole milk
3 T. cocoa powder, unsweetened	3/4 tsp. pure vanilla extract
1/4 c. cornstarch (or flour)	2 T. butter, room temperature
1/4 tsp. iodized salt	opt. Cool Whip, for topping

Piecrust: A pastry piecrust, or a graham cracker piecrust, or a chocolate wafer piecrust may be used. If the piecrust needs to be baked, then bake the piecrust following the piecrust instructions.

Instructions: In a medium bowl combine sugar, cocoa powder, cornstarch, and salt, and stir until well blended.

Separate the cold egg yolks from the egg whites in a bowl. Beat the egg yolks until smooth. Transfer the egg yolks to a medium size nonstick saucepan. Add the half & half and stir until well blended. Gradually add the sugar mixture and stir until well blended. Heat the mixture over medium heat, stirring constantly, for about 6 to 8 minutes, or until the mixture just barely begins to boil. When it starts to bubble and thicken, immediately remove it from the heat. Add vanilla extract and butter, and stir until everything is well blended and smooth. Pour into the piecrust and level the filling inside the piecrust. Refrigerate for at least 4 hours or until firm. If desired, serve with a large spoonful of thawed Cool Whip on each slice.

Key Lime Pie - First-Place Award Recipe

This Recipe won the First-Place Award in the 1999 American Pie Council's National Pie Championship in the Quick and Easy Category

2 (14 oz.) cans sweetened condensed milk	4 egg yolks, beaten
3/4 c. key lime juice	1 graham cracker piecrust

Substitution: If you cannot find key lime juice, then you may use lime juice, or you may use half lemon juice and half lime juice.

Egg Free Recipe: Use 1/2 cup sour cream (1 small 8 ounce container) instead of the egg yolks and bake at 350°F for 10 minutes. Allow to cool and then refrigerate for 4 hours.

Egg Yolk Key Lime Pie Instructions for First-Place Award Pie:

Preheat oven to 375°F.

Put the milk and the lime juice in a large bowl. Use a spoon to remove all the milk from the bottom of each can of milk. Stir until well blended and smooth.

In a different small bowl, separate the cold egg yolks from the whites. Only use the yolks. If any short firm white pieces are clinging to a yolk then remove and discard them. Beat the egg yolks until smooth. (Do not include the egg whites because they will alter the taste of the pie.)

Gradually "temper" the egg yolks by adding 1 tablespoon of the lime and milk mixture to the eggs in the small bowl and stir until well blended. Now wait 1 minute. Add another 1 tablespoon of the lime and milk mixture to the eggs and stir until well blended. Wait another minute. Add 2 tablespoons of the lime and milk mixture to the eggs and stir until well blended. Wait another minute. Your eggs should no longer be a bright yellow. Now add the small bowl of "tempered" eggs to the lime and milk mixture in the large bowl and stir until well blended. (Note: If you add all the citric acid lime juice to the eggs at the same time then you will partially "cook" the eggs and your pie will contain tiny pieces of scrambled egg pieces.)

Pour the mixture into an unbaked graham cracker piecrust.

Bake in a preheated 375°F oven for 15 minutes. Allow to cool and then refrigerate for four hours. If desired, top each slice of pie with a spoonful of Cool Whip and stick a thin slice of lime in the Cool Whip.

Optional Enhanced Green Color: Limes have a green peel but the juice of a lime is not green. Authentic key lime pie is not green. However, visual expectations play an important role in how we perceive the taste of what we eat. An easy way to enhance the color of the pale yellow pie filling is to stir 1 drop of green food coloring into the pie filling.

Optional Fresh Limes: Approximately 20 fresh key limes will yield enough lime juice for this recipe. Allow the fresh limes to come to room temperature. Then roll each lime around on a table or countertop with the palm of your hand and press down on the lime as you roll. Then slice and squeeze the lime and you will get the maximum amount of lime juice out of each lime.

Lemon Meringue Pie

1 piecrust

Lemon Filling:

4 egg yolks
1 1/4 c. granulated sugar
7 T. cornstarch
1/4 tsp. iodized salt

1 1/2 c. water
1/2 c. lemon juice
2 T. butter, room temperature
opt. 1 drop yellow food coloring

Meringue:

1/4 c. water
2 tsp. cornstarch
4 egg whites

1/4 tsp. cream of tartar
6 T. granulated sugar
1/2 tsp. pure vanilla extract

Bake piecrust following the piecrust package instructions.

Eggs: Carefully separate one cold egg into a yolk and whites. Do not allow even a small speck of yolk into the whites or the whites will not beat properly. If an egg white becomes contaminated, then save that entire egg in a covered bowl in the refrigerator for some other use. Transfer the yolk to a different bowl and the whites to a third bowl. Then separate the next egg. Continue until all the eggs have been separated. Allow the whites to come to room temperature.

Lemon Filling: In a bowl beat the egg yolks until smooth.

In a medium nonstick saucepan, add the sugar, cornstarch, and salt, and stir until well blended. Add water and stir until the sugar and cornstarch are dissolved. Then cook over medium heat, stirring constantly, until the mixture comes to a boil. Continue to stir constantly until mixture thickens. Turn off heat.

Transfer 1/2 cup of the hot sugar mixture to the egg yolks bowl and stir until well blended. Then add another 1/2 cup of hot sugar mixture to the egg yolks bowl and stir until well blended. Then put the egg yolk mixture into the saucepan with the filling mixture. Turn on heat to low. Stir constantly and cook for one minute. Remove from heat. Add the lemon juice, butter, and if desired the optional food coloring. Stir until smooth. Set aside for now but leave the lemon filling in the saucepan.

Meringue: In a different small saucepan combine the water and the cornstarch and stir until all the cornstarch is dissolved. Turn heat to medium and stir until the mixture bubbles and thickens. Remove from heat and set aside until later.

In a large bowl whip the egg whites and cream of tartar until foamy. This is easier to do with an electric mixer. Gradually add sugar, 1 tablespoon at a time, while whipping. Add vanilla extract. Continue to whip until soft peaks form. Add the cornstarch gel mixture, 1 tablespoon at time, while stirring, until all the cornstarch mixture has been added. Continue to beat until the meringue forms stiff peaks. (Note: The cornstarch mixture adds a little firmness to the meringue and it will help prevent the meringue from weeping and shrinking.)

Reheat the lemon filling over low heat, stirring constantly, for 2 minutes. Pour the warm lemon filling into the baked pie shell and push the lemon filling to the edge of the piecrust. Then spread the meringue over the lemon pie filling and be sure to nudge the meringue to the edge of the piecrust so the meringue touches the piecrust all the way around the pie in order to form a seal over the lemon filling, and also to anchor the meringue to keep it from shrinking. This will also help prevent weeping and shrinking. The center of the pie should have the most meringue. Use the bottom back edge of a spoon to create peaks in the meringue all over the top of the pie. Bake in a preheated 350°F oven for 8 to 12 minutes, or until the top of the meringue is a golden brown.

Allow pie to cool in baking pan on wire rack for 2 hours and then put in the refrigerator. Allow pie to cool in the refrigerator for at least 3 hours.

After cooling in the refrigerator, cover the pie with a tent of aluminum foil but do not allow the foil to touch the meringue, and leave a very small opening in the foil so moisture can escape.

Sugar Cream Pie

1 9-inch pastry piecrust	6 T. + 2 T. butter, unsalted
1 c. granulated sugar	1 tsp. vanilla extract
1/4 c. cornstarch	2 T. light brown sugar
2 c. half & half, or whole milk	

Piecrust: Bake piecrust following piecrust package instructions. If you make your own piecrust using a recipe at the end of this chapter, then lightly brown the piecrust in a preheated 450°F oven for 10 minutes.

Filling: In a large saucepan combine sugar, cornstarch, and half & half and stir until smooth. Bring to boil, stirring constantly, and immediately reduce heat. Cook over medium heat stirring constantly until mixture is thick and smooth. Remove from heat. Stir in 6 tablespoons butter until the butter melts and is evenly distributed. Stir in vanilla extract. Pour into a cooked pastry piecrust. Pour 2 tablespoons melted butter over top of pie. Sprinkle top of pie with a very thin layer of light brown sugar. Put on a cookie sheet on middle shelf of preheated 375°F oven for 15 to 20 minutes or until golden brown. Turn on broiler and broil top of pie for about 20 to 40 seconds to caramelize the brown sugar to make it crunchy (do not burn). Cool on wire rack. Then chill in refrigerator.

Peanut Butter Pie - No Cooking

1 c. smooth peanut butter
1 (8 oz.) pkg. cream cheese
3/4 c. powdered sugar

8 oz. Cool Whip, thawed
1 (9-inch) piecrust, your choice

Piecrust: A graham cracker piecrust is normally used. However, a chocolate piecrust, or a "Nutter Butter Cookie" piecrust, or a regular pasty piecrust (baked) may be used. A "Nutter Butter Cookie" piecrust is recommended (recipe near the end of this chapter).

Pie Filling: Remove the cream cheese and Cool Whip from the refrigerator and allow to come to room temperature. In a large bowl mix the peanut butter and the cream cheese. An electric mixer makes the task easier. Blend in the sugar. Finally blend in the thawed Cool Whip. Pour into the piecrust of your choice. Use the bottom back edge of a spoon to make tiny peaks in the filling. Chill in the refrigerator for at least 4 hours (or overnight).

Optional Toppings: Pour thin streaks of chocolate syrup over the top of the pie. If desired, sprinkle a few crushed peanuts on top of the pie.

Peanut Butter Chocolate Pudding Pie - Stovetop

2 (3 oz.) pkgs. chocolate pudding
4 c. whole milk
1/2 c. smooth peanut butter

3/4 c. powdered sugar
8 oz. Cool Whip, thawed
1 (9-inch) piecrust, baked

Combine pudding and milk in a saucepan and cook over medium heat until done (thick and bubby). Remove from heat and allow to cool a little. In a separate bowl combine the peanut butter and the sugar to achieve a crumbly mixture. Set aside 2 tablespoons of the crumbs as a topping for the pie. Sprinkle the rest of the mixture into the bottom of a previously baked piecrust and spread it out so that it evenly covers the bottom of the piecrust. Pour the warm pudding on top of the crumbly mixture in the piecrust. Chill in the refrigerator for at least 4 hours (or overnight) until firm. Spread thawed Cool Whip evenly over the top of the pie and then sprinkle the reserved crumbs over the top of the Cool Whip.

Pecan Pie
and Chocolate Pecan Pie

1 (9-inch) piecrust	1 tsp. pure vanilla extract
3 eggs	1 c. granulated sugar
4 T. butter, melted	1/4 tsp. iodized salt
1 c. corn syrup	1 1/2 c. pecans

For **Chocolate Pecan Pie** add the following two ingredients:
1 c. semi-sweet chocolate chips   3 T. whole milk

Corn Syrup: Either light or dark corn syrup may be used. The dark syrup yields a richer flavor. Or substitute butter flavored pancake syrup instead. For a healthier pie use maple syrup instead of corn syrup.

Sugar: Either granulated sugar or light brown sugar.

Pecans: Either halves, or chopped, or some of both. The pecans may be placed on the bottom of the piecrust, or placed on top of the pie filling, or mixed into the pie filling, or any combination of these options. However, do not exceed a total of 1 1/2 cups of pecans.

Instructions: Prick the piecrust with a fork in several places.

Beat eggs in a medium bowl. Do not over beat or the eggs will have a meringue effect on your pie. Add the melted butter, corn syrup, vanilla extract, sugar, and salt, and stir until the pie filling is well blended.

Chocolate Pecan Pie: If making a Chocolate Pecan Pie then melt the chocolate chips in some milk in a saucepan over low heat and stir until smooth. Pour melted chocolate evenly over bottom of a deep piecrust.

Pecan Pie Continued: If desired, add half (or all) of the chopped pecans to the pie filling and stir until well blended.

Pour the pie filling evenly over the inside of the piecrust.

If desired, arrange pecan halves on top of the pie filling to form an attractive pecan topping for the pie.

Bake: Place pie on a cookie sheet on an oven shelf in the middle of a preheated 350°F oven and bake for 30 minutes. Remove the pie and cover the piecrust edges with aluminum foil to keep them from getting too dark. Return the pie to the oven and bake for another 20 to 30 minutes. The pie is done if the center of the pie springs back when lightly tapped. Remove the pie from the oven and allow to cool.

Serve: Some people prefer the flavor of pecan pie if it is served at room temperature. However, some people prefer to eat chilled pecan pie. Some people enjoy Cool Whip, or a scoop of vanilla ice cream, on top of a slice of pie.

Graham Cracker Piecrust,
or Vanilla Wafer, or Chocolate Wafer Piecrusts

1 1/2 c. graham crackers, crushed   6 T. butter, melted
1/3 c. granulated sugar   opt. 1/2 tsp. ground cinnamon

Cookie Wafer Piecrust: Instead of the graham crackers, use about 35 "Nilla" wafers, or about 24 chocolate cookie wafers, or about 30 gingersnap cookies. Crush the cookies until you have 1 1/2 cups of finely crushed cookie crumbs. Also decrease the butter to 4 tablespoons and completely omit the sugar.

Honey Graham Crackers: If using "Honey Graham Crackers" reduce the sugar to 1/4 cup.

Light Brown Sugar: Use light brown sugar instead of the granulated sugar for a sweeter tasting crust.

Graham Cracker Piecrust: Put the graham crackers in a large plastic zipper bag and crush the crackers with a rolling pin. Add the sugar, melted butter, and cinnamon to the crumbs and mix together inside the bag. (If desired, reserve 3 tablespoons of the crumb mixture for a garnish topping on the finished pie.) Pour the crumb mixture into a 9-inch pie plate and press the mixture evenly over the bottom of the pie plate and up the sides of the pie plate. Use the bottom flat surface of a round drinking glass to firmly press the piecrust down against the bottom of the pie plate. A tight pack helps an uncooked piecrust remain together when cut into serving pieces.

Uncooked Piecrust with Chilled Filling: Chill the piecrust in the refrigerator for one hour. Cover the piecrust if chilling longer than one hour. Then add the filling and chill again. The first slice may be difficult to remove, but future slices will come out more easily.

Cooked Piecrust with Chilled Filling: Preheat oven to 350°F if using a silver pie plate, but preheat oven to 300°F if using a dark pie plate. Bake for 8 to 10 minutes until the crust is lightly browned. Let the hot piecrust cool and then chill it in the refrigerator for one hour. Then add the filling and chill again.

Cooked Piecrust with Hot Filling: Chill the crust for one hour in the refrigerator. Then add the filling and bake the crust and the pie at the same time according to the recipe directions for the pie.

"Nutter Butter Cookie" Piecrust

Nutter Butter cookies, see below   6 T. butter

Use 24 round cookies or 18 peanut shaped cookies.

Crush the Nutter Butter cookies in a large bowl. Then add the butter and mix together. Pour the mixture into the bottom of a pie plate and press the mixture evenly over the bottom of the pie plate and up the sides of the pie plate. Use the bottom of a glass to firmly press the mixture against the bottom of the pie plate.

Piecrust using Butter (Top & Bottom Crust)

2 1/2 c. all-purpose flour   2 sticks (16 T.) cold butter, unsalted
3/4 tsp. iodized salt   8 T. ice cold water

Mix flour and salt together in a large bowl and cut in the cold finely diced butter. Add ice cold water 1 tablespoon at a time and stir. Continue to add ice cold water gradually until the mixture forms a ball. Cover the bowl and refrigerate for 4 hours or overnight. Roll each piece of dough on a floured board to the desired size. When done, roll the dough up and over your rolling pin and this will make it easier to unroll the dough into your pie pan. Put one piece of dough into a 9-inch (or 10-inch) pie pan being careful to **not** stretch the dough. Press the dough up the sides of the pie pan.

After filling the lower piecrust with the desired filling according to the pie recipe you are using, dampen the edges of the lower crust with a little cold water. Cut short slits in the remaining piece of dough with a sharp knife to allow steam to escape during baking. Place the remaining piece of dough over the filled pie. Press the edges of the two pieces of dough together using a fork or your fingers. Flute the edges if desired. Bake the pie according to the directions in your pie recipe.

Optional: You may add two tablespoons of granulated sugar at the same time you add the salt in the above recipe.

Note: Some pie recipes require the lower piecrust to be lightly browned for about 10 minutes in a 450°F oven before adding the pie filling.

Piecrust using Shortening (Top & Bottom Crust)

This Piecrust Recipe won the First-Place Award in the
1999 American Pie Council Pie Championship in the
Fruit and Berry Category as the Piecrust for best Cherry Pie

2 c. all-purpose flour	1 c. shortening
1/16 tsp. iodized salt (pinch)	4 to 8 T. ice cold water

Mix flour and salt together in a large bowl and cut in shortening (or lard). Add ice cold water gradually until mixture will hold together. Cover the bowl and refrigerate for 4 hours or overnight. Divide dough in half. Roll each piece of dough on a floured board to the desired size. When done, roll the dough up and over your rolling pin and this will make it easier to unroll the dough into your pie pan. Put one piece of dough in a 9-inch (or 10-inch) pie pan being careful to **not** stretch the dough. Press the dough up the sides of the pie pan.

After filling the lower piecrust with the desired filling according to the pie recipe you are using, dampen the edges of the lower crust with a little cold water. Cut short slits in the remaining piece of dough with a sharp knife to allow steam to escape during baking. Place the remaining piece of dough over the filled pie. Press the edges of the two pieces of dough together using a fork or your fingers. Flute the edges if desired. Bake the pie according to the directions in your pie recipe.

Optional: You may add two tablespoons of granulated sugar at the same time you add the salt in the above recipe.

Note: Some pie recipes require the lower piecrust to be lightly browned for about 10 minutes in a 450°F oven before adding the pie filling.

Note: Using lard instead of shortening or oil will yield a superior quality piecrust.

Chapter Twenty-Five
Potatoes

French Fries (Long Fries or Waffle Fries),
either Deep-Fried or Baked,
also Baked Seasoned Fries
(2 Servings)

---

1 lb. Idaho or Russet potatoes 2 c. peanut oil, if frying
1/2 tsp. iodized salt   1 T. canola oil, if baking

Seasoning (Optional for Baked Fries):
1/2 tsp. garlic salt   1/2 tsp. paprika
1/2 tsp. onion powder   1/2 tsp. chili powder, or Cajun seasoning

Optional Dip for All Fries (stir together until smooth):
1 T. ketchup   1 T. mayonnaise

Size and Shape: French fries are popular in a variety of sizes, from thin to thick. They are also popular as long stick fries and as waffle cut fries. Finally, some people want the potato peel removed and some people do not. If the fries are too thin (3/16 inch or thinner) then they will be crisp on the inside and crisp on the outside. If the fries are too thick (1/2 inch or thicker) then they will be soft on the inside when the outside is crisp and done. If the fries are of average thickness between 1/4 inch to 3/8 inch then they will be done on the inside and crisp on the outside. The recommended size is 1/4 inch thick and 5/8 inch wide. If the fries are deep-fried then they will be greasy but a lot of people like them fried. Baked fries are healthier and baked fries can be seasoned with the optional seasoning, if you wish to try it.

Instructions: Rinse the potatoes under cold faucet water for sanitary reasons and to remove any foreign particles, such as tiny specks of dirt. If desired, peel the potatoes.

Long Stick Fries: Cut the potato long ways into several 3/8 inch thick slices. Lay each slice flat on the cutting surface and cut each slice into 3/8 inch wide fries. Each fry will be 3/8 square in its center. Try to cut all the fries to the same approximate size so they will all cook evenly for the same amount of time. The length will not change the frying time. However, if a fry is too long to fit in your frying saucepan then cut it in half to reduce its length so it will fit.

Waffle Fries: You will need a special waffle fry slicer. A vegetable slicer will do fine if it has a blade that cuts deep wide ridges. Place the end of the potato against the slicer and push forward to make the first slice (a ridged slice and not a waffle slice). Rotate the potato 90

---

degrees and make the second slice (a waffle slice). Rotate the potato 90 degrees and make the third slice (another waffle slice). Continue to rotate the potato 90 degrees and cut another waffle slice until you reach the end of the potato and the last slice will be a ridged slice and not a waffle slice.

Soak Fries: Put the sliced fries in a bowl and cover with water. Add 1/2 teaspoon salt to the water and stir. Put in refrigerator for one hour and allow the fries to soak in the cold water to extract the starch from the exterior surface of the fries. Removing the starch will allow the fries to cook properly so they can reach their maximum flavor potential.

Rinse Fries: Rinse 1 cup of sliced fries in a strainer under cold tap water for about 12 seconds to rinse off the starch that is clinging to the outside of the fries. Then rinse another 1 cup of sliced fries, and so on. Rinsing in small batches helps to get more of the starch off the outside of the sliced fries quicker with the use of less water.

Dry Fries: Place the sliced fries on a dry paper towel and pat dry with another paper towel to remove as much water as possible.

Seasoning for Baked Fries: Put 1 tablespoon of canola oil in a small bowl. Add 1/2 teaspoon of iodized salt and stir until the salt is blended into the oil. (If desired, add the optional garlic salt, onion powder, paprika, and chili powder and stir until blended with the oil.) Lightly coat the fries with the seasoning oil.

Frying Option: Peanut oil is the best deep frying oil for fries. Pour peanut oil into a small saucepan until the oil is about 2 inches deep. Heat the oil over medium-high heat until its temperature reaches 300°F on a deep fry thermometer. Use tongs and carefully add just enough fries to the hot oil so they are not crowded in the oil. Fry for 4 to 5 minutes, stirring occasionally, or until soft but not brown and not done. Remove from oil using tongs or a slotted spoon and put on a paper towel on a plate to drain. Repeat for the rest of the fries until they are all partially cooked. Increase the heat of the oil to 375°F. Return the fries in small batches to the hot oil and cook about 3 minutes, stirring occasionally, until they are golden brown and crisp on the outside. Remove from the oil using tongs or a slotted spoon, place on a paper towel to drain, and sprinkle with iodized salt while they are still hot. Finish cooking the rest of the fries the same way.

Baking Option: Put a piece of parchment paper, or nonstick aluminum foil, on a baking sheet. Place the seasoned fries on the parchment paper in one thin layer with a little space between the fries. Bake in a preheated 400°F oven for 15 minutes. Remove from oven, turn the fries over with a spatula, and then bake for another 15 to 18 minutes, or until done.

Mashed Potatoes,
Garlic Mashed Potatoes,
Sour Cream Mashed Potatoes,
Cream Cheese Mashed Potatoes (Baked),
Cream Cheese & Sour Cream Mashed Potatoes (Baked)
(4 Servings)

2 lb. potatoes	1/4 tsp. fine grind white pepper
1/4 tsp. salt, for boiling water	1/8 tsp. nutmeg
3 T. butter, soft, room temperature	opt. 2 tsp. garlic powder
6 T. warm half & half, or milk	opt. 7 T. sour cream, room temp.
1 tsp. iodized salt	opt. 4 T. cream cheese, room temp.

Potatoes: Red potatoes, or Yukon Gold potatoes, are recommended. However, baking potatoes (Idaho or Russet) may be used.

Instructions: Rinse potatoes for sanitary reasons and to remove any foreign particles. Peel the potatoes, cut into cubes about 1 inch in size. Place in a nonstick saucepan and just barely cover the potatoes with water. Add 1/4 teaspoon salt to the water. Bring to a boil over medium heat, reduce heat to medium-low, slightly cover pan with a lid at a slight angle, and boil between 15 to 20 minutes, or until soft and the potatoes easily break apart when pierced with a fork.

While the potatoes are boiling, heat the butter in a small nonstick saucepan until the butter is melted. Add the half & half, stir, and heat until the mixture is very warm.

When the potatoes are done, drain off the water and mash the potatoes. Add 1 teaspoon salt, white pepper, and nutmeg, and stir. Add the warm butter and half & half, and stir until the potatoes are creamy and smooth. Do not stir too long or the mixture may become sticky.

If desired, add the optional garlic powder and stir until it is well blended into the mashed potatoes.

If desired, add the optional room temperature sour cream and stir until well blended into the mashed potatoes.

Serve immediately or do the following.

If desired, add the optional room temperature cream cheese and stir until blended into the mashed potatoes. Pour the mashed potatoes into a greased 8-inch square (or 2-quart) casserole dish, spread evenly to the sides of the dish, cover with aluminum foil, and bake in a preheated 350°F oven for 20 minutes. Remove the aluminum foil and bake for another 10 minutes. Allow to cool for 2 minutes and then serve.

Potato and Cheese Casserole (4 to 6 Servings)

1 1/2 lb. potatoes (see below)
3 T. butter
1/2 c. half & half, or whole milk
1/2 tsp. iodized salt
1/4 tsp. fine grind black pepper

3/4 c. sour cream, room temperature
1 c. cheddar cheese, shredded
opt. 1/2 c. onions, finely diced
opt. 1/4 lb. bacon or ham, cooked

Note: This dish can be converted from a side dish to a main dish by using 1 pound of the optional bacon (or ham) instead of 1/4 pound.

Potatoes: Hash brown potatoes are recommended. However, baking potatoes (Idaho or Russet) may be used.

If using hash brown potatoes, then use frozen uncooked hash browns and allow them to come to room temperature. Or convert fresh baking potatoes into uncooked hash browns following the hash browns recipe in the breakfast chapter of this cookbook.

If using fresh baking potatoes, then convert them into mashed potatoes following the mashed potatoes recipe in this chapter.

Instructions: Heat the butter in a small nonstick saucepan over medium heat until the butter is melted. Add the half & half, stir, and heat until the mixture is very warm. Pour into a large mixing bowl. Add the salt and black pepper and stir until mixed with the milk and butter. Add the soft room temperature cream cheese and stir until well blended. Add the potatoes. Add half of the shredded cheese.

If desired, add the optional onions.

If desired, add half of the optional cooked crumbled bacon, or half of the optional cooked diced pieces of ham.

Stir gently until the mixture is well blended. Spoon into a greased 8-inch square (or 2-quart) casserole dish and spread evenly to the sides of the dish.

Sprinkle the rest of the shredded cheese on top of the casserole, and sprinkle the rest of the optional bacon (or ham) on top of the cheese.

Cover with aluminum foil and bake in a preheated 350°F oven for 30 minutes. Remove the aluminum foil and bake for an additional 3 minutes. Allow to cool for 2 minutes and then serve.

Potatoes Au Gratin Casserole (4 servings)

4 large baking potatoes
2 T. butter
2 T. all-purpose flour
2 c. half & half, or whole milk

2 tsp. iodized salt
1/8 tsp. fine grind black pepper
1 1/4 c. cheddar cheese, shredded

Preheat oven to 350°F.

Peel potatoes and cut into 1/8 inch thick slices across the narrow width of the potato.

Melt butter in medium nonstick saucepan over medium heat. Add flour and cook 4 minutes stirring constantly. Gradually add half & half and stir to break up any clumps. Stir constantly to prevent burning half & half, and bring to a boil. Then reduce heat to low, add salt and black pepper, and stir and cook for 2 minutes or until the sauce thickens. Reduce heat to very low and gradually add 1 cup of cheese and stir until the cheese melts and the sauce is smooth. Remove from heat.

Well grease a 1-quart casserole dish that has a cover. Place 1/2 of the potatoes in a layer on the bottom of the dish. Cover with 1/2 of the cheese sauce. Add another layer of potatoes and a final layer of cheese sauce. Bake in a preheated 350F oven for 75 minutes. Remove from oven, remove the cover, sprinkle 1/4 cup shredded cheese on top, and bake uncovered for another 5 minutes.

Potato Cakes (4 pancakes)

1 egg, beaten
opt. 1/3 tsp. iodized salt
opt. 1/4 tsp. fine grind black pepper
2 c. mashed potatoes (leftovers)

1/2 c. all-purpose flour
opt. 1/3 c. cheddar cheese
2 T. butter, for frying

Beat egg in a medium bowl. If the mashed potatoes were not seasoned then add the salt and pepper and stir. Add room temperature mashed potatoes and flour and stir until well blended. If desired add room temperature shredded cheddar cheese and stir.

Melt butter in skillet over medium heat. Form potato mixture into four flat 4 inch circles between 1 to 1.5 inch thick. Fry cakes until bottom of cakes are golden brown and then flip and fry the other side. If you try to flip too soon then the potato cake may fall apart.

Variation: If you have young children then you can use cookie cutters to form shapes for the potato cakes before frying.
Optional Toppings: Diced onions, or chives, or butter, or sour cream.

Potatoes Twice Baked (2 Servings)

2 Idaho baking potatoes
2 tsp. + 2 T. butter
1/4 c. half & half, or whole milk
1/4 tsp. iodized salt
1/8 tsp. fine grind black pepper

1/2 c. Colby Jack cheese, shredded
opt. 3/8 c. sour cream
opt. 1/8 c. onion, diced
opt. 1/4 c. bacon bits, fresh cooked
opt. paprika as a garnish

Potatoes: Select the largest baking potatoes you can find. Either Idaho or Russet potatoes are good choices.

Cheese: Use your favorite shredded cheese or the cheese preferred by each person to customize the potatoes, such as Cheddar, Cheddar Jack, Colby, Colby Jack, Monterey Jack, Swiss, 4 Cheese Mexican, or Italian Blend. Or you may use a combination of cheeses.

Instructions: Rinse each potato under tap water. Wrap each potato in a piece of aluminum foil. Put 1 teaspoon of butter on top of the potato inside the aluminum foil. Bake potatoes in a preheated 375°F oven for 75 minutes or until done (when the aluminum foil is opened and the potato is easily pierced with a fork then it is done). Cut each potato in half lengthwise but do not cut through the bottom peel of the potato. Use a spoon to scoop out the inside of each potato but leave approximately 1/4 inch of potato inside the potato all the way around the inside of the peel. Put the inside of the potatoes in a bowl, add 2 tablespoons butter, and mash the potato with a fork until smooth. Add the half & half, salt, black pepper, and 1/4 cup cheese and stir until well blended.

If you know the taste preferences of everyone who will be eating the potatoes then you may mix in the optional sour cream and/or onions, but not the bacon to keep it crunchy. Or you can provide the optional items in a "potato buffet style" beside the finished baked potatoes so each person can add the optional items as desired.

Spoon the filling back into each potato and put the remaining cheese on top of the filling inside each potato. If desired, sprinkle a small amount of paprika on the top of the cheese. Carefully wrap the aluminum foil around each potato leaving some space at the top so the foil does not make contact with the cheese. Reduce the oven temperature to 300°F and bake the potatoes for another 20 minutes. Carefully open the top of the aluminum foil to expose the baked potato but allow each person to finish removing the aluminum foil because the foil helps to keep the potato hot.

Chapter Twenty-Six
Rice

White Rice

---

1 cup **uncooked** dry rice = 3 cups **cooked** rice
1 cup **uncooked** dry rice requires 2 cups **water**

Measure the white rice. Do **not** rinse the rice. Except in the USA, the cooks in most other countries rinse their rice to remove foreign particles because each country has its own quality standards for packaging rice for sale to consumers.

Boil the rice in twice the volume of water with a pinch of salt. Trickle the white rice into the water so the water doesn't stop boiling. Cover the pot and let it simmer 15 to 18 minutes over very low heat until all the water is absorbed. Do not stir while simmering. Stirring causes the grains to stick together. Do not lift the lid until the rice is almost done or you will release essential steam and moisture. When done, remove the pot from the heat and fluff the rice with a fork. Cover and let stand another 5 minutes. The rice will continue to steam and absorb flavors.

Baked Rice (4 Servings)

---

2 T. butter	2 c. water
1/4 c. onions, finely diced	2 bouillon cubes, chicken (or beef)
1 garlic clove, minced	1 c. white rice

Optional (select none, 1, or 2 of the following):

1/4 c. carrot, shredded	1 (4 oz.) can mushroom pieces, drained
1/4 c. celery, chopped	1/2 c. green bell pepper, finely diced

Melt butter in a nonstick saucepan over medium heat. Add onions. If desired, add the optional carrots and/or celery.
Cook for 3 minutes, stirring constantly. Add the minced garlic and cook for 1 minute, stirring constantly.
Add water and bring to a boil. Add the bouillon cubes and stir until completely dissolved.
Place the rice in the bottom of a lightly greased 8-inch square (2-quart) casserole dish. Pour the boiling mixture over the rice and stir.
If desired, add the optional mushrooms and/or bell pepper and stir.
Cover the dish with aluminum foil.
Bake in a preheated 375°F oven for 15 minutes. Remove the aluminum foil and bake an additional 15 minutes uncovered. Remove from oven, fluff with a fork, and let stand for 5 minutes. Then serve.

Cajun Rice, or Dirty Rice, or Cajun Dirty Rice, or New Orleans Rice, or Louisiana Rice, or Imitation Popeye's Cajun Rice (6 Servings)

1 lb. meat (see below)
1/3 c. onion, finely diced
1/2 c. bell pepper, finely chopped
1/2 c. celery, finely chopped
3/4 tsp. Cajun (Creole) seasoning

opt. 1/3 tsp. garlic powder
1 1/2 c. long-grain white rice
3 c. liquid (see below)
1/2 tsp. iodized salt
1/4 tsp. fine grind black pepper

Trivia: "Cajun" usually refers to the inclusion of Cajun seasoning, or cayenne pepper, or chili powder. However, Cajun seasoning includes cayenne pepper. Most "Cajun Rice" recipes include onions, bell peppers, and celery, and some Cajuns may be personally offended if one of these three ingredients is omitted. Usually long-grain white rice is used but brown rice, basmati rice, or jasmine rice may be used instead. "Dirty" means that the nice pretty white rice has "something" in it, and that "something" is usually meat and vegetables (to make the rice a main dish instead of a side dish.) Sometimes "dirty" refers to the liquid the rice is cooked in because it can change the color and flavor of the white rice.

Liquid: To properly cook 1 1/2 cups of white rice requires 3 cups of liquid. The liquid may be water which will retain the white color of the rice. If using beef then beef broth may be used to impart a tan or "dirty" color and a beef flavor to the white rice. If using chicken then chicken broth may be used to impart a cream or "dirty" color and a chicken flavor to the white rice. Chicken broth is frequently used when chicken giblets or chicken livers are included as one of the meats. Water may be added to a can of broth to yield 3 cups of liquid.

Meat: Most "Dirty Rice" recipes, and about half the "Cajun Rice" recipes, include both ground beef and ground pork sausage. About half the "Dirty Rice" recipes, and half the "Cajun Rice" recipes, include either a package of chicken giblets (includes chicken liver, heart, and gizzard), or chicken livers as one of the meats. Sometimes a turkey giblet package is used instead of chicken just because it is available.

The recommended meat for this recipe is any one of the following:
1. 1 pound lean ground beef.
2. 1/2 pound lean ground beef and 1/2 pound ground pork sausage.
3. Either of the above plus a chicken giblet package or 1/4 c. chicken livers.

Imitation Popeye's Cajun Rice: Decrease the meat to 3/4 pound of ground beef without any pork sausage or chicken livers. Only use 1/4 cup diced onion and 1/3 cup finely diced bell peppers. Use 1/3 teaspoon dried celery flakes instead of fresh celery. Increase the Cajun seasoning to 1 teaspoon and add 1/4 teaspoon black pepper. Include the optional 1/3 teaspoon garlic powder. Use water to cook the rice.

Instructions: Put the onions in a nonstick skillet. Crumble the ground beef and the optional ground pork sausage into the skillet with the onions. Cook over medium heat until the meat is no longer pink, stirring frequently. Use the edge of the stirring spoon to break the meat into smaller pieces as it is cooking. Drain off the grease. Reduce heat to low. Add the bell peppers, celery, Cajun seasoning. If desired, add the optional garlic.

Cook over low heat, stirring frequently, while the rice is cooking in a different pot.

If using chicken giblets or chicken livers then rinse them under faucet water. Put the heart and gizzard in one nonstick saucepan and cover with water. Cook over low heat about 20 minutes or until tender. Pat the liver dry with a paper towel. Sprinkle a tiny bit of salt on the liver. Melt 1 teaspoon butter in a different nonstick saucepan over low heat, add the liver, and cook about 4 minutes, and then turn over and cook the other side about 4 minutes, or until tender and completely done. Remove all the chicken parts from their saucepans and dice into small pieces. Add to the other ingredients at the last step when everything is combined together.

Cook the white rice in the desired liquid following the white rice cooking instructions at the beginning of this chapter.

Add the salt and black pepper to the meat mixture and stir.

Combine the cooked white rice with the cooked meat mixture and toss until everything is well blended. Serve immediately.

Indian Rice (4 Servings)

---

2 T. butter	1/2 tsp. iodized salt
opt. 3 T. almonds, slivered	1/4 tsp. fine grind black pepper
1/4 c. onions, finely diced	1 c. white rice
1/2 tsp. ground cinnamon	2 c. water
1/4 tsp. turmeric, or rosemary	opt. 1/3 c. raisins

Melt butter in 2-quart nonstick saucepan over medium heat.

If desired, add the almonds and cook for 3 to 4 minutes, stirring constantly, or until golden brown. Use a slotted spoon to transfer the almonds onto a paper towel to drain.

Add onion to the saucepan and cook for 3 minutes, stirring constantly.

Add cinnamon, turmeric (or rosemary), salt, and black pepper, and stir. Add water and heat to boiling. Gradually trickle in the white rice so the water does not stop boiling. Reduce heat to low. Cover pot and simmer for 15 to 18 minutes without stirring until all the water is absorbed. Fluff the rice with a fork.

If desired, stir in the raisins (if you are not using the almonds).

Replace the cover on the pot and let stand 5 minutes. Then serve.

Rice Pilaf (4 Servings)

2 T. butter	2 c. chicken broth
1/2 c. onions, diced	1/4 tsp. iodized salt
1 c. white rice	1/4 tsp. fine grind black pepper

Optional (select none, 1, or 2 of the following):

1/2 c. green peas	1 (4 oz.) can mushroom pieces, drained
1/2 c. celery, chopped	1/2 c. bell pepper, finely diced
1/2 c. carrots, shredded	1/4 c. raisins

Optional Bell Pepper: If using green peas then use a red bell pepper. But if using carrots then use a green bell pepper.

Melt butter in a medium size nonstick saucepan over medium heat. Add onions and cook for 3 minutes stirring constantly. Add rice and cook 3 minutes stirring constantly. Add chicken broth, salt, and black pepper, and stir.

If desired, add the green peas and stir.

Bring to a boil, stirring occasionally. Reduce heat to low.

If desired, add celery, carrots, and/or drained mushroom pieces, and stir to combine the ingredients.

Cover pot, and cook for 16 minutes without removing the cover from the pot. Remove cover and fluff the rice with a fork.

If desired, add the finely diced bell peppers and/or raisins, and toss with the rice.

Replace the cover on the pot and let stand for 6 minutes. Then serve.

Rice-A-Roni (4 Servings)

1 c. angel hair pasta

Follow the recipe for Rice Pilaf but add 1 cup of angel hair pasta noodles broken into small pieces one-inch or shorter. Brown the broken pasta noodles in the butter with the diced onions at the beginning of the above Rice Pilaf recipe.

Chapter Twenty-Seven
Salads, Salad Dressings, and Dips

Croutons

3 slices of bread, cubed
6 T. butter, unsalted

1/2 tsp. garlic powder
1/2 tsp. onion powder

Preheat oven to 325°F.
Use a nonstick cookie sheet, or spray a cookie sheet with nonstick oil.
The crust may be left on each slice of bread or the crust may be cut off depending on your preference. Use a sharp knife to cut the slices of bread into 1/2 inch cubes. Place the bread cubes on a cookie sheet and bake at 325°F for 15 minutes or until the cubes are dry and a light brown.
Melt the butter in a skillet over low heat. Add the garlic powder and the onion powder to the melted butter and stir well. Add the dry bread cubes and toss to coat them with the butter and seasoning. Cook over low heat until the bread cubes are crisp.

Blue Cheese Dip

1/2 c. (2 oz.) blue cheese, crumbled
1 1/2 c. mayonnaise
1/2 tsp. lemon juice
1/2 tsp. Worcestershire sauce

1/2 tsp. garlic powder
1/2 tsp. onion powder
1/2 tsp. iodized salt
1/4 tsp. fine grind black pepper

Cheese: Gorgonzola cheese may be used instead of blue cheese.
Combine blue cheese, mayonnaise, lemon juice, and Worcestershire sauce in a medium bowl. Use your spoon to crush the crumbled blue cheese so the blue cheese blends with the other ingredients as you stir. (Or use a blender.) Then add the garlic, onion, salt, and black pepper and mix well.

Blue Cheese Dressing

1 c. (4 oz.) blue cheese, crumbled
1 c. mayonnaise
1/4 c. half & half
1/4 c. sour cream
1/2 tsp. Worcestershire sauce

1/2 tsp. dry mustard
1/2 tsp. garlic powder
1/2 tsp. onion powder
1/2 tsp. iodized salt
1/4 tsp. fine grind black pepper

Cheese: Gorgonzola cheese may be used instead of blue cheese.
Divide the crumbled blue cheese in half.

Combine 1/2 cup (2 oz.) blue cheese, mayonnaise, half & half, sour cream, and Worcestershire sauce in a medium bowl. Use your spoon to crush the crumbled blue cheese so the blue cheese blends with the other ingredients as you stir. (Or use a blender.) Then add the mustard, garlic, onion, salt, and black pepper and mix well. Finally had the remaining 1/2 cup (2 oz.) crumbled blue cheese and gently mix throughout the dressing. May be used immediately but most people prefer cold blue cheese dressing. Refrigerate any leftover dressing.

French Dressing

1 c. oil	1/2 tsp. onion powder
3/4 c. ketchup	1 1/2 tsp. lemon juice
1/2 c. granulated sugar	1 tsp. paprika
1/2 c. white vinegar	1 tsp. iodized salt

Oil: Extra virgin olive oil, or corn oil,, or canola oil, or vegetable oil.

Add the oil, ketchup, sugar, vinegar, onion powder, lemon juice, paprika, and salt into a blender and blend until smooth. Refrigerate in an airtight container for one hour or until needed.

Italian Dressing

1 tsp. Italian seasoning	1/4 tsp. fine grind black pepper
1 tsp. granulated sugar	1/3 c. oil
1 tsp. garlic powder	1/4 c. vinegar
1/2 tsp. dried parsley flakes	2 T. water
1/2 tsp. iodized salt	1 tsp. grated Parmesan cheese

Italian Seasoning: If you don't have Italian seasoning then substitute equal amounts of onion powder, dried oregano, dried thyme, dried basil, and celery salt.

Oil: Extra virgin olive oil, or canola oil, or vegetable oil.

Vinegar: Red wine vinegar, or white vinegar, or cider vinegar, or balsamic vinaigrette.

Parmesan Cheese: Parmesan cheese or Romano cheese.

Italian Dressing Instructions: In a medium bowl combine the Italian seasoning, sugar, garlic, parsley, salt, and black pepper. Mix well. Add the oil, vinegar, and water and mix well. Add the cheese and stir. Pour the dressing into a small jar (jelly jar or mason jar), attach the lid, and refrigerate at least overnight to give the flavors a chance to blend together. Shake the jar of dressing immediately before using because the ingredients have a tendency to separate inside the jar.

Imitation Olive Garden Salad Dressing

3/4 c. canola oil
5 T. white vinegar
1/4 c. water
1 1/2 T. mayonnaise
1 pkg. Italian dressing mix
1/2 tsp. Italian seasoning

1/2 tsp. granulated sugar
1/4 tsp. garlic powder
1/2 tsp. iodized salt
1/4 tsp. fine grind black pepper
opt. 1 drop yellow food coloring
opt. Parmesan or Romano cheese

In a medium bowl add the oil, vinegar, water, and mayonnaise and stir until well blended and there are no clumps of mayonnaise. Add the Italian dressing mix and the Italian seasoning and stir until well blended. Add the sugar, garlic powder, salt, and black pepper and stir until well blended. If you desire for the dressing to be yellow then add 1 drop of yellow food coloring and stir to blend completely. Refrigerate for at least 2 hours to give the flavors a chance to blend together.

Optional Salad Garnish: After putting the salad dressing on your salad, you may top with 4 tablespoons shredded Parmesan cheese, or 4 tablespoons shredded Romano cheese, or a combination of half of each type of cheese.

Any leftover salad dressing can be stored in an airtight container in the refrigerator for up to 10 days.

Ranch Dip and Dressing

1 tsp. parsley
1 tsp. onion powder
1/2 tsp. dill weed
1/2 tsp. chives
1/4 tsp. garlic powder

1/4 tsp. iodized salt
1/8 tsp. fine grind black pepper
1/2 c. mayonnaise
1/2 c. sour cream
3/8 c. buttermilk

Thick Dip or Thin Dressing: The above quantities yield a good vegetable dip. To make the dip into a thinner salad dressing add an additional 1/8 cup buttermilk and stir. To make the salad dressing even thinner add another 1/8 cup buttermilk and stir.

Ranch Dry Mix: Combine the parsley, onion powder, dill weed, chives, garlic powder, salt, and black pepper in a small bowl. Stir until everything is well blended. You may save this dry mixture in an airtight container until you need it, or you may use it immediately.

Ranch Dressing: Mix the mayonnaise, sour cream, and buttermilk in a medium bowl until well blended. Add the above ranch dry mix and stir until the dry mix is evenly distributed throughout the mixture.

Or you can put everything into a blender and blend on a low setting until the dressing is smooth.

Refrigerate the dressing for at least three hours and it will thicken and the flavors will merge together. It is even better a day or two later. The dressing may be stored in the refrigerator for two weeks (or longer) depending on the expiration dates of the original mayonnaise, buttermilk, and sour cream that are used.

Optional Flavor Variation: Add a tablespoon of Parmesan cheese and/ or a teaspoon of lemon juice (or red wine vinegar).

Russian Dressing (1/2 cup)

1/3 c. mayonnaise	2 tsp. onion powder
2 T. chili sauce	3 tsp. dill pickle finely minced
1 tsp. horseradish	1/2 tsp. iodized salt
1/2 tsp. Worcestershire sauce	1/4 tsp. fine grind black pepper

In a small bowl combine the mayonnaise, chili sauce, horseradish, and Worcestershire sauce and stir well. Add the onion, dill pickle, salt, and black pepper, and mix well the distribute the ingredients throughout the dressing. Use immediately of store in an airtight container in the refrigerator.

Thousand Island Dressing

1 egg, hard boiled	2 T. sweet pickle relish
3/4 c. mayonnaise	1/4 tsp. iodized salt
3 T. ketchup	1/8 tsp. fine grind black pepper

Hard boil the egg for seven minutes. Allow to cool and remove the shell. Dice the egg into very tiny pieces and then crush the pieces with the edge of a spoon. In a small bowl add the crushed egg, mayonnaise, ketchup, pickle relish, salt, and black pepper and stir until everything is well blended. May be used immediately but most people prefer cold thousand island dressing. Refrigerate any leftover dressing.

Broccoli and Raisin Salad (4 Servings)

2 1/2 c. broccoli florets, fresh   1/4 c. carrots, finely shredded
1/4 c. onions, finely diced   1/8 c. cheddar cheese, grated

Last Minute Ingredients:
1/3 c. raisins   opt. 1/4 c. pecans, crushed
2 slices bacon, crisp, crumbled

Dressing:
1/3 c. of your favorite salad dressing

Rinse the broccoli florets under cold faucet water. Cut the florets off the main stems. Break any extremely large florets in half.

In a large bowl toss the broccoli with the onions, carrots, and cheese.

Just before serving, add the raisins, crisp crumbled bacon, and if desired, the crushed pecans. (Note: Do not add the raisins, bacon, or the optional pecans, until the salad is ready to be served or they will become soggy.)

Toss to blend everything together. Serve cold.

If everyone likes the same type of salad dressing then you can mix your favorite salad dressing into the salad. However, if different people like different flavors of salad dressing then allow each person to add the salad dressing they prefer.

Caesar Salad with Caesar Dressing (6 Servings)

1 head Romaine lettuce

Caesar Dressing:
3/4 c. extra virgin olive oil   1/4 T. dry mustard
3 T. red wine vinegar   1/4 T. garlic powder
1 tsp. Worcestershire sauce   1 T. lemon juice
1/2 tsp. iodized salt   1 egg

Garnish:
1/4 c. grated Parmesan cheese   freshly ground black pepper
1 1/2 c. croutons

Lettuce: Separate the lettuce leaves and rinse thoroughly. Dry the lettuce leaves between paper towels or clean dish towels. Refrigerate for at least one hour until the leaves are crisp.
Caesar Dressing: Combine oil, vinegar, Worcestershire, salt, mustard, garlic, and lemon juice and mix thoroughly to make the dressing.

Egg: Boil 3 cups of water in a small saucepan. "Coddle" the egg by carefully lowering the egg into the boiling water with a spoon and boil for 1 minute. Remove the egg and let the egg cool. Discard the boiling water. Crack the egg and discard the shell. Whisk the egg into the dressing until it is well blended.

Caesar Salad Instructions: Remove the lettuce from the refrigerator and tear the lettuce leaves into pieces about 3 inches long. Arrange the leaves in the bottom of a shallow salad bowl. Top with the grated cheese, croutons, and some freshly ground black pepper. Serve immediately.

Chef's Salad (2 Servings)

3 c. salad greens, bite size	2 slices cooked ham
6 cherry tomatoes, halved	2 slices cooked turkey
4 thin slices of cucumber	1 slice Swiss cheese
1 radish, sliced	1 slice cheddar cheese
1/4 c. celery, sliced	4 strips bacon, cooked, crumbled
1 slice of onion, 1/4 inch thick	10 croutons
2 eggs, hard boiled, sliced	salad dressing of your choice

A Chef's Salad is usually a complete one-dish meal and it is extremely versatile. Different chefs do not agree on exactly what should be in it. Therefore the above list of ingredients should be adjusted to your specific tastes and you should omit anything you do not enjoy and you may add something different that you do enjoy. Although freshly sliced mushrooms are usually not included in a Chef's Salad, you may add 2 or 3 mushrooms if you wish.

Deletions: Except for the salad greens, most people will not miss the omission of one or two of the other salad ingredients.

Salad Greens: Use a small bag of salad greens, or any combination of Boston, bibb, red or green leaf lettuce, or iceberg head lettuce. Rinse and dry the lettuce leaves. Tear the lettuce by hand into bite size strips about 3 inches long.

Tomatoes: If you do not have cherry tomatoes, then you may use a Roma tomato, or a full size tomato, cut into smaller bite size pieces.

Onion: A white, yellow, or purple onion may be used. Cut a 1/4 thick slice out of the onion, and then separate the slice into rings. Cut each ring in half.

Ham: A thin slice of black forest ham, honey ham, or smoked ham, cut into strips about 2 inches long and 1/4 inch wide.

Turkey: A thin slice of oven roasted turkey, or honey roasted turkey, or smoked turkey, or mesquite smoked turkey, cut into strips about 2 inches long and 1/4 inch wide.

Other Meats: Ham and turkey are the traditional meats used in a Chef's Salad. However, you may add or substitute chicken (rotisserie seasoned chicken or chipotle chicken) or roast beef. The thin meat slices should be cut into strips about 2 inches long and 1/4 inch wide.

Bacon: The bacon is optional. It can be bacon bits or strips of bacon that have been cooked and crumbled into small pieces.

Cheese: Any two different types of cheese may be used. A good substitute for Swiss cheese is provolone cheese. A good substitute for cheddar cheese is Colby Jack cheese. Other options are muenster cheese or pepper jack cheese or something else. The cheese may be shredded, or you can cut a thin slice of cheese into pieces about 2 inches long and 1/4 inch wide.

Salad Dressing: Each person should choose their own salad dressing. Common choices are ranch, thousand island, blue cheese, or oil and vinegar.

Chef's Salad Instructions: Arrange the lettuce greens in the bottom of a salad bowl. Add the tomatoes, cucumber slices, radishes, celery, and onion pieces on top of the lettuce. Alternate the sliced eggs, ham, turkey, Swiss cheese, and cheddar cheese like the spokes on a wheel around the top of the salad, partially overlapping as necessary. Sprinkle the bacon and the croutons on top. Serve with the salad dressing of your choice. Allow each person to individually add freshly ground black pepper if desired. (Note: Everything in the Chef's Salad should be bite size and a person should be able to eat the salad with a fork. A knife should not be needed to reduce the size of anything in the salad.)

Buffet Style Chef's Salad: Instead of combining the salad ingredients yourself, you can arrange all the ingredients in a buffet style and allow each person to create their own special version of a Chef's Salad.

Fruit Salad (5 Cups)

1/2 c. strawberries, sliced	1/2 c. cantaloupe, chunks
1/2 c. seedless grapes, halved	1/2 c. honeydew, chunks
1/2 c. apples, peeled, sliced	1/2 c. blueberries
1/2 c. peaches, peeled, sliced	1/2 c. fresh pineapple chunks
1/2 c. pears, peeled, sliced	1 firm banana, sliced

Combine all the above fruits and refrigerate for 4 hours. May be served with or without the optional Fruit Salad Cream Dressing (next recipe).

Note: Fruit salad is very flexible and you can omit fruits, add fruits, and change the amount of each fruit to suit your family's taste preferences. The above recipe uses 10 different fruits but you only need about 4 different fruits to make a reasonable Fruit Salad.

Fruit Salad Cream Dressing

1 (8 oz.) pkg. cream cheese   1/4 c. granulated sugar
1 c. powdered sugar   2 or 3 T. lemon juice
1 c. whipping cream

Allow the cream cheese to come to room temperature until it softens. In a medium bowl, blend the cream cheese with the powdered sugar.

In a different bowl, combine the whipping cream and the granulated sugar and whip until soft peaks form. Add to the first bowl with the cream cheese and stir. Add 1 tablespoon lemon juice and stir. Continue to gradually add a little more lemon juice until the dressing reaches the desired cream consistency. May be used as a dip for individual fruit pieces, or it may be poured over a Fruit Salad.

Garden Green Salad (2 Servings)

3 c. salad greens, bite size   1/4 bell pepper, sliced into rings
2 tomatoes, cut into wedges   1 slice of onion, 1/4 inch thick
1/4 cucumber, sliced   1 T. grated Parmesan cheese
1 carrot, shredded   12 croutons

Salad Greens: Use a small bag of salad greens, or any combination of Boston, bibb, red or green leaf lettuce, or iceberg head lettuce. Rinse and dry the lettuce leaves. Tear the lettuce by hand into bite size strips about 3 inches long.

Tomatoes: Cut into wedges.

Cucumber: Cut 1/8 inch thick slices off 1/4 of a cucumber.

Carrot: Buy shredded carrots or rinse a carrot and cut off its top. Shave off and discard its outer skin, and shred the carrot into long thin pieces.

Green Bell Pepper: Cut two 1/4 thick slices out of the pepper, remove and discard the inner membrane and the seeds. Cut each ring into quarters.

Onion: A white, yellow, or purple onion may be used. Cut a 1/4 thick slice out of the onion, and then separate the slice into rings. Cut each ring in half.

Instructions: Place the salad leaves in the bottom of a salad bowl. Add the tomatoes, cucumber, carrot, green bell pepper, and onion and toss the ingredients to mix them together. Top with Parmesan cheese and croutons. Serve with your favorite salad dressing.

Greek Salad (2 Servings)

Salad:

1/8 c. red onion, 1/4 inch rings
1 c. cucumber, quartered slices
1 c. cherry tomatoes, halved
1/8 c. pitted black olives, halved

1/4 c. feta cheese, crumbled
opt. 1/2 c. green bell pepper, sliced
opt. 1 1/2 c. Romaine lettuce, torn

Dressing:

2 T. extra virgin olive oil
1 T. red wine vinegar
opt. 1 T. lemon juice, fresh

1/2 tsp. dried oregano
1/8 tsp. iodized salt
1/16 tsp. fine grind black pepper

Red Onion: Cut two 1/4 inch thick slices. Save the rest of the onion for another use inside a zipper plastic bag. Cut each slice in half across its center. Separate into individual ring pieces. Put the small pieces into a small bowl of cold water with ice cubes and allow them to soak for 10 minutes to help reduce the sharpness of the onion. Remove and pat dry with a paper towel.

Long Thin Cucumber: A long thin almost seedless English cucumber is recommended. Cut the cucumber in half at its center and save half the cucumber for another use inside a zipper plastic bag. Peel the cucumber and discard the peel. Cut cucumber into 3/8 inch thick slices. Cut each slice into 4 quarters.

Cherry Tomatoes: Rinse under cool tap water. Slice each cherry tomato in half.

Pitted Black Olives: Kalamata black olives are recommended. Slice each pitted black olive in half.

Feta Cheese: Crumble the feta cheese.

Optional Green Bell Pepper: Cut in half from top to bottom and save half the pepper for another use inside a zipper plastic bag. Remove and discard the inner bitter tasting membrane and the seeds. Rinse under cool tap water. Cut into 1/4 inch thick slices. Pat dry with a paper towel.

Optional Romaine Lettuce: Rinse the individual lettuce leaves under cool tap water. Pat dry with a paper towel. Tear into bite size pieces.

Dressing Instructions: Combine the oil, vinegar, and optional lemon juice in a bowl and stir. Add the oregano, salt, and pepper and stir.

Greek Salad Instructions: A Greek salad should have at least one or both of the two optional items (bell pepper and/or lettuce). Combine the onion, cucumber, tomatoes, olives, and at least one of the two optional items (bell pepper and/or lettuce) in a large bowl and toss. Pour the dressing over the salad and sprinkle the feta cheese on top.

Imitation Olive Garden House Salad (6 Servings)

1 (12 oz.) bag salad blend
6 onion rings, red or purple
6 black olives, pitted, whole
3 Roma tomatoes, quartered
3 mild pepperoncini peppers, chopped

1/2 c. croutons
1/4 c. Parmesan cheese, grated
opt. freshly grated black pepper
salad dressing, your choice

Salad Blend: The appropriate mixture of different types of lettuce is in the "Dole American Salad Blend" bag. It is a combination of iceberg lettuce and Romaine lettuce, with a small quantity of grated carrots, chopped red cabbage, and radishes (either sliced or slivered). A bag of "Iceberg Garden Salad Mix" is also acceptable.**Onion:** Slice the onion very thin and then separate the onion rings.

Pepperoncini Peppers: Pepperoncini is the English word for the Italian word peperoncini, which are hot chili peppers. If you enjoy hot peppers, then you may substitute jalapeño peppers. Or you may substitute a sweet banana pepper, or a bell pepper. The Italian word for sweet peppers is peperoni.

Dressing: An imitation Olive Garden house dressing is in this chapter. Or you may use the dressing of your choice.

Instructions: Put a large salad bowl in the freezer for 30 minutes and let it get cold. This will enhance the crispy fresh texture and flavor of the salad.

Empty the bag of "salad blend" into the cold bowl. Add the onion rings, olives, tomatoes, pepperoncinis, and croutons. Toss the salad.

Serve immediately with the Parmesan cheese and black pepper as a garnish for those who want them. Allow each person to select the salad dressing they prefer.

Italian Antipasto Salad (2 Servings)

3 oz. romaine lettuce, torn
3 oz. baby spinach leaves
1/2 c. artichoke hearts, sliced
1/2 c. salami, cubed
2 tomatoes, coarse chopped
1/4 c. olives, pitted, sliced

1/4 c. green bell pepper
1/4 c. red bell pepper
1/3 c. provolone cheese, cubed
1/2 tsp. iodized salt
1/4 tsp. fine grind black pepper
1/4 c. Italian dressing

Italian cooks do not agree on what should be in an antipasto salad. However, the above ingredients do yield a very nice antipasto salad that can be enjoyed by most people, except perhaps for native born Italians who have a lifetime of experience eating true 100% Italian foods.

Lettuce: Tear into bite size pieces.

Artichoke Hearts: Use part of a jar of marinated artichoke hearts, sliced and drained.

Salami: Either salami or pepperoni, cut into 1/4 inch cubes.

Tomatoes: Either 2 large tomatoes, or 4 Roma tomatoes, or 12 cherry tomatoes. Coarse chop the large tomatoes and the Roma tomatoes but only cut the cherry tomatoes in half.

Olives: An equal amount of black and green olives, or use Kalamata olives. Cut each olive in half or slice each olive into 3 or 4 pieces.

Peppers: A combination of two sweet peppers, or one sweet pepper and one hot pepper. Cut the peppers in quarters. Remove and discard the inner membrane and seeds. Rinse the peppers. Cut the peppers into thin strips about 1.5 inches long. May be used uncooked, or they may be cooked in a skillet over low heat for 2 or 3 minutes. Allow to cool and then chill in the refrigerator.

Provolone Cheese: Cut the cheese into 1/4 inch cubes.

Italian Dressing: Either Italian dressing or red wine vinaigrette.

Antipasto Salad Instructions: In a large bowl combine the lettuce, spinach, and artichoke hearts and toss. Add the salami, tomatoes, and olives and toss. Add the peppers and cheese and toss. Divide into two salad bowls. Allow each person to add salt, freshly ground black pepper, and Italian dressing as desired.

Mexican Avocado Tossed Salad (4 Servings) with Spicy Oil & Vinegar Dressing

Salad:

2 c. iceberg lettuce, torn	8 strips cooked bacon, crumbled
2 c. Romaine lettuce, torn	1/4 c. purple onion, sliced, separated
4 Roma tomatoes, 1/4" cubes	1/4 c. Pepper Jack cheese, 1/4" cubes
1 large avocado, peeled, 1/4" cubes	

Tear the iceberg lettuce and the Romaine lettuce into bite size pieces about 2 inches long. Put in a large serving bowl and toss. Cut the tomatoes into 1/4 inch cubes and add to the salad. Cut the avocado in half around the pit. Grab one half of the avocado in each hand and twist in opposite directions and pull apart. Remove the pit with a spoon or a knife. Remove the peel. Cut the avocado into 1/4 inch cubes and add to the salad. Crumble the cooked bacon and add to the salad and toss the salad again. Cut two 1/4 inch thick slices out of the onion. Separate the slices into individual rings. Cut each onion ring into four pieces. Add to the salad. Cut the Pepper Jack cheese into 1/4 inch cubes. Add to the salad and toss again.

Prepare the dressing (on top of the next page) in a separate bowl.

Spicy Oil & Vinegar Dressing:
1/4 c. canola oil or olive oil   1 tsp. iodized salt
1/8 c. vinegar   1/4 tsp. fine grind black pepper
1 T. Tabasco sauce or salsa

Combine oil, vinegar, Tabasco sauce, salt, and pepper and stir until the dressing is well blended.

When ready to serve, pour the dressing over the salad and toss again to distribute the dressing throughout the salad. Serve immediately.

Note: The salad should be eaten immediately after the dressing is added because the dressing will gradually reduce the crispness of the salad.

Mexican Tortilla Chip Salad (4 Servings) With Avocado Dressing

Salad:
6 c. iceberg or bibb lettuce   1/4 c. black olives, sliced
12 cherry tomatoes, quartered   1/4 c. shredded sharp cheddar cheese
1/4 c. green olives, sliced   1 c. tortilla chips, crushed

Tear the lettuce into bite size pieces about 2 inches long. Put in a large serving bowl. Cut each cherry tomato into four pieces and add to the salad. Slice the olives and add to the salad. Add the cheese and toss the salad to mix everything together. Prepare the following dressing.

Avocado Dressing:
1 medium avocado, ripe, peeled, mashed   1/2 tsp. garlic salt
1/4 cup finely shredded white onion   1/2 tsp. granulated sugar
1 T. lemon juice   1/2 c. canola oil

Cut the avocado in half around the pit. Grab one half of the avocado in each hand and twist in opposite directions and pull apart. Remove the pit with a spoon or a knife. Scoop out the inside flesh with a spoon and put in a bowl. Mash the avocado with a fork until creamy but with some very small chunks still remaining. Use the smallest slots on a vegetable shredder and shred 1/4 of a white onion above the avocado bowl so the onion and its juices fall into the avocado bowl. Add the lemon juice, garlic salt, sugar, and oil and stir until well blended.

When ready to serve, pour the dressing over the salad and toss again to distribute the dressing throughout the salad. Finally, add the crushed tortilla chips to the salad and toss again to distribute the chips throughout the salad. Serve immediately.

Note: This salad needs to be eaten immediately after the dressing and the chips are added because the dressing will gradually reduce the crispness of the salad and the tortilla chips.

Mexican Veggie Salad (4 Servings)
with Spicy Ranch Dressing

Salad:

2 c. Romaine lettuce, torn
1 c. endive lettuce, torn
1 can cooked black beans, chilled
1 can cooked sweet corn, chilled

3 Roma tomatoes, 1/4 inch cubes
1/4 c. celery, 1/4 inch cubes
1/4 c. shredded 4 Cheese Mexican
opt. 1 can (10 oz.) chicken chunks

Tear the Romaine lettuce and the endive lettuce into bite size pieces about 2 inches long. Put both in a large serving bowl and toss. Add the chilled black beans and the chilled sweet corn and toss again. Cut the tomatoes and the celery into 1/4 inch cubes and add to the salad and toss again. Add the cheese. If desired, open a small can of chicken breast white meat chunks, drain, and cut the larger chunks of chicken into 1/4 cubes. Toss the salad again. Prepare the following dressing.

Spicy Ranch Dressing:

1/4 c. ranch salad dressing
1/4 c. canola oil or olive oil

2 T. sour cream
1/4 c. salsa

In a separate bowl combine the ranch dressing, the oil, the sour cream and the salsa and stir until the dressing is well blended.

When ready to serve, pour the dressing over the salad and toss again to distribute the dressing throughout the salad. Serve immediately.

Note: This salad needs to be eaten immediately after the dressing is added because the dressing will gradually reduce the crispness of the salad.

Neptune Crab Salad (4 to 6 Servings)

1 lb. imitation fresh crab meat chunks
3/4 c. finely diced celery
opt. 1/8 c. chopped green onions
5/8 c. mayonnaise

3/4 T. lemon juice
1 tsp. dill
1/2 tsp. iodized salt
1/4 tsp. fine grind black pepper

Tear the crab meat into thin pieces or strips. In a large bowl combine the crab meat, celery, and green onions (optional) until well mixed.

In a separate bowl mix the mayonnaise, lemon juice, dill, salt, and black pepper until they are well blended into a smooth dressing. Then add the mayonnaise dressing to the crab meat bowl and toss until everything is evenly coated with the mayonnaise dressing. Serve chilled.

The salad be eaten by itself or served with your choice of crackers.

Pasta Salad (4 Servings)

1 lb. pasta noodles	1 (2.25 oz.) can black olives
2 large tomatoes	1/2 lb. pepperoni
1 bell pepper	4 oz. Caesar Italian dressing
1 small onion	1/2 lb. mozzarella cheese

Pasta Noodles: Either bow tie pasta or tri-color spiral pasta for visual appeal. Cook pasta in salted boiling water until "molto al dente" (just a little undercooked so the pasta can more easily absorb some of the dressing later and not get soggy). Rinse the cooked hot pasta under cold water and then drain.

Tomatoes: Either 2 large tomatoes, or 4 Roma tomatoes, or 12 cherry tomatoes. Dice the large tomatoes and the Roma tomatoes but only cut the cherry tomatoes in half.

Bell Pepper: Either a green, or red, or yellow bell pepper. Cut the pepper in quarters. Remove and discard the inner membrane and seeds. Rinse the pepper. Chop the pepper.

Onion: Either a white, yellow, or purple onion. Remove the outside layer of the onion and then dice the onion.

Black Olives: Slice the black olives. If some people in your family do not care for black olives, then keep them separate and offer them in a small bowl placed beside the pasta salad.

Cheese: Either mozzarella cheese, or Swiss cheese, or provolone cheese, or Pepper Jack cheese. Cut the cheese into 1/4 inch cubes.

Pepperoni: Either pizza style sliced pepperoni (cut each round slice in half), or diced 1/4 inch cubes of cooked ham, or diced 1/4 cubes of cooked salami.

Pasta Salad Instructions: In a large bowl combine the pasta, tomatoes, pepper, onion, black olives, and pepperoni. Toss until well mixed. Pour the Caesar Italian Dressing over the pasta salad. Toss the salad again to distribute the dressing. Cover the bowl and refrigerate at least overnight or for up to 48 hours. Add the cheese when ready to serve so the cheese does not get soggy. Allow each person to add freshly ground black pepper, if desired.

Potato Salad (4 Servings)

3 cups potatoes, peeled, cubed
1/2 c. mayonnaise
1 1/2 tsp. yellow mustard
2 tsp. vinegar, white or cider
1 1/2 tsp. granulated sugar
1/2 tsp. iodized salt

1/8 tsp. fine grind black pepper
1/2 c. celery, diced
1/4 onion, finely diced
2 eggs, hard boiled
opt. 1 T. sweet pickle relish
opt. paprika sprinkled as garnish

Potatoes: Red skin potatoes are recommended. However, baking potatoes may be used. Peel the potatoes and discard the peels. Cut the potatoes into 1/2 inch cubes.

Instructions: Put the potato cubes in a medium nonstick pot and add water until it is 1 inch above the potatoes. Add a pinch of salt to the water. Bring to a boil over medium heat. Reduce heat to medium low and cook, uncovered, for 10 to 15 minutes or until the potato cubes are done when pierced with a fork but still firm. Drain the potatoes.

In a medium bowl, add mayonnaise, mustard, vinegar, and sugar and stir until well blended. Sprinkle in the salt and black pepper and stir until well blended. Add the celery and onions and mix gently.

Optional Pickle Relish: If desired, mix in the optional sweet pickle relish. Or add diced dill pickles instead.

Consistency: If a chunky potato salad is desired then add the cooked cubed potatoes and toss gently with the other ingredients. However, if a smoother potato salad is desire then mash the cooked cubed potatoes with a fork and then stir into the other ingredients.

Hard Boiled Eggs: The eggs may be chopped or sliced as you prefer. Add chopped eggs now and mix gently. Or wait and place sliced eggs on top of the finished potato salad just before sprinkling with paprika.

Serve: Some prefer room temperature potato salad. And some prefer chilled potato salad. If everyone likes it the same way then serve it that way. Or divide the potato salad into two bowls, refrigerate one bowl, and allow the other bowl to remain at room temperature. However, any leftover potato salad must be refrigerated in a covered container.

Optional Paprika: If desired, sprinkle a little paprika over the top over the potato salad.

Russian Garden Salad (4 Servings)

Salad:

12 Romaine lettuce leaves, torn   1/3 c. onion, sliced, separated
4 tomatoes, chopped   4 radishes, sliced
1/2 cucumber, sliced   1/4 cup fresh parsley, chopped

Put torn lettuce leaves in large bowl. Add chopped tomatoes and sliced cucumber. Cut onion into 1/4 inch thick slices and separate slices into rings. Cut each ring in four pieces. Add onion pieces to the salad. Add sliced radishes and chopped parsley. Toss the salad to mix ingredients.

Dressing:

1/2 c. sour cream   1/2 tsp. iodized salt
1 T. extra virgin olive oil   1/4 tsp. fine grind black pepper
1 T. lemon juice

In a small bowl combine sour cream, oil, lemon juice, salt, and black pepper. Stir to mix all the ingredients. Refrigerate until needed.

When ready to serve, pour dressing over the salad and toss again.

Strawberry and Spinach Salad (4 Servings)

Dressing:

1/4 c. extra virgin olive oil   1/4 c. fresh strawberries, sliced
1/4 c. balsamic vinegar   1/4 tsp. iodized salt
2 T. granulated sugar   1/8 tsp. fine grind black pepper

Strawberries: Frozen strawberries may be used in the dressing.
Dressing: Combine oil, vinegar, sugar, strawberries, salt, and black pepper in a blender and purée. Refrigerate dressing for one hour.

Salad:

10 oz. fresh baby spinach   1/4 c. nuts (see below)
3 c. fresh strawberries, sliced   opt. 1/4 c. cheese, crumbled
opt. 1/4 c. red or purple onion slices

Spinach: If baby spinach is not available then regular spinach may be used but tear the large leaves into bite size pieces.
Fruit: Do not use frozen strawberries. You may substitute mandarin oranges or pineapple chunks for fresh strawberries. You may also add blueberries and/or sliced bananas in addition to the strawberries.
Nuts: Blanched slivered almonds, or chopped pecans or walnuts.
Cheese: Goat cheese, or feta cheese, or blue cheese, or a combination.
Salad: In a large bowl toss the spinach, fruit, onions, nuts, and cheese. Refrigerate 15 minutes before serving. Toss with dressing when served.

Chapter Twenty-Eight
Sandwiches

Beef Tex-Mex Sandwich (Two Sandwiches)
---

1 can (12 oz.) roast beef with gravy
1 tsp. Tex-Mex dry seasoning mix
2 T. warm water
1/4 tsp. iodized salt
1/8 tsp. fine grind black pepper
2 sandwich buns (see below)
4 slices cheese (see below)

opt. 1/4 c. onion, slices or diced
opt. 4 slices of tomato
opt. lettuce as desired
opt. 2 T. sliced black olives
opt. 2 T. sour cream
opt. 2 T. mayonnaise
opt. 2 tsp. hot sauce or salsa

opt. pepper, such as banana, bell, cayenne, chipote, or jalapeño, sliced

Gourmet Delight: A Tex-Mex sandwich can be a true gourmet delight if you will allow each person to create the sandwich exactly the way they prefer by putting the optional items on a buffet style side bar.

Roast Beef with Gravy: Different brands of canned roast beef have different amounts of gravy and fat. A brand with no or almost no fat is recommended. Less gravy is recommended because if the can contains more gravy then it will contain less meat. A Tex-Mex sandwich should be a meat sandwich with minimal gravy. If you wish you may drain the gravy off the beef and not use any gravy.

Tex-Mex Dry Seasoning Mix: If you wish you can make your own using the recipe in the sauces chapter of this cookbook. Or substitute taco seasoning or burrito seasoning or fajita seasoning mix.

Buns or Bread: A Tex-Mex sandwich is delicious if you use the type of bread you personally prefer, such as white, wheat, or sourdough. You may use 6 inch buns, or hamburger rolls, or sliced bread, either with or without seeds.

Cheese: 4 cheese Mexican, or Monterrey Jack, or Colby, or Colby Jack, or Pepper Jack, or whatever you prefer, either sliced or shredded.

Instructions: Heat roast beef and gravy in skillet over medium heat. Use the edge of the stirring spoon to break the big chucks of beef into smaller pieces. Dissolve Tex-Mex seasoning in warm water and add to the skillet. Add salt and black pepper and stir to evenly coat the meat.

Put the desired amount of cheese on the bread you prefer. If desired, toast the bread and melt the cheese briefly using your oven broiler.

Transfer the roast beef onto the sandwich bread. Add the optional items of your choice. Close the bun and enjoy the sandwich.

Barbecue Sandwich (One Sandwich)

2 T. barbecue sauce	1 bun, with or without seeds
Beef Barbecue:	
1/4 to 1/3 lb. beef (see below)	1/2 tsp. onion salt (or powder)
Pork Barbecue:	
1/4 to 1/3 lb. pork (see below)	1/4 tsp. fine grind black pepper
1/4 tsp. garlic salt	

Barbecue Sauce: Make your own barbecue sauce, or purchase your favorite brand of barbecue sauce at the grocery store. Restaurants that specialize in barbecue make their own unique sauce that appeals to their customers. This is one reason why some people praise the barbecue at one restaurant whereas other people praise the barbecue at other restaurants. Some restaurant chains sell their special barbecue sauce in small quantities at the local grocery store so you do not have to make your own barbecue sauce unless you want to. A recipe for homemade barbecue sauce is in the sauce chapter of this cookbook.

Meat: Either beef or pork is used. Some people prefer beef, some people prefer pork, and some people like both. Barbecue restaurants usually specialize in either beef or pork barbecue, and this is another reason why some people prefer a specific barbecue restaurant. And each barbecue restaurant uses its own method of preparing the meat, and seasoning the meat, and cooking or smoking the meat. All of these factors influence whether or not a person likes the barbecue at a specific barbecue restaurant.

Ground Meat or Shredded Meat: Barbecue is usually made from shredded meat. However, it can also be made from ground meat.

1. **Ground Meat:** Ground beef and ground pork have the following advantages: the percentage of fat in the ground beef is clearly shown on the package (usually between 7% to 25%), ground meat is easier to prepare, and it more completely absorbs the barbecue sauce and its flavor. Follow the "Preparation Instructions" below.

2. **Shredded Meat:** Purchase one boneless ribeye steak, or one boneless pork loin chop, that is between 1/4 to 1/3 pound. If you enjoy barbecue with a fatty flavor then buy a steak or chop with more fat on it. Begin by trimming off all the fat and either dice the fat into small pieces or discard the fat. Use a fork to hold the meat steady and use a sharp serrated knife to cut the meat into thin slices about 1/8 inch thick. Use a fork to hold each slice of meat and cut each slice into pieces about 1/8 inch wide. Each sliver of meat

should be no longer than 1-inch long. Now follow the "Preparation Instructions" below.

Preparations Instructions:

a. **Beef Barbecue Instructions:** In a bowl mix 2 tablespoons of barbecue sauce with 1/2 teaspoon of onion salt (or powder). Stir the sauce to blend the ingredients. Put the crumbled ground beef, or the shredded beef and if desired some or all the optional fat, in the sauce bowl and stir to blend with the beef. Put in the refrigerator for one hour to give the beef a chance to absorb the flavors.

b. **Pork Barbecue Instructions:** In a bowl mix 2 tablespoons of barbecue sauce, 1/4 teaspoon garlic salt, and 1/4 teaspoon black pepper. Stir the sauce to blend the ingredients. Put the crumbled ground pork, or the shredded pork loin and if desired some or all the optional fat, in the sauce bowl and stir to blend the sauce with the pork. Put in the refrigerator for one hour to give the pork a chance to absorb the flavors.

Cooking Instructions: Remove the meat from the refrigerator and cook the meat in its sauce in a nonstick skillet over low heat until the meat is done, stirring frequently. Put the cooked meat on the bottom of a bun. If desired, add the optional topping of your choice. Put the top on the bun and serve.

Optional Toppings: Room temperature coleslaw, or a slice of your favorite type of cheese (room temperature or melted).

Serve with: Potato chips, or coleslaw, or dill pickle, or sweet pickle.

Chicken Cordon Bleu Sandwich (One Sandwich)

Sandwich:

bread, see below
1/4 lb. chicken, see below
1 slice cooked ham, see below
1 slice cheese, see below

1/16 tsp. iodized salt
1/16 tsp. fine grind black pepper
opt. toppings of your choice

Optional Special Sauce:

2 T. mayonnaise
1/4 tsp. mustard, yellow or Dijon

1 1/2 tsp. pure honey
1 1/2 tsp. horseradish sauce

Trivia: In French the words "cordon bleu" literally mean "ribbon blue." In the 1700s during the reign of the Bourbon Kings it referred to the sky blue ribbon that was worn as an Emblem by the Knights of the Holy Ghost, the highest order of Knighthood in France. Later it was used to describe a cook that adhered to the highest standards of cookery. Today it is used to describe a dish of either veal or chicken, rolled, filled with cheese and either ham or bacon, breaded, and then either fried or baked.

Special Sauce Instructions: Combine mayonnaise, mustard, honey, and horseradish and stir until well blended. May be spread on the underside of the top half of the bun before putting the top on the sandwich.

Sandwich Bread: Select the type of bread you enjoy most. The bread may be seeded or unseeded. Some options include hamburger buns, sourdough rolls, Kaiser rolls, baguettes, French bread, or 2 slices of loaf bread (white or whole wheat).

Heated - Unheated: The sandwich may be served at room temperature, or it can be baked, or toasted under the broiler of an oven. If you use 2 slices of loaf bread then you could fry it in a skillet with some butter like a ham and cheese sandwich.

Chicken: The easiest option is to purchase frozen breaded chicken patties and cook according to the package instructions. If using 2 slices of loaf bread then you can use 3 slices of your favorite deli sliced chicken. Or you can use boneless skinless chicken tenders, and bread them and fry them yourself. The chicken should be about 1/2 inch thick and the size of the bread you are using. If you use fresh chicken tenders then rinse under cold tap water and remove all the pieces of fat. Dip each piece in milk and then coat with breadcrumbs. Put the chicken on a piece of nonstick aluminum foil in a baking pan. Preheat broiler. Allow to sit for 10 minutes. Broil for 2 or 3 minutes, rotating the baking pan so the chicken cooks evenly. Turn the chicken over and broil the other side the same way for 2 or 3 minutes or until the chicken is done and its internal temperature is at least 165°F.

Ham: Use your favorite deli sliced ham, or Canadian bacon.

Cheese: Use your favorite cheese but it should be a cheese that goes well with ham. The most common choice is Swiss. However, provolone, or mozzarella, or muenster, or cheddar, or something else will be fine as long as it is a cheese you really enjoy.

Optional Toppings: Whatever you enjoy. The special sauce is really good and if you wish to experiment then make it and taste a little of it to decide if it appeals to you. If you like it then use it, and if not then discard it. Other options include mayonnaise, or yellow mustard, or brown Dijon mustard, or Romaine lettuce, or watercress, or tomatoes, or onions, or pickles, or mushrooms.

Sandwich Instructions: Slice the bread into a top and bottom half. If you wish, put the top and bottom pieces crust side down on a baking pan and broil in an oven until lightly browned. Place the chicken on the bottom half of the bread. If desired, broil until the chicken is heated. Add a slice of folded ham. If desired, broil until the ham is heated. Add a slice of cheese that has been cut to fit the shape of the bread. If desired, broil until the cheese is melted. Remove from the oven. Add salt and black pepper as desired. If desired, spread the optional special sauce on the underside of the top half of the bun. If desired, add any optional toppings you desire. If you are serving a hot sandwich then sauté the sliced onion and/or sliced mushrooms before adding to the sandwich. Put the top on the sandwich and serve.

Recommended Side Dishes: Serve with potato chips and/or a dill pickle, or with fresh fruit.

Chicken Salad Sandwich, or Egg Salad Sandwich, or Ham Salad Sandwich, or Tuna Salad Sandwich, or Turkey Salad Sandwich (2 Sandwiches)

Salad: Select and make the salad of your choice following the appropriate recipe in the appetizer chapter in this cookbook.

Bread: Multigrain whole wheat bread is recommended but you may use the type of bread you prefer. You may select a hamburger bun (with or without seeds), a hotdog bun, a 6-inch long roll, or two slices of loaf bread.

Toasted: The sandwich bread may be toasted or not toasted. It is your choice.

Sandwich Instructions: Select the type of bread you prefer and toast it if you wish. Select the type of salad you prefer and put it on the bread. If you wish you may add torn lettuce leaves, sliced tomatoes, your choice of sliced cheese, thin rings of onion, bell pepper pieces, avocado slices, or something else on top of the salad inside the sandwich. Finally you may add mayonnaise, canola oil, salt, and/or black pepper as desired. May be eaten with your choice of chips or some other side item.

Hawaiian Ham & Cheese Sliders (4 Sandwiches)

4 Hawaiian Sweet Dinner Rolls	1/4 tsp. Worcestershire sauce
4 slices deli ham	1/3 tsp. onion powder
1 slice Swiss cheese, quartered	opt. 1/2 tsp. black poppy seeds
4 tsp. butter, barely melted	opt. 4 T. pineapple, finely diced
2/3 tsp. brown Dijon mustard	opt. 4 T. mayonnaise

King's Original Hawaiian Sweet Dinner Rolls: They are sold 4 per package and 12 per package. One person can easily eat two of these small sandwiches. Therefore plan on two or three small sandwiches per person.

Instructions: Very lightly grease or spray the inside of a baking dish. Separate the package of rolls into individual rolls. Slice the top half off the rolls and place the bottom half of the rolls in a nonstick baking pan. Fold the slices of ham in half and put one folded slice of ham on each roll. If necessary, trim the ham so it will fit on the bottom half of the roll. Cut one slice of Swiss cheese into 4 quarters and put 1/4 slice of cheese centered on top of each slice of ham. If desired, place a few small pieces of pineapple on each piece of cheese. Place the top half of the rolls back into position above the sandwiches.

In a bowl combine the barely melted butter, mustard, Worcestershire, and onion powder. If desired, add the optional black poppy seeds. Stir until well blended. Pour or brush the butter sauce on the tops of the sandwiches. Cover with nonstick aluminum foil.

Bake in a preheated 350°F oven, covered, for 12 minutes. Remove the foil and bake for another 3 to 5 minutes, or until the tops of the buns are lightly browned and crisp. Remove from the oven. Serve immediately.

Allow each person the option of spreading some of the optional mayonnaise on the underside of the top half of the bun.

If these small sandwiches are being served as appetizers, or as a food items on a buffet, then push a toothpick down through the top center of each sandwich to hold the sandwich together on the serving tray.

Meatball Sandwich (One Sandwich)

1/4 lb. lean ground beef
1/2 tsp. garlic salt
1/4 tsp. fine grind black pepper
1/4 c. sauce, marinara or spaghetti

1 T. canola oil for cooking
1 slice cheese (see below)
1 bread roll, 6-inches long

Meatballs: The diameter of a normal meatball can vary from 1.5 inches to 1.75 inches, with an average diameter of 1 5/8 inches. Each meatball normally contains about 1 1/3 ounces of ground beef. If you wish you may follow the recipe for Asian Meatballs or for Italian Meatballs in this cookbook. However, you may wish to make the meatballs smaller so the meatballs more evenly cover the bread from end to end and from side to side and the sandwich is easier to bite into.

Cheese: Any type of cheese may be used, such as provolone or mozzarella. The cheese may be sliced or shredded.

Bread: Any type of 6 inch long bread roll may be used, such as white, wheat, French, Hoagie, or Semolina rolls. The bread may be soft or crusty and the bread may or may not have seeds.

Sauce: Use your favorite brand of marinara or spaghetti sauce. Or make your own sauce following the instructions in the sauce chapter.

Instructions: Mix the garlic salt and the black pepper into the ground beef. Form ground beef into three, four, or more meatballs depending on how large you want them to be. Bake in a preheated 350°F oven for 10 to 20 minutes until done in the center. While the meatballs are cooking heat the sauce in a saucepan. When the meatballs are done, put them into the sauce and spoon the sauce over the meatballs and allow the meatballs to simmer in the sauce for 3 minutes. Put the cheese on the inside of the bread roll and toast it until the cheese melts. Put meatballs and sauce onto the melted cheese on the bread and serve.

Philly Cheese Steak Sandwich (One Sandwich)

1/3 lb. ribeye steak, 3/8 inch thick 2 slices of onion, 1/4 inch thick
1/2 tsp. garlic salt 2 slices white American cheese
1/4 tsp. fine grind black pepper 1 white bread roll, 6-inches long
1/2 tsp. seasoned meat tenderizer 1 T. canola oil for cooking

Steak: Ribeye, sirloin, London broil, filet mignon, or round steak. Ribeye is recommended because it has the best distribution of fat in the steak. The fat helps the meat cook in the skillet and it adds moisture and its own special flavor to the finished Philly Cheese Steak sandwich.

Onion: Either a yellow or a white onion may be used. Either color onion will have a slightly golden brown caramel color after it has been properly cooked in a skillet. The yellow onion is usually selected because it already has more of the correct color that is associated with a Philly Cheese Steak sandwich and this helps the cooked onion pieces to look okay even if they were not cooked properly, or long enough.

Cheese: American, provolone, and Cheez Whiz are the traditional cheeses used by the good restaurants in Philadelphia. Elsewhere almost any type of cheese may be used, such as Swiss, mozzarella, Pepper Jack, Havarti, and cheddar. Taste is a very personal experience and each person should select their preferred cheese for a Philly Cheese Steak sandwich because the cheese is one of the three traditional items on the inside of the sandwich. Sliced cheese is recommended but you may use cheese spread, shredded cheese, or cheese cubes if you prefer.

Bread Roll: The preferred bread should have a thin crust and a soft fluffy interior. White bread without any seeds is the traditional bread used in Philly but you may select whatever appeals to you.

Other Items: The traditional sandwich in Philadelphia only has steak, onions, and cheese on the sandwich. But in other areas some people add mushrooms, diced green bell peppers, and/or some type of sauce.

Instructions: Put the ribeye steak in a plastic zipper bag in the freezer for 30 to 40 minutes and the partially frozen raw steak will be much easier to slice. Slice across the grain to make the steak slices easier to chew. Cut the steak into the thinnest slices you can. A bread knife with a serrated cutting edge will make it easier to cut very thin slices. When done, cut any slices longer than 1.5 inches into shorter pieces. Sprinkle the raw meat slices with garlic salt, black pepper, and seasoned meat tenderizer and put the seasoned meat in the refrigerator for 30 minutes so the meat can absorb the flavors and become more tender. Most of the seasonings will cook off the meat in the skillet so do not skimp on the seasonings because their purpose is to tenderize and flavor the meat.

Slice the bread long ways from end to end in the center of one side (like a hot dog bun) but do not cut all the way through the bun. Open up the bun and place one slice of cheese on one end of the bun and the other slice of cheese on the opposite end of the bun. It is okay if the cheese overlaps a little in the center. If the cheese is laid square on the bun it will cover the bun from end to end and from side to side. However, if the cheese is laid in a diamond pattern it will leave parts of the bun unprotected and the juices from the cooked meat and onions can make the bun soggy before you finish eating the sandwich. The choice is yours: diamond pattern for visual appeal or square pattern for a great tasting sandwich from beginning to end. Later the hot meat and onions will melt the cheese but the layer of cheese will help the bun to stay dry long enough for you to eat it. If you wish you may put the bun and cheese in a hot oven for 30 or 40 seconds to pre-melt the cheese but this will also crisp the bread and make the crust a little harder. (In Philly the cheese is put in the skillet after the meat has been cooked so that the cheese mixes with the meat and onions. Then when the mixture is put on the bread the juices make the bread soggy before you can eat it all.)

Cut two 1/4 inch thick slices from an onion. Remove and discard the thin exterior ring from the outside of the onion for sanitary reasons. Cut the two slices in half through the center. Dice the onion so the pieces are about 3/8 inch long. Separate the diced pieces of onion.

Preheat a skillet over medium heat. When the skillet is hot, add the oil and spread the oil over the bottom of the skillet using the end of a spatula. Toss the diced onion pieces into the skillet. If desired, sprinkle a little iodized salt on top of the onions. Cook the onions for 3 or 4 minutes or until they have a golden caramel color.

Add the seasoned tenderized meat slices to the skillet with the onions and continue cooking over medium heat. Stir the meat around inside the skillet with the onions and some of the flavor of the onions will mix with the meat. Do not cook the meat too long. The very thin pieces of meat should be done after cooking for one or two minutes in the hot skillet (if you are only making one sandwich at a time). When the meat has browned slightly, immediately remove the meat and the onions from the skillet with a spatula and put them on top of the cheese inside the sliced bun. Most of the oil, grease, and seasonings will remain in the skillet. Close the sandwich and eat it immediately because the hot meat and onions will gradually start to melt through the cheese and begin making the bread a little soggy.

Philly Cheese Steak Sloppy Joes Sandwich (One)

1 tsp. extra light olive oil
1 1/2 T. onion, chopped
1 1/2 T. green peppers, chopped
opt. a few mushroom slices

1/4 lb. 80% lean ground beef
3 T. beef broth
1 T. steak sauce, A-1
1 bun, plain or seeded

Hybrid Sandwich: This is a hybrid sandwich and therefore you may adjust any part of the sandwich to make it more appealing to you.

Onion: Yellow or white. Without the onion this could no longer be called a Philly Cheese Steak hybrid sandwich. However, the amount of onion can be increased or decreased to suit your tastes. If the onion is deleted then this sandwich is a Sloppy Joes with Cheese.

Green Bell Peppers: The green peppers are a traditional part of this sandwich but they may be omitted if you do not like them.

Sliced Mushrooms: Mushrooms are usually not included in the traditional sandwich but you may add them if you wish.

Meat: 80% lean ground beef is recommended. Or use 90% lean.

Steak Sauce: Instead of steak sauce you may substitute 1 Tablespoon ketchup plus 1 teaspoon Worcestershire sauce.

Bread: White hamburger bun (plain or seeded), hotdog bun, 6-inch long roll. The bread can be brown or whatever you prefer.

Cheese: Cheese sauce (next recipe), Cheez Whiz, sliced provolone cheese, shredded provolone cheese. Or you can substitute the type of cheese that appeals to you. Use 1 slice of cheese, or 1/4 cup of shredded cheese, or 3 Tablespoons of cheese spread. The cheese is listed in the ingredients of the cheese sauce recipe that follows.

Optional Toppings: Shredded lettuce, sliced tomato, sliced raw onion, ketchup, mayonnaise, salt, or black pepper. If you add a sliced raw onion on the sandwich then you may wish to reduce or delete the chopped onions that are cooked with the meat.

Sandwich Instructions: Put the oil, chopped onions, and chopped green peppers (no inner membrane or seeds) in a skillet. If desired, add the optional mushroom slices.

Cook over medium heat until the onions begin to brown and become soft and transparent. Add the ground beef and cook until the meat turns brown. Drain off the grease. Add the beef broth and the steak sauce. Bring to a boil and then immediately reduce the heat and simmer until the liquid is gone but the meat is still moist.

If you are using cheese sauce then make it at this time (next page.)

If you wish you may open the bun and lightly toast it in an oven.

Spoon the meat mixture onto the bottom of the bun. Put the cheese on top of the meat (sliced cheese, shredded cheese, cheese spread, or cheese sauce). If you are not using hot cheese sauce then put the sandwich under the broiler in an oven and melt the cheese.

If you wish you may now add other toppings to the sandwich.

Close the bun and enjoy. If desired, you may serve the sandwich with a side item, such as the chips of your choice, or coleslaw, or a pickle.

Cheese Sauce:

1 tsp. butter, unsalted	1/4 c. whole milk
1 tsp. all-purpose flour	1/4 c. provolone cheese, shredded

Melt the butter in a skillet over medium heat. Add the flour and stir. Add the milk and continue to cook, stirring continuously, until the mixture thickens and bubbles. Remove from heat and add the cheese and stir until the cheese melts into a smooth cheese sauce.

Sloppy Joes Sandwich (One Sandwich)

1/4 lb. 80% lean ground beef	1/8 tsp. chili powder
1 1/2 T. finely diced onion	1/8 tsp. garlic powder
1/8 c. ketchup	1/8 tsp. iodized salt
1 tsp. light brown sugar	1/16 tsp. fine grind black pepper
1 tsp. Worcestershire sauce	1 hamburger bun, plain or seeded

Add the lean ground beef and the diced onion to a skillet and cook over medium-low heat. Stir while cooking and continually break the larger pieces of beef into smaller pieces with the edge of your stirring spoon. When the beef is done add the ketchup, sugar, and Worcestershire sauce to the skillet and stir. Add the chili powder, garlic powder, salt, and black pepper to the skillet and stir. Now bring to a boil while stirring and then immediately reduce heat, cover the skillet, and simmer over very low heat for 10 minutes until the mixture is slightly thickened, stirring occasionally. Serve on the hamburger bun of your choice.

Reuben Sandwich (One Sandwich)

2 tsp. butter, softened
2 slices rye bread
2 slices Swiss cheese

3 oz. cooked corned beef brisket
2 oz. sauerkraut, drained, dried
opt. 1 T. Russian dressing

Some people do not enjoy the taste of a traditional Reuben sandwich because of one part of the sandwich. The good news is that you can customize a Reuben sandwich to please your taste preferences by substituting a different ingredient for the one you don't like.

Bread: Rye bread is the traditional choice. However, pumpernickel bread may be substituted if desired.

Cheese: Swiss cheese is the traditional choice. However, Gruyère cheese may be substituted if desired.

Meat: Corned beef brisket is the traditional choice. However, cooked pastrami may be substituted if desired.

Sauerkraut: Sauerkraut is the traditional choice. However, cooked cabbage may be substituted if desired.

Dressing: Dressing is optional. It may be omitted, or Russian dressing, or Thousand Island dressing may be used.

Instructions: Remove the butter, cheese, meat, sauerkraut, and dressing from the refrigerator, measure the quantity you need, and allow everything to come to room temperature.

Drain most of the moisture off the sauerkraut and then use a paper towel to squeeze the remaining moisture out of the sauerkraut.

Preheat a skillet or griddle over medium-low heat.

Spread one teaspoon of butter on one side of a slice of bread. Place the slice of bread butter side down in the skillet. Place a slice of cheese on top of the slice of bread. Put half the meat on the slice of cheese. Put the sauerkraut on the meat. If desired put one tablespoon of dressing on top of the sauerkraut. Then put the rest of the meat on the sandwich. Put the second piece of cheese on the meat. Spread one teaspoon of butter on the other slice of bread and put the buttered side face up on top of the cheese. Press down gently on the top piece of bread with a spatula to help contain the heat inside the sandwich. Cook the bottom slice of bread until it is golden brown and the bottom slice of cheese is melted and then use a spatula to carefully flip the sandwich over in the skillet. Press down gently on the top piece of cooked bread with a spatula to help contain the heat inside the sandwich. Cook the other side of the bread until it is golden brown and the other piece of cheese is melted and the inside of the sandwich is warm. Use a spatula to transfer the sandwich from the skillet onto a plate. Cut the sandwich in half diagonally and serve.

Chapter Twenty-Nine
Seasonings, Sauces, and Gravies

Dried Herbs: You may use fresh herbs that you dry yourself, or you may use dried herbs available at a grocery store. The choice is yours. If you have an average palate then you will probably not be able to detect a significant difference in a blind taste test. This is especially true if the grocery store dried herbs were recently purchased and the homemade dried herbs were freshly dried a few months ago.

Homemade Dry Seasoning Mixes: Most homemade seasoning mixes contain some very small granules and some larger flakes. Some are heavier and some are lighter. Therefore homemade seasoning mixes have a tendency to settle and the smaller heavier particles will fall to the bottom of the dry mix and this leaves the larger lighter ingredients on top. When it is time to use some of the dry mix it is difficult to get the correct combination of the original items. Therefore it is better to only make just enough dry mix for one recipe so you can use all of the dry mix in that one recipe.

Cajun (Creole) Seasoning Dry Mix (2 1/2 Tablespoons)

1 1/2 T. paprika
1/2 tsp. onion powder
1/2 tsp. iodized salt
1/2 tsp. fine grind black pepper
1/2 tsp. dried oregano

1/2 tsp. dried thyme
1/4 tsp. cayenne pepper
1/4 tsp. garlic salt
1/4 tsp. celery salt

Mix all ingredients in a small bowl until well blended. Use immediately or store in an airtight container at room temperature in a dark area, and write the name on a small piece of paper and tape it to the container.

Chili Powder (4 Tablespoons)

2 T. paprika
2 tsp. dried oregano
1 1/2 tsp. ground cumin

1 1/2 tsp. garlic powder
3/4 tsp. onion powder
1/2 tsp. cayenne pepper powder

Mix all ingredients in a small bowl until well blended. Use immediately or store in an airtight container at room temperature in a dark area, and write the name on a small piece of paper and tape it to the container.

Chili Seasoning Dry Mix - Mild (3 Tablespoons)

1 T. chili powder
1 tsp. crushed red pepper
1 tsp. onion powder
1 tsp. garlic powder
1 tsp. ground cumin

1 tsp. cornstarch
1/2 tsp. granulated sugar
1/4 tsp. iodized salt
1/2 tsp. fine grind black pepper

Mix all ingredients in a small bowl until well blended. Use immediately or store in an airtight container at room temperature in a dark area, and write the name on a small piece of paper and tape it to the container. Makes enough seasoning for one pound of ground beef.

Italian Seasoning Dry Mix (3 Tablespoons)

1 T. dried basil
1 T. dried oregano
1 tsp. dried rosemary

1 tsp. dried marjoram
1 tsp. dried thyme

Mix all ingredients in a small bowl until well blended. Then grind them together in a spice grinder, or crush them together in the bottom of the mixing bowl using the back of a spoon until they become a powder. Use immediately or store in an airtight container at room temperature in a dark area, and write the name on a small piece of paper and tape it to the container.

Other Ingredients: Salt, black pepper, garlic powder, onion powder, parsley, sage, and red pepper flakes are not in the above recipe because you can add these herbs yourself to a recipe and this allows you to add the exact amount of these other herbs as appropriate for each recipe.

Advantages of Italian Seasoning: The herbs are already mixed in the proportions commonly preferred by most good Italian-American cooks. By using the premixed Italian Seasoning in your recipes you will be creating a consistent Italian flavor in those recipes that you can depend on and that is consistently pleasing to the people you serve. If you personally prefer a little more of a specific herb then you can easily add a little more of that specific herb to your Italian recipes.

Imitation Lawry's® Seasoned Salt (2 Tablespoons)

2 2/3 tsp. popcorn salt
1 1/4 tsp. granulated sugar
3/4 tsp. paprika
1/3 tsp. cornstarch

1/3 tsp. garlic powder
1/4 tsp. onion powder
1/4 tsp. turmeric
1/4 tsp. celery salt

Trivia: Lawry's® Seasoned Salt was created in 1938 for use in the world-famous Lawry's® Prime Rib Restaurant in Beverly Hills, California to season prime rib beef. It is currently used to season prime rib, beef, chicken, potatoes, and casseroles.

Instructions: Mix all ingredients in a small bowl until well blended. Use immediately or store in an airtight container at room temperature in a dark area. Write the name on some paper and tape it to the container.

Imitation Longhorn Steakhouse Steak Seasoning, and Imitation Outback Steakhouse Steak Seasoning (3 Teaspoons or Enough for 2 Steaks)

1 tsp. coarse Kosher salt
3/4 tsp. paprika
1/2 tsp. fine grind black pepper
1/4 tsp. onion powder

1/4 tsp. garlic powder
1/16 tsp. coriander, freshly ground
1/16 tsp. turmeric
opt. 1/16 tsp. cayenne pepper

Mix all ingredients in a small bowl until well blended. Use immediately or store in an airtight container at room temperature in a dark area, and write the name on a small piece of paper and tape it to the container.

Imitation Longhorn Steakhouse Prairie Dust for Shrimp (4 Tablespoons)

4 tsp. paprika
3 tsp. iodized salt
2 1/2 tsp. fine grind black pepper

1 1/2 tsp. garlic powder
3/4 tsp. cayenne pepper
1/4 tsp. onion powder

Mix all ingredients in a small bowl until well blended. Use immediately or store in an airtight container at room temperature in a dark area, and write the name on a small piece of paper and tape it to the container.

Imitation Old Bay Seasoning (4 Tablespoons)

7 tsp. celery salt
1 1/3 tsp. fine grind black pepper

1/4 tsp. cayenne pepper
1/4 tsp. ground ginger

1 1/4 tsp. paprika   1/4 tsp. cardamom
1 1/4 tsp. dry mustard   1/8 tsp. cinnamon
1/3 tsp. allspice

Trivia: Old Bay seasoning was created in 1939 by a German immigrant named Gustav Brunn in the Chesapeake Bay area in order to season crabs with a salt mixture that would encourage restaurant customers to purchase more beverages. It gradually became a standard seasoning on Navy ships. It was named after the passenger ship called "The Old Bay Line" that sailed the Chesapeake Bay in the early 1900s between Baltimore, Maryland and Norfolk, Virginia. The seasoning is primarily used to season crabs and shrimp, and sometime clams and oysters.

Mix all ingredients in a small bowl until well blended. Use immediately or store in an airtight container at room temperature in a dark area, and write the name on a small piece of paper and tape it to the container.

Imitation Taco Bell®
Taco Seasoning Dry Mix (4 Tablespoons)

---

1 T. all-purpose flour   1 tsp. paprika
1 T. dried onion flakes (or 1 tsp. onion salt) 1 tsp. ground cumin
1 tsp. beef bouillon cube finely crushed   1/4 tsp. cayenne pepper
1 tsp. chili powder   1/4 tsp. granulated sugar
1 tsp. garlic salt (or 1/4 tsp. garlic powder and 3/4 tsp. iodized salt)

Mix all ingredients in a small bowl until well blended. Use immediately or store in an airtight container at room temperature in a dark area, and write the name on a small piece of paper and tape it to the container. The above quantities will season one pound of ground beef for use in a Mexican recipe.

Tex-Mex Seasoning Dry Mix and Dip (3 Tablespoons)

---

1 T. chili powder   1/2 tsp. iodized salt
1 T. ground cumin   1/4 tsp. fine grind black pepper
1 tsp. onion powder   1/8 tsp. cayenne pepper powder
1 tsp. garlic powder

Mix all ingredients in a small bowl until well blended. Use immediately or store in an airtight container at room temperature in a dark area, and write the name on a small piece of paper and tape it to the container. Use on beef, chicken, burritos, fajitas, and taco.

Tex-Mex Dip: Combine dry mix with 6 tablespoons mayonnaise and 6 tablespoons of room temperature sour cream. Stir until smooth.

Alfredo Sauce (2 Cups)

4 T. butter, unsalted
1 c. heavy whipping cream
opt. 1 T. cream cheese
2 tsp. garlic powder

1/8 tsp. iodized salt
1/8 tsp. white pepper
opt. 1/2 tsp. Italian seasoning
3/4 c. Parmesan cheese

Parmesan cheese: Shredded cheese or Kraft grated Parmesan cheese in the green container. Freshly shredded cheese is highly recommended.

Pepper: Either black pepper or white pepper will produce the correct flavor in the finished sauce. However, white pepper is recommended for visual appeal because it is not visible in the finished sauce.

Instructions: Melt butter in a nonstick saucepan over low heat. Add the heavy cream and the optional cream cheese, stir, and cook for about 3 minutes stirring frequently. Add the garlic powder, salt, white pepper, and the optional Italian seasoning. Stir for one minute. Add the Parmesan cheese, and cook over very low heat stirring frequently until the sauce thickens and the sauce is smooth.

Asian Chow Mein Sauce (3 Tablespoons)

2 1/2 tsp. soy sauce, all-purpose
2 1/4 tsp. oyster sauce
2 tsp. rice wine (see below)
1 tsp. cornstarch

2/3 tsp. sesame oil
2/3 tsp. granulated sugar
1/8 tsp. white pepper

The above sauce recipe was not created to match the recipe of any one restaurant. Instead it was designed to blend the different restaurant cuisines into a single recipe that would appeal to the largest number of people. However, it will not appeal to everyone because some people are accustomed to the sauce flavor of a specific restaurant.

Soy Sauce: Regular all-purpose soy sauce is recommended. If you use sweet soy sauce then use 3 teaspoons of sweet soy sauce and do not add the sugar.

Rice Wine: Any rice wine, or sake, or Sherry, may be used. It is added for its flavor and not for its alcohol because the alcohol will cook off quickly when heated. If you do not wish to use alcohol then you may substitute apple juice or grape juice. Or you may use 1 1/2 teaspoon chicken broth and 1/2 teaspoon white vinegar.

Instructions: Combine the soy sauce, oyster sauce, wine, cornstarch, sesame oil, sugar, and white pepper, and stir until well blended. This recipe will yield 3 tablespoons of sauce or enough for 2 servings.

Uses: Use when cooking noodles, or beef, or chicken, or shrimp.

Barbecue Sauce (1 1/2 cups)

3/4 c. ketchup
2 1/2 T. vinegar, white or cider
2 T. lemon juice
1 T. Worcestershire sauce
2 tsp. canola oil

3/8 c. water
3 T. brown sugar, light or dark
1 tsp. garlic powder
1 tsp. onion powder
1 tsp. fine grind black pepper

Introduction: There is no such thing as a "universal" barbecue sauce that appeals to everyone. Instead there are lots of different flavors of barbecue sauce as can be seen by the number of different brands and special flavors available in the average grocery store. The ingredients, smoothness, thickness, and "hotness" of these sauces is what makes each one unique. The above recipe will yield a sauce of "average barbecue" flavor that is acceptable to the average person. It can easily be modified by adding any additional flavors you enjoy. (No salt is included because the ketchup contains salt.)

Instructions: In a medium nonstick saucepan, add the ketchup, vinegar, lemon juice, Worcestershire, oil, and water and stir until well blended. Add the sugar, garlic powder, onion powder, and black pepper and stir until well blended. Bring the sauce to a boil and then immediately reduce the heat to low. Cook uncovered, stirring frequently, for 20 to 25 minutes to thicken the sauce and meld the flavors. Remove from heat. If not using immediately then refrigerate in an airtight container for up to two weeks.

Brown Butter Sauce (French: Beurre Noisette)

4 T. butter, unsalted, when melted will yield 3 T. brown butter

Cut butter into 1 tablespoon slices and put in nonstick saucepan. A light colored pan or pot allows you to easily see when the butter is properly browned. Melt the butter over medium heat. Stir constantly to prevent overcooking. The butter will begin to foam, the water will gradually be cooked off, and only the milk solids will be left. When the butter has turned a light tan color pour the butter into a bowl. The butter will continue to cook as it cools and it will become a little browner with a toasty aroma. Very dark butter has a slightly bitter taste and is called "beurre noir." If overcooked it will scorch, turn black, and have a very bitter taste.

Use immediately or save in an airtight container in the refrigerator. Pour melted brown butter over cooked fish, seafood, pasta, Brussels sprouts, or broccoli just before serving. Or add to dessert recipes.

Butter - Lemon Butter Sauce, Garlic Butter Sauce, and Lemon Garlic Butter Sauce (4 Tablespoons)

4 T. butter, unsalted, melted

Lemon Butter Sauce:
1 tsp. lemon juice

Garlic Butter Sauce:
1/8 tsp. garlic powder   opt. 1/16 tsp. paprika
opt. 1/8 tsp. Italian seasoning

Lemon Garlic Butter Sauce:
1 tsp. lemon juice   1/8 tsp. garlic powder

Cut butter into one tablespoon slices and put in nonstick saucepan. Melt butter over low heat. Add the appropriate ingredients (see above) and stir until well blended.

Pour warm butter sauce over cooked chicken, fish, pasta, or vegetables just before serving. *Melted hot butter sauce is one of the important secret ingredients of a gourmet cook.*

Cheese Sauce (1 1/3 cups)

1 T. butter   1/16 tsp. iodized salt
1 T. all-purpose flour   3/4 cups cheese, shredded
1/2 c. half & half, or whole milk, room temperature

Cheese: Use any block cheese and shred it when you make the sauce. The type of cheese will flavor the sauce so select a cheese based on how you will use the sauce. Sharp cheddar cheese is recommended. Or you may use American, brie, gouda, mozzarella, Parmesan, Romano, or something else. Or use 2 different cheeses to create a unique flavor.

Instructions: Melt the butter in a medium nonstick saucepan over medium heat. Add the flour and cook for 4 minutes stirring constantly. Gradually add the half & half and stir to break up any clumps. Stir constantly to prevent burning the half & half, and bring to a boil. Then reduce the heat to low, add the salt, and stir and cook for 2 minutes or until the sauce thickens. Reduce the heat to very low and gradually add the cheese and stir until the cheese melts and the sauce is smooth.

Possible Uses: Pour on any vegetable such as broccoli, cauliflower, and baked potatoes, or on macaroni, pasta, nachos, open faced sandwiches, chicken, or pork chops.

Cocktail Sauce (3/4 Cup)

1/2 c. ketchup	1/4 tsp. Worcestershire sauce
1 1/2 T. horseradish	1/4 tsp. iodized salt
2 T. lemon juice	1/8 tsp. fine grind black pepper

Combine the ketchup, horseradish, lemon juice, Worcestershire, salt, and black pepper in a bowl and stir until everything is well mixed and the sauce looks uniform. Chill in the refrigerator and then serve. May be stored in an airtight container in the refrigerator for up to one week.

Fry Sauce (3/4 to 1 Cup)
Utah Fry Sauce (3/4 to 1 Cup)
Imitation Artic Circle Restaurant Fry Sauce (1 1/2 Cups)

Traditional Basic Fry Sauce (1941):

1/2 c. mayonnaise	between 1/4 c. to 1/2 c. ketchup

Imitation Artic Circle Restaurant Fry Sauce (1950):

1/2 c. mayonnaise	1/2 c. ketchup
1/2 c. buttermilk	(never any pickle flavor)

Utah Fry Sauce:

1/2 c. mayonnaise	between 1/4 c. to 1/2 c. ketchup
1/4 tsp. onion powder	1/2 T. pickle juice

Trivia: This sauce has contested origins. In the USA, Don Carlos Edwards is credited with creating this sauce in 1941 in his first restaurant in Salt Lake City, Utah. In 1950 he named his second restaurant the Arctic Circle Restaurant and customers stood in line to eat one of his famous creations. Today there are many versions of this recipe but most use equal amounts of mayonnaise and ketchup (a pink sauce), or double the mayonnaise to ketchup (a whiter sauce). This sauce is used as a dipping sauce for French fries and fried onion rings, and as a spread on hamburgers.

Instructions: Mix all ingredients until well blended. Serve at room temperature. Refrigerate any unused sauce in an airtight container.

Honey Mustard Dipping Sauce for Chicken (1 1/8 Cups)

1/2 c. mayonnaise
2 T. yellow mustard
1 T. brown Dijon mustard

1/4 c. honey
2 T. orange juice
1 T. lemon juice

In a small bowl, combine the mayonnaise, yellow mustard, brown mustard, honey, orange juice, and lemon juice, and stir until well blended. Use immediately of store in an airtight container in the refrigerator.

Hot Dipping Sauce (1 1/8 Cups)
for Chicken Nuggets, Tenders, and Wings

1/2 c. mayonnaise
1/2 c. sour cream
2 T. horseradish
1/2 tsp. cayenne pepper

1/4 tsp. chili powder
1/2 tsp. iodized salt
1/4 tsp. fine grind black pepper

In a medium bowl mix the mayonnaise and sour cream until smooth. Add the horseradish and stir until well blended. Add the cayenne pepper, chili powder, salt, and black pepper and stir until well blended.

Use immediately or store in an airtight container in the refrigerator until needed.

Hot Fudge Sauce (1 1/2 Cups)

1/3 c. heavy cream
1/4 c. light brown sugar
1/4 c. light corn syrup
2 T. cocoa powder

1/8 tsp. iodized salt
2 tsp. pure vanilla extract
4 oz. semi-sweet chocolate

Put the cream, sugar, corn syrup, cocoa, salt, and vanilla extract in a saucepan and stir. Cook over medium heat. Then reduce the heat to a simmer and add the finely chopped chocolate and continue to stir and simmer for another 3 or 4 minutes until the chocolate melts and the sauce is thick. Allow the hot fudge sauce to cool for a few minutes before using.

Imitation Outback Steakhouse Blooming Onion Dipping Sauce for Onion Rings and Fries (2/3 Cup)

1/3 c. mayonnaise
2 T. sour cream
1 1/2 T. horseradish sauce
1 1/2 T. ketchup

1/4 tsp. paprika
1/8 tsp. garlic salt
1/8 tsp. cayenne pepper

In a medium bowl mix the mayonnaise and sour cream until smooth. Add the horseradish and ketchup, and stir until well blended. Add the paprika, garlic salt, and cayenne pepper, and stir until well blended.

Use immediately or store in an airtight container in the refrigerator until needed.

Remove from refrigerator and allow to come to room temperature before using as a dip for fried onion rings, French fries, or tater tots.

Marinara Sauce and Spaghetti Sauce (about 3 cups)

1 T. extra light olive oil
1/2 c. onion, finely diced
1 (4 tsp.) garlic clove, minced
1 (14.5 oz.) can crushed tomatoes
1 (6 oz.) can tomato paste
1 (8 oz.) can tomato sauce

1T. granulated sugar
2 tsp. dried basil
1/2 tsp. iodized salt
1/2 tsp. fine grind black pepper
opt. 1 T. chicken bouillon cube
Spaghetti: add 3 T. Italian seasoning

Bouillon Cube: Adds a subtle meat flavor. A chicken bouillon cube imparts a neutral but pleasant meat flavor. If preferred, a beef bouillon cube may be used instead to impart a beef flavor.

Spaghetti Sauce Option: Add the optional Italian seasoning at the same time as the basil to create spaghetti sauce.

Marinara Sauce Instructions: Put the olive oil and the onions in a large nonstick pot and cook over medium heat for 4 minutes. Reduce the heat to low and add the garlic and simmer 2 minutes. Add the crushed tomatoes, tomato paste, and the tomato sauce and stir well. Add the sugar, basil, salt, black pepper, and the crushed bouillon cube. Stir well. Bring the sauce to a boil and then immediately reduce heat to low and simmer on very low heat for 45 minutes, stirring frequently.

Mexican Hot Sauce (3 1/3 cups)

1 c. dried red chili peppers, diced
1/8 cup white onion, minced
2 T. white vinegar
1 c. water
1/2 T. chili powder

1/2 tsp. cumin powder
1/2 tsp. garlic powder
1/2 tsp. oregano
1/2 tsp. iodized salt
1 (8 oz.) can tomato sauce

Remove the stems from the dried red chili peppers (if they have not been previously removed). Add the chili peppers, onion, vinegar, water, chili powder, cumin powder, garlic powder, oregano, and salt to a saucepan. Stir to combine the ingredients. Bring the mixture to a boil and then immediately reduce the heat to a simmer. Simmer uncovered for 10 minutes, stirring occasionally. Remove from heat and allow to cool. Transfer to a blender, add the tomato sauce, and blend until smooth. If the hot sauce is too thick then add a little more water and blend again.

Mexican Smooth Red Salsa (about 2 1/3 Cups)

2 (14.5 oz.) cans diced tomatoes
1 whole green jalapeño, finely diced
3 T. fresh cilantro leaves, finely diced

1/2 tsp. garlic powder
1/2 tsp. onion powder
1/4 tsp. iodized salt

Trivia: In English the word "salsa" means sauce. Traditional Mexican salsa is smooth, either red or green, and it is not chunky. Red salsa is "salsa rojo" and green salsa is "salsa verde." On the other hand, "pico de gallo" is a combination of chunky tomatoes, onions, peppers, cilantro, and seasonings. This recipe is for "salsa rojo" and not "pico de gallo."

Canned Tomatoes: Recommend diced Mexican tomatoes with green chilies and chipotle peppers.

Onion Powder: May replace with 1/8 cup finely grated fresh onion.

Garlic Powder: May replace with 1 fresh minced garlic clove.

Instructions: In a medium bowl mix the tomatoes, jalapeño, cilantro, garlic, onion, and salt. Stir until well blend. If desired, put mixture into a blender or food processor, and blend until smooth.

Refrigerate for at least 60 minutes, or overnight, to allow time for the flavors to merge together.

Serve with the chips of you choice, or on tacos, burritos, or enchiladas.

Note: The hot flavor of this salsa will gradually increase with time.

Pizza Sauce (1 1/2 Cups for One 12 inch Pizza)

1 (15 oz.) can tomato puree	1/3 tsp. marjoram
1/4 c. water	1/3 tsp. basil
1 1/3 tsp. granulated sugar	1/3 tsp. garlic powder
1 tsp. extra light olive oil	1/4 tsp. thyme
1/2 tsp. oregano	1/2 tsp. iodized salt
1/3 tsp. lemon juice	1/8 tsp. fine grind black pepper

Sauce per Pizza: There is no standard for the thickness of a layer of sauce on a pizza. Different restaurants will put more or less sauce on top of their pizzas and this is one of the major reasons why different people prefer one restaurant's pizza to the pizzas served at other restaurants because different people prefer more or less sauce on their pizzas. Less sauce increases the taste impact of the cheeses and toppings on the pizza, and less sauce is usually easier on the digestive system. Only you can decide how much sauce you prefer on your homemade pizzas.

Grandpappy's Gourmet Pizza Sauce: Use the above quantities of all the ingredients and follow the instructions below.

Domino's Imitation Pizza Sauce: Omit the lemon juice and the thyme. Add 2 1/4 cups finely shredded mozzarella cheese and 1/8 teaspoon cayenne pepper. Yield will increase to 3 1/2 cups of sauce but the sauce will contain a lot of cheese so keep this in mind when you add shredded cheese on top of the sauce.

Little Caesar's Imitation Pizza Sauce: Omit the oil, lemon juice, marjoram, and thyme. Decrease the sugar to 1/4 teaspoon. Increase the oregano to 1 1/2 teaspoons. Add 1/4 teaspoon onion powder.

Papa John's Imitation Pizza Sauce: Omit the marjoram and the black pepper.

Pizza Hut Imitation Pizza Sauce: Omit the oil and the black pepper. Increase the oregano to 1 teaspoon.

Instructions: Combine all ingredients in a nonstick saucepan and bring to a boil over medium heat while stirring. Reduce heat to very low and simmer, stirring occasionally, for 15 to 60 minutes, or until the sauce is the consistency you prefer. Simmering for 60 minutes is recommended because the longer you simmer the sauce the more completely the flavors meld together, the thicker the sauce will become, and there will be less sauce to cover the top of the pizza. If you use too much sauce, or if the sauce is too thin, then the melted cheese on the finished pizza may slide off the sauce onto the plate.

Orange and Butter Sauce
for Seafood (1/2 Cup)

1 orange

1 stick (8 T.) butter, unsalted

1/4 tsp. iodized salt

1/4 tsp. white pepper

Scrape 1 teaspoon of zest off the peel of the orange and be very careful to not get any of the underlying white pith in the zest. Squeeze the juice out of the orange into a cup until you have at least 1/3 cup of orange juice.

Heat the orange juice and the zest in a nonstick skillet over medium heat. Gradually add the butter 1 tablespoon at a time and as the butter melts stir it into the orange sauce. Continue to add 1 tablespoon of butter at a time, wait for it to melt, and stir it into the sauce. If you add the butter slowly it will make a smooth orange sauce. Do not allow the sauce to boil or it will separate. After all the butter has been added, continue to heat the sauce until it has been reduced down to approximately 1/2 cup of sauce. Then stir in the salt and white pepper. Keep the sauce warm until you are ready to serve it.

Serve with trout, crab, lobster, scallops, or other shellfish.   The sauce may be poured over the seafood or it may bee served as a dipping sauce beside the seafood.

Southwest Dipping Sauce
for Onion Rings, Chips, or Vegetables (2/3 Cup)

1/2 c. mayonnaise

1 T. ketchup

1 1/3 T. horseradish sauce

1/4 tsp. paprika

1/8 tsp. dried oregano

1/4 tsp. iodized salt

1/16 tsp. fine grind black pepper

In a small bowl, combine all ingredients and stir until well blended. Use immediately or store in an airtight container in the refrigerator.

Tartar Sauce
for Fried Fish (6 Servings)

1 c. mayonnaise

1/4 c. pickle relish (sweet or dill)

1 T. onion, finely diced

1 T. lemon juice

2 tsp. dill weed or dried parsley

1/4 t. iodized salt

1/4 t. fine grind black pepper

Combine all ingredients and stir until well blended. Chill for 1 hour.

Teriyaki Sauce (about 1 1/3 cups)

opt. 4 T. Mirim (Japanese sweet rice wine)

1/2 c. soy sauce — 1 tsp. garlic powder

3 T. dark brown sugar — 2 tsp. fresh ginger, minced

1 1/2 T. pure honey — opt. 4 T. water

opt. 1 1/2 tsp. sesame oil — opt. 2 tsp. cornstarch

Consistency: Traditional Japanese teriyaki sauce is thin. Japanese-American teriyaki sauce is usually thicker and somewhat sticky.

Japanese Wine: Mirim has less alcohol than vanilla extract. If you wish you can substitute sake, or white wine, or cooking sherry, instead. When the Mirim is boiled the alcohol quickly boils off into an almost non-alcoholic liquid. Mirim is used to add its flavor to the sauce and not its alcohol. If you wish you may simply omit the Mirim from the recipe and nothing has to be added in its place.

Instructions: Pour optional Mirim into a nonstick sauce pan and bring to a boil over medium-high heat. Immediately reduce heat to medium-low and simmer for 1 minute. Add soy sauce, brown sugar, honey, and the optional sesame oil, add stir. Add the garlic and ginger, and stir.

Option 1: If you desire a thinner traditional Japanese teriyaki sauce then add the optional water.

Option 2: If you intend to use the sauce as a marinade for meat then add 2 teaspoons of cornstarch to 4 tablespoons of cold water and mix until the cornstarch is completely dissolved. Then add it to the sauce. This will help the sauce stick to the meat.

Instructions Continued: Simmer over medium-low heat for another 5 minutes or longer, stirring frequently. The longer you simmer the sauce the thicker it will become.

Use immediately or store in an airtight container in the refrigerator.

Meat Marinade: This sauce will add a distinctive Japanese flavor to poultry, fish, beef, and vegetables.

Gravy, White, Country Style (1 1/4 Cups)

1 T. butter	1/8 tsp. iodized salt
2 T. all-purpose flour	1/16 tsp. fine grind black pepper
1 c. whole milk	

Melt butter in a medium nonstick saucepan over medium heat. Add flour, 1 tablespoon at a time, and stir after adding each tablespoon of flour. Cook for 2 minutes, stirring constantly, to prevent the mixture from burning. Stir in milk, 1/2 cup at a time, stirring constantly. Bring to a boil while stirring and then reduce to heat to low. Add salt and black pepper and continue stirring until gravy thickens. If gravy becomes too thick then add just a little more milk to thin the gravy.

Possible Uses: Pour over biscuits, mashed potatoes, pork chops, or turkey. Or mix with a little crumbled cooked pork sausage before using.

Gravy, Brown (1 1/4 Cups)

2 T. butter	1/4 tsp. garlic powder
2 T. all-purpose flour	1/4 tsp. iodized salt
1 (14 oz.) can beef broth	1/4 tsp. fine grind black pepper
2 tsp. Worcestershire sauce	

Melt butter in a medium nonstick saucepan over medium heat. Add flour and cook 4 minutes stirring constantly. Gradually add beef broth and stir until smooth without any lumps. Add Worcestershire sauce, garlic powder, salt, and black pepper and stir. Continue to stir and cook over medium heat for 5 minutes or until sauce thickens.

Possible Uses: Pour over mashed potatoes, beef, pork, or turkey. Or add sliced sautéed mushrooms to the brown gravy before using.

Sautéed Mushrooms (Sliced or Whole)

1/2 lb. fresh mushrooms	1/8 tsp. garlic powder
1 T. olive oil or canola oil	1/8 tsp. iodized salt
1 T. butter	1/16 tsp. fine grind black pepper

Mushrooms: Button, cremini, portabella, shiitake, or a combination. Briefly rinse mushrooms. Gently dry mushrooms with paper towel. If serving whole, remove the stems. If serving sliced, leave stems on and cut into 1/4 inch thick slices. Heat oil and butter in skillet over medium heat until fat sizzles. Add mushrooms, garlic powder, salt, and black pepper. Cook 5 minutes. Reduce heat to low and simmer 5 minutes.

Gravy, Turkey Giblet (5 1/2 Cups)

3 c. turkey stock
2 c. water
1 giblet package
3 T. butter

3 T. all-purpose flour
3/4 tsp. iodized salt
1/4 tsp. fine grind black pepper

Turkey Stock and Water. If you have normal turkey stock then use 3 cups of stock and 2 cups of water. If you have a thick turkey stock then use 2 cups of turkey stock and 3 cups of water. If you don't have turkey stock then you can substitute chicken stock.

Giblets: Giblets include the heart, liver, gizzard, and neck of a turkey or a chicken. They are usually included in a small package inside the cavity of the whole bird. Turkey giblets are bigger and therefore they contain more meat. Remove the meat from the neck. Cut the heart, and gizzard into smaller pieces. You may discard the liver, or you can mince it and put it in the refrigerator for later. If you use the liver it will change the final taste of the gravy.

Instructions: Put the water in a large pot. Add the cut up giblet meat, except for the liver meat. Bring to a boil over medium heat. Reduce heat to low and cook for 20 to 25 minutes, or until the meat is done. Remove from heat. Strain the turkey broth through a fine mesh sieve into a large bowl. Transfer the small pieces of meat into another bowl and mince them. Then put the minced meat in the large bowl with the turkey broth.

Melt the butter in a medium nonstick saucepan over medium heat. Add the flour and cook for 4 minutes stirring constantly. Gradually add the turkey stock and stir. Add the salt and black pepper and stir. Add the bowl of turkey broth with the minced giblet meat. If desired, add the minced liver meat. Simmer over low heat for 30 minutes, stirring occasionally, until the broth thickens into a gravy of the desired consistency. If too thin, add a little more flour and cook for another 30 minutes.

Chapter Thirty
Side Dishes

Coleslaw (4 Servings)

---

3 c. cabbage, shredded or chopped   1/8 tsp. fine grind black pepper
1/3 c. carrot, shredded   opt. 1/3 tsp. celery seed
1/3 c. mayonnaise   opt. 2 tsp. onion, finely diced
1 T. vinegar, white or apple cider   opt. 4 tsp. whole milk
4 tsp. granulated sugar   opt. 1 1/2 tsp. lemon juice
1/4 tsp. iodized salt

Cabbage: Coleslaw may be made using only green cabbage, or using a combination of one-half green cabbage and one-half red cabbage. The cabbage can be shredded into long pieces, or it can be finely chopped into small pieces about 1/4 inch long. More finely chopped cabbage will fit into one cup because there is less air space between the small pieces of cabbage. Most fast food restaurants finely chop their cabbage.

Kentucky Fried Chicken finely chops their cabbage and they add the optional onion, milk, and lemon juice but not the celery seed.

Instructions: Either shred or chop the cabbage. Peel and shred the carrot. Mix together in a large bowl.

In a separate small bowl, combine the mayonnaise, vinegar, sugar, salt, and black pepper, and stir until well blended. If desired, add the optional celery seed, onion, milk, and/or lemon juice and stir until well blended.

Combine the mayonnaise mixture and the cabbage mixture and toss until the cabbage is evenly coated. Refrigerate for at least 2 hours before serving. Refrigerate any leftover coleslaw.

Fettuccini Alfredo (4 Servings)

---

16 oz. Fettuccini dry noodles   2 c. Alfredo sauce (sauce chapter)

Cook the fettuccini noodles following the package instructions. While the noodles are cooking prepare the Alfredo sauce following the instructions in the sauce chapter of this cookbook. When the noodles are done, drain the noodles. Immediately stir in the Alfredo sauce and thoroughly coat the noodles with the sauce.
Serve immediately.
If desired, this side dish can be made into a main dish by adding meat (chicken, or sausage, or shrimp) following the instructions in the Italian recipes chapter.

Hush Puppies (about 24 Hush Puppies)

1 c. yellow cornmeal	1/4 tsp. fine grind black pepper
1/2 c. all-purpose flour	1 egg, beaten
1 1/2 tsp. baking powder	1/2 c. buttermilk
2 T. granulated sugar	1/2 c. onion, grated
3/4 tsp. iodized salt	canola oil for frying

In a large bowl combine the cornmeal, flour, baking powder, sugar, salt, and black pepper. Stir until well blended. Then sift the dry ingredients to break up any lumps and to blend them together more evenly.

In a different bowl beat the egg until smooth. Add the buttermilk and stir until well blended. Add grated onion with its juice and stir. Add the egg mixture into the large bowl with the cornmeal. Stir until the dry ingredients are moistened and then stop. Let the batter stand for 1 hour. The thicker the batter the easier it is to work with.

Moisten your hands and form hush puppies into balls between 1 inch to 1 1/4 inches in diameter. If the hush puppies are too large the inside will still be moist when the outside is done. If they are too small the inside will be done before the outside turns a golden brown.

Put oil in a saucepan to a depth of 3 inches. Heat over medium-high heat until a deep-fry thermometer reads 375°F. If the temperature is too high the outside burns before the inside is done. If the temperature is too low they absorb too much oil and taste greasy. Reduce heat to medium. Moisten the end of a long metal spoon with oil and pick up one hush puppy on the spoon. Lower the spoon into the oil and allow the hush puppy to slide off the spoon. Moisten the spoon and repeat until about 6 hush puppies are in the oil. Do not crowd the hush puppies in the oil. Fry for about 3 or 4 minutes. Some of the hush puppies may flip over by themselves. Use a spoon to flip the other hush puppies so the other side will fry. Continue to fry until the hush puppies begin to turn a golden brown. Do not overcook. They are done when they look like they might need to fry just a little longer. Use a slotted spoon to remove hush puppies from the oil, allow the hot oil to drip back down into the pot, and put the hush puppies on a paper towel to absorb some of the excess oil. Repeat until all the hush puppies have been cooked. The hush puppies should be crisp on the outside and soft of the inside. Serve immediately.

Macaroni and Cheese - Baked or Stovetop

8 oz. pasta (see below) 1/4 tsp. iodized salt
1 1/4 c. half & half, or whole milk 1/4 tsp. fine grind black pepper
3 T. butter 1 1/2 c. Cheddar Jack cheese
2 1/2 T. all-purpose flour

Additional Topping Ingredients for Baked Macaroni and Cheese:
1 1/2 T. butter 1/4 c. Cheddar Jack cheese, grated
1 c. Panko breadcrumbs

Pasta: Elbow macaroni is the traditional pasta used in this recipe. However, you may use twists or bowties or another type of pasta to enhance an old recipe with a new exciting different visual appearance.

Cheese: Four ounces of cheese by weight is one cup of finely shredded cheese. Finely shredded Cheddar Jack cheese melts into a smoother sauce than 100% cheddar cheese. Or use Velveeta cheese because it was designed to melt into a smooth cheese sauce. Or use mozzarella cheese, or Monterey Jack cheese, or a combination of cheeses.

Instructions: Bring a pot of lightly salted water to a boil over medium heat. Add macaroni and stir for about 6 minutes or until the macaroni is tender but still firm (al dente). Drain and set aside.

In a small saucepan warm the half & half over medium heat until tiny bubbles form around its edges but do not let it come to a boil. Remove from the heat and set it aside.

In a medium saucepan melt the butter over medium low heat. Add the flour and cook for 3 minutes while stirring constantly. Gradually add the warm half & half and stir constantly for about 3 minutes until the sauce thickens. Add the salt and pepper and stir. Increase the heat to medium and gradually add the cheese and stir each time cheese is added to make a cheese sauce.

Now you will need to follow the instructions below based on how you wish to finish cooking the macaroni and cheese.

Stovetop Macaroni and Cheese: Reduce heat to low and add the cooked macaroni and stir to thoroughly coat the macaroni with the cheese sauce. Simmer over low heat for 2 minutes. Serve immediately.

Baked Macaroni and Cheese: Remove the cheese sauce from the heat. Add the cooked macaroni and stir to thoroughly coat the macaroni with the cheese sauce. (Note: If you cooked 8 ounces of macaroni then use an 8-inch baking pan. If you doubled the recipe then use a 13-inch by 9-inch casserole dish.) Pour the macaroni and cheese into a lightly buttered baking dish. Make the topping in a small saucepan by melting the butter over medium low heat. Put the Panko breadcrumbs in a small bowl and pour the melted butter over the breadcrumbs. Stir to coat the breadcrumbs with butter. Add the finely grated cheese and stir until well blended. Pour the mixture evenly over the top of the macaroni and cheese. Bake in a preheated 350°F oven for 30 minutes. Then set the oven to broil and broil for about 5 minutes or until the top surface is a light golden brown.

Onion Rings, Deep-Fried

1 sweet onion, such as Vidalia	1/4 tsp. paprika
2 c. ice cold water	1/4 tsp. dried oregano
1 egg, beaten	1/8 tsp. cayenne pepper
3/4 c. whole milk, or buttermilk	1/2 tsp. iodized salt
1 c. all-purpose flour	1/4 tsp. fine grind black pepper
1/4 tsp. garlic powder	2 c. canola oil, for deep frying

Cut the onion into consistent 1/4 inch, or 3/8 inch, or 1/2 inch thick slices depending on how thick you like them. 3/8 inch thick slices are recommended. Separate into rings. Place into a bowl of ice cold water and put the bowl in the refrigerator for 20 minutes.

Beat the egg in a medium bowl until smooth. Add the milk and stir until well blended.

In a medium bowl add the flour, garlic powder, paprika, oregano, cayenne pepper, salt, and pepper. Stir until well blended. Add the egg and milk mixture and stir until the batter is well blended.

Put oil in a small sauce pan until it is 2 inches deep. Heat over medium-high heat until the oil is hot (about 375°F). Coat one onion ring in the batter and leave it in the batter. Repeat until there are 5 coated onion rings in the batter. Transfer the onions one at a time into the hot oil until all 5 onions are cooking. Deep-fry for about 2 minutes or until the bottom side of the onions are golden brown. Turn the onions over in the oil and fry the other side of the onions for about 1 or 2 minutes or until the other side is golden brown. Use a slotted spoon or spaghetti ladle to lift the onions up above the hot oil, allow the hot oil to drip into the saucepan, and then put the onions onto a paper towel to absorb some of the excess oil. Keep the fried onions warm in a preheated 225°F oven until all the onions have been deep-fried the same way.

Serve with Onion Ring Dipping Sauce (recipe in sauce chapter).

Sautéed Apples (2 Servings)

1 large apple (see below)	2 T. light brown sugar
1 T. butter, unsalted	1/8 tsp. ground cinnamon
1/2 tsp. cornstarch	opt. pinch nutmeg
2 T. water	

Trivia: In the 1950s we lived with my mother's parents for two years. At least once each month my Granny would serve sautéed apples as part of the evening meal. She would put the apples on our dinner plates beside some type of meat and some type of vegetable and fresh baked bread. I do not have my Granny's recipe but the recipe below yields apples that taste very similar to the apples she cooked. I didn't know what sautéed meant in the 1950s so I just called them fried apples.

Apples: Almost any type of apple may be used, such as Gala, Golden Delicious, Granny Smith, Honeycrisp, Pink Lady, or Red Delicious. Different types of apples will yield uniquely delightful flavors.

Instructions: Rinse the apples to help remove any residual insecticide spray. Peel and discard the peels for the same reason. Slice the apple into pieces between 1/4 inch to 1/2 inch wide. Remove and discard the core and the seeds. Each time you make this recipe if you will slice the apples differently, such as thin slices, or thick slices, or into chunks, or diced, then you will create different dishes, each with its own unique visual appeal. Just slice the apples to a uniform consistent size so all the pieces arrive at the desired degree of tenderness at the same time.
Melt butter in a large nonstick skillet over medium-high heat. Add the apples in a single layer and stir constantly (sauté). Do not crowd the apples in the skillet. Flip the apples over in addition to stirring them around. Cook until the apples are almost tender, between 5 to 8 minutes depending on how the apples were sliced and the heat of the skillet. Dissolve the cornstarch completely in the water and then add to the apples. Sprinkle brown sugar, cinnamon, and nutmeg over the apples and stir. Bring to a boil for 2 minutes, or until the sugar melts, stirring constantly. Serve warm.

Serving Options: May be served at any meal with almost any meat, such as in the evening with pork chops or steak, and with most vegetables, such as potatoes. May be served at breakfast on top of pancakes, or beside pancakes, or beside fried ham. May also be put on top of vanilla ice cream (upside down pie "à la mode").

Stuffing (or Dressing) - Stovetop (4 Servings)

bread or croutons (see below)
3 T. butter
1/4 c. onion, diced
1 c. celery, diced
1 c. chicken stock
1 T. dried parsley

1/2 tsp. garlic powder
1/2 tsp. sage (or poultry seasoning)
1/4 tsp. marjoram
1/4 tsp. iodized salt
1/8 tsp. fine grind black pepper
opt. 1/2 c. shredded cooked chicken

Stovetop or Baked Stuffing: Both include the same ingredients in the same amounts. Stovetop stuffing requires about 8 minutes of cooking time on the stove, whereas baked stuffing requires about 40 minutes of cooking time in the oven. Stovetop stuffing is usually moister, softer, and tastier because it is easier to control the moisture content (dryness) of stovetop stuffing. If the stovetop stuffing is too moist for you, then it can easily be put into a baking pan in the oven for a few minutes to bake off some of the moisture and the next time you make it you can use a little less chicken stock.

Sliced Bread, or Bread Cubes, or Croutons: 10 slices of bread (white or wheat), or 4 cups of bread cubes, or 4 cups of normal croutons (not brittle and hard).

Instructions: If using sliced bread then toast the bread in a toaster or in the oven until brown but not burned. Trim off and discard the crust and cut each slice of bread into 3/8 inch cubes.

Melt butter in a large nonstick saucepan over medium heat. Add the diced onions and diced celery and cook for about 4 minutes or until the onions become soft and translucent. Add the chicken stock, parsley, garlic, sage, marjoram, salt, and black pepper. If desired, add shredded cooked chicken. Stir to blend all the ingredients. Bring to a boil. Remove the saucepan from the heat, add the bread cubes, and stir to mix the bread cubes in the liquid. Cover the saucepan and let it sit for 5 minutes. Remove the cover and stir with a fork to fluff up the stuffing.

Chapter Thirty-One
Soups

Broccoli Cheese Soup (4 Servings)

---

6 T. butter
1/3 c. all-purpose flour
2 1/2 c. half & half, or whole milk
1/2 tsp. iodized salt
1/4 tsp. fine grind black pepper

2 c. chicken stock
2 c. broccoli, finely diced
1/4 c. carrot, peeled, grated
1/3 c. onion, finely diced
2 c. cheese, see below

Cheese: The cheese should be freshly grated from a block of cheese. Grated cheese will melt easier into a soup consistency. The flavor of the soup will be significantly influenced by the type of cheese used. The flavor of broccoli blends well with most types of cheeses, such as mild cheddar, sharp cheddar, Cheddar Jack, Colby Jack, Monterrey Jack, or Velveeta, or a combination of different cheeses. Pick your favorite.

Instructions: Melt the butter in a large nonstick saucepan over medium heat. Add the flour and cook for 4 minutes stirring constantly. Gradually add the half & half and stir to break up any clumps. Stir constantly to prevent burning the half & half, and bring to a boil. Then reduce the heat to low, add the salt and black pepper, and stir. Simmer for 2 minutes. Reduce the heat to very low and whisk in the chicken stock. Cook for 20 minutes, stirring occasionally. Increase the heat to low and add the finely diced broccoli, the grated carrot, and the finely diced onion. Continue to cook over low heat for 20 to 25 minutes or until the broccoli is tender when pierced with a fork. Reduce heat to very low and gradually stir in the grated cheese. Stir gently until the cheese is melted. Serve in soup bowls.

Optional Garnishes: Sprinkle a few crushed croutons, or a little crumbled bacon, or a little grated cheese, on top of a bowl of soup.

Goes Good With: Sliced French bread, sliced tomatoes, or a rotisserie chicken.

Soup Consistency: The above recipe yields a slightly chunky soup. If you prefer a more liquid soup then allow the soup to cool before adding the cheese and put the soup in a blender and blend to the consistency your prefer. Then return the soup to the saucepan and cook over low heat while adding the grated cheese.

Chicken (or Turkey) Vegetable Soup (4 Servings), or Chicken and Rice Soup, or Chicken Noodle Soup

3 1/3 c. chicken (turkey) stock
3/4 c. water
4 tsp. canola oil for cooking
1/2 c. onions, chopped
1 c. carrots, chopped

2/3 c. celery, chopped
1/8 tsp. fine grind black pepper
1 3/4 c. cooked chicken, or turkey
opt. 2/3 c. cooked long grain white rice
opt. 2/3 c. cooked noodles

Chicken (or Turkey) Stock and Water. If you have normal chicken (or turkey) stock then use 3 1/3 cups of stock and 3/4 cup of water. If you have a thick chicken (or turkey) stock then use 2 cups of the stock and 2 cups of water.

Instructions: Heat the oil in a large nonstick saucepan over medium heat. Add the onions and cook for 4 to 5 minutes or until the onions are golden brown and soft. Add the carrots, celery, chicken stock (or turkey stock), water, black pepper, and reduce heat to low and simmer, stirring frequently, until the vegetables are cooked but still slightly firm. Add the cooked shredded chicken (or turkey).

Chicken (or Turkey) and Rice Soup: If Chicken (or Turkey) and Rice Soup is desired then add 2/3 cup of cooked white rice.

Chicken (or Turkey) Noodle Soup: If Chicken (or Turkey) Noodle Soup is desired then add 2/3 cup of cooked noodles.

Simmer the soup over low heat for 5 minutes. Serve.

French Onion Soup (4 Servings)

2 T. extra light olive oil
4 c. onions, sliced 3/4 inch wide
2 T. butter
1/2 tsp. granulated sugar
1/2 tsp. iodized salt
1 garlic clove, minced
1/2 tsp. dried thyme

1/4 tsp. fine grind black pepper
4 c. beef stock
4 thick slices French bread
4 thin slices provolone cheese
4 thin slices Swiss cheese
1/4 c. Parmesan cheese, garnish

Onions: Onions are one of the two primary ingredients that give this soup its distinctive flavor. Properly cooking and caramelizing the onions is a critical step in the preparation of this soup. A Spanish white onion yields a good flavor. A Vidalia onion yields a more subtle flavor.

Beef Stock: Beef stock is the other primary ingredient that gives this soup its distinctive flavor. Do not buy a cheap brand or you may be disappointed with the results. Instead invest in a well known brand, such as Kitchen Basics, or Campbell's Double-Rich Beef Consumme.

Cheese: The Provolone and Swiss cheeses may be replaced with grated Swiss Gruyere cheese and Romano cheese.

Instructions: In a large nonstick saucepan heat 1 1/2 tablespoons oil over medium heat. Add the sliced onions and toss to coat with oil. Cook for 15 to 20 minutes, stirring often, until the onions have softened. Add the butter. Stir and cook for about 15 minutes, stirring often, until the onions begin to turn brown. Sprinkle in the sugar and the salt and stir. Cook about 10 or 15 minutes, stirring often, until the onions are well browned but not burnt. Add the minced garlic, thyme, and black pepper, and stir. Reduce heat to very low, add the beef stock, stir, cover the pot, and simmer for 30 minutes, stirring occasionally.

While the soup is simmering, put a piece of aluminum foil on a baking sheet. Put an oven rack in the upper third of the oven and preheat the oven to 450°F. Brush a little olive oil on both sides of each slice of French bread. Put in the oven and toast about 5 to 7 minutes, or until lightly browned. Remove from the oven, turn the toast over on the aluminum foil, and put 1 thin slice of provolone cheese, and 1 thin slice of Swiss cheese, on each slice of French bread. Just before serving the soup, return the bread to the oven and bake until the cheese is bubbly and a light brown.

Serve: Transfer the soup into soup bowls and put a slice of cheesy French bread on top of the soup in the bowl. Sprinkle a little grated Parmesan cheese on top of each slice of bread in each bowl. (Or you can slice the French bread into 1/4 inch cubes and drop them on top of the soup.)

Potato Soup (4 servings)

3 c. potatoes, peeled, cubed	3/4 c. half & half, or whole milk
1 1/2 c. chicken stock	1/2 tsp. iodized salt
1/8 c. onion, diced	1/8 tsp. fine grind black pepper
1/8 c. celery, diced	1/2 c. sharp cheddar cheese, grated
2 T. butter	opt. 4 slices cooked crisp bacon
2 1/2 T. all-purpose flour	

Potatoes: Red skin potatoes are recommended. However, baking potatoes may be used. Peel the potatoes and discard the peels. Cut the potatoes into 1/2 inch cubes.

Instructions: In a medium nonstick pot, add the potato cubes, chicken stock, onions, and celery. Bring to a boil over medium heat. Reduce heat to medium low and cook, uncovered, for 15 to 20 minutes or until the potato cubes are soft when pierced with a fork.

While the potato cubes are cooking, melt the butter in a different medium nonstick saucepan over medium heat. Add the flour and cook for 4 minutes stirring constantly. Gradually add the half & half and stir to break up any clumps. Stir constantly to prevent burning the half & half, and bring to a boil. Immediately reduce heat to low, add the salt and black pepper, stir, and simmer until the potato cubes in the other pot are done. Then add the half & half mixture to the pot with the potato cubes, reduce the heat to low, and stir for one minute. Gradually add the grated cheese and stir while the cheese melts. Continue to stir and simmer over low heat until the soup is the consistency you prefer.

Serve: Transfer the soup into soup bowls. If desired, sprinkle one finely crumbled slice of cooked crisp bacon over the soup in each bowl.

Tomato Soup (4 servings)

4 c. tomatoes, peeled, chopped
3 T. butter, unsalted
2 c. water
3 vegetable bouillon cubes
1 medium onion, quartered
opt. 2 carrots, cut lengthwise

opt. 1 T. granulated sugar
1/2 c. heavy cream, or half & half
3/4 tsp. iodized salt
1/4 tsp. fine grind black pepper
opt. 1/2 tsp. grated parmesan cheese

Rinse tomatoes under running water to help remove insecticides. Dunk tomatoes in boiling water for 30 seconds and the tomatoes will be easy to peel. Discard skins. Chop tomatoes into pieces while still warm and many of the seeds will fall out onto the cutting board and can be discarded. It is okay for some tomato seeds to end up in the soup because the soup will be blender processed after it is cooked.

Melt butter in a large nonstick saucepan. Stir in water. Add vegetable bouillon cubes, chopped tomatoes, quartered onion, carrots sliced in half from end to end, and sugar. Bring to a boil and immediately reduce heat to low. Simmer uncovered for 30 minutes, stirring occasionally, or until the soup is the thickness you prefer.

Allow to cool slightly. Remove onions and carrots. The onions added flavor to the soup. The sweetness of the carrots offset the acid in the tomatoes. Stir in cream, salt, and black pepper. Put half the soup in a blender. Hold top down on blender and blend until the texture is almost smooth. A few very small chunks of tomato will give the soup some personality. Blend the other half of the soup. Reheat the soup for serving. If desired, top with a sprinkle of grated parmesan cheese.

Serving Suggestions: Soup crackers, oyster crackers, or mini saltines are good with soup. Grilled cheese sandwiches are also recommended.

Chapter Thirty-Two
Vegetables

A Few Suggestions for Cooking Vegetables

Salt: If a bean or corn recipe calls for salt, then wait and add the required amount of salt when the beans or corn are at the midpoint of their required cooking time. This will help to minimize the final toughness of the beans or corn.

Above Ground Vegetables: Vegetables that grow above ground should be boiled with **no** cover on the cook pot.

Soaking Vegetables: If fresh vegetables need to be soaked then do so **before** slicing in order to retain as much of their nutritional value as possible.

Asparagus, Oven Roasted (2 Servings)

1/2 lb. fresh asparagus spears
4 tsp. extra light olive oil
1/4 tsp. iodized salt
1/8 tsp. fine grind black pepper

opt. 1 tsp. garlic salt
opt. 1 T. Parmesan cheese
opt. 1 tsp. lemon juice

Asparagus: Invest in high quality fresh asparagus spears. Thinner spears are usually more tender than thicker spears. Use both hands to grab each uncooked spear at both ends and bend until it breaks. It will normally break where it begins to get tough at its thick end. If you wish to use the thick ends then peel them.

Instructions: Place a sheet of nonstick aluminum foil on a baking pan with a raised edge to contain the juices while cooking. Spread the asparagus in a single layer on the foil with the spears touching each other lengthwise. Drizzle the oil over the asparagus. Lightly sprinkle with salt and black pepper. If desired, lightly sprinkle with garlic salt and/or Parmesan cheese.

Bake in a preheated 400°F oven for 6 minutes. Remove from oven and turn the asparagus spears over using a spatula. Return to the oven and bake for another 4 to 6 minutes until crisp, depending on the thickness of the asparagus and the desired tenderness is achieved.

Remove from oven. If desired, drizzle lemon juice over the asparagus.

Baked Beans (6 to 8 servings)

1 lb. (or 4 cans) beans (see below) 1 tsp. dry mustard, or Dijon
3 T. molasses   1 tsp. iodized salt
3 T. light brown sugar   1/4 tsp. fine grind black pepper
1/2 c. ketchup   1/4 c. sweet onion, finely diced
1 T. Worcestershire sauce   6 slices bacon, cooked crisp

Beans: Navy beans are normally used. However, some people prefer canned pork and beans. An interesting option is to use 1/2 black beans plus 1/2 of either pinto or light red kidney beans. Either 1 pound of dried beans or 4 cans (15 oz. each) of beans may be used. This recipe includes instructions for dried beans. If using canned beans then skip the preparation instructions for dried beans.

How to Prepare Dried Beans: Look through the dry beans and remove any small foreign particles. Rinse the dry beans thoroughly and discard the rinse water. For each cup of dry beans add 3 cups of water and soak overnight in the refrigerator. Drain the beans and discard the soak water for health and safety reasons because even though the soak water will contain some vitamins and nutrients, it may contain some undesirable chemicals. If the beans are not thoroughly cooked then they are more difficult to chew and digest, and they will generate more gas during the digestive process. In order to neutralize any minor amount of toxins that may still be in the beans, add the beans to the cook pot, cover with 2 inches of cold water, bring to a boil, and boil for 10 minutes. Then reduce the heat to very low. Put a lid or cover on the cook pot. The slower the beans are cooked the easier it is for the human body to digest them. Slowly simmering the beans over very low heat for between 3 to 8 hours is ideal. Check the beans every hour and add more hot water if necessary. Do not add cool water or cold water to the beans while they are cooking because the cool water shock will toughen the beans and they will require a longer cooking time and the beans will be a little harder to digest. Instead heat the extra water in a separate cook pot and then add the hot water to the bean pot. When the beans are soft and a bean can be easily mashed with a fork using just a little pressure, then the beans are done.

Baking Instructions for All Beans: Lightly grease a 2-quart (8-inch square) casserole dish. Pour the beans into the bottom of the dish. In a separate nonstick saucepan, combine the molasses, brown sugar, ketchup, Worcestershire sauce, mustard, salt, black pepper, and diced onions, and bring to a boil over medium-high heat while stirring. Pour over the beans in the casserole dish. Crumble the crisp bacon and spread evenly over the beans. Bake uncovered in a preheated 325°F oven for 2 hours. Remove from oven and allow to cool for at least 15 minutes before serving.

Broccoli Steamed, with or without Cheese Sauce (4 to 6 servings)

1 bunch of broccoli florets   1/3 tsp. fine grind black pepper
About 1 c. water   2 T. butter, room temperature

Rinse the broccoli florets under cold faucet water. Cut the florets off the main stems. Break any extremely large florets in half.

If using a folding steamer insert, then unfold it and put it into the saucepan.

Add 1 cup of water to the saucepan. The water should be below the steamer basket. Bring to a boil over medium-high heat. Reduce heat to medium-low. Put the florets in the steamer basket and cover the pot. Boil for 5 to 6 minutes but never longer than 6 minutes. Transfer to a serving bowl, sprinkle with black pepper, and put butter on top of the florets so the butter can melt.

Instead of butter, pour cheese sauce on top of the broccoli. A cheese sauce recipe is in the sauce chapter.

Or crumble 2 slices of crisp bacon into small pieces and sprinkle over the steamed broccoli.

Corn on the Cob (2 Servings)

2 ears of corn, still on the cob   2 T. butter, for serving
1 T. granulated sugar   1/4 tsp. iodized salt
1/2 T. lemon juice   1/8 tsp. fine grind black pepper

Recommended: Invest in a pair of "corn on the cob skewers" for each member of your family. After cooking the corn, stick one holder into each end of each cob so it will be easier for a person to hold and eat the corn without burning their fingers or getting butter on their fingers.

Cooking Time: Fresh corn that has just been picked off the stalk takes less time to cook than older corn. Corn still in its husks remains fresher than corn without its husks because the husks help to prevent the corn from drying out. As corn ages it gradually becomes tougher and drier and it takes longer to cook than when it was fresh. Corn picked the same day it is cooked will be done in about 5 or 6 minutes. Older corn can take up to 10 minutes to cook.

If the corn is still in its husks, then leave the husks on the corn until you are ready to cook it. Pull the husks down and tear them off the bottom thick end of the cob. Pull off and discard all the silky threads. If the corn has a narrow tapered end with tiny corn kernels on it then use a sharp knife to cut the end off to leave a straight piece of cob exposed.

If desired, hold each end of a long ear of corn in each hand and break it in half so the halves will fit better in the cook pot and they will be easier to control while eating. One-half ear of corn is also a full serving for a young child.

Fill a medium-size cook pot approximately 1/2 full of water. Add sugar and lemon juice and stir until the sugar is completely dissolved. Do not add any salt to the water. (Note: You will not be able to taste the sugar or the lemon juice in the cooked corn. The sugar and lemon juice simply help the corn to retain its natural flavor during cooking and they help the corn to remain tender and to not become chewy. Lemon juice is better than vinegar in this application, but you can experiment with vinegar instead of lemon juice if you wish.)

Bring the water to a boil over medium-high heat. Use tongs and carefully add the corn, one corn cob at a time, until all the corn is in the pot. Bring the water to a boil again and boil for 5 seconds. Then turn off the heat and cover the pot. Wait at least 8 minutes and then remove the corn from the pot and serve. (If you do not know how old the corn is then you can wait 10 minutes before removing it from the pot.)

Allow each person to add butter, salt, and pepper as desired.

Creamed Spinach (4 Servings)

1 lb. spinach, fresh or frozen	1 T. garlic, minced
3 T. butter, for fresh spinach	1/2 tsp. iodized salt
3 T. butter, for sauce	1/8 tsp. fine grind black pepper
3 T. all-purpose flour, for sauce	1/4 tsp. ground nutmeg
2/3 c. half & half, or whole milk	opt. 1/4 c. Parmesan cheese, grated
1/4 c. sweet onion, minced	

Spinach: Fresh baby spinach is recommended. However, regular fresh spinach, or frozen chopped spinach, may be used.

Frozen Spinach: If using frozen spinach then cook according to the package instructions. Drain the cooked spinach. Gently press as much liquid as possible out of the spinach. Return drained spinach to the nonstick saucepan in which it was cooked.

Fresh Spinach: If using fresh baby spinach then it does not need to be chopped. If using regular size leaf spinach then roughly chop the big leaves into smaller pieces. To cook the spinach, melt 3 tablespoons of butter in a nonstick saucepan over medium heat. Add half the fresh spinach and stir until coated with butter. Add the rest of the fresh spinach and stir to coat with butter. Cook for about 4 or 5 minutes or until the spinach is wilted but not soggy.

Cooked Spinach: Keep the cooked spinach warm in its saucepan over very, very, low heat while preparing the sauce. Very gently stir the spinach once per minute while the sauce is cooking. Just before adding the spinach to the sauce, heat it just a little until the cooked spinach is very warm.

Sauce: Melt 3 tablespoons butter in a nonstick saucepan over medium heat. Add 3 tablespoons flour and whisk together until the flour is well blended with the butter. Cook 5 minutes, or until golden brown. Add half & half, onion, garlic, salt, and black pepper and whisk gently for 5 minutes. Remove from heat. Add ground nutmeg and stir to mix it into the sauce.

If desired, add the optional freshly grated Parmesan cheese and stir to blend it with the sauce.

Add the very warm spinach to the sauce and stir gently to coat the spinach with the sauce. Serve immediately.

Italian Green Beans (2 Servings)

1 (14 1/2 oz.) can Allen's Cut Italian Green Beans

Seasonings:

1 T. onion, minced	opt. 1 T. bacon grease
1/3 tsp. Italian seasoning	opt. 2 slices bacon, cooked, crumbled
1/4 tsp. garlic salt	opt. 1 T. Parmesan cheese, grated
1/4 tsp. fine grind black pepper	

Italian Green Beans: Allen's Cut Italian Green Beans in the 14.5 ounce can are highly recommended instead of every other brand of Italian green beans. Or, if you prefer, you can purchase a different brand of canned green beans, or you can purchase fresh green beans and cook them yourself. If you purchase the big 28 ounce can of Allen's Cut Italian Green Beans then use twice the amount of seasoning.

Instructions: Heat the fully cooked cut Italian green beans in a medium nonstick saucepan over medium heat until the water begins to boil. Reduce heat to low and cook for 2 minutes. Then drain beans in a strainer but save 2 tablespoons of the hot water in a small bowl. Allow the water to cool a little.

Seasoning: Add the onion, Italian seasoning, garlic salt, and fine grind black pepper to the water in the bowl and stir until well blended.

Bacon Grease: If using the optional bacon grease, then put the bacon grease in the now empty saucepan in which the green beans were heated. If using cold bacon grease that has solidified, then melt the bacon grease over low heat.

Instructions Continued: Add the seasoning solution to the saucepan.

Return the drained green beans to the saucepan and stir to mix the seasoning with the green beans. Heat over very low heat for 2 minutes.

Remove from heat.

If desired, add the crumbled cooked bacon to the beans and toss to mix.

If desired, add the Parmesan cheese to the beans and toss to mix.

Serve immediately.

Index of Recipes

About the Author

Robert Wayne Atkins, P.E. (Grandpappy)

Born in 1949. Accepted Jesus Christ as Savior in April of 1976.

B.S. Degree in Industrial Engineering & Operations Research, Virginia Polytechnic Institute and State University, June 1972.

Master of Business Administration, Georgia State University, 1985.

Licensed Professional Engineer (P.E.), Florida 1980, Georgia 1982.

Professor of Industrial Engineering and Industrial Engineering Technology, Southern Polytechnic College of Engineering and Engineering Technology, Kennesaw State University, 1984-2021.

Member of The Gideons International continuously since 1979.

Ordained Deacon in Christian Church, Ocala, Florida, 1980.

Author of Nine Computer Software Games including **"The Lost Crown of Queen Anne,"** 1988-1991.

Contributing Author to **"Maynard's Industrial Engineering Handbook,"** Fifth Edition, pg. 5.10, 2001

Contributing Author to **"Maynard's Industrial & Systems Engineering Handbook,"** Sixth Edition, pg. 102, 2023.

Listed in **"Who's Who in America,"** 64th Edition, 2010.

Listed in **"Who's Who in the World,"** 29th Edition, 2012.

Recipient of **"Who's Who"** Lifetime Achievement Award, 2019.

Other Books by this Same Author:
1. Handbook of Industrial, Systems, and Quality Engineering (English).
2. Manual de Ingeniería Industrial, de Sistemas y de Calidad (Spanish).
3. Engineering Statistics and Applications.
4. Engineering Economy and Financial Analysis.
5. Introduction to Industrial and Systems Engineering.
6. Instructor's Manual: Introduction to Industrial & Systems Engineering.
7. Work Measurement and Ergonomics.
8. Instructor's Manual: Work Measurement and Ergonomics.
9. Facilities Design and Plant Layout.
10. Instructor's Manual: Facilities Design and Plant Layout.
11. The Common Sense Diet.
12. The Food Book.
13. Grandpappy's Recipes for Hard Times.
14. Grandpappy's Campfire Survival Cookbook (English).
15. Recetas del Abuelo para la Supervivencia al Acampar (Spanish).
16. Grandpappy's Survival Manual for Hard Times, Third Edition.
17. The Most Important Survival Skills of the 1800s.
18. How to Tan Animal Hides and How to Make High Quality Buckskin Clothing.
19. How to Live Comfortably for Several Years in a Hostile Wilderness Environment.
20. Some Difficult Questions Answered Using the Holy Bible.
21. Religion and Christianity in the Twenty-First Century.
22. Grandpappy's Christian Poems.
23. The New Heaven and the New Earth (English).
24. El Cielo Nuevo y La Tierra Nueva (Spanish).
25. Grandpappy's Stories for Children of All Ages.
26. Ancient Board Games and Solitaire Games from Around the World.
27. The Four Pillars of Prosperity: Government, Business, Religion, and Banks.

Made in the USA
Monee, IL
29 December 2023

50766535R00162